D1562897

PHILO OF ALEXANDRIA
AN EXEGETE FOR HIS TIME

SUPPLEMENTS TO
NOVUM TESTAMENTUM

VOLUME LXXXVI

PHILO OF ALEXANDRIA
AN EXEGETE FOR HIS TIME

BY

PEDER BORGEN

BRILL
LEIDEN · NEW YORK · KÖLN
1997

This book is printed on acid-free paper.

Library of Congress Cataloging-in-Publication Data

Borgen, Peder.
    Philo of Alexandria : an exegete for his time / by Peder Borgen.
        p. cm. — (Supplements to Novum Testamentum, ISSN 0167-9732 ;
    v. 86)
    Includes bibliographical references and indexes.
    ISBN 9004103880 (cloth : alk. paper)
    1. Philo, of Alexandria. 2. Bible. O.T.—Criticism,
interpretation, etc., Jewish—History. 3. Philosophy, Ancient.
4. Philosophy, Jewish. I. Title. II. Series.
BS1161.P5B67   1997
221.6'092—dc21
                                                        97-29997
                                                            CIP
                                                            r97

Die Deutsche Bibliothek - CIP-Einheitsaufnahme

Borgen, Peder:
Philo of Alexandria - an exegete for his time / by Peder Borgen. -
Leiden ; New York ; Köln : Brill, 1997
    (Supplements to Novum testamentum ; Vol. 86)
    ISBN 90–04–10388-0
[Novum Testamentum / Supplements]
Supplements to Novum testamentum – Leiden ; New York ; Köln :
Brill
    Früher Schriftenreihe
    Fortlaufende Beiheftreihe zu Novum testamentum
    Vol. 86. Borgen, Peder: Philo of Alexandria - an exegete for his
time. - 1997

ISSN   0167-9732
ISBN   90 04 10388 0

PRINTED IN THE NETHERLANDS

Dedicated to NILS ALSTRUP DAHL
and
HOWARD CLARK KEE

formerly my treasured teachers
presently my treasured colleagues

CONTENTS

PREFACE

While writing my monograph on the concept of manna in the Gospel of John and the writings of Philo, entitled *Bread from Heaven* (1965), I became convinced that a clue to Philo's writings lay in the appreciation of the relationship between exegesis, exegetical traditions, contemporary ideas, and historical context. Over the years I have explored various aspects from the same perspective. In the present monograph I build on insights gained from these preceding studies and bring the analysis further into a monograph on Philo as an exegete for his time.

This approach to Philo makes it possible to understand Philo's two historical treatises, *Against Flaccus* and *On the Virtues, that is On the Embassy to Gaius*, closely together with his expository writings. Those two treatises demonstrate that a central context for Philo, as also for the Alexandrian Jews in earlier times, was the relationship and interaction between the Jewish community and its non-Jewish surroundings. This context is in various ways reflected in his expository writings.

The majority of Philo's extant treatises is of expository nature. The analysis of their structures, of the various exegetical forms, and of exegetical methods and terminology used, is only in its infancy. In this area the contribution made in this monograph is meant to suggest avenues for further research.

Philo is a representative of Diaspora Judaism and of Judaism as such in the late Second Temple period. At the same time he also illuminates the background and the wider context of the New Testament and the early Church. At some points this perspective is indicated in the monograph.

Biblical quotations in English are taken from *The Holy Bible Containing the Old and New Testament*, Revised Standard Version (New York: Nelson & Sons, 1952), and quotations in English from Philo's writings are taken from *Philo with an English Translation* by F.H. Colson, 1–10, Loeb Classical Library (Cambridge, Mass.: Harvard University press, 1929–62), and from *Philo, Supplements*, 1–2, translated from Ancient Armenian Version of the Original Greek by R. Marcus, Loeb Classical Library (Cambridge, Mass.: Harvard University Press, 1953). In some cases modifications of these translations have been made on the basis of the Greek text.

The preparation of this book was made possible thanks to a grant from the Norwegian Research Council. The Norwegian Research Council, the Joint Committee of the Nordic Research Councils for the Humanities (NOS-H), and the University of Trondheim with its Department of Religious Studies have over the years given me support and encouragement in my research.

A personal note is to be added about my former teachers, Professor em. Nils Alstrup Dahl and Professor em. Howard Clark Kee. They taught me and encouraged me when I was a young student. They introduced me to New Testament research and to the study of Judaism seen within a Graeco-Roman context. They helped me to pay attention to the primary sources and to interpret them in their social historical setting. My period as student is now in the far past, but as one of their colleagues and now also as an emeritus as they are, I wish to express my appreciation and thanks by dedicating the book to them.

Trondheim, Autumn 1997.

Peder Borgen

INTRODUCTION

MYSTIC? PHILOSOPHER? EXEGETE?

Mysticism or Pharisaic philosophy?

The point of departure of the present study of Philo as an exegete for his time is the survey of research I wrote in the 1984 volume on Philo in the series *Aufstieg und Niedergang der römischen Welt*.[1] One of the questions discussed was how to characterize Philo's basic profile, whether he was primarily to be seen as a mystic, a philosopher or an exegete. Aspects of this discussion can serve as an introduction to the present study, and at the same time bring the survey up to date.

H. Leisegang interpreted Philo on the basis of Greek mysticism and the mystery cults.[2] Thus Philo was basically seen not as a Jew, but as a Greek mystic wearing Jewish robes. With variations in approach and emphasis, R. Reitzenstein, É. Bréhier, and J. Pascher set the Egyptian mystery cult in the center of their interpretation.[3]

E.R. Goodenough also stressed the importance of the mystery cults, but he did not think that Philo himself originated this interpretation. Philo was rather a witness to a wider tendency within Hellenistic Judaism to regard itself as a mystery. Goodenough formulates his hypothesis in this way:[4]

> The shreds of literature we have from Greek Judaism before Philo, and the full achievement recorded by Philo's time, indicate that the Jews were captivated by their neighbour's religion and thought. Yet since a Jew could not now simply become an initiate of Isis or Orpheus and remain a Jew as well, the amazingly clever trick was devised, we do not know when or by whom, of representing Moses as Orpheus and Hermes-Tat, and explaining that the Jewish 'Wisdom' figure, by translation 'Sophia', was identical with that 'Female Principle in nature' which Plutarch identified as Isis![5]

---

[1] See Borgen (1984A).
[2] Leisegang (1919); Leisegang (1941).
[3] See Borgen (1984A) 139.
[4] Goodenough (1935) 6–10.
[5] *Ibid.*, 7.

By Philo's time, and long before, Judaism in the Greek-speaking world, especially in Egypt, had been transformed into a Mystery.

The objective of this Judaism was salvation in the mystical sense. God was no longer only the God presented in the Old Testament:

> He was the Absolute, connected with phenomena by His Light-Stream, the Logos or Sophia. The hope and aim of man was to leave created things with their sordid complications, and to rise to incorruption, immortality, life, by climbing the mystic ladder, traversing the Royal Road of the Light-Stream.[6]

The commandments of the Law were still carefully followed by most Jews, but they were secondary to the true Law in a Platonizing sense, the streaming Logos-Nomos of God. Philo is the chief source for knowledge of details of this Mystery. He is, however, far beyond a crude stage of syncretism. He is looking not directly at gentile mythology but at the Hellenistic mystic philosophy which made any mythology only a typology for its doctrines. The allegories of Philo are then not attempts at making Abraham, Moses, Sophia, and the Logos types of Orpheus, Isis or the Persian pleroma, but rather types of the ideas which Greek thinkers were forcing upon all mythology.

Is then Philo's mystery a real mystery, or, as an ideological rather than a ritualistic mystery, only a figurative one? Goodenough finds this dilemma to be false, since real mystery in ancient usage is to be understood as teaching, with or without rites, which would lead the 'initiate' or 'disciple' out of matter into the eternal. And if mystic Judaism made use of rites, it would have used Jewish rites, transformed with pagan ideology, but externally unchanged. According to Goodenough, this latter alternative proves to be Philo's approach to the Jewish festivals. There is no trace of an initiatory rite for Jews into the Mystery. But for the proselytes Philo changed circumcision into a sacrament, just as he made every festival into a sacrament in the sense that it was a visible sign of an invisible, a mystic, grace.

In his work *Jewish Symbols* Goodenough tries to trace evidence for this widespread Judaism by means of archaeological data on the use of mystical symbols.[7] In order to recover the theology of this Jewish mystery religion, one has to rely on Philo's writings. But most of the Jews were not theologians. They only felt and experienced by means of symbols and rites what Philo tried to explain.

---

[6] *Ibid.*
[7] Goodenough (1953–68).

Goodenough's research has many merits:[8] He interpreted Philo as a representative of a movement in Judaism, and not as an isolated individual. Although he thought that pagan philosophy and mysteries had conquered this kind of Judaism, he nevertheless managed at the same time to observe that Philo was a patriotic Jew. It is also important that he drew on archaeological material to throw light on Judaism. Finally, Goodenough is right in his emphasis on Philo's practical aim, namely, to lead men to the vision of God.

Many points of criticism can also be given: Goodenough's notion of a widespread pagan sacramental mystery was an exaggeration. And his attempts to show that there existed an empire-wide, anti-rabbinic Judaism based on the idea and rites of a mystery, have failed. Although he was aware of G. Scholem's research on early Jewish mysticism, his schematic and uniform understanding of rabbinic and normative Judaism over against mystic Judaism, made it impossible for him to see the variety of Judaism, also in Palestine, before A.D. 70, and also after that time.[9] Moreover, Goodenough did not offer much help on Philo's exegetical activity and method.

S. Sandmel follows Goodenough's basic contention that Philo's view of Judaism differed from that of the rabbis, as philosophical mysticism differed from halakhic legalism.[10] Philonic Judaism was the result of a Hellenization which was as complete as was possible for a group which retained throughout its loyalty to the Torah. Sandmel does not, however, accept Goodenough's view that Philo represented a large movement within Judaism. He thinks that Philo and his associates reflected a marginal, aberrant version of Judaism. Sandmel has rightly moved away from Goodenough's emphasis on the transformation of Judaism into the model of mystery religions. Sandmel rather defines Philo's practical aim as an existential actualization of the Biblical material: Philo's exegesis of Scripture includes his reading Scripture in full accord with his own view of Jewish religiosity;[11] The philosophical matters were only secondary to Philo. They illustrated his principal purpose, to exhort his reader to travel on the 'royal road' to perfection.[12]

---

[8] Borgen (1984A) 140.
[9] *Ibid.*
[10] Sandmel (1971); Sandmel (1979).
[11] Sandmel (1954) 248–253.
[12] Sandmel (1971) XX–XXIV.

A different approach to that of Goodenough and Sandmel was
attempted by H.A. Wolfson.[13] His study on Philo is part of a comprehensive project under the general title "Structure and Growth of
Philosophic Systems from Plato to Spinoza", and he finds in Philo's
writings the "foundations of religious philosophy in Judaism, Christianity, and Islam" as it is said in the sub-title of his two volumes work.

While Goodenough thought that Hellenization had transformed
Judaism into a mystery, Wolfson says that Philo represents "a Hellenization in language only, not in religious belief or cult . . . it did
not cause them [the Jews] to change their conception of their own
religion".[14] Philo uses terms borrowed from the mysteries in the
same way he uses terms borrowed from popular religion and from
mythology, all of them because they were part of common speech,
not because Philo meant Judaism to be a mystery.[15]

According to Wolfson, Philo was a great and unique philosopher:
Philo ushered in the period of 'Mediaeval Philosophy' which was
based on Scripture and revelation. In this way mediaeval philosophy
was the history of the philosophy of Philo.[16] Philo was the first religious thinker to make philosophy a handmaid to religion, and he
first formulated the problem of the reconciliation of faith and reason: Just as the truths of revelation are embodied in Scripture, so the
truth discovered by reason are embodied in a philosophic literature
written primarily in Greek. Since God is the author both of the truths
made known by revelation and of the truths discovered by reason,
there can be no real conflict between them.[17]

In Wolfson's interpretation Philonic thoughts are a philosophical
derivation and development of Pharisaic Judaism. In his use of Greek
philosophy Philo is rather critical of Stoicism, although he draws
heavily on Stoic expressions. His philosophy of religion comes closer
to Platonic ideas, but every Platonic teaching is examined critically.

With his belief derived from Scripture that from eternity God was
alone, and hence that God alone is uncreated, Philo gave his own
version of the philosophy of Plato, partly as an interpretation of Plato
and partly as a departure from him. According to Philo God is superior to virtue and knowledge, and he created the intelligible world as

---

[13] Wolfson (1948).
[14] *Ibid.*, 1:13.
[15] *Ibid.*, 1:45–46.
[16] *Ibid.*, 2:439–460.
[17] *Ibid.*, 2:446ff.

well as the visible world.[18] One of the most important features of Philo's revision of the Platonic theory of ideas is his application of the term *Logos* to the totality of ideas and his description for it as the place of the intelligible world, which in turn consists of the ideas.[19] With regard to the doctrine of God as such, Philo was the first philosopher known to have stated that God, in His essence, is unknowable and undescribable. Scripture teaches that God is not to be named, and under the influence of philosophic reasoning, this notion came to mean that God cannot be described or known. Those terms which in Scripture are predicated of God are according to Philo either used only for the purpose of instruction, or they are what philosophers call properties.[20] In this way Wolfson step by step discovers in Philo's writings a comprehensive and consistent system of philosophy of religion, a system of religious ethics included.

Wolfson's work is a rich collection of important material on Philo, Judaism, Greek philosophy, etc. In spite of his main interest in philosophy of religion, he also pays attention to the actual situation of Hellenistic Judaism, with special reference to Alexandrian Judaism and Philo. Moreover, the large amount of parallels to Philonic ideas from rabbinic traditions give support to the hypothesis that Philo and at least parts of Palestinian Judaism had traditions in common and also that there are points of kinship where the ideas are formulated in different and independent ways. Wolfson's critics are right, however, when they maintain that he is much more systematic than Philo ever was. Thus a Philonic system rather than Philo has been reconstructed.[21]

Gnostic and Middle Platonic interpretations

Since Philo draws on philosophical and religious ideas from various backgrounds, some scholars interpret him against the background of religious syncretism, as in Gnosticism, or the mixture of philosophical schools in Middle Platonism.

Hans Jonas places Philo within the context of Gnosticism. According to Jonas, 'Gnosis' is to be described as an understanding of existence.

---

[18] *Ibid.*, 1:200−17.
[19] *Ibid.*, 1:293.
[20] *Ibid.*, 2:149ff.
[21] See Feldman (1963) 7.

As a phenomenon in Late Antiquity it is syncretistic and eclectic, and he finds several Gnostic features in Philo.[22] Philo follows basically a Gnostic dualism between the human-earthly-cosmic realm and the divine and transcendental realm. Though theoretical knowledge of God's essence is not accessible to man, his existence, that He is, can be known. Through mystical knowledge man can have an unmediated access to God through Himself above and beyond the world and its way of knowledge.

As for man, self-knowledge means knowledge of one's own nothingness. Thus Philo's dualistic contrast between God and man reflects the basic Gnostic dualism between God and the world. According to Jonas Gnostic elements are seen in Philo's use of the term 'virtue', ἀρετή. He thinks that in Philo the Stoic-Platonic concept of virtue is hollowed out by Jewish and crypto-Gnostic motifs on the basis of the dualism between heaven and earth, soul and body. This transformation is seen by the non-Greek idea that virtue comes from above, like the manna, without co-operation by men, leaving the soul to have no goodness of its own.[23]

In connection with his interpretation of the manna in *Mut.* 253–263, Philo has no such dualism. Jonas is right when he thinks that the Greek concept of virtue has been transformed. The transformation is due to the problem of the relation of the Jewish understanding of revelation to Greek philosophy of education. The virtue and wisdom of revelation comes, like the manna, from above without co-operation by men. Philo clearly says that the earthly and human-centered education of the *encyclia* also has its virtue: "Thus each virtue, one where the teacher is another, one where the teacher and learner are the same, will be open to human kind" (*Mut.* 263). Thus, Jonas is positively wrong when he refers to *Mut.* 258 to show that Philo does not leave any goodness to man.[24]

Scholars such as M. Simon, S. Sandmel, R.McL. Wilson and B. Pearson, although admitting that Philo has elements which are akin to Gnostic thought and attitudes, agree that Philo is not to be understood as a Gnostic. S. Sandmel characterizes the difference between Philo and Gnosticism in this way: "I see no traces of a fallen god; I see, however, fallen man in Eden. I see no benighted creator;

---

[22] Jonas (1954) especially 70–121.
[23] *Ibid.*, 38; Jonas (1967) 374–375. Thyen (1955) 243, accepts Jonas' interpretation.
[24] Borgen (1984A) 144.

I see, however, the logos as the creator. As to a sinister creation, I see in Philo the view that this world of appearance is rather sinister, and that the sage is indeed an alien soul in this world. I do not see cosmic captivity or acosmic salvation; I do see salvation of the prison of the body. I do not wonder at the absence of a fallen God, for Philo was a staunch Jew; in light of Genesis 1, and the repeated refrain of 'God saw and it was good', Philo could scarcely admit of a benighted creator".[25] B. Pearson concludes correspondingly that "Philo is not dependent upon, or influenced by, Gnosticism. Rather, the earliest Gnostic writings show a clear dependence upon Jewish sources, not only the Old Testament, but also Jewish traditions of exegesis and Jewish haggadic and apocryphal traditions. Indeed the Jewish element in Gnosticism – which at the same time is *anti*-Jewish in its thrust – is so prominent as to suggest that Gnosticism origi- nated within Judaism as a revolutionary protest movement against traditional Jewish religion. Philo is an important source for some (not all) of the Hellenistic Jewish elements borrowed by the Gnostics".[26]

B. Pearson himself follows the scholars who place Philo within the context of Middle Platonism. Some among these scholars should be mentioned. A main presentation of this interpretation of Philo is found in J. Dillon's book on the *Middle Platonists*. Dillon devotes almost fifty pages of his book to what he himself characterizes as a partial study of Philo.[27] He attempts to isolate in his thought those elements which may derive from contemporary Alexandrian Platonism. His conclusion is that Philo adapted Alexandrian Platonism which was heavily influenced by Stoicism and Pythagoreanism to his own exegetical purposes. Moses is in this way a "fully fledged Middle Platonist".[28]

Philo's views on 'ideas' and 'logos' can illustrate this interpreta- tion. Philo saw in Genesis a double creation, first that of the *noetic* world as model, then that of the sensible world, which was produced by God from the model. Philo draws here on Platonic thoughts which he has modified. While the model of Plato's *Timaeus* was something independent of the *Demiurg*, the model in Philo's exegesis becomes God's creation. Philo's interpretation has, according to Dillon, probably

---

[25] Sandmel (1971) XVI. Cf. also Simon (1967) 359–374; Wilson (1972); Wilson (1993); Pearson (1984).
[26] Pearson (1984) 341.
[27] Dillon (1977) 139–183.
[28] *Ibid.*, 143.

been furthered by similar trends in Middle Platonism in Alexandria, as for example in Antiochus of Ascalon. Antiochus identified the *Demiurg* with the Stoic *Pneuma-Logos*, and thus the paradigm of the *Timaeus* is but the content of the intellect of the *Logos*, on the pattern of which the physical world was constructed. Philo is the first, however, known to explicitly state that the model, the *noetic* world, is God's creation. In agreement with such Middle Platonists as Eudorus of Alexandria, Philo makes ample use of Pythagorean philosophy of numbers in his understanding of the order of the cosmos.[29]

How then is Philo's relationship to Middle Platonism to be defined? This question was not raised by Dillon in a direct way, however. He was primarily concerned with Philo as a witness to contemporary Platonism, so that he only wrote a partial study on him. More recently Dillon has clarified his position further and expressed his agreement with the formulation of D. Runia "that Philo is a Platonizing expositor of scripture, showing a marked preference for using Middle Platonist doctrines in his exegesis". Dillon himself points to the basic problem in dealing with Middle Platonism, namely the fragmentary pieces of information that we have about the doctrines of the later Platonists, as well as of the Aristotelians and the Stoics.[30]

In his comments on this interpretation of Philo within the context of Alexandrian Middle Platonists, D. Runia finds it to be a setback for this theory that J. Glucker has shown that there is no direct connection between Antiochus and Alexandrian philosophy. Eudorus' sympathy for Pythagorean theology is certainly reflected in Philo's work, however. Although Runia sees extensive correspondences between Philo and the Middle Platonist, he argues against calling Philo a Middle Platonist. The reason is because Philo is doing his own thing. He sees his own task as giving a philosophically orientated exegesis of the words of Moses, and for this undertaking the doctrines of Plato, and in particular the *Timaeus*, are an indispensable aid.

The numerous Platonic ideas and motifs are not, in Philo's view, read into scripture or used to illustrate Mosaic ideas, but are genuinely present in the sacred word and must be brought to the light in the exegetical process.[31]

As for the views of D. Winston, D. Runia characterizes him in

---

[29] *Ibid.*, 93–95, 158–160. See Borgen (1984A) 149.
[30] Runia (1993) 125–26; Dillon (1995) 123.
[31] Runia (1986) 499, 505–519.

this way: Winston represents the view that Philo is *de facto* Middle Platonic. Philo does not belong to the school, but has a philosophical stance which is fundamentally Platonic.[32]

Although Runia finds H.A. Wolfson's study on Philo's philosophy misleading because it credits Philo with a dogmatic and systematic certainty, he thinks that Wolfson's main thesis is fundamentally correct. Philo's attempt to bring together scripture and philosophy marks a pivotal point in the history of thought, the result of which only gradually became apparent in the centuries after his death.[33]

Exegesis and tradition

In his understanding of Philo as an exegete of the Laws of Moses, Runia follows a growing trend in Philonic scholarship.[34] The pioneering work here was already published in 1875, written by C. Siegfried.[35] From 1960 onwards the present author has followed this approach, analysing the ways in which Philo worked as an exegete and wove together elements from various writings and traditions into his exposition. Philo was one among several interpreters of the Pentateuch in the Jewish community in Alexandria. Some differences and agreements among them are reflected in his writings. Moreover, Philo's Pentateuchal interpretations have been produced within the context of his own and his compatriots' historical situation. Philo draws on the expository activity in the synagogue.[36]

A comprehensive study along this line was done by V. Nikiprowetzky in his book *Le commentaire de l'Écriture chez Philon d'Alexandrie*, published in 1977.[37] For Philo philosophy basically means the content of the Laws of Moses. Thus, the study of these scriptures is the right way to appropriate this philosophy. Philo's commentaries are always designed to explain the biblical text. Also Nikiprowetzky finds that his commentaries reflect exegesis in the synagogue, and that they are to be seen within the context of their historical situation.

---

[32] Runia (1993) 125–26.
[33] Runia (1986) 552.
[34] See Runia (1986) 535–38; Runia (1984) 236–41; Runia (1987) 112. Both essays are also published in Runia (1990), in IV:236–41 and in V:112 respectively.
[35] Siegfried (1875).
[36] Borgen (1960); Borgen (1963), reprinted in Borgen (1987) 121–29. See also Borgen (1965).
[37] Nikiprowetzky (1977).

Philo intended to interpret the Laws of Moses in a way acceptable to Hellenistic thinking, but within the limits imposed by the role of the exegete. Greek philosophy supplies a language of reason used by Philo as exegete to examine the deeper meaning present in the Scriptures themselves. The task of the Philonic scholars is therefore to concentrate on the exegetical themes, without severing them from the scriptural passages as a set of independent ideas.

It should be added to this characterization of the approach of V. Nikiprowetzky that he and other scholars have attempted to analyse the structure of Philo's commentaries as *commentaries*.[38] Such analysis can give us a better understanding of Philo's works and will therefore be discussed further in the present study.

An analysis of Philo's expositions as the work of an exegete seems more adequate than examining his treatises mainly against the background of ancient rhetoric. This latter approach does not sufficiently take as starting point the circumstances that these writings are commentaries on Scripture.[39] Within this framework rhetorical analysis may prove to be helpful, however.

The emphasis on Philo as exegete has led several scholars to search for exegetical traditions and examine the way in which he builds the various kinds of traditional material into his exegesis. The present author has done this in his analysis of some of the passages in which Philo interprets the biblical texts about the manna.[40] R. Hamerton-Kelly and B. Mack, have proposed a comprehensive program for such an enterprise. Mack's proposal is built on the following basic supposition: "Philo used traditional exegetical methods and materials. These materials are diverse and may reflect stages of exegetical history or "schools" of exegesis which are in debate with one another. Philo employed these traditions with varying degrees of acceptance, and he reworked them with varying degrees of consistency".[41] By analysing the entire Philonic corpus it may be possible to identify some coherent exegetical traditions from their previous existence in the synagogal community. The assumption is that Philo stands at the end of the development of scriptural exegesis in the Alexandrian synagogue.[42]

---

[38] Nikiprowetzky (1983) 5–75.
[39] Mack (1984) 81–115; Conley (1987); Conley (1984) 343–371.
[40] Borgen (1965).
[41] Mack (1974–75) 75; cf. Hamerton-Kelly (1972) 3–26.
[42] Mack (1974–75) 71–112; Mack (1984A) 227–271.

T.H. Tobin follows the program suggested by R. Hamerton-Kelly and B. Mack in his analysis of the various interpretations of the creation of man found in Philo's writings.[43] Tobin attempts to reconstruct the history of the interpretation of the biblical texts, and reaches the following conclusion: The interpretation of the creation of man developed in two major phases. The first of these major phases involved the development of a consistent, Platonically oriented interpretation of the creation of man, an interpretation that was coordinated with an equally Platonically oriented interpretation of the creation of the world. Within this phase one finds both the interpretation of Gen 1:27 and Gen 2:7 as the creation of a single man and later the interpretation of Gen 1:27 and Gen 2:7 as the creation of *two* men, one heavenly and the other earthly. Both of these developments represent attempts to interpret the account of the creation of man in a way that is consistent with analogous developments within the Middle Platonism of the latter half of the first century B.C. in Alexandria. The second major phase, the level of Philo himself, involves the introduction of the allegory of the soul. In this type of interpretation, the text of Genesis is taken to refer not to events of the external world but to conflicting elements within the individual human being, especially to the soul. The man becomes a symbol of mind, the woman of sense perception, and the serpent of pleasure. This type of interpretation is similar to the Middle Platonic interpretation of the *Odyssey* which seemed to have made its appearance toward the end of the first century B.C. But unlike the allegorical interpretations of Homer, Philo's use of the allegory of the soul did not involve the rejection of the literal level of interpretation. Both levels were to be maintained since both levels of interpretation were divinely inspired.[44]

Although one must agree with Tobin's call for further studies on the traditions employed by Philo as well as the view of other exegetes referred to by him, D. Runia's objections to Tobin's thesis carry weight: It is quite improbable that Philo should faithfully have preserved the original structure, content and key vocabulary of previous interpretations. Moreover, given our ignorance concerning the origins of Middle Platonism, the correlation between its development and stages of development of the diverse exegetical interpretations is

---

[43] Tobin (1983).
[44] *Ibid.*, 177–178.

too hypothetical.[45] Still, the task of examining traditions employed
by Philo and the way in which he treats them, remains central in
Philonic research, and it is significant that Tobin suggests that the
synagogue was the institutional framework of transmission and development of such traditions.[46]

In the survey of Philonic research since World War II the present
author also discussed Philo's use of tradition with special reference to
haggada and halaka.[47] One conclusion drawn was as follows: "Since
no sharp distinction can be drawn between Palestinian Judaism and
Hellenistic Judaism, it is a subordinate question to ask whether Philo
was dependant on Palestinian traditions or the Palestinian Jews drew
on Alexandrian traditions, as exemplified in Philo's writings. The main
question is then to uncover traditions current in Judaism at that time
and examine the various usages, emphases and applications within
this common context".[48]

N.G. Cohen takes this understanding as point of departure and
maintains that Philo's major works are to be placed within the main-
stream of Jewish midrashic tradition.[49] Although there are significant
differences between Philonic midrash and the rabbinic midrashic tradition in its present form, the two have more in common than appears
at first glance. According to Cohen Palestinian midrash contemporary
to Philo was even closer to Philo's expositions than would appear on
the basis of the extant midrashic texts in the midrashim, which are
for the most part summary abstracts from many homilies.[50]

Philo's endeavour to assign the highest Greek philosophical value
to what he considered important in Judaism demonstrates the over-
whelming degree to which he was both a product of, and a protagonist
in, the Hellenistic culture of his day.[51] In general, Cohen's approach
is promising and further studies should be made along the same line.

Against the background of this survey of research the task is to
explore further Philo's work as an exegete, and look into the ways
in which he interprets his Jewish background and setting within

---

[45] Runia (1986) 556–58.
[46] Tobin (1983) 172–176.
[47] Borgen (1984A) 124–26.
[48] Borgen (1984A) 124.
[49] Cohen (1995) 8–10.
[50] *Ibid.*, 18–19. Cf. Borgen (1965) 57 about sections from *Exodus Rabba*: "So, although authentic sermons are not preserved here, the homiletic pattern has been
the collecting basin for material of different kinds from the tradition".
[51] Cohen (1995) 286.

the context of non-Jewish surroundings. The question to be raised is therefore this: What can be known about Philo and the context in which he lived? How are his expositions and his expository writings to be defined? Is it possible to define Philo's criteria, his hermeneutical key, which would provide us with some threads to follow in the analysis of the complex expository material in his treatises?

CHAPTER ONE

PHILO AND HIS WORLD

The man and his family

In a presentation of Philo as an exegete for his time it is necessary first to characterize the person and his outlook. Although the sources do not give us much information about Philo himself, some points can be collected from various places in his writings and also in the writings of Josephus.

Philo was a prominent member of the Jewish community of Alexandria, the largest Jewish settlement outside Palestine.[1] The only certain date known from his life comes from his account of the great pogrom in Alexandria which started in A.D. 38 under the prefect Flaccus, during the reign of the Roman emperor Gaius Caligula. Philo was then chosen to head a delegation of five men (*Legat.* 370) sent in A.D. 39/40 by the Jewish community to Gaius Caligula in Rome.[2] They were to report to Emperor Gaius Caligula on the sufferings of the Jews and present their claims (*Legat.* 178–79). Philo's mission failed, and the Emperor sent the envoys away as foolish people who refused to believe that he had the nature of a god (*Legat.* 367). Gaius Caligula died in A.D. 41, and his successor, Claudius, issued an edict to normalize conditions in Alexandria. Claudius confirmed the particular religious and judicial rights of the Jews, but denied them equal rights with the Greek citizens.[3]

A few other datable events are found in his writings. In *Alexander, or Whether the Animals Have Reason* 27, Philo speaks of the celebrations in various places given by Germanicus Iulius Caesar, probably in A.D. 12, when he entered on his first term of consulship. The horse race account in *Anim.* 58 is found also in Pliny *Historia Naturalis* 8:160–

---

[1] *Legat.* 182. Concerning Philo's family and life, see especially Schwartz (1953) 591–602 and Schwartz (1967) 35–44.

[2] See Schürer (1973) 1:388–98, and Schürer (1986) 3:1, 136–37. According to Josephus, *Ant.* 18:257, the Jewish and the Greek embassies each consisted of three men.

[3] Schürer (1973) 388–98.

61, where the event is said to have occurred during the games of Claudius Caesar in A.D. 47.

There are points in Philo's writing which indicate that he had also been engaged in the political life of the Jewish community in Alexandria earlier in his life. It is impossible, however, to give a precise description of his function. In a rather general way he says that envy had plunged him into the ocean of civil cares, *Spec.* 3:1–5. It seems clear that his engagement in politics was reluctant. He advises his fellow-Jews to be cautious in their dealings with the non-Jewish political authorities (*Somn.* 2:78–92).[4]

Philo belonged to one of the wealthiest Jewish families in Alexandria. Josephus tells that Philo's brother, Alexander, was "foremost among his contemporaries at Alexandria both for his family and his wealth" (*Ant.* 18:259 and 20:100). Alexander was probably chief of customs (*alabarch*) and guardian of the Emperor Claudius' mother's properties in Egypt (*Ant.* 19:276 and 20:100). Alexander was rich enough to lend money to the Jewish king Agrippa 1 and his wife Cypros (*Ant.* 18:159–60), and to plate the gates of the Temple of Jerusalem in gold and silver (*J.W.* 5:205). Alexander's son Marcus Julius Alexander ran a large business firm which had important business dealings with Arab countries and India. He married Berenice, the daughter of king Agrippa (*Ant.* 19:276–77).[5]

Another son of Alexander, Tiberius Iulius Alexander, was born ca. A.D. 15. He had a public career which took him to the highest post of a Roman official in Egypt, that of prefect (A.D. 66–70). He had then already served as procurator of Judaea (A.D. 46–48) and served as chief of staff under Titus during the siege of Jerusalem A.D. 70.[6] From Josephus we learn that he deserted his Jewish religion (*Ant.* 20:100).

---

[4] See Goodenough (1938) 5–7. For similar views among some Pharisees, see Alon (1977) 18–47.
[5] See Fuks (1951) 207–16. Marcus Julius Alexander was one of the best customer of Nicanor and his family.
[6] Schürer (1973) 1:456–57.

On the basis of information from Philo and Josephus, A. Terian has set up the following tables about Philo's family:[7]

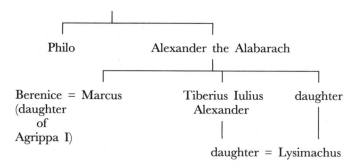

Genealogical chart of Philo

Philo was a learned person. He had a wide Greek education, and was acquainted with many Greek philosophers and writers. In his youth he received the Greek general education of the encyclia, which he treats of extensively in *On the Preliminary Studies*. He described his own training in this way:

> For instance when first I was incited by the goads of philosophy to desire her I consorted in early youth with one of her handmaids, Grammar, and all that I begat by her, writing, reading and study of the writings of poets, I dedicated to her mistress. And again I kept the company with another, namely Geometry, and was charmed with her beauty, for she shewed symmetry and proportion in every part. Yet I took none of her children for my private use, but brought them as a gift to the lawful wife. Again my ardour moved me to keep company with a third; rich in rhythm, harmony and melody was she, and her name was Music, and from her I begat diatonics, chromatics and enharmonics, conjunct and disjunct melodies, conforming with the consonance of the fourth, fifth or octave intervals. And again of none of these did I make a secret hoard, wishing to see the lawful wife a lady of wealth with a host of servants ministering to her (*Congr.* 74–76).

Philo thought Greek encyclical education should prepare for true philosophy, the 'lawful wife', Sarah, who has handmaids. In this he follows an allegorical interpretation of Homer's Penelope, such as found in ps.-Plutarch, *De Liberis Educandis*, 7D: those who wear themselves out in general studies and fail to master philosophy, are like

---

[7] Terian (1984) 282–83.

the suitors who could not win Penelope and contented themselves
with her maids. Philo adapts this to his interpretation of Sarah and
Hagar (Gen 16:1–6). When Abraham failed at first to have a child
by Sarah (= philosophy), he took the maid Hagar (= encyclical studies) in her place.

Philo's writings show that he had a broad education also beyond
the encyclia. He not only had excellent command of Greek language
and literary style, but was well acquainted both with Greek authors
and philosophers. Among Greek authors mentioned are: Aeschylus,
Aristotle, Boethus, Chrysippus, Cleanthes, Democritus, Diogenes, Euripides, Heraclitus, Hesiod, Hippocrates, Homer, Ion, Ocellus, Panaetius,
Philolaus, Pindar, Plato, Solon, Sophocles, Xenophon, Zeno.[8]

Philo gives glimpses of his public social life. He took part in banquets, *Leg. all.* 3:155f., frequented the theatre, and heard concerts,
Ebr. 177 and *Prob.* 141. He watched boxing, wrestling and horse-
racing, *Prob.* 26 and *Hypothetica* in Eusebius *Praep. ev.* 7:14, 58.

Philo was a religious Jew who identified himself with the Jewish
laws and customs: "our ancestral customs . . . and especially the law
of the Seventh Day which we regard with most reverence and awe"
(*Somn.* 2:123). In *Somn.* 2:123–32 Philo reports on an occasion when
the Roman governor tried to disturb their customs, and in particular
to do away with the law of the Seventh Day. He tried to compel
men to do service to him on it. In this connection Philo refers to the
Jews sitting in their conventicles, reading their holy books, and expounding any obscure point and discussing at length their ancestral
philosophy. The Jews reacted strongly against the governor's inter-
ference with the Sabbath. They "were intensely indignant and shewed
themselves as mournful and disconsolate as they would were their
native city being sacked and razed, and its citizens being sold into
captivity . . ." (§ 124).

Philo tells of many synagogues in each section of Alexandria, and
that one synagogue was very large and notable (*Legat.* 132–34). This
synagogue may have been the 'double colonnade' of Alexandria
mentioned in *b. Sukkah* 51b and *t. Sukkah* 4:6. Philo understood the
synagogues to be schools of philosophy. His writings prove that his
philosophical interest was expressed largely in exegesis of the Laws
of Moses. Although it cannot be demonstrated that his interpretations of the Laws of Moses originated in the expository activity in

---

[8] See Earp (1929–62) 269–433. Cf. Alexandre (1967) 105–29.

the synagogues, they obviously in various degrees had this activity as background, and even, at places, as source.

At times Philo relates that he had mystical experiences in connection with his exegetical activity. In *Spec.* 3:1–6 Philo recounts his mind's inspired ascents, in which he either travels together with the sun, moon and the other heavenly bodies or in the upper air. The ascents lift him up from earthly cares, give him a bird's eye's perspective and a hermeneutical key to the Laws of Moses. Moreover, according to *Cher.* 27–29 Philo at times hears a voice in his soul. Often this soul is god-possessed and prompts the mind to grasp a deeper meaning. Finally, under divine inspiration he had ecstatic experiences with loss of consciousness and with an experience of light (*Migr.* 34–35). The variety of forms of these ecstatic experiences support the understanding that they refer to real experiences and are not only literary compositions made up by Philo as an author.

He had been to Jerusalem and worshipped in the Temple: "There is a city on the sea coast of Syria called Ascalon. While I was there at a time when I was on my way to our ancestral Temple to offer up prayers and sacrifices . . ." (*Prov.* 2:64). According to Philo Moses had ordained that since God is one, there should also be only one temple (*Spec.* 1:67), alluding to Deut 12's words about the centralization of the temple worship in Jerusalem. Deuteronomy 12 is also the basis for the similar view expressed by Josephus in *Ant.* 4:200 and *Ag.Ap.* 2:193.

Philo is polemical against pagan temples both by emphasizing monotheism and by arguing against the existence of many temples either in many places or many in the same place (*Spec.* 1:67). In this statement there seems, moreover, to be an implicit rejection of the temple of the Jew Onias as a legitimate temple for Jewish worship besides the worship in the Jerusalem Temple.

Scholars, such as J.J. Collins and A. Mendelson, maintain that although the Temple played crucial roles in Philo's thought, he made realistic accommodation to the exigencies of life. For example, in *Leg. all.* 3:11, commenting on Deut 16:16, he was more concerned to expatiate on the true (allegorical) meaning of the Temple feasts than he was to inform his fellow Diaspora Jews how to fulfill their traditional religious obligations.[9] This understanding needs to be modified:

---

[9] Mendelson (1988) 18–21; Collins (1983) 116.

Although the distances made pilgrimages to Jerusalem from the Diaspora difficult and strenuous, the direct ties with the Jerusalem Temple were strong also on the level of the regular religious life, as can be seen from the circumstance that at stated times selected envoys brought the money for the first fruits and sacrificed in the Temple. And the hopes of the pious Jews rested on this (*Legat.* 156). Thus it is surprising that Mendelson only refers in passing in a footnote to this religious and economic practice which involved the Diaspora Jews in a personal way and made them participate actively and regularly in the network centered around the Jerusalem Temple.[10]

Philo's geographical horizon

In his book, *Ptolemaic Alexandria*, P.M. Fraser states that an adequate understanding of the outlook of an individual in antiquity depends to a considerable extent on our ability to assess his geographical horizon.[11] Thus, in order to understand the situation of Philo and Alexandrian Judaism as a whole, it is of interest to examine the main points of their geographical world perspective. As reflected in Philo's writings, his world comprised the area from India in the east to Libya, Rome and the Atlantic ocean in the West, and from Scythia and Germany in the north to Ethiopia in the south.[12]

In this world three centers are emphasised by Philo:

1   Jerusalem;
2   Greece, with Athens as the main city;
3   Alexandria and Egypt, where Philo lived.

A fourth center is generally presupposed, and is explicitly mentioned in connection with the pogrom in Alexandria in A.D. 38: Italy and Rome.

With regard to Jerusalem Philo presents the common Jewish view:[13] Jerusalem and the Temple are the center of all Judaism, whether in the Diaspora or in Judea. Philo is an important source for knowledge of the Jewish Diaspora as well as for knowledge of the role of

---

[10] Mendelson (1988) 62, n. 16.
[11] Fraser (1972) 1:520; Borgen (1983A) 59–71.
[12] *Somn.* 2:59.121f.; *Spec.* 3:15–23; *Quod Deus* 173–75; *Ebr.* 133; *Aet.* 141; *Jos.* 134–36; *Mos.* 2:18–20; *Legat.* 10, 356.
[13] See Safrai (1974) 184–215.

Jerusalem in this period.[14] In a letter attributed by Philo to King
Agrippa,[15] the king writes:

> While she [the Holy City], as I have said, is my native city she is also
> the mother city not of one country Judaea but of most of the others in
> virtue of the colonies sent out of divers times to the neighbouring lands
> Egypt, Phoenicia, the part of Syria called the Hollow and the rest as
> well, and the lands lying far apart, Pamphylia, Cilicia, most of Asia up
> to Bithynia and the corners of Pontus, similarly also into Europe, Thes-
> saly, Boeotia, Macedonia, Aetolia, Attica, Argos, Corinth and most of
> the best parts of Peleponnese. And not only are the mainlands full of
> Jewish colonies, but also the most highly esteemed of the islands Euboea,
> Cyprys, Crete. I say nothing of the countries beyond the Euphrates,
> for except for a small part they all, Babylon and of the other satrapies
> those where the land within their confines is highly fertile, have Jewish
> inhabitants. So that if my own home-city is granted a share of your
> goodwill the benefit extends not to one city but to myriads of the others
> situated in every region of the inhabited world whether in Europe or
> in Asia or in Libya, whether in the mainlands or in the islands, whether
> it be seabord or inland (*Legat.* 281–83).[16]

In this list Philo shows special interest in the Jewish colonies in Greece,
as various parts of Greece and the Greek islands are listed in particular detail. No mention is made, however, of the Jewish community
of Rome nor of the Jews in Italy as a whole. In connection with his
visit to Rome due to the Alexandrian pogrom, Philo speaks about
the Jews in Rome (*Legat.* 155–57).[17]

Like Josephus, Philo gives evidence of the fact that Jerusalem was
the center of a network which tied the Palestinian and the Diaspora
Jews together. In his praise of the Emperor Augustus Philo emphasizes that he did not prevent the Jews of Rome from collecting money
for sacred purposes from their firstfruits and send them to Jerusalem
by persons who would offer the sacrifices (*Legat.* 156–57). Philo was
aware that the Jews had this privilege in the various places of their
diaspora:

> In fact, practically in every city there are banking places for the holy
> money where people regularly come and give their offerings. And at
> stated times there are appointed to carry the sacred tribute envoys se-
> lected on their merits, from every city those of the highest repute, under
> whose conduct the hopes of each and all will travel safely. For it is on

---

[14] See Stern (1974) 117–83.
[15] See Smallwood (1961) 292.
[16] See Smallwood (1961) 293–96.
[17] Stern (1974) 118.

these firstfruits, as prescribed by the law, that the hopes of the pious rest (*Spec.* 1:78.[18] See also Josephus *Ant.* 18:312–13, and *J.W.* 7:218).

Moreover, Jews from the Diaspora went on pilgrimages to Jerusalem. Philo writes:

> Countless multitudes from countless cities come, some over land, others over sea, from east and west and north and south at every feast. They take the temple for their port as a general haven and refuge from the bustle and great turmoil of life. . . . Friendships are formed between those who hitherto knew not each other, and the sacrifices and libations are the occasion of reciprocity of feeling and constitute the surest pledge that all are of one mind (*Spec.* 1:69).[19]

Finally, Philo seems to give evidence for the expectation that God some day would gather together in the homeland the exiles from the end of the earth.[20]

This material in Philo shows that he regarded the Jews as one nation whether they lived in Jerusalem and Judea or were scattered around in the other parts of the world. His main aim was therefore not to assert the independence and greatness of Alexandrian Judaism over Palestinian Judaism. Consequently, when he refers to other Jewish scholars, he does not classify some as Alexandrian teachers in distinction from Palestinian rabbis. For example, when Philo in *Mos.* 1:4 refers to the elders who transmitted to him traditions about Moses, he calls them elders of the nation, although probably they were in fact largely Alexandrian teachers. The picture given above of pilgrimages (*Spec.* 1:69) indicates, however, that Jerusalem to some extent served as a pool of information and a place of exchange of traditions and news about Jews from Judea and from the various Diaspora communities.

It has already been noted that Philo shows special interest in Greece, since in *Legat.* 281–83 he listed various parts of Greece and the Greek islands in particular detail. In several places he expresses a high regard for Athens and Greece and their contribution to civilisation. He frequently uses the Greek division of the world: Greeks and barbarians.[21] Although the importance of Athens had diminished in Hellenistic and Roman times, it still was one of the most celebrated and honoured cities. In accordance with this view, Philo says

---

[18] See also *Legat.* 216, 291, 311–12. Smallwood (1961) 237–39.
[19] Safrai (1974) 191ff.
[20] *Praem.* 117. Cf. Safrai (1974) 185.
[21] *Opif.* 128; *Ebr.* 193; *Conf.* 6, 190; *Mut.* 35–36; *Abr.* 136, 267, etc.

that Athens ranks highest in Greece: ". . . the Athenians, the keenest
in intelligence among the Greeks – for Athens is in Greece what the
pupil is in the eye and reason in the soul . . ." (*Prob.* 140). The dry
climate of Greece, though bad for vegetation, is good for intellect
(*Prov.* 2:66). Thus, Greece was a center for learning (*Mos.* 1:21–23).

Consequently, Philo draws extensively on Greek authors, many of
whom he also names explicitly. Apart from Biblical names, most of
the personal names mentioned by Philo belong to Greek culture.
Also, most of the pagan gods referred to by name are Greek ones:
Koré, Demeter, Poseidon, Hera, Hephaestus, Apollo, Artemis, Aphrodite, Hermes, Bacchus, Heracles, and Zeus.[22]

Besides Jerusalem and Athens, Rome is also of central significance
to Philo, though in a different way. In Philo's view Rome and the
Romans have no culture or learning of their own, but serve as pro-
moters of Greek culture. Rome's importance is in the political sphere.
Philo describes the Roman empire as a dominion not confined to
the really vital parts of the world – the world between the Euphrates
and the Rhine – but a dominion extending from the rising to the
setting of the sun. The Roman emperors are chief actors in Philo's
treatises *Against Flaccus* and *On the Embassy to Gaius.*[23]

A main problem was the worship of the emperor. Philo recognised
that Augustus was venerated as God, and he refers explicitly to the
worship of him in the temple Sebasteum in Alexandria. Philo stresses
that Augustus did not directly claim to be god. Although the Jews
regarded emperor-worship with horror, Augustus still approved of
them and permitted them to live in accordance with their Laws and
worship only their one God. Philo interpreted this to mean that
Augustus was never elated or puffed up by the vast honours given to
him. The emperor Gaius Caligula, on the other hand, made a direct
claim to divinity, and enforced the worship of himself. The Jews
were not to be exempted. Philo makes it clear that the Jews opposed
him on principle, since they acknowledged only one God, the creator. In Philo's judgment, Gaius Caligula overstepped the bounds of
human nature in his eagerness to be thought a God (*Legat.* 75).[24] In

---

[22] *Opif.* 100; *Prob.* 102.127.130; *Aet.* 81; *Prov.* 2:7.24; *Legat.* 188.265.346.

[23] Augustus, Gaius Julius Caesar Octavianus: *Flac.* 23.49.81.103f.; *Legat.* 48.149.322;
Augustus, Gaius Caesar Caligula: *Flac.* 9–15, etc.; *Legat.* 32–39, etc.; Claudius Germanicus Caesar: *Legat.* 206; Julius Caesar is mentioned in *Prob.* 118.

[24] *Legat.* 75–165. For details of Gaius' conflict with the Jews, see Smallwood (1976)
174–80; 236–45.

this context Philo expressed his high evaluation of the *pax romana* created by Augustus, and charged Gaius Caligula with causing war and strife to flourish (*Legat.* 143–49).

As for Philo's picture of Alexandria and Egypt, he states that Egypt is delineated by the sea in the north, by Libya in the west, and by Ethiopia in the south (*Flac.* 43; *Mos.* 1:99). Philo knows that Alexandria with its environs has status as a city in its own right distinct both politically and culturally from Egypt proper. He uses the double name, Alexandria and Egypt.[25] Moreover he knows that the Roman prefect of Alexandria and Egypt also rules over Libya (*Flac.* 152).

In passing Philo reports that Egypt is divided into provinces, the nomes (*Mos.* 1:21; *Vit.cont.* 21). It is surprising, however, that he names very few of the locations of Egypt. He tells that the Nile flows from Ethiopia through the whole of Egypt, and that the Egyptians have deified it.[26] Outside Alexandria the Mareotic Lake was located (*Vit.cont.* 22). A few Egyptian towns and cities, such as Memphis, are mentioned as places of history.[27]

At times Philo can express positive appraisals of the Egyptians. They are men of high learning, as teachers of arithmetic, geometry, the love of metre, rhythm and harmony, etc. (*Mos.* 1:214). Mostly, however, his characterization of the Egyptians is of a negative nature. He offers sharp criticism of their worship of animals and of the Nile. He specifies the animal worship as worship of bulls, rams, goats, lions, crocodiles, asps, dogs, cats, wolves, and birds, as well as ibises and hawks, and also fishes.[28] The bull Apis is by Philo identified with the golden calf in Exod 32.[29] It is to be noted that other main Egyptian gods, such as Isis, Osiris, Hathor, etc. are not explicitly mentioned by Philo.

Philo is harsh in his criticism of the character of the Egyptians: they are arrogant whenever they have experienced good fortune (*Agr.* 62). Jealousy is part of the Egyptians' nature, and the Egyptians have an ancient and innate hostility to the Jews (*Flac.* 29). They are fools who prefer ease to toil and are at enmity with those who would

---

[25] *Flac.* 163. See Fraser (1972) 2:197f.

[26] *Mos.* 1:6.98–101, 114–18, 202, 2:195; *Conf.* 29f.; *Heres* 315f.; *Fug.* 179f.; *Somn.* 2:255–59, 278, 300; *Praem.* 90; *Prov.* 2:65. See Lambdin (1962) 3:549–51.

[27] Memphis, *Mos.* 1:118; other places are mentioned in *Post.* 54–58; *Somn.* 1:77f.

[28] *Dec.* 76–80; *Legat.* 139.163. Cf. Moore (1950) 1:197–98, about the emphasis on animal worship in the Greek and Roman periods.

[29] *Sacr.* 130; *Post.* 2:158–67; *Ebr.* 95–124; *Migr.* 85; *Fug.* 90; *Mos.* 2:161–73, 270–4; *Spec.* 3:79, 124–27.

advise them to their profit (*Mut.* 170). Thus, the Egyptians represent body and passion, evil and rebellion against God.[30] They are a seed-bed of evil in whose souls both the venom and the temper of the native crocodiles and asps are reproduced.[31]

Among the cities of the Roman Empire, Philo describes only Alexandria, his home city, in any detail. The city has five quarters named after the first letters of the alphabet (*Flac.* 55). The locations most clearly identifiable from Philo's writings are the island Pharos and the temple Caesareum. Both places have an ideological importance. The island Pharos was the place where, according to tradition, the Laws of Moses were translated into Greek, an event which Jews and Greeks celebrated together on the island every year as a sign of the coming universal recognition of the Laws of Moses.[32] The Caesareum, in turn, was a glorious temple for the worship of the emperor:

> For there is elsewhere no precinct like that which is called Sebasteum, a temple to Caesar on shipboard, situated on an eminence facing the harbours famed for their excellent moorage, huge and conspicuous, fitted on a scale not found elsewhere with dedicated offerings, around it a girdle of pictures and statues in silver and gold, forming a precinct of vast breadth, embellished with porticoes, libraries, chambers, groves, gateways and wide open courts and everything which lavish expenditure could produce to beautify it – the whole a hope of safety to the voyage either going into or out of the harbour.[33]

Among the other places in the city Philo mentions the gymnasium, with a statue said to be dedicated to Cleopatra. Other places are the market place, the palace, theatre, numerous synagogues in all parts of the city, especially one large and notable one.[34] Beaches, dunghills and tombs are also part of Philo's picture of the city as also are the harbours of the river Nile.[35]

Philo makes the prefect Flaccus praise Alexandria in the lament of his own downfall: "I am Flaccus, who but now was governor of Alexandria, that great city, or multitude of cities. . . ." In another place Philo tells that the city was close to the heart of Gaius. Gaius thought that this large city was admirably situated for commanding

---

[30] *Leg. all.* 3:38; *Somn.* 2.255; *Post.* 156; *Abr.* 103; *Jos.* 151f.; *Conf.* 88; *Congr.* 118.
[31] *Legat.* 166: Philo here contemptously characterises the Alexandrian 'Greeks' as Egyptians. See Smallwood (1961) 225 and 246.
[32] *Mos.* 2:35–44. See also *Flac.* 27.110.
[33] *Legat.* 150–51. See Smallwood (1961) 231–32.
[34] *Flac.* 34.37.45–48.64.74.84.92.95; *Legat.* 131–35.
[35] *Flac.* 56; *Legat.* 127–29.

or serving the habitable world. He therefore wanted to make the city into a center for the worship of himself as god. Such praise of Alexandria's universal role was part of Ptolemaic ideology, but was also continued in Roman time.[36]

As for the Jews in Alexandria, some details are to be added to the points already mentioned. The Jews were organised as a community with their own council of elders, the gerousia.[37] The names of three of these elders are given: Euodus, Trypho and Andro. Many professions were represented among the Alexandrian Jews, such as tradesmen, farmers, shipmen, merchants and artisans (*Flac.* 57). At other places, however, Philo's writings reflect that many of the Jews were poor.[38]

Although Philo may at times divide the population of Alexandria into two groups, the Jews and the others, he also makes it clear that there were three main groups in the city:

a   the Alexandrians proper,
b   the Egyptians, and
c   the Jews.

Thus, Philo tells at one point that there were differences between the scourges used in the city. The Egyptians were scourged with a lash, which was different from the one used when the Alexandrians were punished by scourging. The Jews used to be treated like the Alexandrians in this respect, but during the pogrom they were treated like Egyptians.[39]

From this survey of Philo's world, it becomes clear that religiously and culturally he identified himself with Jerusalem and Athens; politically he gave a positive evaluation of the *pax romana*, but in his relationship with the Roman government he was nevertheless in a deep quandary since the very existence of Alexandrian Jewry was threatened by the tragic pogrom of A.D. 38. Alexandria played a universal role to Philo, both politically and religiously. Her central role for the Jews was especially made manifest in the Greek translation of the Laws of Moses.

Within this geographical horizon the historical perspective illumi-

---

[36] *Flac.* 163; *Legat.* 338; cf. 173. See Fraser (1972) 1:513; 2:702, n. 58, and 740, n. 160.

[37] *Flac.* 38.74.76. See Applebaum (1974) 473–76.

[38] *Spec.* 3:159ff.

[39] Acts 2:9–11; concerning the biblical names of Medes and Elamites, see Conzelmann (1963) 26. Philo, *Somn.* 2:59.

nates Philo's context further, especially the history of the Jews of Alexandria. This is the theme of the next chapter.

A comparison between the geographical horizons of
Philo and in Luke–Acts

Philo's geographical world perspective is viewed from the stand point of a Jew who is located in the Diaspora southeast of the Mediterranean. As comparison one might look for the geographical perspective of an author whose location is northeast of the same ocean. A relevant approach is then to examine the horizon of Luke–Acts, since also Luke–Acts has the Jewish Diaspora as its setting. Already in the first volume of Luke–Acts, the Gospel of Luke, the world perspective is apparent. The birth of Christ is seen within the context of the whole Roman empire: "In those days a decree went out from Caesar Agustus that all the world (*oikoumene*) should be enrolled" (Luk 2:1). The universal perspective is emphasised in the second volume, the Acts of the Apostles, where the horizon is "the ends of the earth" (Acts 1:8), "every nation under heaven" (2:5), and "all Asia and the world" (19:27).

What are then the border areas of the world in Luke–Acts? In the East, the outermost areas mentioned are the biblical nations of the Medes and the Elamites (Acts 2:9–11). Philo goes even further East and refers to India and the Indians (*Somn.* 2:56, 59; *Probus* 74). In the north Pontus and Bithynia at the Black Sea are listed by Luke in Acts 2:9–11; 16:7, and by Philo in *Legat.* 281–83.

In Acts the regions north of Macedonia are not specified, while Philo names the Scythians and Germans.[40] In the West Rom and Libya are names common both to Acts and Philo.[41] Vaguely, Philo refers to areas further West beyond Rome, but Rome is the most western place identified by him, besides Carthage, which he mentions in passing.[42] In the South Luke and Philo have knowledge of Ethiopia.[43]

---

[40] *Somn.* 2:59, 121.
[41] Acts 2:9–11; 28:12–31; *Legat.* 283; *Somn.* 2:54; *Leg. all.* 1:62.
[42] Carthage: *Immut.* 174. Philo knows of the Atlantic Ocean, *Ebr.* 133.
[43] Acts 8:26–39; *Immut.* 174; *Flac.* 43, etc.

Luke joins Philo in regarding Jerusalem, Athens and Rome as the main centers of the world. Both in the Gospel and in Acts Luke is very occupied with Jerusalem. Both Luke and Philo tell about people coming to worship in the Temple of Jerusalem. Philo shows how Jews from all the world meet and enjoy fellowship in Jerusalem, and Luke informs us that Jews from all nations live in Jerusalem.[44] Travel to and from Jerusalem in Acts moreover serves the aims and needs of the emerging Christian movement.[45] The central and universal role played by Jerusalem in Luke and Philo is due, of course, to the fact that both represent the geographical outlook of Diaspora Judaism.

As for Athens, Luke depicts her in Acts 17:10–34 as the central representative of non-Jewish culture and religion. It was here that Paul presented the gospel to Epicurean and Stoic philosophers.[46] In spite of the respect for Athens expressed by both Luke and Philo, Philo's admiration of the city is even more marked, just as Greek philosophy and literature to a much greater extent have penetrated his writings.

In Luke–Acts the Greek division of the people of the world into "Greeks and barbarians" is not utilised, and the Jewish distinction between Jews and gentiles prevails, and occasionally the term used is "Jews and Greeks".[47] In this way Luke limits himself to the typically Jewish terminology more than do Philo and Paul.

Acts 28:16–31 tells of Paul's coming to Rome, where he lived two years, teaching about the Lord Jesus Christ openly and unhindered. The precise role of Rome in this concluding section of Luke–Acts is much debated. One might here see the fulfilment of Acts 1:8: in Rome the gospel has reached the ends of the earth.[48] Roloff follows this interpretation in a modified form. According to him, Rome replaces Jerusalem in Acts. The eschatological people of God do not any longer have Jerusalem as their center. God leads Paul to Rome, the center of the gentile world.[49] Some scholars will not interpret "the ends of the earth" in Acts 1:8 as a reference to Rome. Thornton, for one, states that there is no evidence that any Jew, Greek or Roman around the first century A.D. ever conceived of Rome as being at

---

[44] For example Luke 2:41–51; 9:51–22:38; Acts 8:27–39; 21:15–36; 2:9–11; 6:1–9; Philo, *Spec.* 1:69.
[45] For example Acts 15:1–30.
[46] See Haenchen (1968) 454–55; Conzelmann (1963) 95–96; Schneider (1982) 2:231.
[47] Acts 13:45–46; 14:1–2; 18:6; 28:28, etc.
[48] Haenchen (1968) 112, n. 6; 654.
[49] Roloff (1981) 289, 371.

the end of the earth. All would have agreed that beyond Rome there
lay other countries, Spain to the West and Gaul and barbarian Bri-
tannia to the North. Thornton suggests an alternative interpretation
of "the ends of the earth" in Acts 1:8: the phrase points to the Ethio-
pian eunuch who, after having been baptised, returned to his country, Acts 8:26–39.[50]

Although knowledge of the regions West and North of Rome was
widespread, as evidenced in Philo's writings, Thornton is mistaken
when he says that no one around the first century conceived of Rome
as being at the end of the earth. Thornton overlooks Psalms of Solomon 8:15: "He brought him [Pompey] that is from the end of the
earth [i.e. Rome], that smiteth mightily."[51] Moreover, Philo, who lived
in Alexandria, only identifies and describes one city in the West,
Rome, and both in Philo's writings and in Luke–Acts Rome is the
most westerly place where Jews reside. Actually, no certain evidence
is found for the existence of a Jewish colony in the first century A.D.
West of Rome, apart from one in Carthage.[52]

On the basis of these data the most probable conclusion is: Rome
and her Jewish colony represent in Acts 28:16–31 "the ends of the
earth" (Acts 1:8), because that city is the one place in the extreme
West which stands out and is well known.[53]

Philo's home city, Alexandria, is also mentioned in Luke–Acts.
The fact that she was a main center for shipping and commerce is
reflected in Acts 28:11, which states that Paul sailed from Malta on
board a ship of Alexandria. From Acts 6:9 we learn that Alexandrian
Jews had settled in Jerusalem and shared a synagogue with other
Diaspora Jews. The impact of Alexandria is also seen in the Christian movement, through Apollos, who was an Alexandrian Jew, an
eloquent man, well versed in the scriptures. Luke associates him with
Corinth and Ephesus (Acts 18:24–19:1).[54]

The major stage of the events recorded in Acts is not Alexandria,
however, but Asia Minor, Macedonia and Achaia, besides Jerusalem
and the surrounding area. In these regions it seems that Luke attributes

[50] Thornton (1977–78) 374–75.
[51] See Hammershaimb (1970) 5:574, n. 15a. The English translation is taken from
Charles (1913) 2:641.
[52] Cf. Stern (1974) 117–83.
[53] Cf. Noack (1968) 82.
[54] See further 1 Cor 1:12; 3:4–6, 22; 4:6; 16:12; Tit 3:13. – The use of the Septuagint in Luke–Acts may also be listed as an influence from Alexandrian Judaism;
cf. Stendahl (1954) 158, 161–62.

a special role to Ephesus. Several observations point in this direction:

1. Luke reports the universal claim of the worship of Artemis, as stated by the silversmith Demetrius: Artemis "whom all Asia and the world worship". For comparison one might mention the way in which Philo makes non-Jews express the universal claim of Alexandria (*Flac.* 163; *Legat.* 338).

2. According to Acts 19:9f. Paul lectured for two years in Tyrannus' auditorium "so that all the residents of Asia heard the word of the Lord, both Jews and Greeks". As a result of his work in Ephesus "the word of the Lord grew and prevailed mightily" (Acts 19:20).

3. Most important, Paul's farewell discourse, Acts 20:17–38, was addressed to the elders of the Ephesian church. At the close of his church founding activity and missionary travel, Paul gives his 'testament' and his legacy to the church at Ephesus. This testament had paradigmatic character, and the Ephesian congregation thereby became the bearers of Paul's legacy.[55]

These points give a basis for the following hypothesis to be formulated. The horizon of Luke–Acts may be defined as the geographical perspective of the world as seen from the standpoint of pagans, Jews and Christians in Ephesus. If so, Ephesus has to Luke a function corresponding to that of Alexandria to Philo.

Paul's farewell speech offers the clue to the rest of Acts. His travel to Jerusalem, and then to Rome in the extreme West, is the completion of his ministry of preaching the gospel of the grace of God (Acts 20:24). His legacy to the church, however, he left with the church of Ephesus, and not with churches in Jerusalem and Rome.

Thus, two corresponding perspectives can be seen, that of Philo, seen from the standpoint of the great city south of the Mediterranean, Alexandria, and that of the author of Luke–Acts, mainly seen from the great city north of the same sea, Ephesus. In both cases the focus is placed on the areas around the eastern part of the sea, with Jerusalem as the main center. A special interest for Athens is evident, and also for Rome. Philo pays more attention to Athens than the author of Luke–Acts does, while to him the city of Rome has more of a principal function than it does for Philo. These different emphases reflect on the one hand Philo's philosophical bent and on the other hand the central role of the theme of mission to the ends of earth in Luke–Acts.

---

[55] Conzelmann (1963) 117; Schneider (1962) 2:293 ("Testament für die Kirche").

CHAPTER TWO

THE HISTORICAL PERSPECTIVE

The period of growth

As Philo looked back into Alexandrian history he shared with earlier generations of Jews their positive evaluation of the Ptolemaic rulers. In Ptolemaic times this positive attitude was seen in various ways: Aristobulus had an exegetical dialogue with King Ptolemy. *Letter of Aristeas* tells how King Ptolemy II Philadelphus wanted copies of Jewish books for his Library and how he entertained the Jewish scholars. In Book 3 of the *Sibylline Oracles* a Ptolemaic king, probably Ptolemy VI Philometor or his anticipated successor, is endorsed as a virtual Messiah. Similarily, Philo expressed his praise of Ptolemy II Philadelphus in *Mos.* 2:28–31. His positive evaluation of the Ptolemaic kings in general is seen in *Legat.* 138:

> Take first the kings of Egypt. In three hundred years there was a succession of some ten or more of these, and none of them had any images or statues set up for them in our meeting-houses by the Alexandrians, although they were of the same race and kin as the people and were acknowledged, written and spoken of by them as gods.

A survey of the history of the Jews in Egypt during the Ptolemaic and early Roman periods will make it possible to place Philo and his community better in context. Against that background it becomes evident that Philo is to be seen as the climax of exegetical trends which already began when the Laws of Moses were translated into Greek.[1]

Philo's writings are based on the Laws of Moses. As shown in the preceding chapter the geographical locations referred to in his treatises are mainly the regions east and north of Egypt and Egypt itself. Philo and the Jewish communities in Egypt lived within the same geographical confines as those of their ancestors.

Alexander the Great conquered Egypt in 332 B.C.[2] After his death in 323 B.C. his senior generals, the Diadochi, formed a collective

---

[1] See Borgen (1984) 279–80.
[2] For the following, cf. Borgen (1992A) 1062–72.

group of rulers. One of the generals, Ptolemy, was satrap of Egypt. When the collective leadership broke up, the empire was divided into three main parts, the kingdom of Antigonid Macedonia, the Seleucid kingdom in Western Asia and the Ptolemaic kingdom in Egypt.

Ptolemy I, called Soter, managed to defend his position in Egypt and founded the Ptolemaic dynasty. Egypt became an independent "Macedonian" kingdom, engaged in hard struggle for maintaining its independence and for playing a leading role in the affairs of the Hellenistic world. The city founded by Alexander, Alexandria, became the capital, and from this northern center of Egypt, in close approximity to the other centers of Greek civilization, the Ptolemies ruled over the long and narrow country created by the river Nile. Since the native Egyptians regarded the Ptolemies as an alien government – in spite of all the Egyptian traditions taken over by these rulers –, the Ptolemies employed Macedonians, Greeks and people from other non-Egyptian nations in their administration and army. Moreover, many prisoners of war from various nations were brought to Egypt as slaves.[3]

The government of Ptolemaic Egypt became a highly centralized and more ruthlessly efficient version of the ancient Pharaonic system. This reorganization took mainly place during Ptolemy I Soter ((323)304–284 B.C.) and Ptolemy II Philadelphus (284–246 B.C.). The whole land was the personal possession, the "house", of the king.

The encounter of the Jews with Hellenistic Egypt took place within the framework of the Ptolemies' military and economic expansions. Ptolemy I Soter conquered Palestine for the first time in 320 B.C.; he conquered it again in 312 B.C., 302 B.C., and finally in 301 B.C. It is probable that in the course of these wars numerous Jewish prisoners were taken into Egypt. Some Jews seemed to follow Ptolemy I voluntarily. The Jews settled all over Egypt, in the towns and in the country. Although living in Egypt, their ties with Jerusalem and Palestine remained strong and communication was made the easier by the circumstance that for about one hundred years (301–198 B.C.) Palestine was one of the Ptolemies' foreign possessions.

What was the nature of these Jewish communities? The dedication of the synagogues to the king show that the Jewish communities recognized the king and were recognized by him. The dedications are on behalf of the reigning sovereign in the same way as are the

---

[3] Rostovtzeff (1941) 1:1–43, 255–422.

pagan dedications, but direct ruler worship was avoided by the Jews.[4]
The recognition of the synagogue by the king implied that he had
given the Jews a legal status as a community, most probably in the
form of a *politeuma*.

The settlers from various ethnic groups were in many places organized as such *politeumata*. Such communities in Egypt were the *politeumata*
of Idumaeans, Phrygians, Cretans, Lycians, Cilicians, and Boeotians.
The legal status of such a *politeuma* has not been clarified at every
point, but basically it was the confirmation by the king that an ethnic
community was permitted – within limits – to live in accordance with
its ancestral laws. In the case of the Jews, this meant the right to live
according to the Laws of Moses.[5] It is probable that the High Priest
Hezekiah, who joined Ptolemy in 312 B.C., received the charter of
such a *politeuma*. Josephus cited Hecataeus, who told that Ptolemy I
gathered Jews who were prepared to follow him to Egypt, and read
them from a document: "For he possessed (the conditions) of their
settlement and their political constitution (drawn up) in writing"
(Josephus, *Ag.Ap.* 1:189). A variant of the formula 'to live according
to their ancestral laws' was also used by the Seleucid King Antiochus
III on the occasion of his conquest of Jerusalem in 198 B.C.[6] Moreover, in the *Letter of Aristeas* 310 the Jewish community of Alexandria
is called *politeuma*.

The largest Jewish community in Egypt was this one in Alexandria. The Alexandrian literature, especially the translation of the Bible
into Greek, testifies to the strength and vitality of the Jewish community of Alexandria already from the third century B.C.

The main occupation for the Jews in Egypt were military service
and agriculture. Numerous Jews served in the army as soldiers on
duty or as soldiers in the reserves. To lessen the cost of maintaining
an army, and to make the military forces identify themselves with
the government, the Ptolemies adopted the policy of settling large
numbers of soldiers in special military colonies, where in return for
a plot of farm land they were obliged to return to active service
upon call. This plot of land was liable to be withdrawn and restored
to the king's possession. Yet, in the process of time, these plots of

---

[4] Fraser (1972) 1:226–227, 282–283, 298–299. Cf. Philo, *Legat.* 137–138, 141–
142, 356–357; Josephus, *Ant.* 13:67; Kasher (1985) 30 and 257, n. 92.
[5] *CPJ* (1957) 1:6–8; Tcherikover (1966) 299–301; Kasher (1985) 30, 41.
[6] *CPJ* (1957) 1:7 and note 19; Josephus, *Ant.* 12:142.

land became gradually permanent possessions for all practical reasons, and could as such be inherited by the leaseholder's (the *cleruch*'s) children. The terms used to designate such military colonies were *katoikiai* or *cleruchies*.[7]

The other main area of occupation of the Jews in the third century B.C. was that of agriculture. Having received allotments from the king, many soldiers were at the same time farmers. Other Jews were leaseholders, 'king's peasants', field hands, vine-dresssers, shepherds, and so on. Jews also held positions in the police and in the governmental administration. A renegade Jew, Dositheos, son of Drimylos, had a great career. He served as one of the two heads of the royal secretariat, and later was called to the highest priestly office in Egypt, that of being priest in the ruler-cult, as the eponymous priest of Alexander and the deified Ptolemies. He served during the reigns of Ptolemy III Euergetes I (246–221 B.C.) and Ptolemy IV Philopator (221–204 B.C.).[8]

As the Jews penetrated into Ptolemaic Egypt, Hebrew and Aramaic gradually ceased to serve as spoken and literary languages, especially in Alexandria, but also increasingly in other parts of Egypt, as seen from inscriptions and papyri written in Greek. Since the Jewish communities within limits were permitted to follow the ancestral laws, the knowledge of the Laws of Moses was a fundamental need for the Jews themselves, and to a varying degree also for their sovereigns and employers, the different levels of the Ptolemaic administration. Thus, it seems somewhat artificial to ask whether the needs of the Jewish communities or the interest of the Ptolemaic administration made it necessary to translate the Torah into Greek.

The period of power

The Jews of Egypt did not only consolidate their positions during the period from Ptolemy VI Philometor (181–145 B.C.) to the Roman conquest in 30 B.C. They became a considerable military and political force. The background was the weakening of the Ptolemaic government, since Ptolemy IV Philopator (221–204 B.C.). Ptolemy V Epiphanes (204–181 B.C.) mismanaged the Egyptian economy, and the

---

[7] *CPJ* (1957) 1:11–15.
[8] *CPJ* (1957) 1:230–236; Kasher (1985) 60.

relationship with the native Egyptians deteriorated so that local revolts took place. Moreover, the foreign policy of the Seleucids in Antioch grew more aggressive, and they consistently were on the attack militarily. Family quarrels and court intrigues drained the strength of the Ptolemaic dynasty from the inside. When the Ptolemaic kings called for assistance from the new power in the West, Rome, Egypt became almost a client of Rome. In 198 B.C. Antiochus III (222–187 B.C.) conquered Palestine, and in 170 B.C. Antiochus IV Epiphanes (175–164 B.C.) invaded Egypt, but had to withdraw upon the ultimatum given him by the Roman envoy Popilius Laenas.[9]

When the relation between Jerusalem and the Seleucid occupants grew tense, pro-Ptolemaic sympathies developed in the city, and shortly before the Maccabean revolt, which started against the Seleucid government in 167, many Jews emigrated to Egypt. Of special importance is the emigration of Onias of the high priestly family in Jerusalem, probably about 162–160 B.C.[10] Onias IV and his sons Helkias and Hananiah had a remarkable career in Egypt. Onias was priest and warrior and was given an important role to play in Ptolemy VI's counter-move against the threatening power of the Seleucids. Onias and his Jewish followers formed a military force of some size, and they were settled in the Leontopolis district about 190 kilometers south east of Alexandria. Onias built a temple, and the area along the eastern branches of the Nile Delta was called 'the Land of Onias'. The settlement and the temple were probably built some years after Onias and his followers had emigrated to Egypt, that is, when Onias had gained a reputation as a good general and had organized around him a Jewish force of military value. The location of this military center was strategically important, and the fact that the Jews were assigned the defence of such a sensitive area for about a hundred years, indicate their strong position in Ptolemaic politics.[11] Their alliance with the Ptolemaic rulers also proved that they favoured a centralized government and wanted to mark themselves off from the native Egyptians.

Jewish leaders were especially influential during the reign of Cleopatra III, 116 to 101 B.C. Cleopatra chose her younger son Ptolemy X

---

[9] Tcherikover (1966) 73–89; Rostovtzeff (1941) 2:705 and 871; Wilson (1962) 2:55–56; Fraser (1972) 119–120.
[10] Tcherikover (1966) 228–231, 276–277; Kasher (1985) 7; See also Hayward (1982) 429–43.
[11] Kasher (1985) 7–8.

Alexander I to reign with her. The Alexandrians compelled her to depose him and accept the older son, Ptolemy IX Lathyrus to share her throne. In the subsequent tension, and conflicts among the Queen, her sons and the population, the Queen's control of the capital and the country was largely built on the loyal support of the Jews. The sons of Onias IV, Helkias and Hananiah, were appointed high officers in the Queen's army.[12] When Ptolemy Lathyrus, having fled to Cyprus, conducted a campaign against his mother with Seleucid help, Cleopatra entered into an alliance with the Hasmonean king Alexander Janneus.[13]

The Jewish leaders were not only military supporters of the Queen. They also influenced her in her political decisions. When Cleopatra in the years 104–102 B.C. went to Palestine against the Seleucids and Ptolemy Lathyrus, and some of her advisers recommended that she betray her ally, king Janneus, and seize the country for herself, Hananiah said: "I would have you know, that this wrong to the king will turn all the Jews who dwell in your kingdom into your foes" (Josephus, *Ant.* 13:354). Moreover, this incident shows that Hananiah, although of high priestly family from Jerusalem, recognized the Hasmonean government and did not try to return to Jerusalem and its temple. Hananiah's brother, Helkias, was killed in one of the battles fought in Palestine.[14]

The reign of the Ptolemaic dynasty was approaching its end, however. After the Roman Antony and the Egyptian Queen Cleopatra VII were defeated by Octavian in the battle at Actium in 31 B.C., and Antony and Cleopatra subsequently ended their lives, the Romans annexed Egypt in 30 B.C. and made it into a province.

Hopes and disaster

In many respects the transfer into Roman rule meant discontinuity with the Ptolemaic past.[15] The Ptolemaic capital had become a provincial city in the Roman Empire. The Roman prefect in the *praetorium*

---

[12] Josephus, *Ant.* 13:349 says that Cleopatra appointed the two Jewish generals "at the head of the whole army". Although probably an exaggeration, the statement testifies to their leading position in the army also beyond the Jewish units.

[13] *CPJ* (1964) 3:141–142; Tcherikover (1966) 283; *CPJ* (1957) 1:23.

[14] Tcherikover (1966) 283–284; Kasher (1985) 11.

[15] For the following, see especially *CPJ* (1957) 1:55–65; Tcherikover (1963) 1–8; Kasher (1985) 18–20.

replaced the Ptolemy and his court in the palace. The Roman legions replaced the multi-ethnic Ptolemaic army. From now on, the resources of Egypt and Alexandria had to serve the needs and aims of the new rulers and their home base, Rome. Nevertheless, the victory of Augustus had brought to an end the Ptolemaic dynasty which had proved itself unable to rule effectively. At first, therefore, the Roman conquest meant fresh life for a decaying administration. The result was economic progress. Apart from the appointment of the prefect, Augustus and his early successors only changed so much as was necessary to control the buraucracy and make it more efficient.

A few Jews continued the tradition of Dositheus, Onias, Helkias and Hananiah and had high posts in the government of the country, now in the Roman administration. The most prominent examples were Philo's brother Alexander and his son Tiberius Iulius Alexander.[16]

During the period between 30 B.C. and A.D. 117 three armed uprisings and revolts demonstrate that the situation of the Egyptian Jews were deteriorating and moved towards their extermination: the armed uprising at the death of emperor Gaius Caligula in A.D. 41, the impact of the Jewish war in Palestine on the tensions in Egypt, A.D. 66 and 70–73, and the suicidal Messianic revolution of Jews in Cyrene and Egypt in the years A.D. 115–117.

In A.D. 66 the Alexandrian Greek *polis* wanted the emperor Nero to cancel the Jews' rights in the city. (In the same year Nero decided to recognize the exclusive sovereignty of the Greek polis in Caesarea Maritima over all residents in the city, thereby cancelling the rights of the Jewish community.) According to Josephus a number of Jews entered the amphitheatre in Alexandria where the members of the *polis* were deliberating on the subject of an embassy to be sent to Nero. The Greeks tried to capture the Jews, got hold of three of them, and took them away to be burned alive. This caused the whole Jewish community to rise and attempt to set fire to the amphitheatre. The Roman Prefect, Philo's nephew Tiberius Alexander, crushed the Jewish revolt. The soldiers killed the Jews, burned and plundered their houses. The Jews tried to oppose the Roman troops with arms, but they were totally routed. According to Josephus 50,000 Jews were killed.[17]

---

[16] *CPJ* (1957) 1:49, n. 4; *CPJ* (1960) 2:188–190; Smallwood (1976) 257–259; Kasher (1985) 347.
[17] *CPJ* (1957) 1:78–79.

The Jewish community structure was not abolished, however. The council of elders as an institution remained intact. In A.D. 73 some Jewish guerilla-fighters, the *sicarii*, fled from Palestine to Egypt, and instigated the Egyptian Jews to revolt under the slogan "No lord but God". After they had killed some of the moderate Jews of rank, the leaders of the council of elders in Alexandria called a general assembly and charged the *sicarii* for causing dangerous trouble. The assembly seized 600 *sicarii* on the spot. The *sicarii* who escaped into Egypt were arrested and brought back to Alexandria. All were put to death by the Romans. Moreover, the Romans, fearing that the Jews might again join together in revolutionary actions, demolished Onias' temple. This indicates that this temple was still a center of militant Judaism.[18]

The suicidal revolution in A.D. 115–117 involved the Jews in Alexandria and Egypt, in Cyrene and on Cyprus.[19] The Jews attacked their Greek and Egyptian neighbours. At first the Jews were victorious, but then began to suffer defeats, and when it developed into a war with the Romans they were crushed. All who participated in the war fought to exterminate the enemy.

The Jewish revolt was Messianic in character. Its aim was to destroy pagans and their polytheistic temples, and to establish Jewish control of the entire area, and probably also with the final aim of delivering Judaea and Jerusalem from Roman occupation. The aim was the liquidation of the Roman regime and the setting up of a new Jewish commonwealth, whose task was to inaugurate the Messianic era. In Cyrene a Jewish Messiah appeared, King Loukuas-Andreas.

The revolution was crushed by the Roman legions. In many places the Jewish population was almost totally annihilated. The great synagogue as well as other synagogues and buildings in Alexandria and in all of Egypt were demolished. Some Jews, mainly in Alexandria, it seems, survived, but the strength of Egyptian Jews had been broken for ever. In this way the more than 700 years of Jewish settlement and history in Egypt had virtually come to an end, and it took more than a century for Jewish life in Egypt to reawaken – never to achieve again its former strength.

---

[18] Josephus, *J.W.* 7:409–420 and 433–436.
[19] *CPJ* (1957) 1:89–90; Tcherikover (1963) 28–32; Hengel (1983) 655–686; Smallwood (1976) 397.

Jewish Alexandrian literature

Philo based his work on the Greek translation of the Hebrew Bible. This Greek translation, the Septuagint (the Translation of the Seventy), probably was initiated during the reign of Ptolemy II Philadelphus (284–246 B.C.) and was completed towards the mid-second century B.C. The Greek spoken and written by the Jews reflected their background. The Septuagint contains many Hebraisms, and a learned Greek, Cleomedes, gibes at the rude folk-dialect used in the synagogues. The translators to some extent modified the Hebrew text, at times drawing on some of the current exegetical traditions.[20]

The Septuagint served as basis not only for Philo's writings, but for the Jewish Alexandrian literature in general. The pieces preserved of this literature from the third century are largely found in Eusebius, *Praeparatio Evangelica*. Eusebius has five fragments of Demetrius, and Clement of Alexandria preserves still another fragment. Demetrius wrote in the third century B.C. under Ptolemy IV Philopator (221–204 B.C.), probably in Alexandria. His work was apparently called *On the Kings of Judaea*. The fragments are mainly concerned with the patriarchal history of the Septuagint Pentateuch and were probably part of the preface to an account of the Judaean monarchy. He formulates the biblical history in the form of Greek chronological historiography, corresponding to the chronological presentation of Egyptian history by the Egyptian priest Manetho, who also lived in the third century B.C. The goal which Demetrius and Manetho had in common was to demonstrate the considerable age of the respective national traditions.[21] Demetrius is also an exegete. He builds his book on the Septuagint and raises exegetical problems and gives answers, a method which became widely used in the exegetical form of *quaestiones et solutiones*. This method and this form played a central role in Philo's exegesis.

Eusebius has also preserved parts of the drama *The Exodus* written in Greek iambic trimeter by one Ezekiel, otherwise unknown. The tragedy covered most of the life of Moses in a version which for the most part followed the Septuagint translation quite closely, from Moses' birth and to the Exodus with the crossing of the Red Sea,

---

[20] *CPJ* (1957) 1:30–32; Tcherikover (1966) 348; Fraser (1972) 1:689–690.
[21] Hengel (1974) 1:69; Fraser (1972) 1:690–694; Attridge (1984) 161–62; Doran (1987) 248–251.

the destruction of the Egyptians, and closing with a description of the oasis Elim. A remarkable departure from the Septuagint text is found in a dialogue between Moses and his father-in-law, in which Moses describes a dream. In his dream Moses is conveyed to Sinai's peak, where he sees a gigantic throne and upon it, God himself in human semblance. God bids him approach the throne, gives him the sceptre, seats him on the throne and crowns him. From the throne, Moses beholds the whole universe. According to the interpretation, Moses will cause a great throne to arise, and he himself will rule over mortals. Moreover, he will see all things in the present, past and future. The fragments place emphasis on the Passover, and they express a cosmic understanding of Jewish existence. Moses' cosmic kingship implies a claim by the Jewish nation to be the ruler of the world. Accordingly, the opposing Egyptians who fought against the Jews, were destroyed. The tragedy shows how an Egyptian Jew employs Greek literary form to interpret Jewish self-understanding. The tragedy was written during the second half of the third century or the first half of the second century B.C.[22] This picture of Moses' heavenly ascent and divine kingship shows that Philo's corresponding understanding of Moses was not an innovation made by him.

Philo's writings testify to the existence of hostility felt and polemic expressed against the Jews. Such anti-Jewish sentiments were already formulated by the Egyptian priest Manetho, who counselled Ptolemy I Soter on native religion, and who in his history of Egypt gave a polemical interpretation of the Exodus of the Hebrew people. He represented them as mixed up with a crowd of Egyptian lepers and others, who for various maladies were condemned to banishment from Egypt. Manetho's work reflects the hostility of Egyptians to foreigners, and especially to Jews.[23] At the same time his polemic against the Jews testifies to the fact that they already represented an important factor in Egyptian society.

A book probably written in Alexandria in the 2nd century B.C., *On The Jews*, by Artapanus, shows kinship with Ezekiel the Tragedian in giving Moses divine attributes, but he does it in a syncretistic way. In his glorification of Moses and in his version of the salvation of the Jews in the Exodus, Artapanus is in direct opposition to the

---

[22] See Nickelsburg (1984) 125–130; Fraser (1972) 1:707–708; cf. Borgen (1984) 267–268.

[23] Josephus, *Ag.Ap.* 1:229; 2:1–15; Aziza (1987) 41–52; Fraser (1972) 1:508–509.

anti-Jewish account of Moses given by the Egyptian priest Manetho.

Aristobulus came from a high-priestly family and lived at the time of Ptolemy VI Philometor (181–145). His work has the form of an exegetical dialogue, in which he answers questions raised by the Ptolemaic king.[24] The author of the *Letter of Aristeas*, addressed to Aristeas' brother Philocrates, presents himself as a Greek courtier of Ptolemy II Philadelphus (284–246 B.C.). He tells about a series of events connected with the Greek translation of the Torah. According to the letter the translation took place during the early part of the reign of Ptolemy II Philadelphus, and was done by seventy Jewish scholars sent from the High Priest in Jerusalem upon request from King Ptolemy. The date when the Letter was written is uncertain, but it presupposes the existence of the Septuagint translation. A date in the middle or second half of the second century B.C. is probable, and in spite of its own claim to have been written by a non-Jew, a Jew must have been the real author.[25] The *Sibylline Oracles* also use a pagan figure as medium, the prophetess named Sibyl. Book 3 in the standard collection of Sibylline Oracles is Jewish. Its main corpus has been dated to the time of Ptolemy VI Philometor (181–145 B.C.).[26]

The Wisdom of Solomon was probably written sometime between 200 B.C. and A.D. 50, most probably during the first century B.C.[27] The central theme is the view that God's cosmic Wisdom is sought and made known to the King of Israel, Solomon, and is seen to be at work in the history of Israel and its worship of the one God. God's deliverance of the righteous and his warfare against the ungodly is the subject of the first part (Wisd 1:1–6:11).

The *Third Book of Maccabees* is an aetiological romance probably written at the beginning of the Roman period to explain an already existing festival, and to provide the Jews of Alexandria with ammunition in their struggle against the resident Greeks.[28] The main basis for the book seems to have been an older aetiological legend, recorded by Josephus in *Ag.Ap.* 2:5. According to this legend Ptolemy VIII Physcon (145–116 B.C.) cast the Jews, who supported Cleopatra, before drunken elephants. These turned instead against the king's friends, and the king changed his plans.

[24] See Borgen (1987) 1–16.
[25] Walter (1987) 83–85; Fraser (1972) 1:698–704; Kasher (1985) 208–211.
[26] See Collins (1984) 357–381, and bibliography.
[27] Schürer (1986) 3:1, 568–579; Nickelsburg (1982) 175–185.
[28] Schürer (1986) 3:1, 537–542, with criticism of Kasher (1985) 211–232; Nickelsburg (1982) 169–172.

In the *Third Book of Maccabees* this story seems to have been transferred back to the time of Ptolemy IV Philopator (222–204 B.C.) and woven together with the problems the Jews faced when that king wanted the Jews and others to worship Dionysus as condition for giving them full citizenship. The book offers support to the view that the Jews had an intermediate status higher than the native Egyptians, but lower than the full citizens of Alexandria. The King removed the privileges of the Jews and degraded them to the rank of natives. Their previous state was that of an ethnic *politeuma* in exile "worshipping God, and living according to his law they held themselves apart in the matter of food". They had the Jerusalem Temple as their religious center. On the condition that they entered into the royal cult of Dionysus they could obtain full citizenship. The end result was that the King issued a letter of protection for the Jews to all the governors in the provinces and permitted the Jews to put to death apostates among their own people.

Philo, an Alexandrian Jew

Philo lived during the early phase of the Roman period, and his writings reflect this historical situation. He tells that Augustus confirmed the rights of the Jewish community to live in accordance with their ancestral laws (*Flac.* 50 and *Legat.* 152–158, etc.). Nevertheless, the Jews entered into a new situation in important areas. They were eliminated as a military factor together with the Ptolemaic army as a whole. Although they, being dependent on the central government, had in time changed their allegiance from the Ptolemaic dynasty to the Romans, the Romans nevertheless used the Greeks in their administration and gave them privileges.

The deterioration of the situation for the Alexandrian Jewish community was demonstrated in the pogrom which took place when Gaius Caligula was Roman emperor and Flaccus was governor of Alexandria and Egypt. These disastrous events caused Philo to write the treatises *Against Flaccus* and *On the Embassy to Gaius*. The main reason for that crisis, which took place A.D. 38–41, was the growing conflict between the Jews and the Greeks in Alexandria, and Gaius Caligula's enforcement of emperor worship.[29]

---

[29] For the following, see Philo's two books *Against Flaccus* and *On the Embassy to Gaius*. See further Bell (1926) 1–30; Smallwood (1976) 237–250; *CPJ* (1957) 1:65–74; Barraclough (1984) 429–436.

The Greeks wanted a ruling from the prefect Flaccus on the con-
stitutional question of Jewish status in the city, and they succeeded
in getting Flaccus to issue an edict making the Jews to be "foreigners
and aliens". The Jews were now aliens without the right of domicile,
and without the rights to have an administration of their own under
the leadership of the council of elders.

Flaccus issued this edict after the anti-Jewish forces exploited the
visit of the Jewish king Agrippa by setting up a lunatic named Carabas
in royal robes in the gymnasium, saluting him as king in a mocking
scene. Then the crowd claimoured for the installation of images of
the emperor in the synagogues. A cruel progrom followed. The Jews
were driven together into a ghetto, and members of the Jewish council
of elders were arrested and tortured so severely that some died. The
Jewish embassy, headed by Philo, was sent to Rome for the purpose
of explaining to Gaius Caligula the traditional rights of the Jewish
community. The Greeks sent a counter-embassy, headed by the anti-
Jewish writer Apion. Philo's mission was a failure.

Suddenly the situation changed. In A.D. 41 Gaius Caligula was
assassinated and Claudius succeeded him. The Alexandrian Jews
started an armed uprising against the Greeks, and they received help
by Jews from Egypt and from Palestine. Roman intervention put an
end to the conflict, and Claudius issued an edict giving back to the
Jews the rights held before the pogrom started, reinstating the *politeuma*
and protecting the synagogues. The struggle before the emperor
continued. Finally he settled the questions in a letter.[30] He confirmed
the rights of the Jews, chastised both ethnic groups for their share in
the disturbances in Alexandria, forbade Jews to participate in the
activities in the gymnasium and recive gymnasium education. Claudius
stated explicitly that the Jews lived "in a city not their own".

Philo accordingly was divided in his attitudes towards the Roman
rule. Although he was sharp in his criticism of Gaius Caligula, he
had a positive view to the Roman rulers Augustus and Tiberius (*Legat.*
141–61). This positive attitude was conditioned upon their recognition of the rights of the Jews to live in accordance with the Laws of
Moses and worship the One God. On the other hand, the Roman
emperor Gaius Caligula and the prefect Flaccus were under the judge-
ment of God for abolishing the privileges of the Jews. In this respect

---

[30] *CPJ* (1960) 2:36–55; Bell (1924) 1–37.

he continued the general tradition of Alexandrian Jews in so far as it was reflected in their literature.

Also in other areas Philo continued trends from the earlier period. As shown above the Jews expressed a feeling of superiority in their writings: Aristobulus stated that Jewish philosophy, found in the Laws of Moses, had many points of agreement with the Greeks, whose philosophers and legislators learned from Moses; the pagan Aristeas made King Ptolemy express admiration of the Jewish Temple, worship, wisdom and Laws; the Jewish sages exceeded the philosophers in their wisdom; the Sibyl appeals to the Greeks to refrain from idolatry and adultery and prophesies that people from all countries will send gifts and worship in the Temple in Jerusalem. The Jews carry the moral leadership of the human race. The book Wisdom of Solomon outlines the cosmic significance of Jewish existence, interprets the universal role of Israel, represented here by the king, presumably Solomon. Some Greek philosophical concepts have been 'conquered' and made to serve Jewish self-understanding and Jewish imperial ideology.[31]

Philo followed the same tradition and emphasized the God-given role of the Jewish nation. His view suggests that he did not only fight for equal rights for the Jews, but claimed that the call of the Jews was to be the head nation with other nations as their vassals. According to Philo, Moses was appointed king of a nation destined to offer prayer forever on behalf of the human race (*Mos.* 1:149). The quality of the life of the Jewish nation will bring victory over their enemies, and the Jewish people will be the head of the nations (*Praem.* 79–172). Philo oscillates between military and spiritual warfare, but he testifies to the continuation of a militant eschatology in the Jewish community, ideas which probably inspired some Jews to take up arms at the death of Gaius Caligula in A.D. 41, and in the revolts of A.D. 66 and A.D. 115–17.[32]

Philo continues the approach seen especially in the *Letter of Aristeas*, in Aristobulus, and the Wisdom of Solomon to interpret the Laws of Moses and Jewish existence by means of Greek ideas and religious traditions. Thus both Aristobulus and Aristeas agreed that when the

---

[31] See Gilbert (1984) 309–12.

[32] Although Tcherikover and Fuks, *CPJ* (1957) 1:78, have ignored Philo's eschatological claim, they rightly stress that the Alexandrian Jews aimed at acquiring Alexandrian citizenship. See Borgen (1984A) 109–11.

Greek poets and philosophers speak of Zeus, they mean the true God, whom the Jews worship.[33] Of special importance is the circumstance that Aristobulus, in his use of Greek philosophy and quotations, and in his use of the allegorical method represented a trend towards Philo's developed expositions. Like Philo, he stresses the cosmic significance of Judaism, and shows that Philo's philosophically influenced exegesis was not an isolated case. According to Philo, the authentic philosophy was formulated by Moses, and Greek philosophy contained elements of this true philosophy and was in some points derived from the teachings of Moses.

The sharp polemic against polytheistic cults expressed in writings such as the *Letter of Aristeas*, the *Sibylline Oracles* 3, the Wisdom of Solomon, and *3 Maccabees* is also found in Philo's interpretations of the Laws of Moses. In *Aristeas* the one God, the Creator, is contrasted with the idols and idolatry of the Egyptians. The *Sibyl* in book 3 offers very sharp criticism of Romans and Greeks for their idolatry and adultery. Also in the fragments of *Aristobulus* there is a pointer in the same direction: Orpheus and Aratus, in quotations given, had no holy concepts of God since they used polytheistic names of the One God. Harsh criticism is found in the Wisdom of Solomon 13–15, and is a predominant theme of *3 Maccabees*. As for Philo, he often levels sharp criticism at polytheistic idolatry, as for example in his exposition of the first of the Ten Commandments (*Dec.* 52–81 and *Spec.* 1:12–20). Differing from all these writings, Artapanus represented a syncretistic form of Judaism.

Philo testifies to the continuation of ideological attacks on the Jews by the non-Jews. Such attacks were already seen in the writings of the Egyptian Manetho. In this connection it should be mentioned that Josephus, *Against Apion*, the anti-Jewish *Acts of the Alexandrian Martyrs*, and Gnostic writings prove that there was a broad stream of anti-Jewish traditions, attitudes and literature in Egypt. The Jewish polemic against aspects of pagan culture and against some of the other ethnic groups, such as the Egyptians, was at times as pointed. Thus, *Sybilline Oracles* 5, written towards the end of the first century A.D., is openly hostile to the gentiles in Egypt and Rome.[34]

---

[33] In two Jewish inscriptions from Ptolemaic times in Upper Egypt the god Pan, as the universal God, seems to be identified with the God of the Jews. See Hengel (1974) 1:264.

[34] Cf. Schürer (1986) 3:1, 595–608; Kasher (1985) 327–345; Pearson (1984) 340–341; Collins (1987) 436–438; Tcherikover (1963) 1–32; Hengel (1983) 655–86.

Philo's treatises *On the Confusion of Tongues* and *On the Change of Names* defended the Laws of Moses and Jewish institutions against apostates who were inclined to mock. And in *Hypothetica (Apology of the Jews)* he defended the Jews against attacks and criticism akin to the negative interpretation of Moses by the Egyptian historian Manetho and others. He had as presupposition traditional exegetical activity based on the Laws of Moses, a cosmic (and historical) interpretation of Judaism, involvement with issues on the borderline between the Jewish community and other peoples, and a conviction of the superiority of the Jewish nation. Thus, this survey suggests that Philo should not be understood as an isolated individual outside the broad stream of Jewish outlooks, convictions and attitudes which existed in the history of the Alexandrian Jewish community. It is the task of the present study to substantiate this understanding further.

CHAPTER THREE

REVIEWING AND REWRITING BIBLICAL MATERIAL

In the preceding chapter it was shown that the Septuagint played a central role in the Alexandrian Jewish community. Accordingly, many of Philo's writings are expositions of the Laws of Moses in this Greek translation. As a necessary background for a study of Philo as exegete, a brief preliminary survey of these expository writings will be given. They fall into two main groups:

A) Rewriting the Pentateuch.

The Exposition of the Laws of Moses:

In these exegetical works, Philo paraphrases and expands the biblical text. The extant writings here are: *On the Creation; On Abraham; On Joseph; On the Decalogue; On the Special Laws 1–4; On the Virtues*, and *On Rewards and Punishments*. Scholars have named this collection of treatises the *Exposition of the Laws of Moses*.[1]

On the Life of Moses:

On the Life of Moses was formerly classed in a group of miscellaneous writings, but E.R. Goodenough has shown that these treatises and the *Exposition* were companion works.[2]

Hypothetica (Apology of the Jews):

The preserved fragments of *Hypothetica (Apology of the Jews)* deal with events and laws which cover parts of the Pentateuch from Jacob (Genesis 25) to the conquest of Palestine in the books of Joshua and Judges. The emphasis in this work is placed on a characterization of Judaism in Philo's own time, especially serving as a response to criticism levelled against the Jews.

B) Exegetical Commentaries.

The Allegorical Commentary on Genesis,

which consists of *Allegorical Laws 1–3; On the Cherubim; On the Sacrifices of Abel and Cain; The Worse Attacks the Better; On the Posterity and Exile of Cain; On the Giants; On the Unchangeableness of God; On Hus-*

---

[1] Cf. Goodenough (1933) 109–25.
[2] *Ibid.* See further Morris (1987) 854–55.

bandry; On Noah's Work as Planter; On Drunkenness; On Sobriety; On the Confusion of Tongues; On the Migration of Abraham; Who is the Heir of Divine Things?; On Mating with the Preliminary Studies; On Flight and Finding; On the Change of Names; On God; On Dreams. This series covers the main parts of Genesis 2–41. In general they have the form of a verse-by-verse commentary on the biblical texts.

Questions and Answers on Genesis and Exodus:

This is a brief commentary in the form of questions and answers on sections of the two first books of the Pentateuch.[3] The extant text of *Question and Answers on Genesis* begins at Gen 2:4 and ends at 28:9 (with *lacunae*), and *Questions and Answers on Exodus* covers parts of Exod 12:2 to 28:34 (LXX). All but a small portion of the Greek original has been lost and for the bulk of the work we must depend upon the ancient Armenian version.[4]

Various expository forms are found in these writings. A comprehensive study of the forms used is needed. Only a beginning can be made in the present book.

Some of these forms may be characterized as direct exegesis in the meaning that either the biblical material may be interpreted by means of rewriting as a paraphrase, or a cited biblical text may be explained without a question being formulated. The first area to be analysed is Philo's paraphrastic rewriting and reviewing of smaller and larger units, even up to the rewriting of the larger parts of the Pentateuch as a whole.

Blessings and Curses:

Philo has taken the form and content of blessings and curses from the Bible. He also draws on biblical material as to content. In the book of Deuteronomy the theme of blessings and curses is of special importance. In some passages both are presented close together in antithetical form, such as in Deut 11:26–29 and in 28:3–6 and 16–19. As an example parts of Deut 11:26–28 may be quoted: "V. 26 'Behold, I set before you this day a blessing and a curse; (v. 27) the blessing, if you obey the commandments of the Lord your God . . . (v. 28) and the curse, if you do not obey the commandments of the Lord your God. . . .'"

Philo builds on this form in his rewriting of biblical material in

---

[3] The original work may have taken in other books of the Pentateuch, see Morris (1987) 826–30.

[4] See for example Hilgert (1991) 1–15.

Praem. 79–162, mainly drawing on parts of Lev 26 and Deut 28. The future blessings are surveyed in *Praem.* 85–125. Philo uses various words for blessings, such as blessing (εὐλογία, *Praem.* 79 and 113), gift (δωρεά, §§ 79 and 163), good thing(s) (τὸ ἀγαθόν/τὰ ἀγαθά, §§ 87–88, 102, 105, 118), grace, gift (χάρις, 101, 111, 126), and also the term εὐχή as it is used in § 126, cf. *Mos.* 1:278–94. The description of the curses follows in *Praem.* 127–62. The main term is curse (ἀρά, 126–27, 157, 162).

Philo ties the two sections together in *Praem.* 126: "These are the blessings (εὐχαί) invoked upon good men, men who fulfil the laws by their deeds, which blessings will be accomplished by the gift (χάρις) of the bounteous God, who glorifies and rewards moral excellence because of its likeness to Himself. We must now investigate the curses (ἀραί) delivered against the law-breakers and transgressors".

In *Heres* 177 Philo includes the biblical duality of blessings and curses in the lengthy section on equality, §§ 161–206. This section is to a large extent a collection of scriptural examples which illustrate the term equality, a term which has a Greek background. Thus the section has kinship with the section on *Virt.* 51–174, where biblical examples are collected to illustrate the term *philanthropia*, which has a Greek background just as the concept of equality does.

Philo paraphrases Deut 27:11–13 where Moses tells the 12 tribes that they were to divide themselves into two groups, one to gather on one mountain (Gerizim) and pronounce blessings, the other on another mountain (Ebal) to pronounce curses. This shows that curses are equal in number to blessings, and praises given to the good and censure given to the bad are equally beneficial, *Heres* 177.[5]

Lists of biblical examples

In Jewish and early Christian literature there were numerous reviews of biblical history. Such reviews vary in content and length and each is adapted to its own context and interpretative function. Some of them have the form of a series of examples, such as a series of persons and events listed to positively exemplify a given theme and concern, while in others the themes are exemplified by contrasting pairs of persons and groups. The order in which persons and events

---

[5] Cf. *1 QS* 2:2–10, where the priests pronounce blessings and the levites curses.

are listed may follow the sequence found in the biblical books, or they may be selected thematically and be rendered in a different order.[6] Lists of biblical persons are found among other places in Sirach 44:1–49:16, Wisd 10:1–21; 1 Macc 2:49–64; *3 Macc* 2:1–20; 6:1–15; *4 Macc* 16:16–23; 18:11–13; *Apocalypse of Zephaniah* 9:4; *4 Ezra* 7:106– 10; Hebr 11:1–39; *1 Clement* 4:7–6:4; 9:2–12:8.

Philo lists a series of biblical persons in *Virt.* 198–210. Here Adam, Noah, Abraham and Isaac are surveyed and characterized. The structure of *Virt.* 198–210 is as follows:

Thesis (Virt. 198). Unworthy children of excellent parents:

> That he [Moses] held nobility (τὸ εὐγενές) to depend on the acquisition of virtue and considered that the possessor of virtue and not anyone born of highly excellent parents is noble, is evident from many examples.

Examples common to all humankind:

1 Cain, son of Adam and Eve, cf. Gen 4:1–16 (*Virt.* 199–200): The sons of the earth-born were of high birth. They sprung from the first bridal pair. One of the sons murdered his younger brother.

2 The three sons born to Noah, cf. Gen 6:11–9:25 (*Virt.* 201–02): One of the worthiest men was saved with his family in the deluge. One son cast shame on his father and was laid under a curse.

3 Adam, cf. Gen 2:15–24 (*Virt.* 203–05): Why leave out Adam, whose Father was the eternal God? He chose evil and changed immortality for mortality.

Examples peculiar to the Jews:

"But besides these common examples, the Jews have others peculiar to themselves" (206):

1 Abraham's many children and Isaac, cf. Gen 25:5–6 (*Virt.* 207): Abraham was father of many children, begotten with three wives, but only one inherited the patrimony.

2 Isaac and Esau and Jacob, Gen 27:5–40 (*Virt.* 208–10): Isaac begat two twins. The elder was disobedient and became a renegade, while the younger was obedient.

---

[6] See Attridge (1989) 30–37. Schmitt (1977). Concerning lists and catalogues in Antiquity in general, Fitzgerald (1997) 275–93.

Worthy children of men of guilt (Virt. 211):

1   Abraham, cf. Gen 11:31–23:6 (*Virt.* 212–19):
    Abraham, son of a father who was a polytheist was trans-
    formed and became the standard of nobility for all proselytes.
2   Women (*Virt.* 220–25):
    Also women aspired to this nobility (*Virt.* 220), such as a)
    Tamar, cf. Gen 38:6–11 (*Virt.* 221–22), and b) the concu-
    bines of Jacob and their daughters and sons, Gen 29:24, 29
    and 30:3, 9 (*Virt.* 223–25).

Conclusion (226–27):

> Must we not then absolutely reject the claims of those who assume as
> their own precious possession the nobility which belongs to others, who,
> different from those just mentioned, might well be considered enemies
> (ἐχθροί) of the Jewish nation (τοῦ τῶν Ἰουδαίων ἔθνους) and of every
> person in every place?
> Enemies of our nation, because they give their compatriots licence
> to put their trust in the virtue of their ancestors and despise the thought
> of living a sound and steadfast life.
> Enemies of people in general, who even if they reach the very sum-
> mit of moral excellence, will not benefit thereby, if their parents and
> grandparents were not beyond reproach.
> I doubt indeed if any more mischievous doctrine could be propounded
> than this, that avenging justice will not follow the children of good par-
> ents if they turn to wickedness, and that honour will not be the reward
> of the good children of the wicked, thus contradicting the law, which
> assesses each person on his own merits and does not take into account
> the virtues or vices of his kinsmen in awarding praise or punishment.

In this collection of examples the focus is on the dynamics between
generations and not on individuals as such. Thus no names are given,
although their identities can easily be recognized. As a parallel, one
might refer to the list of examples in Wisd 10:1–21 where persons
are characterized but not named. In these two passages the biblical
persons are characterized, respectively as nobly born, virtuous, err-
ing, etc. (*Virt.*) and righteous and unrighteous, etc. (Wisd). Thus the
persons explicitly exemplify certain qualities or lack of qualities and
therefore their names are not of importance.[7]

This series of cases from the Laws of Moses in *Virt.* 198–210 serves
as an argument against the view that nobility of ancestry as such is

---

[7] Schmitt (1977).

a criterion of nobility, and in favour of the view that the criterion is rather the virtuous life of the person himself.

It is worth noticing that, although Philo here illustrates a general principle, he at the same time explicitly applies it to the relationship between the Jewish nation and others. Accordingly he divides the examples in two groups: (1) Examples common to all humankind, and (2) examples peculiar to the Jews. Those who refer to their noble ancestry in order to assert themselves over against the Jewish *politeia*, are enemies of the Jewish nation. At the same time Philo keeps the idea of Jewish superiority, since he maintains that non-Jews obtain nobility by following Abraham's example and becoming proselytes.

A list of examples from biblical history is also found in the *Allegorical Commentary*, for example in *Leg. all.* 3:(65)69–106. The exposition of Gen 3:14–15 in *Leg. all.* 3:65–68 has the form of question and answer. The problem is the contradiction between two biblical words: God curses the serpent without giving it the opportunity to defend itself (Gen 3:14–15), while he gave Eve the opportunity to defend herself by asking her "What is this that you have done" (Gen 3:13). Philo's answer to the question is that the woman, meaning sense-perception, may be good or bad, while the serpent, meaning pleasure is always and everywhere guilty and foul. In this way the theme of predestination is introduced and a chain of biblical examples is listed to exemplify and prove the point. The theme is repeated in the transitions among the examples.

A parallel to the predestined punishment of the serpent is seen in the story of Er, Gen 38:6–7, *Leg. all.* 3:69–76. Philo's transition reads: "For this reason in the case of Er also God knows him to be wicked and puts him to death without bringing an open charge against him" (*Leg. all.* 3:69).

As a contrast Philo from *Leg. all.* 3:77–106 lists examples of predestination of good persons. At some points wicked persons are mentioned as a contrast. The examples are selected on the basis of the theme, so that the order does not in general follow the same sequence as that found in the Pentateuch. The exception is the sequence of the patriarchs Abraham, Isaac and Jacob.

The cases included are:

Leg. all. 3:77–78: Noah, Gen 6:8:
The transitional statement, *Leg. all.* 3:77, reads: "Exactly, then, as God has conceived a hatred for pleasure and the body without giving

reasons, so too has he promoted goodly natures apart from any manifest reason, pronouncing no action of theirs before bestowing his praises upon them". The example is Noah and the conclusion is (3:78): "For all things in the world and the world itself is a free gift and act of kindness and grace on God's part".

Leg. all. 3:79–82: Melchizedek, Gen 14:18:
The transition, *Leg. all.* 3:79, reads: "Melchizedek, too, has God made both king of peace, for that is the meaning of 'Salem', and His own priest. He has not fashioned beforehand any deed of his, but produces him to begin with as such a king, peaceable and worthy of His own priesthood". Melchizedek is pictured as a king in contrast to a despot. Subordinate biblical references are Deut 4:39 and 23:3–4.

Leg. all. 3:83–84: Abraham, Gen 12:1:
The transition, *Leg. all.* 3:80, reads: "What good thing had Abram already done, that He bids him estrange himself from fatherland and kindred . . ."? The example listed is Abram who turned away from what is base, contemplated the universe and explored the Deity and His nature.

Leg. all. 3:85–87: Isaac, Gen 17:17–19:
The transition reads (*Leg. all.* 3:85): "Some even before their birth God endows with a goodly form and equipment, and has determined that they shall have a most excellent portion". The example given is Isaac, whom God held worthy of his name, meaning joy, even before he was begotten.

Leg. all. 3:88–89: Jacob and Esau, Gen 25:23:
The transition reads (*Leg. all.* 3:88): "Once again, of Jacob and Esau, when still in the womb, God declares that the one is a ruler and leader and master, but that Esau is a subject and a slave". The examples are Jacob, who is endowed with reason and Esau, who represents what is base and irrational.

Leg. all. 3:90–93: Manasseh and Ephraim, Gen 48:19:
The transition is found in *Leg. all.* 90: "What led this same Jacob, when Joseph brought to him his two sons, the elder Manasseh and the younger Ephraim, to cross his hand and place his right hand on Ephraim, the younger son and his left hand on Manasseh, the elder . . ."? The examples are Ephraim, the younger son, who received the first place, and Manasseh, the elder, who was counted worthy of second place.

Leg. all. 3:94: The sacrificers of the Passover, Num 9:1–8:
The transition reads: "Moses also, to take another case, awards special praise among the sacrificers of the Passover to those who sacrificed the first time [i.e. in the first month], because, when they had separated themselves from the passions of Egypt by crossing the Red Sea, they kept to the crossing and no more hankered after them, but to those who sacrificed the second time [i.e. in the second month], he assigns the second place, for after turning they retraced the wrong steps they had taken and, as though they had forgotten their duties, they set out again to perform them. . . ." The examples are the faithful and the forgetful sacrificers of the Passover.

Leg. all. 3:95–99: Bezalel, Gen 31:2–4:
The transition in *Leg. all.* 3:95 reads: "This, moreover, is the reason of God's proclaiming Bezalel by name, and saying that He has given him wisdom and knowledge, and that he will appoint him artificer and chief craftsman of all the work of the Tabernacle, that is of the soul, though He has so far pointed to no work or deed of Bezalel, such as to win him even commendation". The example, Bezalel, means 'shadow'. He represents those who discern the Artificer by means of His works. Gen 1:27 is cited as a secondary biblical reference.

Leg. all. 3:100–03: Moses, Exod 25:40 and 33:13; Num 12:6–8:
The transition is given in *Leg. all.* 3:100: "There is a mind more perfect and more thoroughly cleansed . . . a mind which gains its knowledge of the First Cause not from created things, as one may learn the substance from the 'shadow', but lifting its eyes above and beyond creation obtains a clear vision of the uncreated One, so as from Him to apprehend both Himself and His 'shadow'". The examples recorded are Moses, who is the artificer of the archetypes, and Bezalel, the artificer of the copies of these.

Conclusion, Leg. all. 3:104–06.
The exposition in *Leg. all.* 3:65–76 of the cursing of the serpent, Gen 3:14–15, and the list of biblical examples (*Leg. all.* 3:77–103) illustrate that there are two different natures created. On the basis of this biblical documentation Philo gives an exhortation in the 1st person plural, *Leg. all.* 3:104:

> Seeing then that we have found two natures (δύο φύσεις) created, undergoing moulding, and chiselled into full relief by God's hands, the one essentially hurtful, blameworthy, and accursed, the other beneficial and praiseworthy, stamped the one with a counterfeit, the other with

a genuine impression, let us offer a noble and suitable prayer (εὐχὴν εὐξώμεθα), which Moses offered before us, 'that God may open to us His own treasury' (Deut 28:12) . . ., and that He may close up the treasuries of evil things.

This exhortation receives further motivation by a didactic epilogue (*Leg. all.* 3:105–06), about the treasury of evil things and the treasury of good things. The conclusion points to the possibility of repentance for those who sin: "For he [Moses] says that the treasuries of evil things were sealed in the day of vengeance, the sacred word thus showing that not even against those who sin, will God proceed at once, but gives time for repentance and for the healing and setting on his feet again of him who had slipped" (*Leg. all.* 3:106). Thus the biblical examples of cases of predestination do not prevent Philo from concluding with a call for prayer and with a word about the possibility of repentance. Thus a paraenetic motive is traceable in this chain of biblical cases. As secondary quotations Deut 28:12 and 32:34–35 are cited in this concluding paragraph.

This list gives parallel examples to the case of the serpent (*Leg. all.* 3:65–68), largely in the form of its contrast. Words from the biblical story about the serpent are not woven into the exposition of the parallels. In the conclusion (*Leg. all.* 3:104), after all the examples have been presented, the word "accursed" from the quotation about the serpent, Gen 3:14–15, is brought into the exposition again. Thus, rather than giving a number of subordinate quotations, Philo here has a chain of parallel cases, placed side by side, using the case of the serpent, Gen 3:14–15, as a literary *inclusio* for the large section of *Leg. all.* 3:65–106. Within the context of each biblical case in the chain, some subordinate texts are included, such as Deut 19:17 and Gen 3:13 in *Leg. all.* 3:65–66, Deut 23:3f. in *Leg. all.* 3:81, Deut 4:39 in *Leg. all.* 3:82, Num 9:6ff. in *Leg. all.* 3:94, Gen 1:27 in *Leg. all.* 3:96, Exod 25:40 and Num 12:6–8 in *Leg. all.* 3:103, and Deut 28:12 and 32:34 in *Leg. all.* 3:104–05.

Outside of Philo's works, one might especially mention as a parallel Paul's discussion of predestination in Rom 9, in which he gives a brief list of God's election in vv. 7–18 referring to Abraham, Isaac, Jacob and Esau, and Pharaoh:[8]

---

[8] Concerning Rom 9:7–17, see commentaries, such as Dunn (1988) ad loc. and Fitzmyer (1993) ad loc. Haacker (1997) 211–15 compares Rom 9:6b–13 with *Virt.* 207–10 and *Praem.* 58–60. He has overlooked the parallel in *Leg. all.* 3:88.

(V. 7) not all are children of Abraham because they are his descendant, but 'Through Isaac shall your descendant be named'. . . . (10) . . . when Rebecca had conceived children by one man, our forefather Isaac, (11) though they were not yet born and had done nothing either good or bad, in order that God's purpose of election might continue, not because of works but because of his call, (12) she was told, 'The elder will serve the younger'. As it is written, 'Jacob I loved, but Esau I hated'. . . . . . . (16) So it depends not upon man's will or exertion, but upon God's mercy. (17) For the scripture says to Pharaoh, 'I have raised you up for the very purpose of showing my power in you, so that my name may be proclaimed in all the earth'.

In Rom 9:7 and 10–13 the relationship between generations is pictured in the cases of Abraham and his children with only Isaac as heir, and Rebecca and Isaac and the beloved Jacob and the hated Esau are pictured parallel to the discussion of the generations Abraham and his children, with Isaac as the heir, and Isaac and the obedient Jacob and disobedient Esau, in *Virt.* 207–08.

The idea of predestination is common to *Leg. all.* 3:77–106 and Rom 9:6–25, and there are close agreements between *Leg. all.* 3:88 and Rom 9:10–12, 20–23:

Leg. all. 3:88:

> Once again, of Jacob and Esau, when still in the womb, God declares that the one is a ruler and a leader and master, but that Esau is a subject and a slave. For God the modeller of living beings (ζωοπλάστης) knows well the different pieces of his own handiwork (τὰ δημιουργή-ματα), even before He has thoroughly chiselled (διατορεῦσαι) and consummated them, and the faculties which they are to display at a later time, in a word their deeds and experiences. And so when Rebecca, the soul that waits on God, goes to inquire of God, He tells her in reply, 'Two nations are in your womb, and two peoples shall be separated from your belly, and one people shall be above the other people, and the elder shall serve the younger' (Gen 25:23).[9]

Rom 9:10–12:

> (10) And not only so, but also when Rebecca had conceived children by one man, our forefather Isaac, (11) though they were not yet born and had done nothing either good or bad, in order that God's purpose of election might continue, not because of works but because of His call, (12) she was told, 'The elder will serve the younger' (Gen 25:23).

---

[9] The translation in *PLCL* is modified.

In both passages there is a short report on the case followed by a
Scripture quotation from Gen 25:23. As for content, the idea illustrated is God's foreknowledge and election of two contrasting persons, Jacob and Esau, even before their birth. Moreover, in both
cases God is pictured as a modeller in clay. Philo tells that God is a
modeller of living beings, chiselling them as his own handiwork. Paul,
in Rom 9:20–22, is even more explicit in comparing God with a
modeller in clay: "But, who are you, a man, to answer back to God?
Will what is moulded say to its molder, 'Why have you made me
thus?' Has the potter no right over the clay, to make out of the
same lump one vessel for beauty and another for menial use"? (20–
21). These agreements make it probable that Philo and Paul here
draw on a common expository tradition of Gen 25:23.

Rewriting biblical events and laws

Reviews of material from the Old Testament may also have the form
of continuous rewriting, as a written Bible. In an essay Ph.S. Alexander attempts to give a definition of the genre 'rewritten Bible'.
One criterion suggested by him is: "Rewritten Bible texts are narra-
tives, which follow a sequential, chronological order. Their framework is an account of events, and so they may be described broadly
as histories. They are not theological treatises, though an account of
events may incidentally serve theological ends".[10]

This is a fruitful attempt to define the genre, but the fact that the
Bible contains an extensive body of laws needs to be brought into
the definition of a 'rewritten Bible'. The relevance of this point is
seen from the fact that Alexander himself notices that Josephus in
his *Jewish Antiquities* wants to acquaint the Greek-speaking world with
the entire ancient history and the political constitution (i.e. the laws)
of the Jews, *Ant.* 1:5. Thus Alexander recognizes that Josephus covers
in reasonable detail the content of the Law of Moses.

Philo has sections in which he rewrites biblical events and laws
together. An example is *Virt.* 51–174 which deals with the virtue
philanthropia, 'the love of men', 'philanthropy'. Philo illustrates the topic
both with incidents from biblical history and with a selection of laws.
He exalts Moses' *philanthropia* by recording some events in his life

---

[10] Alexander (1988) 116.

and by presenting a selection from the Mosaic Laws, taken from Exodus, Leviticus, Numbers, and Deuteronomy. Referring back to his story of Moses given in the previously written two books *On the Life of Moses*, Philo adds in *Virt.* 51–79 some incidents at the close of Moses' career. Then a selection of laws is presented under the outline of specimens of the kindness to be shown (a) to fellow Israelites (§§ 80–101), (b) to strangers, settlers, enemies, and slaves (§§ 102–24), (c) to animals (§§ 125–47), and (d) to plants (§§ 148–60). *Virt.* 51–174 will receive further attention below in a separate chapter.

There seems basically to be a corresponding structure in parts of the preserved fragments of Philo's *Hypothetica*: In the fragment 8:6:1–9 a review of biblical history is given, from Abraham to the Exodus and to the Hebrews' settlement in the land. Then Philo describes the Mosaic constitution and presents the admonitions, prohibitions, and injunctions, 6:10–7:20.

Corresponding to the praise of the *philanthropia* expressed in the Laws in *Virt.*, the qualities of the Laws of the Jews are also praised in *Hypothetica* 7:1a), but here their severity is stressed in contrast to the evasive nature of the laws of the Gentiles: "Do we find any of these things or anything similar among the Jews; anything which so savours of mildness and lenity, anything which permits of legal proceedings or extenuations or postponements or assessments of penalties and reduction of assessments? Nothing at all, everything is clear and simple".

In *Hypothetica* 7:1b) a list of offenses is given. Then in 7:3–5 Philo gives a list of rules directed to wives, parents, sons, rulers, etc., and in 7:6a) Philo summarizes what has already been given and what follows, things which belong to unwritten customs and institutions and the laws themselves. A further list of various injunctions follows in 7:6b)–8. They include treatment of the poor, animals, dead people, abortion, etc. After this a list of less serious matters follows, 7:9. The survey of the Laws concludes with a longer section on the Sabbath and the sabbatical year, 7:10–19.

Josephus gives a corresponding account of the Jewish Laws in *Ag.Ap.* 145–56. His stated purpose was to refute pagan criticism by Apollonius Molon, Lysimachus and others. Corresponding to the outline of *Virt.* 51–174 and *Hypothetica* 8:6:1–7:19 Josephus too begins with a characterization of Moses and events connected with the Exodus from Egypt (*Ag.Ap.* 2:157–63). In a direct way Josephus gives a polemic response to his critics in 2:164–89, and then a selection of the Laws follows.

Josephus' outline of this selection of laws and regulations is: In *Ag.Ap.* 2:190–98 God and the worship of God are in focus. God is the Creator. "Him must we worship by the practice of virtue". In a pointed way it is stressed that there is but one Temple. In *Ag.Ap.* 2:199–208 laws for the Jewish society are reviewed: laws relating to marriage, education of children and funeral ceremonies. Honour to parents, etc. The theme of the laws in *Ag.Ap.* 2:209–14 is the goodness and generosity which are to be shown to all, also to aliens, enemies, nature, etc. In *Ag.Ap.* 2:215–17a death penalties for offences against laws, such as adultery, etc. are listed. As for the eschatological outlook, in *Ag.Ap.* 2:209–14 it is stated that for those who live in accordance with the Jewish Laws, the reward is a future life.

G.P. Carras has collected a list of ten agreements between Philo's *Hypothetica* and Josephus' *Against Apion*:[11]

1   Animals are to be treated humanely, and are even to be granted refuge in one's own home.
2   Women are to have a subservient role to their husbands.
3   Instruction in the Torah serves the religious and social function of learning the Jewish tradition, advancing in piety, and the avoiding ignorance.
4   Helping the needy is a religious duty.
5   People are to be given help with basic necessities such as water and fire.
6   Abortive measures against the generative process are prohibited.
7   Impiety towards God and parents is punishable by death.
8   Burying the dead is a duty.
9   The authority of parents is acknowledged.
10 Confidentiality should be observed in friendship; misuse of information that has been divulged in trust is not permissible, even if a time of estrangement should arise.

Carras states that points 8, 9, 1, 3, 4, 7 are drawn from the Old Testament. So also points 6 and 2 are based on the Old Testament, but they came to fuller expression in later literature. Thus points 5 and 10 are shared exclusively by *Hypothetica* and *Against Apion*.

---

[11] Carras (1993) 24–47; Kamlah (1974). Cf. Sterling (1990), who thinks that the content and the basic work were determined by a previous work of Lysimachus, in which severe criticism was levelled against Judaism.

This parallel selection of material from the Laws of Moses, the points of similarities as to elaborations as well as the distinctive notions they have in common, suggest that Philo and Josephus shared a common source and body of traditions, which were part of common Judaism.

It should be added that there are also agreements between *Virt.* and *Ag.Ap.* These similarities are of a more general nature, however. In *Virt.* 102 and in *Ag.Ap.* 2:210, and especially in 2:261 the acceptance of proselytes by the Jews is seen as a proof of the Jews' equity and love for humanity and their magnanimity. Both Philo, *Virt.* 125–47 and Josephus, *Ag.Ap.* 2:213 can apply the term *philanthropia* not only to attitudes and behaviours among humans, but also to their proper behaviour to animals. This use of the term is also found in Plutarch, *Cato Maior* 5:5; *De sollertia animalium* 6:964A, and 13:970A. In general Josephus may, just as Philo does in *Virt.* 51–174, state that the Laws of Moses are characterized by *philanthropia*, love of humankind (*Ag.Ap.* 2:145–46 and 211–14). These similarities suggest that Philo and Josephus, as a response to their non-Jewish surroundings, interpret the Laws of Moses in a way commonly done by Jews.

The conclusion is that Philo in *Virt.* 51–174, *Hypothetica* 6:1–7:19 and Josephus in *Ag.Ap.* 2:157–219 utilize a conventional form of reviewing Mosaic history and laws, and they partly draw on common traditions and share the same apologetic tendencies.

The basic structure of this form is already to be found in the Book of Deuteronomy, which contains a revised repetition of a large part of the history and laws of the first four books of the Laws of Moses.[12] This model can also be traced in Josephus' *Jewish Antiquities*, as in *Ant.* 4:176–331, where Josephus in §§ 199–301 gives a summary of the laws and events from biblical history, drawing largely on the Book of Deuteronomy.

Also in the treatises *On the Decalogue* and *On the Special Laws*, books 1–4 Philo rewrites biblical events and laws. In the opening scene, *Dec.* 1–49, the people are assembled in the desert, and related to that event some questions are raised: Why was the Law given in the desert? Why ten commandments? What was the nature of the voice? Why was the singular number "thou" used? In conclusion Philo describes the grandeur of the scene. Against this background Philo presents the Laws.

---

[12] Weinfeld (1992).

The outline of *On the Decalogue* is:

Dec. 1: Transition; §§ 2–49: The people assembled in the desert. Questions and answers are given (see Exod 12–14; 19–20).

Dec. 50–51: Introduction. The ten commandments are divided into two sets of five.

Dec. 52–120: The first table with the first five commandments: The first commandment, against idolatry (§§ 52–65). The second commandment, against idols (§§ 66–81). The third commandment, on not taking God's name in vain (§§ 82–95). The fourth commandment, the sacred seventh day (§§ 96–105). The fifth commandment, the honour due to parents (§§ 106–20).

Dec. 121–53: The second table with the second five commandments: The first commandment, against adultery (§§ 121–31). The second commandment, to do no murder (§§ 132–34). The third commandment, against stealing (§§ 135–37). The fourth commandment, against false witness (§§ 138–41). The fifth commandment, against covetousness (§§ 142–53).

Dec. 154–75: The Decalogue, a summary of the special laws.

Dec. 176–8: The question of penalties.

It should be added here that in *Heres* 167–73 Philo almost gives a condensed version of the treatise *On the Decalogue*. In this short version he shows how the Decalogue is determined by the principle of equality, as expressed both in the fact that there were two tables and in the division of the commandments into two sets of five, the one set comprising duties to God, and the other duties to men. In this way Philo interprets the Decalogue within the context of the long section on equality (*Heres* 133–206).

Then in *On the Special Laws*, Books 1–4, the usual procedure is to begin with an elaboration on a given commandment, similar though fuller than in *On the Decalogue*, and then go on to discuss particular enactments which Philo thinks may be set under it.

In *Dec.* 175 as well as in *Praem.* 1–3; *Spec.* 4:132 and *Mos.* 2:188f. Philo says that the Decalogue was given by God in His own person and the particular laws were given by the mouth of Moses. The Decalogue was then a summary of the special laws which in turn depended on these ten oracles directly from God. Since this view occurs in summaries and in a transitional statement in the introduction to *Praem.* 1–3, Philo identifies himself with this understanding. Is he then here developing thoughts also found elsewhere, or has he himself conceived this theory?

H.A. Wolfson has noted that in rabbinic literature it is similarly said that the Ten Commandments contain all the laws of the Torah. This method of classification is adopted by Philo in his direct discussion of the Laws of Moses. First, in his *On the Decalogue* he enumerates and discusses the Ten Commandments. Then in his *On the Special Laws*, he discusses the special laws which he arranges under the Ten Commandments.[13] Wolfson bases his view on *Cant. Rab.* 5:14, 2, where it is stated that the 613 commandments are implied in the Decalogue.

E. Urbach has argued against Wolfson's view. According to him, in *Cant. Rab.* 5.14, 2 and corresponding passages "it is not asserted that the Ten Commandments incorporated all precepts in the Torah, only that each commandment forms the basis of interpetations... all the Halakha originated in the Oral Law was, as it were, written beside each commandment".[14]

R.D. Hecht has pointed out that Urbach has overlooked the evidence of the Targums, especially that found in *Targum Pseudo-Jonathan*, Exod 24:12: "And the Lord said to Moses, come up before me to the mountain and be there and I will give you the tablets of stone upon which are hinted the rest of the law and the six hundred and thirteen commandments which I have written for their instruction".[15]

On the basis of this debate among Wolfson, Urbach and Hecht, the conclusion can be drawn that Philo seems to develop in a more systematic fashion a notion also found in Palestinian tradition, that the Decalogue contained *in nuce* all the commandments of the Mosaic Laws.[16] Thus, Philo has a Jewish concept as organizing principle.

As for Philo's systematic interest it is seen also in the rewriting of the Mosaic Laws in *Virt.* 51–174 from the perspective of the Greek concept of *philantropia*. To some degree also in the *Hypothetica* and in Josephus' *Ag.Ap.* 145–56 selections of laws are made on the basis of certain concerns and perspectives. Here the apologetic interests are especially evident. By developing the systematization on such a broad

---

[13] Wolfson (1948) 2:201.
[14] Urbach (1975) 1:361. Cf. Amir (1973).
[15] Hecht (1978) 3–17.
[16] See Borgen (1984A) 126; Borgen (1984) 239–240, and n. 30, and Borgen (1987) 26–27.

scale as in *On the Decalogue* and in *The Special Laws*, Philo has approached the form of a Greek codex of laws.[17]

Summary

In this chapter it has been shown that in the rewriting of parts of the Pentateuch Philo utilizes both shorter reviews and surveys and bodies of comprehensive rewriting of Mosaic history and Mosaic laws. The rewriting can elaborate on the form of blessings and curses, and can have the form of a chain of biblical cases which serves the purpose of argumentation in support of a thesis (*Virt.* 198–210) or which provides documentation of a certain theme which leads to a concluding exhortation (*Leg. all.* 3:77–106). The purpose can also be to demonstrate the superior quality of the Laws of Moses as an apologetic response to critical attacks, as in the *Hypothetica*.

In his systematic work Philo can draw on traditional Jewish notions, such as blessings and curses and the view that the Decalogue is a summary of the other laws. He can also use Greek notions as his organizing theme, such as *philanthropia* in *Virt.* 51–174 and the theme of equality in *Heres* 161–206. In this way the Greek notions are 'Judaized' as well as the perspective of the biblical material is 'Hellenized'.

This chapter has included some preliminary observations on the treatises *On the Decalogue* and *On the Special Laws*. The next task is to expand the perspective to comprise all of the treatises called the *Exposition of the Laws of Moses*, i.e. the large body of writings of which *On the Decalogue* and *On the Special Laws*, Books 1–4, are parts.

---

[17] Cf. Amir (1973), 1–8, and Amir (1983) 67–76, who stresses the influence from the Greek context.

CHAPTER FOUR

REWRITTEN BIBLE?

Introduction

Philo did not only interpret small biblical units, but gave comprehensive presentations of the Laws of Moses to such an extent that one might claim that he largely rewrote the Pentateuch in the set of treatises called the *Exposition of the Laws of Moses*. Does he here place himself within the wider context of Jewish expository traditions? It has been attempted to group such traditions into a genre. In his definition of the 'rewritten Bible' genre Ph.S. Alexander states that its framework is an account of events, and so they may be described broadly as histories. This genre is different from theological treatises, though the account of events may serve theological ends.[1] Does Philo's *Exposition* agree with this criterion?

Philo begins with the story of Creation. He writes the whole treatise *Opif.* on Gen 1–3, using the biblical form of *hexaemeron*, and rewrites in biblical sequence the stories about the Garden, the Serpent, the Fall and its consequences. He follows the biblical order in *Abr.* 7–16 in his account of Enos, Enoch, Noah and the Deluge, and in *Abr.* 17–276 on Abraham. Several events in the life of Abraham are recorded, his migration, his adventures in Egypt, the three angelic visitors, the destruction of the cities of the Plain, the sacrifice of Isaac, the settlement of the dispute with Lot, his victory over the four kings, Sarah and Hagar, and Sarah's death. In *Jos.* 1 Philo refers back to Abraham, Isaac and Jacob, and in *Jos.* 2–156 he deals with the story of Joseph.[2] Several events in Joseph's career are included in the treatise: Joseph's dream, his being sold to merchants, who in turn sold him to Potiphar. The history in Potiphar's house is recorded, so also Joseph's imprisonment, his life in prison, his interpretation of dreams and his release and exaltation. Joseph's activities as viceroy are told, and the story

---

[1] Alexander (1988) 116.

[2] The treatises on Isaac and Jacob are lost, but Philo refers to them in the introduction to *On Joseph, Jos.* 1.

about his brothers and his father and about Joseph's death.

Philo omits events from the experiences of the Israelites in Egypt, and also the story of the Exodus. He gives a separate account of the story of Moses and events in Egypt and the Exodus in the treatises *On the Life of Moses* 1–2, however. But in the *Exposition* he moves from the accounts of the Patriarchs Enos, Enoch, Noah, Abraham, Isaac, Jacob and Joseph to the scene where the people are assembled in the desert and receive the Law. An extensive presentation of the Law follows in *Dec.* and *Spec.* 1–4. In spite of the systematic outline of Philo's treatment of the virtues in *Spec.* 4:132–238 and *On the Virtues*, their extensive exemplification consists largely of biblical events and laws. Finally the treatise *On the Rewards and Punishments* reviews some biblical stories and develops an eschatological scenario.

Thus Philo's *Exposition* is in agreement with Alexander's criterion that the framework of the rewritten Bible genre is an account of events which largely follows the chronology of the Bible. Also the circumstance that Philo is selective and that he omits passages does not undercut this conclusion, although his omission of events about the Israelites in Egypt and their Exodus creates a chronological hiatus. As already stated the lacking sections are written down separately in *On the Life of Moses*.

Philo's comprehensive presentation of the Mosaic Laws makes the *Exposition* also to a code of law. From this viewpoint the story of the Creation serves as a *proem*, and the story of the Patriarchs is integrated into the law code by regarding them as embodiments of unwritten law and as archetypes that preceded the written law. Y. Amir understands Philo's *Exposition* on this basis without including the chronological rewriting of the biblical history in his characterization.[3] Amir's view makes it difficult to classify the *Exposition* as a rewritten Bible in the sense suggested by Alexander, in particular since he in principle excludes explicit theological and philosophical statements and aims from his definition.

Alexander's definition seems to be too restrictive, however, since Josephus in his rewritten Bible, the *Antiquities*, formulates theological and philosophical views.[4] For example, both Philo and Josephus entertain the idea that the Law is in harmony with the universe, *Opif.* 3 and *Ant.* 1:24, and both give a cosmic interpretation of the tabernacle and the clothing of the high priest (*Spec.* 1:84–96; *Mos.* 2:88,

---

[3] Amir (1988) 424–26.
[4] Niehoff (1996) 31–45.

101–35 and *Ant.* 3:179–87). Philo goes further than Josephus in expressing theological and philosophical ideas which according to him are present in the biblical material.

The analysis so far points to the following characterization of Philo's *Exposition*: The core of these treatises is a chronological sequence of events. The connection between biblical history and law is kept by Philo, with an emphasis on an interpretative rewriting of the Law. Theological and philosophical aims are made explicit and in this way Jewish and Greek traditions and ideas are fused together. At places Philo relates the biblical material to his own time.

Philo's own interpretation

In the formation of the biblical material and Jewish and Greek notions Philo is not just an editor but an author who follows certain overarching perspectives. If this is the case, there is a need for exploring further Philo's own views and perspectives as they are expressed in the exposition. Of special importance in this context is the circumstance that Philo has divided this rewritten presentation of the Laws of Moses into treatises which he ties together by transitional statements. In these transitions he gives his own perspective and understanding.[5] Thus we find in them systematic motifs which demonstrate that Philo is not just an eclectic editor but is largely an author.

The introductory and transitional statements in the *Exposition of the Laws of Moses* indicate that Philo in the *Exposition* has organized and interpreted traditional material with five systematic aspects in view:

1   The creation of cosmos and humans, *On the Creation* (cf. *Praem.* 1).
2   A record of good and bad lives and sentences passed in each generation on both, *On Abraham; (On Isaac; On Jacob); On Joseph* (cf. *Praem.* 2a).
3   Having related the lives of the good men, the Patriarchs (and their contrasting persons and groups), who are portrayed in the Sacred Books as archetypes and founders of 'our nation', Philo presents the written laws of Moses, starting in *On the Decalogue* with the Ten Commandments understood as the main headings delivered by the voice of God. The particular

---

[5] Cf. Borgen (1996C).

laws, which are derived from the Decalogue and had Moses as the spokesman, are written down in *On the Special Laws*, Books 1:1–4:132. (Cf. *Praem.* 2b).

4   The virtues which Moses assigned to peace and war are common to all commandments, *On the Special Laws* 4:133–238 and *On the Virtues* (cf. *Praem.* 3).

5   After having related the particular laws and the virtues they have in common, Philo proceeds to the rewards and punishments which the good and the bad respectively have to expect. The treatise *On Rewards and Punishments* covers both aspects. (Cf. *Praem.* 3b).

These points indicate that Philo in the transitional statements suggests that there are some uniting threads which tie these treatises together. One might even suggest that he followed some overriding concepts when he interpreted various traditional material in his *Exposition.* Although Philo is not a systematic philosopher, he has some overarching perspectives when he fuses Jewish and Greek traditions, ideas and notions together.

The created order and the good lives of the patriarchs (and bad lives of others)

On the Creation; On Abraham; (On Isaac; On Jacob; On Joseph).
   Philo opens the second treatise, *On Abraham* 1–2a, with a characterization of the Book of Genesis:

> The first of the five books in which the holy laws are written bears the name and inscription of Genesis, from the genesis of the world, an account of which it contains at its beginning. It has received this title in spite of its embracing numberless other matters; for it tells of peace and war, of fruitfulness and barrenness, of dearth and plenty; how fire and water wrought great destruction of what is on earth; how on the other hand plants and animals were born and throve through the kindly tempering of the air and the yearly seasons, and so too men, some of whom lived a life of virtue, others of vice. But since some of these things are parts of the world, and others events which befall it, and the world is the complete consummation which contains them all, he dedicated the whole book to it.

This opening summary of the Book of Genesis suggests that Philo sees as one unit his treatises *On the Creation, On Abraham,* the lost treatises *On Isaac* and *On Jacob,* and the treatise *On Joseph.* They are all based on the Book of Genesis, and in Philo's view the cosmic framework of creation comprises all aspects of its content.

In accordance with Philo's survey in *On Abraham* 1–2a, his preceding treatise, *On the Creation*, deals with creation proper. Philo refers explicitly back to this treatise in *Abr.* 2b: "The way in which the making of the cosmos was arranged (διατέτακται), we set forth in detail, as well as was possible, in the preceding treatise (ἡ σύνταξις) . . ." (trans. mine).

On the Creation covers Gen 1–3 and deals with the creation and the sin committed by Adam and Eve. After an introductory section (*Opif.* 1–12) Philo tells the creation story, following the scheme of six days, the *hexaemeron*, Gen 1:1–31, and then adding the story of the seventh day, Gen 2:1–3, and using Gen 2:4–5 as a concluding summary (*Opif.* 13–130). Subsequent points from Gen 2 and 3 are then elaborated upon in *Opif.* 131–70a, including an interpretation of the sin of Adam and Eve and their punishment. The conclusion of the treatise in *Opif.* 170b–72 makes explicit the teachings drawn from the creation story. He develops the *hexaemeron* form into an expanding paraphrase, as is also done in other *hexaemerons* in Jewish writings, such as in 4 *Ezra* 6:38–59; *Jubilees* 2:1–21; 2 *Enoch* 24–30, etc.

Ideas in *On the Creation* show many similarities with Platonic as well as Stoic views; in addition, there are parallels found in Jewish writings. A central Stoic notion is formulated already in Philo's opening paragraphs to the treatise, *Opif.* 3: The lawgiver Moses has introduced his Laws with an exordium which consists of an account of the creation of the cosmos, implying that the cosmos is in harmony with the Law, and the Law with the cosmos. The Stoics postulated behind the particular laws the rational law of nature.[6] When Moses begins his Law with an account of the creation, the meaning is that the Jewish Laws are in direct accordance with the law of the cosmos. Also in rabbinic writings the Torah has a cosmic role to play but formulated in less abstract ideas: The world was created with Torah in view (*Gen. Rab. 1:2*), and heaven and earth cannot exist without Torah (*b. Nedarim* 32a). Stoic ideas are also the view of the world as a city and man as a cosmopolite (*Opif.* 3 and 19),[7] the understanding

---

[6] See Cicero *De nat. deor.* 1:36; *Diog. Laert.* 7:87. Cf. *De Mundo* 6. For the debate on the idea of 'natural law', see Köster (1968) 521–41; Horsley (1978) 35–59 and Runia (1986) 466–67.

[7] *Diogenes Laertius* 6:63.

that time is measured space (*Opif.* 26),[8] and the idea of a fourfold hierarchical order of creatures (*Opif.* 66–68).[9]

The correspondence between Moses' cosmogony and Plato's *Timaeus* is exploited to demonstrate that the cosmos was created as a result of God's goodness (*Opif.* 21; *Timaeus* 29E), that the creational sequence could tell us much about its hierarchical structure and that an intelligible world of forms transcends the visible world (*Opif.* 16, etc; *Timaeus* 30C; 33B). Corresponding ideas are found in Wisd 21:24, where God's love and creation are related and even in *Gen. Rab.* 12:15 and 21:7 where God's mercy is seen behind creation. The simultaneity of time and the world (*Opif.* 26) agrees with the Platonic view (*Timaeus* 38B), but this is also a rabbinic idea (*b. Hagigah* 12a).[10]

It must be added that more than a quarter of *On the Creation* is devoted to arithmological excursus on the tetrad and the hebdomad (*Opif.* 47–52, 89–128). Thus the treatise betrays an extensive use of Pythagorean-like speculations on numbers.[11] By his use of such speculations on numbers he shows how the cosmic order is made manifest in Jewish Laws and practices. Thus the number seven, which reveals the structure of all of the cosmos is revealed in the Sabbath and the Jewish observance of the Sabbath. The Jews in this way celebrate the birthday of the world (*Opif.* 89, with reference to Gen 2:2–3). Philo's interpretation here is not new. Already in the second century B.C. Aristobulus made the number seven serve as the ordering principle of the cosmos, and he linked this order to the Jewish Sabbath (Eusebius, *Praeparatio Evangelica*, 13, 12:12–13).[12]

Philo begins the treatise by drawing a contrast between on the one hand Moses and his Laws and on the other hand the other lawgivers and their laws (*Opif.* 1ff.), and in *Opif.* 170–72a he concludes his treatise with criticisms of the Sceptic view that God's existence is doubtful, the Aristotelian view (*Aet.* 10) that the world is without beginning, and the Epicurean idea of a plurality of worlds and denial of Providence.[13]

---

[8] *SVF*, 2:509f.; Philo, *Aet.* 4 and 52; *Diog. Laert.* 7:141.
[9] See further *Leg. all.* 2:22–23 and *Immut.* 35–48. *SVF*, 2:457–60.
[10] See especially Runia (1986); Theiler (1965); Theiler (1965A) 199–217; Theiler (1971) 25–35; Grumach (1939) 126–131.
[11] Staehle (1931); Moehring (1978) 191–227; Früchtel (1968).
[12] See Borgen (1987) 11.
[13] See *PLCL* 1:476; Mendelson (1988) 29–49; cf. Runia (1986) 426–27. Polemic against Epicurean denial of providence also occurs in rabbinic writings. See Fischel (1973). A similar polemic is found as early as Sirach. See Hengel (1974) 1:141ff.

In this way *On the Creation* deals with the creation proper, Gen 1–3, with focus upon the aspect of order. The next point in Philo's survey, *Abr.* 1–2a gives the referential background for *On Abraham*, (*On Isaac, On Jacob*), and *On Joseph*.

On Abraham does not only tell about Abraham, but also contains the stories of Enos, Enoch and Noah. Thus, while *On the Creation* covered Gen 1–3, *On Abraham* begins with Gen 4 and draws on parts of Gen 4–26. Although the treatises *On Isaac* and *On Jacob* are lost, the opening paragraph of the treatise *On Joseph* refers back to them as well as to *On Abraham*: "Since I have described the lives of these three, the life which results from teaching, the life of the self-taught and the life of practice, I will carry on the series by describing a fourth life, that of a statesman" (*Jos.* 1). *On Joseph* covers Gen 37–47, and *On Isaac* and *On Jacob* then presumably related the remaining parts of Genesis.

In the interpretation of these patriarchs Philo brings Jewish and Greek motifs and ideas together. A Jewish motif is the correspondence between the practices of the Patriarchs and the Mosaic Law. For example, according to the *Book of Jubilees*, Noah, Abraham and others observed and enjoined the laws inscribed on heavenly tablets which were later given to Moses. Also in rabbinic writings such views are expressed.[14] A similar correlation is found in Philo, but here the Platonizing element makes the lives and words of the Patriarchs archetypes (ἀρχέτυποι), and the particular Mosaic laws copies (εἰκόνες) (*Abr.* 3).[15] S. Sandmel draws a contrast between the views of the Rabbis and of Philo: "The rabbis say that Abraham observed the Law; Philo says that the Law set forth as legislation those things which Abraham did".[16] Philo indicates himself, however, that he modifies and interprets the view that Abraham obeyed the Law: "Such was the life of the first, the founder of the nation, one who obeyed the Law, some will say, but rather, as our discourse has shown, himself a law and an unwritten statute" (*Abr.* 276).

As stated above, in *Jos.* 1 Philo interprets the three Patriarchs in this way: Abraham means wisdom or virtue acquired by teaching,

---

[14] *Jubilees* 6:17; 15:1; 16:28, etc.; See Bousset (1926) 125, n. 3 and 126, n. 1. The idea that the Patriarchs kept the commandments of the Torah is familiar in rabbinic dicta as well. See Urbach (1975) 1:335ff.

[15] Sandmel (1971) 49.

[16] *Ibid.*, 108.

Isaac by nature, and Jacob by practice.[17] Here Philo draws on a broad Greek tradition about education, in which instruction, nature and practice are discussed in relation to virtue. Ps.-Plutarch associates the triad with Pythagoras, Socrates and Plato.[18]

To Philo, however, these aspects of virtue and wisdom which Abraham, Isaac and Jacob represented, characterize the Jewish people and its religion: "while Moses represented the first man, the one born on earth, as father of all that were born up to the deluge, and Noah who with all his house alone survived that great destruction because of his justice and excellent character in other ways as the father of a new race which would spring up afresh, the oracles speak of this august and precious trinity [Abraham, Isaac and Jacob] as parent of one species of that race, which species is called 'royal' and 'priesthood' and 'holy nation' (Exod 19:6). Its high position is shewn by the name; for the nation is called in the Hebrew tongue Israel, which, being interpreted, is 'He who sees God'" (*Abr.* 56–57).[19]

Joseph, who represents the life of the statesman (ὁ πολιτικός), is added to the three chief patriarchs, and is also understood to be a living law before the Laws were given at Mt. Sinai, *Jos.* 1.

It is of interest to note that Philo's transitional summary in *Abr.* 1–2 does not only refer to those who lived a life of virtue, but also others who lived a life of vice. Thus all through *Abr.* and *Jos.* evil is pictured as a contrast. A few glimpses should be given as examples: Enos, the true Man, is seen as a contrast to his fathers and grandfathers who were the founders of a mixed race, *Abr.* 9; Enoch, representing repentance, is seen within the contrast between the worthless man, who is a hater of good and lover of evil and the man of worth who has rejected vice which is welcomed by the multitude, *Abr.* 19–25; Noah was 'just' at a time when every country and nation and city and every private individual was filled with evil practices, and they were punished through the Deluge, *Abr.* 40–46.

Abraham departed from the Chaldean misconception that the world itself was god, *Abr.* 68–71. He was hospitable, while the Egyp-

---

[17] See also *Mos.* 1:76, etc.

[18] See especially Ps.-Plutarch, *De liberis educandis* 2A–C. See further Hadot (1960) 125–26; Borgen (1965) 103ff.; Borgen (1984A) 115–17; Borgen (1984) 254–56.

[19] Cf. *Abr.* 98: "That marriage [of Abraham and Sarah] from which was to issue not a family of a few sons and daughters, but a whole nation, and that the nation dearest of all to God, which, as I hold, has received the gift of priesthood and prophecy on behalf of all mankind".

tians were inhospitable and licentious, *Abr.* 107–114. The land of the Sodomites was brimful of innumerable iniquities and suffered destruction as a punishment, *Abr.* 133–41. Abraham's courage appeared in his victory over the four kings who had routed the armies of the five cities (*Abr.* 225–35). As an example from the story about Joseph, it may be mentioned how the 'cook', the 'butler' and the 'baker' represent the different ways in which the body-loving mind regards luxuries and necessities (*Jos.* 148–56).

The conclusion is: Basically the treatises contain the history of the lives of virtuous persons and of evil persons, as stated by Philo in *Abr.* 1 and *Praem.* 2. Thus there is basis for classifying these treatises as 'rewritten Bible'. At the same time the lives of the virtuous ones are embodiments of the unwritten cosmic law and represent virtues and qualities, as for example learning from teaching (Abraham), the self-taught (Isaac) and practice (Jacob). Furthermore, a Platonizing influence is seen in the idea that the Patriarchs are archetypes of which the specific laws of Moses are copies (*Abr.* 3).

The particular Laws of Moses

On the Decalogue and *On the Special Laws*, Books 1–4:132.

Having related the lives of the Patriarchs, Philo presents the particular Laws of Moses, comprising the Ten Commandments as their main headings delivered by the voice of God (*On the Decalogue*), and the particular laws dependent on them, of which Moses was the spokesman (*On the Special Laws*, Books 1–4:132). Again the transitional statement builds the bridge between the treatises, now in *Dec.* 1:

> Having related in the preceding treatises the lives of those whom Moses judged to be the men of wisdom, who are set before us in the Sacred Books as founders of our nation (ἀρχηγέτας τοῦ ἡμετέρου ἔθνους) and in themselves unwritten laws, I shall now proceed in due course to give full descriptions of the written laws.

Also here there is a two level view. On the concrete and nationalistic level the lives of the Patriarchs were the lives of "the founders of our nation", i.e. of the Jewish nation. On the general level of law and philosophy they were archetypes and in themselves unwritten laws.

On the basis of the debate among Wolfson, Urbach and Hecht examined in the preceding chapter, the conclusion was drawn that Philo seems to develop a notion from Jewish tradition, that the Decalogue

serves as head of all the commandments of the Mosaic Laws. Philo
has developed this Jewish concept into a broad systematic rewriting
of the Mosaic Laws. Since Josephus in his *Jewish Antiquities* also includes interpretative surveys of the Mosaic Laws, Philo's more extensive survey does not make his *Exposition* fall outside the classification
of being a rewritten Bible. Accordingly, *On the Special Laws*, Book 1,
begins with a reference back to *On the Decalogue*: "The Ten Words,
as they are called, the main heads under which are summarized the
Special Laws, have been explained in detail in the preceding treatise. We have now, as the sequence of our dissertation requires, to
examine the particular ordinances" (*Spec.* 1:1).

The treatise *On the Special Laws*, Book 1, interprets the first and second commandments, against polytheism and idols, and gives details
on knowledge and worship of God. Book 2 covers laws which can
be assigned to the next three commandments: not taking God's name
in vain (regulations on oaths and vows), keeping the Sabbath (special
laws on various feasts), and honouring parents (duties of parents and
children to each other). Thus the two books interpret the commandments of the first table.

In the closing of the second book Philo points forward to his presentation of the laws based on the second table (*Spec.* 2:262): "We
will proceed when opportunity offers to examine the contents of the
second table". In *Spec.* 3:7 Philo makes the connection between *On
the Special Laws*, Book 3, and the preceding Books 1 and 2 and *On the
Decalogue*:

> Since out of the ten oracles which God gave forth Himself without a
> spokesman or interpreter, we have spoken of five, namely those graven
> on the first table, and also of all the particular laws which had refer-
> ence to these, and our present duty is to couple with them those of the
> second table as well as we can, I will again endeavour to fit the special
> laws into each of the heads.

In *On the Special Laws* 4, Philo again links the book to the preceding
treatise:

> The laws directed against adultery and murder and the offences which
> fall under either head have been already discussed with all possible
> fullness as I venture to think. But we must also examine the one which
> follows next in order, the third in the second table or eighth in the
> two taken together, which forbids stealing (*Spec.* 4:1).

In this book paragraph 132 brings the discussion of the Ten Commandments to its conclusion.

Since Philo emphasizes the connection between the story of the Creation and the Laws, some of the connecting ideas should be mentioned: Already in *Opif.* 89–128 the Sabbath law, as inscribed by Moses on the most holy tables of the Law (*Opif.* 128), was seen as a manifestation of the whole of the cosmos, structured as it is on the basis of the number seven. In the actual presentation of the Laws of the two tables, Philo again gives a comprehensive treatment of the Seventh Day and the number seven in *On the Decalogue* 96–105 and *On the Special Laws* 2:40 and 56–70. In *Spec.* 2:40 Philo even makes an explicit cross-reference to a previous section on the number seven: "Now the part played by seven among the numbers has been described at length in an earlier place. . . ." The section referred to is *Opif.* 90–127. Those who live in accordance with the Seventh Day, that is the Jews, are citizens of God's cosmic commonwealth, *politeia*, *Dec.* 97–98. Thus the Jewish commonwealth (*politeia*) and the cosmic commonwealth coincide. Moreover, the Seventh Day is a means of revelation of the Father and maker of all (*Dec.* 105), a view already held by Aristobulus in the second century B.C.[20]

The concept of the true man is another connecting idea which is derived from man created by God. The true men appear in contrast to the many who go astray: Enos, the lover of hope, was the true man, and he was the founder of the race from which all impurity had been strained, the race which is truly reasonable, in contrast to the others who like beasts lack hope (*Abr.* 7–10). In his generation Noah was the true man (*Abr.* 31–33). The Jews are the true men: ". . . out of the whole human race He chose as of special merit and judged worthy of pre-eminence over all, those who are in a true sense men and called them to the service of Himself" (*Spec.* 1:303).

In accordance with the universal perspective of creation, *On the Special Laws* tells about the universal role of the Jewish nation, in this case represented by the high priest in the Jerusalem Temple: The high priest offers prayers and and gives thanks on behalf of the whole human race and also for the various parts of nature, *Spec.* 1:97.

The virtues. Rewards and punishments, blessings and curses

In the transitional words of *Spec.* 4:133–34 Philo defines the meaning and role of virtues in relation to the particular laws:

----

[20] See Borgen (1987) 11.

> We must not fail to know that, just as each of the ten separately has
> some particular laws akin to it having nothing in common with any
> other, there are some things common to all which fit in not with some
> particular number such as one or two but with all the ten Great Words.
> These are the virtues of common utility.[21]

Philo states that he had spoken earlier of the virtues piety or holiness
and wisdom and temperance, (*Spec.* 133). Then he moves on to deal
with justice, and continues in the next treatise, *On the Virtues*, by discussing virtues of courage, philanthropy, repentance and nobility.

Various virtues and lists of virtues are commonplaces in the Graeco-
Roman world. Philo betrays the knowledge of Plato's fourfold division of virtues, wisdom, temperance, justice and courage, φρόνησις,
σωφροσύνη, ἀνδρεία, δικαιοσύνη in *Leg. all.* 1:63,[22] but, as can be
seen from *Spec.* 4:133–238 and the treatise *On the Virtues*, he operates
with some virtues beyond these four. For example, one such addition is *philanthropia*, a virtue which in Philo's time had increased its
importance in the Hellenistic world.[23] Although repentance as a phenomenon may be referred to in Greek philosophy, as by Aristotle in
Eth. Nic. III:1:1110b, 22–23, and by Stoics (*SVF.* 3:548), it was not
seen as a virtue.[24] Due to his Jewish background Philo has brought
the biblical notion of repentance into his list of virtues, *Virt.* 175–86.

Moreover, Philo's emphasis on "piety and holiness", (*Spec.* 4:135,
cf. 147 and *Praem.* 53), as the queen of virtues, shows that he regarded
the worship of God as being basic in a virtuous life. He brought the
Greek terminology of virtues into his exposition because they in his
understanding expressed biblical notions and served as characteristic
qualities of Jewish life. This latter point is demonstrated in *Mos.* 2:216:

> For what are our places of prayer throughout the cities but schools of
> prudence (φρόνησις) and courage (ἀνδρεία) and temperance (σωφροσύνη)
> and justice (δικαιοσύνη), and also of piety (εὐσέβεια), holiness (ὁσιότης)
> and every virtue by which duties to God and men are discerned and
> rightly performed.

---

[21] PLCL: "of universal value".

[22] See Plato, *Laws* 1:631c; *Republic* 4:428b, etc. Concerning other Jewish uses of
the Platonic/Stoic cardinal virtues, see Wis 8:7; 4 *Macc.* 1:2–4. See general survey
in Fitzgerald (1992). For Philo, see Wolfson (1948) 2:200–37, and the discussion of
Philo, *Spec.* 4:133–35 in Cohen (1995) 86–99.

[23] See Winston (1984) 394; Hirzel (1912) 24–25. Philo's emphasis on the virtue of
philanthropia is partly due to an apologetic motif. He wants to defend Judaism against
accusations of misanthropy (*Virt.* 141). See further the chapter on *philanthropia* below
in the present study.

[24] See Wolfson (1948) 2:252–59.

The transitional statement between *Spec.* 133–238 and the treatise *On the Virtues* is given in *Virt.* 1: "The subject of justice and all the relevant points which the occasion requires have already been discussed, and I will take courage next in the sequence". The treatise *On the Virtues* and the preceding *Spec.* 4:133–238, are organized according to subject matter, but the subjects are not treated in an abstract or analytical way but are used to organize biblical material from the Pentateuch. The virtues of justice (*Spec.* 133–238), courage (*Virt.* 1–50), humanity or philanthropy (*Virt.* 51–174), repentance (*Virt.* 175–86) and nobility (*Virt.* 187–227) serve rather as key words and are illustrated from the Pentateuch and elaborated upon in an exhortatory or warning way. The virtue of justice is illustrated by material from parts of Exod 18, Lev 19, Num 20, and several chapters of Deuteronomy; courage from parts of Num 25 and 30, and of Deut 20, 22, and 28; humanity from Num 27 and various laws in Exodus, Leviticus and Deuteronomy; repentance from parts of Deut 26 and 30 and Pentateuchal ideas about proselytes; nobility from passages in Genesis about Adam – Cain, Noah – Ham, sons of Abraham, Tamar, etc.

Philo connects the treatise *On Rewards and Punishments* with the preceding ones in this way: ". . . the virtues which he [Moses] assigned to peace and war have been discussed as fully as was needful in the preceding treatises, and I now proceed in due course to the rewards and punishments which the good and the bad have respectively to expect" (*Virt.* 3). The treatise falls into two main parts: The first main part deals with rewards and punishments, *Praem.* 7–78. The second part of the treatise (*Praem.* 79–172) sets forth blessings and curses. A transitional statement between the two parts is missing.[25]

The first part is largely based on Genesis. The paragraphs *Praem.* 7–66, especially *Praem.* 7–56 are almost a short form of the earlier treatise *On Abraham*, the lost *On Isaac*, and *On Jacob* and in addition to those, *On the Life of Moses*. The second part covers mainly sections from Exodus, Leviticus, Numbers and Deuteronomy not covered by *On the Decalogue*, *On the Special Laws*, and *On the Virtues*. The main emphasis is placed on Lev 26 and 28, and Deut 28. The first half of the treatise is conceived of as a contest for the athletes of virtue in the sacred arena, and the prizes they won as rewards (*Praem.* 4–6). The form of blessings and curses, is based more directly on biblical

---

[25] See Morris (1987) 3:2, 853.

traditions. Thus the category of blessings and curses is already used in Deuteronomy.

This treatise is not attached to the *Exposition* as a kind of epilogue, as J. Morris maintains.[26] It makes clear that the Laws of Moses are to function in the life of individuals and the nation(s). Philo formulates this perspective in *Praem.* 4:

> After having schooled the citizens of his polity with gentle instructions and exhortations and more sternly with threats and warnings he called on them to make a practical exhibition of what they had learned.

At some points Greek life style is reflected. As an example allusions and references to Greek athletic games can be mentioned. Thus in *Praem.* 4–6 Philo has a metaphorical use of athletic imagery to illustrate how Moses after training (συνασκήσας) the citizens of his nation called on them to give a demonstration (ἐπίδειξιν) of what they had learned. They advanced into the sacred games (εἰς ἱερὸν ἀγῶνα). The true athletes (ἀθληταί) did not disappoint the hopes of the laws which had trained (τοὺς ἀλείπτας νόμους) them, the unmanly dropped down, a derision to the spectators (θεατῶν). The victors enjoyed the prizes and proclamations (οἱ βραβείων καὶ κηρυγμάτων). The others were without a crown (ἀστεφάνωτοι) – with a defeat more grievous than those in the gymnastic contests (ἐν τοῖς γυμνικοῖς ἀγῶσιν).[27]

Also elsewhere in the *Exposition of the Laws of Moses* as well as in other writings Philo betrays knowledge of Greek athletics.[28] In *Spec.* 2:230 Philo relates how parents educated their children in gymnasium education: "They have benefited the body by means of the gymnasium and the training there given. . . ." Other examples of terminology from athletics are: round a turningpost in a race and come back to the start (περὶ ὃν ὡς καμπτῆρα εἰλοῦνται καὶ ἀνακάμπτουσι) (*Opif.* 47); those who arrange athletic festivals, before they invite spectators into the stadium, make sure of a supply of competitors (*Opif.* 78); strip and powder oneself (ἐπαποδύεσθαι καὶ κονίεσθαι) (*Abr.* 256); not for blows and violence like those of boxers and pancratiasts (*Spec.* 3:174); exhausted wrestlers have been thrown to the ground (*Virt.* 6); admit defeat like an athlete with his head held in the chancery (ἐκτραχηκιζόμενος) (*Praem.* 29); turn the post and run the double course back (ἀνακάμψουσι διαυλοδρομήσαντες) (*Praem.* 170, cf. *Spec.* 2:122).

---

[26] Morris (1987) 3:2, 853.
[27] *Praem.* 4–6 has here been paraphrased and abridged.
[28] See Harris (1976) 51–95.

Philo's summary survey

It is significant that in his introduction of the last treatise of the *Exposition of the Laws of Moses,* i.e. in *Praem.* 1–3, Philo gives a summary of the whole work, from the story of the Creation to his concluding ideas about rewards and punishments:[29]

> The oracles delivered through the prophet Moses are of three kinds. The first deals with the creation of the world, the second with history and the third with legislation.
>
> The story of the creation is told throughout with an excellence worthy of the divine subject, beginning with the genesis of Heaven and ending with the framing of man. For Heaven is the most perfect of things indestructible as man of things mortal, immortal and mortal being the original components out of which the Creator wrought the world, the one created then and there to take command, the other subject, as it were, to be also created in the future.
>
> The historical part is a record of good and bad lives and of the sentences passed in each generation on both, rewards in one case, punishments in the other.
>
> The legislative part has two divisions, one in which the subject matter is more general, the other consisting of the ordinances of specific laws. On the one hand there are the ten heads or summaries which we are told were not delivered through a spokesman but were shaped high above in the air into the form of articulate speech; on the other the specific ordinances of the oracles given through the lips of a prophet.
>
> All these and further the virtues which he assigned to peace and war, have been discussed as fully as was needful in the preceding treatises, and I now proceed in due course to the rewards and punishments which the good and the bad have respectively to expect.

Here in *Praem.* 1–3 Philo divides The *Exposition of the Laws of Moses* into the story of the creation (cf. *On the Creation*), the historical part (cf. *On Abraham, [On Isaac, On Jacob]; On Joseph*) and the legislative part (cf. *On the Decalogue; On the Special Laws* 1:1–4:132); the virtues assigned to peace and war (cf. *On the Special Laws* 4:133–238 and *On the Virtues*), and rewards and punishments (cf. *On Rewards and Punishments*). The present study of the *Exposition* is very well summed up in this survey made by Philo himself in *Praem.* 1–3.

---

[29] Cf. the similar summary in *Mos.* 2:46–47.

Conclusion

The conclusion is that Philo's treatises designated as the *Exposition on the Laws of Moses* follow in general the chronology of the five books of Moses. At the same time Philo has an emphasis on the aspect of law, and is explicit about his theological and philosophical aims. Although Philo is not a system-building philosopher, he is not just an eclectic editor. He is an expositor who both draws on traditions and brings in various current ideas into his interpretations, and at the same time follows certain identifiable perspectives and uniting threads in his composition. These perspectives are especially seen in his transitional statements by which he ties the treatises together. Accordingly, he combines unevenness and complexity with such systematic pointers. These pointers are so closely woven together with the treatises concerned that they should not be built into an abstracted system. Moreover, to trace some of these perspectives the present study has exemplified how Philo fuses Jewish and Greek ideas and notions together.

In general the *Exposition* meets Ph.S. Alexander's criterion for a rewritten Bible. Features in Josephus' *Jewish Antiquities* as well as Philo's *Exposition* show that Alexander's definition needs to be broadened somewhat, however, so as to more readily comprise surveys of laws as well as explicit theological aims. On the other hand, Y. Amir's characterization of the *Exposition* as just the Laws of Moses, need to be supplemented by an emphasis on the fact that Philo follows the biblical stories in chronological sequence in which both the lives of virtue and the lives of vice are pictured.

Basically, then, Philo follows a Jewish tradition when he retells the biblical story of the Pentateuch. The designation of Moses as a legislator, and the interpretative survey of laws do not as such preclude Philo's *Exposition* from being a rewritten Bible. Both Philo and Josephus see Moses as a legislator (νομοθέτης) and draw a contrast between Moses and other legislators (*Opif.* 1–3; *Ant.* 1:18–23). As for the Mosaic Laws, Josephus tells that he intends to write another treatise about them (*Ant.* 3:223). He nevertheless mentions laws and regulations on purifications, sacrifices, festivals, and various other laws (*Ant.* 3:224–86), and he concludes: "Such was the code of laws which Moses, while keeping his army encamped beneath Mount Sinai, learnt from the mouth of God and transmitted in writing to the Hebrews" (*Ant.* 3:286). In addition to the presentation of the Laws of Moses in *On the Decalogue* and *On the Special Laws*, Books 1–4, Philo gives, as already shown in the preceding chapter, an account of some of the last events in the life of Moses and gives a survey of the Laws which Moses gave to posterity when he deals with the virtue *philanthropia* (*Virt.* 51–174). It is of interest to notice that Josephus in *Ant.* 4:176–331 gives an account of Moses' farewell speech, followed by an extensive survey of laws, and of Moses' death.

According to Alexander the genre of rewritten Bible is different from the genre of theological treatises, though the account of events may serve theological ends.[30] Philo does not comply with this criterion. He is explicit about his systematic, philosophical and theological aims. One might just refer to his theological and philosophical conclusion in *Opif.* 170–72, where he sums up the right ideas about God, creation and providence against opposite views in contemporary philosophies of religion. His theological and philosophical aim is also expressed in many other ways, as in the sections with deeper (allegorical) interpretations, for instance in *Abr.* 68–89 and *Jos.* 28–36, and in organizing his *On the Life of Moses* around Moses as king, legislator, high-priest and prophet. Moreover, the Laws ordain that the priest should be without any bodily deformity (Lev 21:17–21 and 22:4). According to Philo this symbolizes the perfection of his immortal soul, which according to Gen 1:27 was fashioned after the image of the self-existent. And in Philo's exposition the image of God is Logos through whom the whole universe was framed (*Spec.* 1:81). Thus the true heavenly man was present in the priest's immortal soul.

In this *Exposition of the Laws of Moses* Philo basically follows the form also found in other Jewish books in which (parts of) the Pentateuch have been rewritten. Examples are the *Book of Jubilees*, the *Genesis Apocryphon*, the *Biblical Antiquities of Pseudo-Philo*, and Josephus' *Jewish Antiquities*. Philo covers the biblical story from creation to Joshua's succession of Moses. The *Book of Jubilees* narrates the story from creation to the giving of the Laws on Mt. Sinai. The *Genesis Apocryphon* is only preserved in parts, covering Genesis from the birth of Noah to Gen 15:4. The *Biblical Antiquities of Pseudo-Philo* contain an abstract of the biblical story from Gen 5 to the death of Saul. In his *Jewish Antiquities* Josephus begins with creation and relates the whole span of biblical history and goes beyond even to the beginning of the Jewish war in his own time.[31]

---

[30] Alexander (1988) 116.
[31] Borgen (1984) 233–34; Borgen (1987) 18 and 20. See also Nickelsburg (1984) 97–110; Alexander (1988) 99–121.

CHAPTER FIVE

QUESTIONS AND ANSWERS

Introduction

In the previous chapters various forms of direct exegesis have been analysed both with reference to small units as well as the comprehensive rewriting in the *Exposition of the Laws of Moses*. Philo's *Allegorical Commentary* and *Questions and Answers on Genesis and Exodus* display a different structure. They are running commentaries which interpret quoted biblical texts in sequence, verse by verse. Also some of the rabbinic *midrashim* and some of the Dead Sea Scrolls consist of running commentaries on the Pentateuch and other parts of the Hebrew Bible. D. Dimant's comment on the Dead Sea Scrolls is to the point: ". . . the lemmatic structure and the exegetical techniques used by the pesharim link them firmly with other types of lemmatic commentaries, such as the rabbinic midrashim and the commentaries of Philo".[1]

Philo's exegetical commentaries differ at some points from the commentaries which have been found among the *Dead Sea Scrolls*. For example, the *Dead Sea Scrolls* commentaries do not cultivate the form of questions and answers. One of Philo's commentary series, the *Questions and Answers on Genesis and Exodus*, is a collection of questions and answers with reference to quoted texts. Philo employs this form also in his *Allegorical Commentary* and in his *Exposition of the Laws of Moses*, however. Before analysing the structures of three treatises in the *Allegorical Commentary*, his widespread use of the form of question and answer should be examined.

Philo's employment of the form of question and answer in his exegesis has received the increasing attention of scholars. It has been discussed against the background of the history of the form in Greek tradition, the homiletic activity in the synagogal settings, the relationship between Philo's *Questions and Answers on Genesis and on Exodus* and his *Allegorical Commentary*, and the theory that Philo's exegesis in

---

[1] Dimant (1992) 5:250. See Porton (1992) 4:820: "Expositional collections present a running commentary to consecutive verses of the biblical text".

these commentaries have been composed by means of this question-and-answer-technique.[2]

Scholars such as G. Sterling and S. Wan have compared the commentary series *Questions and Answers* with the *Allegorical Commentary*. G. Sterling has suggested that the *Questions and Answers Commentary* is a 'Prolegomena' to the *Allegorical Commentary*.[3] S. Wan reaches the opposite conclusion: the *Allegorical Commentary* and the *Questions and Answers Commentary* are independent of each other. The similar questions and answers draw on traditional material.[4] P. Borgen and R. Skarsten reached in 1967/77 a conclusion similar to that of Wan.[5]

The intention of the present chapter is then to add observations which support this latter view, partly by drawing on material from Philo's *Exposition of the Laws of Moses* and also on some rabbinic parallels. Thus the exegetical form of question and answer is central to a formal analysis of the works of Philo, since it occurs in *On the Life of Moses* and *The Exposition*, as well as in the *Allegorical Commentary* and the commentary *Questions and Answers on Genesis and on Exodus*.[6]

In the *Exposition* such questions and answers are found in *Opif.* 72–75 and 77–88, in *Dec.* 2–17, 36–43 and 176–78. In this rewritten Bible Philo uses the exegetical form of question and answer at the point of the creation story when God has created man (*Opif.* 72–88). He employs the same form in connection with the central event of the giving of the Law at Mt Sinai (*Dec.* 36–43) where the question raised is:

> But we may properly ask why, when all these many thousands were collected in one spot, He thought good in proclaiming His ten oracles to address each not as to several persons but as to one, 'Thou shalt not commit adultery. . . .'

The introductory section to the Sinai event (*Dec.* 2–17) also has the same form. Here the problem was that the desert was an unusual place for setting up a code of laws:

> To the question why he promulgated his laws in the depths of the desert instead of in the cities, we may answer in the first place. . . . . . .

---

[2] See Borgen and Skarsten (1976/77) 1–15; also printed in Borgen (1983A) 191–201; Nikiprowetzky (1977) 170–80; Nikiprowetzky (1983) 5–75; Hay (1991); Wan (1993) 22–53.
[3] Sterling (1991) 99–123.
[4] Wan (1993) 52–53.
[5] See reference in fn. 2.
[6] See Borgen and Skarsten (1976/77) 1–15; Borgen (1983A) 191–201.

He also had a second object in mind. . . . . . . He had a third reason as follows. . . . . . Some too give a fourth reason. . . . .

At the end of the treatise (*Dec.* 176–78), the problem is the difference between the Ten Commandments received from God and the approach of other (non-Jewish) legislators:

> Next let us pass on to give the reason why He expressed the ten words or laws in the form of simple commands or prohibitions without laying down any penalty, as is the way of legislators, against future transgressors. . . .

Thus, Philo at important points in the *Exposition of the Laws of Moses* employs the exegetical form of questions and answers.

In *On the Life of Moses* the form of question and answer is used in *Mos.* 2:47ff. Here the question is raised why Moses in an unusual and unique way made the story of the creation of the world to begin his legislation: "One must now give the reason why he began his lawbook with history, and put the commands and prohibitions in the second place".

In *Mos.* 2:47ff., *Dec.* 2–17 and *Dec.* 176–78 the questions are not based on one or two specific scriptural texts but have a broader scriptural base, such as the relationship between parts of the Pentateuch, the desert location of the Sinai event and the nature of the Decalogue as a whole. In *Dec.* 36, however, three of the ten commandments are quoted and the question raised refers to their formulation in the singular "Thou shalt not commit adultery (οὐ μοιχεύσεις). . . ."

Broadly speaking, Philo's own context is reflected in some of the passages. The questions asked in *Mos.* 2:47ff. and *Dec.* 176–78 refer to some special features (the creation as proem; God has given the Ten Commandments without laying down any penalty) of the Mosaic Law *when compared with other laws.* In the first answer of the question why the laws were given in the desert Philo gives a characterization of the cities as a place of countless evils, such as vanity and pride and polytheistic worship. This point had special relevance against the background of life in a large city such as that of Alexandria.

Parallel usages

Some of the questions and answers in the *Exposition* show similarities with passages in the *Allegorical Commentary*. For example, *On the Creation* 72ff. can be compared with *Conf.* 168ff.:

Opif. 72–75:

Question:

One may not unfitly raise the question what reason there could be for his ascribing the creation in the case of man only not to one Creator as in the case of the rest but, as the words would suggest, to several. For he represents the Father of the universe as speaking thus, "Let us make man after our image and likeness" (Gen 1:26). 'Can it be', I would ask, 'that He to whom all things are subject, is in need for anyone whatever? Or can it be that when He made the heaven and the earth and the seas, he required no one to be His fellow-worker, yet was unable apart from the co-operation of others by His own unaided power to fashion a creature so puny and perishable as man'?

Answer:

The full truth about the cause of this it must needs be that God alone knows, but the cause which probable conjecture seems plausible and reasonable we must not conceal. It is this. . . . .

Conclusion:

So we see why it is only in the instance of man's creation that we are told by Moses that God said 'Let us make', an expression which plainly shows the taking with him of others as fellow-workers. It is to the end that, when man orders his course aright, when his thoughts and deeds are blameless, God the universal Ruler may be owned as their Source; while others from the number of His subordinates are held responsible for thoughts and deeds of a contrary sort: for it could not be that the Father should be the cause of an evil thing to His offspring: and vice and vicious activities are an evil thing.

Conf. 168–79:[7]

Question:

It is worth carefully looking into the question of what is implied by the words which are put into the mouth of God. 'Come and let us go down and confuse their tongue there' (Gen 11:7). For it is clear that He is conversing with some persons whom He treats as His fellow-workers, and we find the same in an earlier passage of the formation of man. Here we have "The Lord God said 'let us make man after our image and likeness'" (Gen 1:26); where the words 'let us make' imply plurality. And once more, "God said, 'behold Adam has become as one of us by knowing good and evil'" (Gen 3:22); here the 'us' in 'as one of us' is said not of one, but of more than one.

---

[7] The translation in *PLCL* is slightly modified.

Answer:

> 1) It is first to be said that no existing thing is of equal honour to God. . . . .
>
> 2) Having reached agreement on this preliminary question the next step will be to gather the relevant considerations into a coherent argument. Let us consider what these are. . . . .
>
> 3) These points were needed as premisses. Now the inferences of these matters must be stated. . . . .

Conclusion:

> Thus it was meet and right that when man was formed, God should assign a share in the work to His lieutenants, as He does with the words 'let us make man' so that man's right actions might be attributable to Him alone, but his sins to others. For it seemed to be unfitting to God the All-ruler that the road to wickedness within the reasonable soul should be of His making, and therefore He delegated the forming of this part to His inferiors. For the work of forming the voluntary element to balance the involuntary had to be accomplished to render the whole complete.

In *Opif.* 72–75 the question in *Opif.* 72 and the answer in §§ 73–75 form the basic structure of the exposition of the text from Gen 1:26. The problem is the difference between the singular and plural forms of the verb. The singular is used of God creating the heaven and the earth; the plural is used in Gen 1:26 when He creates man. The expository answer is summed up in a concluding statement in *Opif.* 75. Here part of the problematic text, Gen 1:26, is quoted again.

In *Conf.* 168–79 the question in §§ 168–169 and the answer in §§ 170–79 also form the basic structure of the exposition. The problem is found in three Old Testament texts, in Gen 11:7 about God confusing the tongues of the builders of the tower, in Gen 1:26 about God creating man, and in Gen 3:22 about God speaking about Adam as knowing good and evil.The problem in all three texts is, as in *Opif.* 72–75, the use of plural about God. The answer in *Conf.* 170–79 is divided into three sections followed by the conclusion, which mainly refers to Gen 1:26 by quoting part of it again. The content of the conclusion in *Conf.* 179 is similar to that of the conclusion in *Opif.* 75.

These examples of question and answer applied to the creation of man according to Gen 1:26 show that the same exegetical problem formulation and form are built into the rewritten presentation of the whole Pentateuch in the *Exposition*, and into the expository commentary upon Gen 11:1–9, the story of the tower of Babel, in the *Allegorical Commentary*. In his answers in *Conf.* 170–79 it should be noted that Philo quotes from Homer's *Iliad* 2:204–205 ("It is not well that many lords should rule . . ."). He refers to a problem also of his own time, polytheism, by levelling criticism against those who have deified the sun, the moon and the whole sky.

Parallel usage of question and answer is found both in the *Exposition* and in the *Questions and Answers on Genesis and on Exodus* as well. Thus, in *Opif.* 77 and in *QG* 2:43 the problem of an unexpected order and rank in the Pentateuchal story is dealt with in the form of question and answer:

Opif. 77–88:[8]

> *Question*:
>
> (§ 77): One should inquire the reason why man comes last in the world's creation; for, as the sacred writings show, he was the last whom the Father and Maker fashioned.
>
> *Answer*:
>
> (§ 77): Those, then, who have studied more deeply than others the laws of Moses and who examine their contents with all possible minuteness, maintain that God, when He made man partaker of kinship with Himself in mind and reason best of all gifts, did not begrudge him the other gifts either, but made ready for him beforehand all things in the world, as for living being dearest and closest to Himself, since it was His will that when man came into existence he should be at loss for none of the means of living and of living well. . . . .
>
> (§ 79): Such is the first reason for which apparently man was created after all things: but we must mention a second that is not improbable. . . . .
>
> (§ 82): Let what has been said suffice for an account of the second reason. A third is this. . . . .
>
> (§ 83): Finally, this is suggested as a cogent reason. . . . .

QG 1:43:

> *Question*:
>
> Why, when they hid themselves from the face of God, was not the woman, who first ate of the forbidden fruit, first mentioned but the man; for [Scripture] says, 'Adam and his wife hid themselves'.
>
> *Answer*:
>
> It was the more imperfect and ignoble element, the female, that made a beginning of transgression and lawlessness, while the male

---

[8] The translation in *PLCL* is slightly modified.

made the beginning of reverence and modesty and all good, since
he was better and more perfect.

Here the exegetical form of question and answer again is evident. In
both cases the problem is that of an unexpected order and rank in
the Pentateuchal story:[9] the woman ate first of the forbidden fruit,
but was nevertheless mentioned last when they hid themselves (*QG*
1:43). In *Opif.* 77–78 it is thought surprising that Adam is the last of
God's creations. The problem of order presupposes the idea that the
last is inferior to the first, a principle explicitly stated in *Opif.* 87:
"The fact of having been the last to come into existence does not
involve an inferiority corresponding to his place in the series". The
answer in *QG* 1:43 is in accordance with the principle that the first
in order is also the one who ranks first: Adam, who was mentioned
first, was better and more perfect. The answer in *Opif.* 77–88 must
reverse itself and argue against this principle in order to understand
man as the superior being even though created last: God had to prepare for all that man would need before He created him. Thus man
came last in the order of creation although he was higher in rank.

Jewish and Greek parallels

The form of question and answer is a common feature both to Philo
and rabbinic exegesis. Philo and rabbinic writings even draw on the
same tradition. In *Opif.* 77 the question is raised why man was created last, and then the answer follows in four points:

1 God provided first for man's means of living, so that man
    would find a banquet ready for him when he came.
2 Just as man found all provisions needed for life, those who
    strive for righteousness will experience peace, order and all
    good things in readiness.
3 Man as miniature heaven ties the end of creation to the
    beginning, heaven.
4 Man came after all created things, as king and master.

The following points show that Philo in parts draws on traditions
which he has in common with rabbinic traditions:

---

[9] The problem of order in the Pentateuchal text is also discussed in *QG* 1:61 and
2:79.

A) The same question, why Adam was created last, occurs several places in rabbinic writings.[10] Of special interest is the parallel in *t. Sanh.* 8:7 and 9:

Opif. 77:[11]

> *Question*:
>
> a) 'επιζητήσειε δ' ἄν τις τὴν αἰτίαν, δι' ἣν ὕστατόν ἐστιν ἄνθρωπος τῆς τοῦ κόσμου γενέσεως.
>
> (One should ask the reason why man comes last in the world's creation)
>
> b) ἐφ' ἅπασι γὰρ τοῖς ἄλλοις αὐτὸν ὁ ποιητὴς καὶ πατήρ, ὥσπερ αἱ ἱεραὶ γραφαὶ μηνύουσιν εἰργάσατο.
>
> (for, as the sacred writings show, he was the last whom the Father and Maker fashioned.)

T. Sanhedrin 8:7 (*Tosefta*, ed. Zuckermandel):

> *Question*:
>
> b) אדם נברא באחרונה
>
> (Man was created last)
>
> a) ולמה נברא באחרונה
>
> (And why was he created last?)

Both in Philo, *Opif.* 77 and in *t. Sanhedrin* 8:7 the problem is one of unexpected order in the scriptural account: why was Adam created last? Both places point a) raises the question, while point b) states the fact that man (according to Scriptures) was created last.

The first of Philo's answers is basically the same as one of the answers given in *t. Sanh.* 8:9, and this answer goes beyond the narrative in Gen 1.

Opif. 78:[12]

> *Answer*:
>
> Just as givers of a banquet, then, do not send out the summonses to supper till they have put everything in readiness for the feast . . . . . in the same way the Ruler of all things, like some

---

[10] *Gen. Rab.* 8:1ff.; *Lev. Rab.* 14:1; *Midrash Ps.* 139; *Tanchuma*, ed. Buber, 32; *t. Sanh.* 8:7; *y. Sanh.* 4:9.

[11] The translation in *PLCL* is modified.

[12] The translation in *PLCL* is modified.

provider ... of a banquet, when about to invite man to the enjoyment of a feast ... made ready beforehand the material ... in
order that on coming into the world man might at once find ...
a banquet ... full of all things that earth and rivers and sea and
air bring forth for use and enjoyment. . . .

t. Sanh. 8:9:

Answer:
Another matter: So that he might enter the banquet at once. They
have made a parable: To what is the matter comparable? To a
king who built a palace and dedicated it and prepared a meal
and [only] afterwards invited the guests. And so Scripture says,
'The wisest of women has built her a house' (Prov 9:1). This
refers to the King of the kings of kings, blessed be He, who built
his world in seven days by wisdom. 'She has hewn out her seven
pillars' (Prov 9:1) – these are the seven days of creation. 'She has
killed her beasts and mixed her wine' (Prov 9:2) – These are the
oceans, rivers, wastes, and all the other things which the world
needs. . . .[13]

B) In both passages the picture of a banquet is used to explain why
Adam was created last. There are even many similarities between
Philo and the Tosephta in wording:[14]

Philo: καθάπερ οὖν ... τὸν αὐτὸν τρόπον Tos: הוא למה הדבר דומה
כן ...
Philo: ἐπὶ δεῖπνον ... πρὸς εὐωχίαν .. συμπόσιον .. Tos: סעודה
Philo: καλοῦσιν ... καλεῖν ... Tos: יכנס ... זימן
Philo: οὐ πρότερον ... προ(ευτρεπίσατο) ... Tos: ואחר כך
Philo: εὐτρεπίσαι ... (προ)ευτρεπίσατο .. Tos: וחינכה והתקין
Philo: ὁ τῶν ὅλον ἡγεμών .... Tos: מלך מלכי המלכים
Philo: γῆ καὶ ποταμοί καὶ θάλαττα ... Tos: ומדברות ונהרות ימים
Philo: εἰς χρῆσιν καὶ ἀπόλαυσιν ... Tos: ושאר צורכי העולם

All these similarities in wording give support to the conclusion that
Philo, *Opif.* 77–78, and *t. Sanh.* 8:7 and 9 render the same tradition.
Moreover, this tradition occurs also in other places in the rabbinic
writings, as in *y. Sanh.* 4:9; *b. Sanh.* 38a; *Jalkut, Shemone* 15, confer
Gen. Rab. 8:6. The tradition was also used by the Church Fathers, as
by Gregor of Nyssa, *De hom. op.*, ch. 2. Thus this tradition was widespread and originated at the time of Philo or before.

---

[13] The translation is taken from Neusner (1981) 224.
[14] Zuckermandel (ed.) (1881) ad loc.

This conclusion is strengthened by the fact that Philo explicitly says that he renders the answer of other scholars on the Laws of Moses. Thus, the tradition originated before Philo recorded it in *Opif.* 77–78, since he wrote: "Those, then, who have studied more deeply than others the laws of Moses and who examine their contents with all possible minuteness, maintain that. . . ."[15]

C) Also with regard to the second answer (*Opif.* 79), to the question why man was created last, Philo utilizes Jewish traditions. Here the answer is: "At the moment of his coming into existence man found all provisions for life". This is a repetition of a point already mentioned in his first answer in *Opif.* 77: ". . . He . . . made ready for him beforehand all things in the world . . ., since it was His will that when man came into existence he should be at a loss for none of the means of living and of living well". A close parallel is found in *Gen. Rab.* 8:6: "Only after He had created what was needed for his food He created him". This idea refers to Gen 1:28 where it is said that living beings exist for the sake of human beings. Philo expresses this understanding at several places in his writings, such as in *Prov.* 2:84 (*SVF* 2:149); 91–92; 103; *Mos.* 1:60–62 and *Spec.* 4:119–21.

Scholars have observed that the question and answer form is found both in the Jewish Alexandrian writer Demetrius, as well as in Greek commentaries on Plato's *Theaetetus* and on the writings of Homer.

In Demetrius' work *On the Kings of Judaea*, fragment 2, preserved in Eusebius, *Praep. Evang.* 9:21:14, the following question and answer occurs:

> *Question*:
>   A crucial question arises as to why (διαπορεῖσθαι δὲ διὰ τί) Joseph gave Benjamin a fivefold portion at the meal even though he would not be able to consume so much meat.
> *Answer*:
>   He did this because seven sons had been born to his father by Leah whereas only two sons had been born to him by Rachel his

---

[15] Runia (1986) 272–4 and 530, discusses *Opif.* 77–8 under the theme "The encomium of sight", based on Plato's *Timaeus* 47a–c. He finds two Platonic themes in the passage, the gift of the gods and the kinship of man's mind with the heavenly bodies. As for the gifts of the gods, Runia expresses surprise that with the partial exception of *Opif.* 77–8 Philo ignores this theme.

As a comment to Runia's work, it must be said that his analysis of this passage shows that it needs be supplemented by a study of Jewish exegetical traditions. It is striking that just Philo's use of the (Platonic) theme of the gifts of the gods, is an elaboration of the common Jewish tradition about God making everything ready for man, like a banquet, before man was created. Runia is himself aware of the need for his study being supplemented in this way (Runia (1986) 6).

mother. For this reason, he served up five portions for Benjamin and he himself took two. Thus there were between them seven portions, that is, as many as all the sons of Leah had taken.[16]

A problem of measurement is also raised and answered in the *Anonymous Commentary on Theaetetus* 34:9–14 and 34:33–35:44. S. Wan arranges the text schematically in this way:[17]

> *Text*:
> And in this way taking every single case in turn up to the root of 17 square feet; but at this point for some reason he came to a halt. Cf. *Theaet.* 147d:5–6.
>
> *Question*:
> There are those who inquire why (ζητοῦσιν διὰ τί) he proceeds to 17 square feet.
>
> *Answer*:
> Some say (τινές φασιν) that Theodorus . . .
> Others (ἔνιοι δή) are of the opinion that . . .
> Perhaps it would be better to affirm (μήποτε ἄμεινον ᾖ λέγειν) that he proceeded to 17 square feet because . . .

The problem of Homer contradicting himself is discussed in *Schol Venetus* A on the *Iliad* 1:52:

> *Text*:
> the pyres of corpses burned thick
>
> *Question*:
> Why, they say, does the poet contradict himself? (πῶς, φασίν, ὁ ποιητὴς ἐναντία ἑαυτῷ λέγαι) For after he earlier said (εἰπὼν γὰρ πρῶτον) 'and he made them prey for dogs' then he now brings forward (νῦν ἐγάγει) 'always the pyres of corpses'.
>
> *Answer*:
> We will say, however, that (ἐροῦμεν οὖν ὅτι) the plague increased the wrath, but the wrath the battles that followed; and those falling in the battles became prey for dogs, but those who were destroyed by the plague, burned.[18]

The question follows after the quoted text and the relevant parts of the text is repeated in the question and contrasted with a seemingly contradicting statement made earlier. The problem is thus a contradition in the text of the *Iliad*. The answer solves the problem.

These parallels demonstrate that in his extensive use of the exe-

---

[16] Translation in Holladay (1983) ad loc.
[17] Wan (1993) 30–31. Cf. the geometrical speculation in Plutarch, *Platonic Questions, Question* 4 (1003Bff.).
[18] Dindorf (1878) 14–15.

getical form of question and answer Philo represents a broad Jewish tradition which is to be seen as part of a widespread Hellenistic usage.

The exegetical form of question and answer is commonly used in the *Allegorical Commentary*. Some examples are: *Leg. all.* 1:33–41; 48–52, 70–71, 85–87, 90, 91–92a; 101–04, 105–08, 2:19–21, 42–43, 44–45, 68–70, 80–81, 3:18–19; 49ff., 66–68, 77–78, 184–85, 188; *Cher.* 21f. and 55ff.; *Sacr.* 11ff. and 128ff.; *Quod Det* 57ff. and 80ff.; *Post.* 33ff., 40ff. and 153; *Gig.* 55ff.; *Immut.* 11f., 60ff., 70ff., 86ff., 104 and 122; *Somn.* 1:5ff., 12f., 14ff., 41f., and 2:300ff.

The 'Question and Answer Commentary'
and the 'Allegorical Commentary'

Furthermore, close parallels exist between the *Questions and Answers in Genesis* and *The Allegorical Commentary*, as can be illustrated by the agreements between *Leg. all.* 1:85–87; 101–04 and *QG* 1:13 and 15.

Just as was the case in *Opif.* 72–75 and *Conf.* 168–69, so also in *Leg. all.* 1:101–04 and *QG* 1:15 the use of both singular and plural poses the problem:[19]

Leg. all. 1:101–04:

Question:

Next there is this further question to be raised. When He is giving the charge to eat of every tree of the garden, He addresses the command to a single person, but when He issues the prohibition against making any use of that which causes evil and good, He speaks to more than one: for in the former case He says, 'Thou shalt eat from every tree'; but in the latter, 'ye shall not eat, and in the day that ye eat' not 'that thou eatest', and 'ye shall die' not 'thou shalt die'.

Answer:

We must accordingly remark in the first place that the good is scarce, the evil abundant. Hence it is hard to find a single wise man, while of inferior men there is a countless multitude. Quite fitly, therefore, does He bid a single man to find nourishment in the virtues, but many to abstain from evil-doing, for myriads practice this.

In the second place, for the acquisition and practice of virtue a single thing only, namely our understanding, is requisite: but the body not only fails to cooperate to this end, but is an actual

---

[19] See Borgen and Skarsten (1976–77) 2–5.

hindrance; for we may almost make it an axiom that the business of wisdom is to become estranged from the body and its cravings: but for the enjoyment of evil it is necessary not only that the mind be in a certain condition, but also the power of perception and of speech, in fact the body; for all these the inferior man requires for the full satisfaction of his particular form of wickedness. For how shall he divulge sacred and hidden truths unless he have an organ of speech? And how is he to indulge in pleasure, if he be bereft of a stomach and the organs of taste? So it is in accordance with the necessities of the case that He addresses the understanding alone about gaining virtue; for, as I said, it alone is needed for its acquisition; whereas in the pursuit of evil, several faculties are needed, soul, speech, senses, body, for wickedness employs all these in displaying itself.

QG 1:15:

Question:
Why does [God] say, when He commands [Adam] to eat of every tree which is in Paradise, 'Eat' in the singular number; but when He forbids eating of the tree which gives knowledge of good and evil, says, in the plural number, 'Do not eat, for on the day when ye shall eat, ye shall die'?

Answer:
First, because though it extends over many things, the good is one, and not less for this reason, namely that He who gave the benefit is one, as is also the one who received the benefit. This "one" I speak of, not with reference to the number which precedes the number two, but with reference to the unitary power, in accordance with which many things are harmonized and agree and by their concord imitate the one, such as a flock, a herd, a drove, a chorus, an army, a nation, a tribe, a household, a city. For all these, extending over many, are one community and embrace lovingly; but when they are unmixed and have nothing in common, they fall into duality and into a multitude and are divided. For duality is the beginning of division. But two who use the same philosophy as one enjoy an unadulterated and clear virtue which is free of evil. But when good and evil are mixed, they have as their beginning a mixture of death.

There are close agreements between these two passages both in form and in the formulation of the exegetical problem in the text. Both have question and answer as basic structure. In both passages the problem is the difference between singular in one verb and plural in another verb in the verses discussed, namely Gen 2:16–17. These agreements show that the exegesis in *Leg. all.* 1:101–04 is of a kind similar to that in *Questions and Answers on Genesis, in casu QG* 1:15. The fact that the answers differ in content in the two passages does not alter this conclusion. This difference only makes clear that Philo (or a synagogal school tradition behind him) could give two different answers to the same question and could express them within the same expository structure.

The question of difference between singular and plural forms of words is also raised in connection with other Old Testament texts. Above Philo's exposition of Gen 1:26 has been analysed. There the problem was also number, why plural was used when God created man, Gen 1:26. As also seen above the same problem was discussed in *Dec.* 36–43. The question is stated in *Dec.* 36 and the answer, divided into three parts, follows in *Dec.* 37–43. Again the problem is the difference between singular and plural: the commandments in Exod 20:13–15 have verbs in the singular, as if addressed to one person, in spite of the fact that many thousands were collected in one spot. The answers given are 1) each individual person is equal in worth to a whole nation; 2) in this way the exhortations are received as a personal message; 3) kings and despots should learn from God not to despise an insignificant private person. It is to be noted that the unexpected use of the singular is not explained here by means of deeper (allegorical) exegesis, as was the case in *QG* 1:15 and *Leg. all.* 1:101–04. Thus it can be seen that such questions may lead either to deeper (allegorical) exposition or not.

The conclusion is that the expository form of questions and answer and similar problem-formulations are used in Philo's *Exposition of the Laws of Moses*, in the *Allegorical Commentary* as well as in his *Questions and Answers on Genesis and Exodus*.

Exegetical terminology

In Philo's exegetical form of questions and answers formulas are being used, even though in a flexible way. Some of such phrases are:

In *Opif.* 77–88 and *Leg. all.* 1:91–92 the questions are introduced by phrases which have (ἐπι)ζητεῖν as the verb followed by words for 'why': ἐπιζητήσειε δ' ἄν τις τὴν αἰτίαν δι' ἥν . . . (*Opif.* 77); and ζητητέον δέ, διὰ τί . . . (*Leg. all.* 1:91). The phrase ζητοῦσιν διὰ τί in the *Anonymous Commentary on Theaetetus* 34:33–35 belongs to this category.

In *Opif.* 72–75; *Leg. all.* 1:85–87, 101–04 and *Dec.* 36–43 the questions are introduced by phrases which have (δι)απορεῖν as verb:

ἀπορήσειε δ' ἄν τις οὐκ ἀπὸ σκοποῦ, τί δήποτε (Opif. 72); ἄξιον δὲ διαπορῆσαι διὰ τί . . . (Leg. all. 1:85); ἑξῆς κἀκείνω διαπορητέον . . . (Leg. all. 1:101); and δεόντως δ' ἄν τις ἀπορῆσαι, τοῦ χάριν, . . . (Dec. 36). According to Eusebius, Praep. Ev. 9:21:14 Demetrius used this same verb in his formulation of the question, διαπορεῖσθαι δὲ διὰ τί.

The answers in Leg. All. 1:85–87, 91–92, 101–04 and Dec. 36–43 are introduced with phrases which contain the word λεκτέον: λεκτέον οὖν ὅτι . . . (Leg. all. 1:86); τί οὖν λεκτέον; (Leg. all. 1:91); λεκτέον οὖν τάδε, ὅτι . . . (Leg. all. 1:102); and λεκτέον οὖν ἕν μέν, ὅτι . . . (Dec. 37).

From this partial survey it may be seen that there are similarities in the wording of the questions and answers. This suggests that Philo is using traditional exegetical formulas, although in a flexible way.

In Opif. 77–88 and 72–75 the answers are introduced by other phrases. In the first of these passages the answer consists of five points, four of which offer positive answers, while the fifth rejects a mistaken interpretation. The various points are introduced as follows:

a λέγουσιν οὖν οἱ τοῖς νόμοις ἐπὶ πλέον ἐμβαθύναντες, καὶ τὰ κατ' αὐτοὺς ὡς ἔνι μάλιστα μετὰ πάσης ἐξετάσεως ἀκριβοῦντες, ὅτι . . . (§ 77). ἥδε μὲν αἰτία πρώτη, δι' ἣν ἄνθρωπος ἐφ' ἅπασι γεγενῆσθαι δοκεῖ.

b δευτέραν δ' οὐκ ἀπὸ σκοποῦ λεκτέον (§ 79). δευτέρα μὲν αἰτία ἥδε λελέχθω,

c τρίτη δ' ἐστὶ τοιάδε (§ 82).

d ἐπὶ πᾶσι μέντοι κἀκεῖνο λέγεται πρὸς ἀπόδοσιν αἰτίας ἀναγκαίας (§ 83).

e χρὴ μέντοι μηδ' ἐκεῖνο ἀγνοεῖν ὅτι . . . (§ 87).

In point b) the form λεκτέον is used, as in the passages mentioned above. In a), b) and d) other forms of the verb λέγειν appear. The reason is that in a) an explicit reference to the views of others is made; in c) and d) the phrases are varied to avoid mechanical repetition. The viewpoint to be rejected e) is then introduced by means of another verb, ἀγνοεῖν.

The answer in Opif. 72–73 has this wording: τὴν μὲν οὖν ἀληθεστάτην αἰτίαν θεὸν ἀνάγκη μόνον εἰδέναι, τὴν δ' εἰκότι στοχασμῷ πιθανὴν καὶ εὔλογον ("The full truth about the cause of this it must needs be that God alone knows, but the cause which by probable conjecture seems plausible we must not conceal".) The reason for this formulation is that the exegete finds his own solution to be conjectural and feels it necessary to indicate this.

Although it is problematic to compare this exegetical terminology with that in *Questions and Answers on Genesis and on Exodus*, some observations can be made. The introductory phrase in *Opif.* 77 (λέγουσιν οὖν οἱ . . .) may be compared with similar phraseology in *QG* 1:8 (cf. "nonnuli dixerunt"), 2:64 (τινὲς δέ φασι) and 3:13 (cf. "quidam dixerunt"). Philo uses phrases like these when he makes explicit that he records the views of others.[20] It would be premature, however, to draw the conclusion that those referred to in this way all belonged to one specific group of exegetes.

The introductory phrases ἐπιζητήσειε δ' ἄν τις τὴν αἰτίαν, δι' ἥν . . . (*Opif.* 77) and ἀπορήσειε δ' ἄν τις οὐκ ἀπὸ σκοποῦ, τι δήποτε . . . (*Opif.* 72), as well as the other phrases listed, are long forms for the corresponding use of διὰ τί, which occurs frequently in the *Questions and Answers* Commentary, as also in the corresponding Hebrew term ולמה, 'wherefore', 'why', is used in *t. Sanh.* 8:7. The Greek fragments to *QG* 1:1; 2:13, 62; 4:144, 145; *QE* 2:64, 65 testify to this use of διὰ τί.

Finally, the phrases with λεκτέον which introduce the answers in *Leg. all.* 1:86, 91, 102 and *Dec.* 37 are employed in cases for which in the *Questions and Answer* commentary there is often no introductory formula, or where διότι or ὅτι is used (*QG* 1:94, 4:145), or where another term (such as 'first', 'second', etc.) may be used.

Complex forms

Philo may use more complex forms of question and answer when he discusses *aporiae* in the biblical texts. One such form occurs when objection is raised against a particular interpretation of a text. An example is found in *QE* 2:49, where Exod 24:18b is interpreted:

QE 2:49:

1 *Question, paraphrasing the text, Exod 24:18b:*

   Why does Moses remain on the mountain forty days and the same number of nights?

---

[20] Aucher (1826) ad loc.; Bréhier (1908) 55, nn. 1 and 2; Bousset (1915) 44.

2   *Answer*:

Concerning the number forty and its place in nature a detailed account was given earlier, so that one need not speak further of this at length. (Cf. *QG* 1:25; 2:14; 4:154).

Perhaps, however, it is necessary to add that the migrant generation was about to be condemned and waste away in corruption for forty years in all after receiving many benefactions and showing ingratitude in many ways. And so, he remains there above for the same number of days as these years, reconciling the Father to the nation by prayers and intercessions, especially at the very time when the laws were given by God and there was constructed in words the portable temple, which is called the Tent of Testimony.

3   *The interpretation is questioned*:
a) *Rhetorical questions with points from the interpretation repeated*:

For whom, then, were the laws (given)?
Was it, indeed, for those who were to perish?
And for whose sake were the oracles (given)?
Was it for those who were to be destroyed a little later?

b) *Problem-question about Moses which might be raised by "some"*:

It seems to me, however, that someone may say, 'Is it possible that he had foreknowledge of the judgment that was to come upon it'?

Answer:

But he who says this should bear in mind that every prophetic soul is divinely inspired and prophesies many future things not so much by reflecting as through divine madness and certainty.

A more elaborate structure occurs in *Mut.* 141a, 142–44, in rabbinic parallels, such as *Mek. Exod.* 12:2 and in the New Testament, John 6:30–48.[21]

Mut. 141a, 142–44:[22]
1   *Text*:

§ 141a: So much for the phrase 'I will give to thee'. We must now explain 'from her' (Gen 17:16).

---

21 See Borgen (1965) 80–83.
22 The translation in *PLCL* is slightly modified.

2 *Interpretation, Mut.* 142b:

> There is a third class who say that virtue is 'the mother' of any good that has come into being, receiving the seeds of that being from nothing that is mortal.

3 *The interpretation is questioned*:

> § 143: Some ask, however, whether the barren can bear children, since the oracles earlier described Sarah as barren,

4 *The questioned interpretation is repeated*:

> and now admit that she will become 'a mother'.

5 *The answer*:

> §§ 143–44: Our answer to this must be that it is not in the nature of a barren woman to bear, any more than of the blind to see or the deaf to hear. But as for the soul which is sterilized to wickedness and unfruitful to the endless host of passions and vices, scarce any prosper in childbirth as she.
>
> For she bears offspring worthy of love, even the number seven, according to the hymn of Hannah, that is grace, who says", The barren hath borne seven, but she that is much in children hath languished" (1 Sam 2:5).
>
> She applies the word "much" to the mind which is a medley of mixed and confused thoughts, which, because of the multitude of riots and turmoils that surround it, brings forth evil past all remedy. But the word "barren" she applies to the mind which refuses to accept any mortal sowing as fruitful, the mind which makes away with and brings to abortion all the intimacies and the matings of the wicked, but holds fast to the "seven" and the supreme peace which it gives. This peace she would fain bear in her womb and be called 'mother'.

A parallel form occurs in midrashic expositions when contradictions are discussed. *Mek. Exod.* 12:2 is an example:[23]

1 *Text*:

> This new moon shall be unto you (Exod 12:2).

2 *The interpretation*:

> the 'new moon', of course, He showed him at nighttime.

---

[23] The translation is taken from Lauterbach (1935) ad loc.

3   *The interpretation is questioned*:

R. Simon the son of Yohai says: Is it not a fact that all the words which He spoke to Moses He spoke only in the daytime?

4   *The questioned interpretation is repeated*:

How then could He, while speaking with him at daytime, show him the 'new moon' at nighttime?

5   *The answer*:

R. Eliezer says: He spoke with him at daytime near nightfall, and then showed him the 'new moon' right after nightfall.

John 6:31–48:
1   *Text*:

v. 31: Our fathers ate the manna in the wilderness; as it is written, 'He gave them bread from heaven to eat'.

2   *The interpretation*:

v. 41: The Jews then murmured at him, because he said (εἶπεν), 'I am the bread which came down from heaven'.

3   *The interpretation is questioned*:

v. 42: They said (καὶ ἔλεγον),
'Is not this (οὐχ οὗτός ἐστιν) Jesus, the Son of Joseph, whose father and mother we know'?

4   *The questioned interpretation is repeated*:

How does he now say (πῶς νῦν λέγει ὅτι)
'I have come down from heaven'?

5   *The answer*:

v. 43: Jesus answered them (ἀπεκρίθη Ἰησοῦς καὶ εἶπεν αὐτοῖς),
'Do not murmur among yourselves.
v. 44–47: No one can come to me unless the Father who sent me draws him. . . . .
v. 48: I am the bread of life'.

These passages discuss an exegetical problem in a sequence of five points: Point 1) has a quotation from the Old Testament, Gen 17:16, Exod 12:2 and Exod 16:4/Ps 78:24(?) respectively. Point 2) gives the interpretation of the quotation. In John 6:41ff. the words 'bread' and 'from heaven' from the Old Testament quotation are repeated. In

Mek. Exod. 12:2 one word from the quotation is interpreted, 'new moon'. No word from the Old Testament quotation is rendered in the interpretation in *Mut.* 142b, but the central term 'mother' clearly refers to 'from her' in the cited text, Gen 17:16. Point 3), then, introduces the objection against the interpretation. In *Mek. Exod.* 12:2 this point precedes point 2). The interpretation in point 2) is repeated in point 4), on the basis of the objection raised. Finally, point 5) gives the answer to the objection and gives the solution to the question raised.

The exegetical and stylistic terminology in these passages show similarities: In *Mut.* 141a, 142b–44 the phrases are: point 1) the Old Testament quotation. 2) τρίτοι δέ εἰσιν οἱ ... λέγοντες 3) πρὸς δὲ τοὺς ζητοῦντας, εἰ 4) οἱ χρησμοὶ νῦν ὅτι ... ὁμολογοῦσι 5) λεκτέον ἐκεῖνο, ὅτι. The corresponding phrases in *Mek. Exod.* 12:2 are: 1) The Old Testament quotation. 2) אומר יוחאי בן שמעון רבי (3 והלא (4 כיצד 5) אומר אליעזר רבי. Finally, the wordings in John 6:31b, 41–48 are: 1) The Old Testament quotation. 2) εἶπεν 3) καὶ ἔλεγον οὐχ οὗτός ἐστιν 4) πῶς νῦν λέγει ὅτι 5) ἀπεκρίθη Ἰησοῦς καὶ εἶπεν αὐτοῖς.

Such a more elaborate sequence of the exegetical question and answer form occurs also elsewhere in the *Mekilta on Exodus*. See *Mek. Exod.* 12:1; 15:5, etc. Thus, it is clear that as far as form is concern, there is no real difference between Philo's approach in Alexandria, and the approach used in Palestinian tradition, as it was written down at a later time in the *Mekilta on Exodus*.

Another form of exegetical question and answer is found in *Virt.* 171–74:

> *The case:*
>> But with the men of windy pride, whose intensified arrogance sets them quite beyond cure, the law seals admirably in not bringing them to be judged by men but handing them over to the divine tribunal only,
>
> *The (proof-)text, Num 15:30:*
>> for it says, 'Whosoever sets his hand to do anything with presumptuousness provokes God'.
>
> *Question and answer:*
>> Why is this?
>>
>> First, because arrogance is a vice of the soul and the soul is invisible save only to God. ...
>>
>> Secondly, the arrogant man is always filled with the spirit of unreason, holding himself, as Pindar says, to be neither man nor demigod, but wholly divine, and claiming to overstep the limits of human nature. ...

> Naturally, such a person will, as the Revealer tells us, have God
> for his accuser and avenger.

Here a case is pictured, namely the appearance of men of arrogance
beyond human limits. Such a case is referred to the divine court.
The quotation from the Law (Num 15:30) shows that this crime is a
crime against God. Then after the quotation is given, the question is
raised "Why is this?", which asks for a rationale for applying the
Law-quotation to the case. The double answer gives the reasoning
behind this application of the law, and draws the conclusion, "Naturally such a person will, as the Revealer tells us, have God for his
accuser and avenger". This passage, *Virt.* 171–74, occurs in Philo's
Exposition, and it is important that this presentation of the Laws contains evidence for the exegetical question and answer form being
used in the legal evaluation of a case.

Conclusion

This analysis has demonstrated the central importance which the
exegetical use of the form of question and answer has in Philo's
expository writings, in his *On the Life of Moses, the Exposition* and *Allegorical Commentary* as well as in the *Questions and Answers Commentary*. It
is the weakness of the essays in the book edited by D. Hay, *Both
Literal and Allegorical* (1993), that the use of the question-and-answer-
form in *On the Life of Moses* and the *Exposition* is ignored and that no
thorough analysis is given of rabbinic usage.

Instead of discussing the relationship between the *Questions and Answers
Commentary* and the *Allegorical Commentary*, one should rather think of
the place of this exegetical method and form in learned settings within
Judaism as well as in the wider Hellenistic context. These learned
settings may be within a Jewish synagogual context, as suggested by
Philo's report on the expository activity among the Therapeutae:

> ... the President of the company ... discusses (ζητεῖ) some questions
> arising in the Holy Scriptures or solves (ἐπιλύεται) one that has been
> propounded by someone else.

Against this background the term διαλέγομαι, 'hold converse with',
'discuss', when used about the expository activity, probably refers to
the use of question and answer method (*Cont.* 31 and 79, *Spec.* 2:62
and *Mos.* 2:215). Against the background of such expository activity

in community sessions, learned persons would themselves employ the same expository method, partly as a rhetorical and literary device. Accordingly, Philo would both draw on traditional questions and answers, as for example in *Opif.* 77 as seen together with *t. Sanh. 8:7* and *9*, and he himself would participate actively in this kind of exegesis as part of his literary efforts. Thus, instead of discussing the possible dependance of the *Allegorical Commentary* on the *Questions and Answers Commentary*, one should discuss how far Philo is dependent on traditions and on learned (synagogual) school activity in his extensive use of this form of exegesis.[24]

V. Nikiprowetzky suggested that the technique of question and answer was behind Philo's expositions in general, and that its background was the expository activity in the synagogual settings.[25] This view seems too onesided. An analysis of Philo's exposition demonstrates that also other forms have been used.

It should be added that the form of questions and answers was frequently used also in Christian exegesis. Early on, it often reflected controversies between orthodox and heretic. From the 4th century on, the commentaries treated traditional problems rather than live issues. The form was also used for personal counselling and pedagogics. Thus, the question and answer form represented a very broad and varied exegetical tradition in Antiquity.[26]

---

[24] Cf. Delling (1974) 141; Nikiprowetzky (1977) 174–77.
[25] Nikiprowetzky (1977) 179–80 and Nikiprowetzky (1983) 15–75.
[26] See Schaublin (1974) 49–51; Dörrie and Dörries (1966) cols. 347–70.

CHAPTER SIX

ON THE GIANTS AND ON THE UNCHANGEABLENESS OF GOD

Introduction

Philo's 'rewritten Bible', the *Exposition of the Laws of Moses*, has been analysed in an earlier chapter. The present task is to examine the structure of his running commentary, the *Allegorical Commentary*. This commentary series is both complex and extensive, so that a selection must be made. The examples chosen are the twin treatises *On the Giants* and *On the Unchangeableness of God* and the treatise the *Allegorical Laws*, Book 1. The task is to exemplify the character of some of the expository forms used and show how they have been composed together into a treatise.

Two questions raised by D. Runia will guide us in the analysis: 1) In his essay "Further Observations on the Structure of Philo's Allegorical Treatises" he asks the following question: "Is there a uniform method (e.g. the *quaestio* and *solutio*) that is repeated over and over again, or does Philo exhibit a diversity of approaches"?[1] 2) Another question asked by Runia is: "The role of the secondary biblical texts which Philo habitually introduces is also controversial . . . do these secondary texts merely function as illustratory material, or do they take on a life of their own?"[2]

In the commentary series *Questions and Answers on Genesis and on Exodus* transitional statements are only used in a limited degree. In the rewritten Bible, called the *Exposition of the Laws of Moses* Philo ties the different parts together by interpretative transitional statements, and he has also given summary statements by which he outlines the content of larger units of the work. There is a kinship between the *Exposition* and the *Allegorical Commentary* in the respect that both have been subject to extensive editorial activity. Thus, both in the *Exposition* and in the *Allegorical Commentary* references and transitions bind various parts

---

[1] Runia (1987) 112.
[2] *Ibid.*

together. At the same time both the *Allegorical Commentary* and the *Questions and Answers* differ from the *Exposition* in their general structure since they appear in the form of running commentaries on parts of the Pentateuchal text and not as a rewritten Bible.

The parts of the *Allegorical Commentary* which are preserved, are:

Gen 2:1–17 *The Allegorical Laws* (*Legum Allegoriae*) 1
Gen 2:18–3:1 *The Allegorical Laws* (*Legum Allegoriae*) 2
Gen 3:8b–19 *The Allegorical Laws* (*Legum Allegoriae*) 3
Gen 3:24–4:1 *On the Cherubim* (*De Cherubim*)
Gen 4:2–4 *On the Sacrifices of Abel and Cain* (*De Sacrificiis Abelis et Caini*)
Gen 4:8–15 *That the Worse Attacks the Better* (*Quod Deterius Potiori Insidiari Soleat*)
Gen 4:16–25 (in parts) *On the Posterity and Exile of Cain* (*De Posteritate Caini*)
Gen 6:1–4a *On the Giants* (*De Gigantibus*)
Gen 6:4b–12 (in parts) *On the Unchangeableness of God* (*Quod Deus Sit Immutabilis*)
Gen 9:20–21 *On Husbandry* (*De Agricultura*)
Gen 9:20–21 *On Noah's Work as a Planter* (*De Plantatione*)
Gen 9:20–21 *On Drunkenness* (*De Ebrietate*)
Gen 9:24–27 *On Sobriety* (*De Sobrietate*)
Gen 11:1–9 *On the Confusion of Tongues* (*De Confusione Linguarum*)
Gen 12:1–6 (in parts) *On the Migration of Abraham* (*De Migratione Abrahami*)
Gen 15:2–18 *Who Is the Heir of Divine Things* (*Quis Rerum Divinarum Heres*)
Gen 16:1–5 *On Mating with the Preliminary Studies* (*De Congressu Quaerendae Eruditionis Gratia*)
Gen 16:6b–14 *On Flight and Finding* (*De Fuga et Inventione*)
Gen 17:1–5.16–22 *On the Change of Names* (*De Mutatione Nominum*)
Gen 18 (in parts) *On God* (*De Deo*) (Fragment)
Gen 28:10–22 and 31:10–13 *On Dreams* 1 (*De Somniis* 1)
Gen 37:8–11; 40:9–11, 16–17 and 41:17–24 *On Dreams* 2 (*De Somniis* 2)

There is some evidence and several indications that Philo wrote other treatises of this nature. The clearest evidence is found in *Heres* 1, where Philo refers to a lost treatise on Gen 15:1; likewise *Somn.* 1:1 is an introduction to a second treatise on dreams, the first one being lost. Still other treatises may have interpreted parts of Genesis which are not covered by the extant writings.[3]

---

[3] See discussion for example in Cohn (1899) 393, 402.

Originally the title of all these commentaries seems to have been *Legum Allegoriae*. This name is now given only to the first three treatises, while the others have received individual names. The basic structure for these treatises is the form of a running commentary on parts of Gen 2:1–41:24. The expositions in the allegorical commentary vary in length and are more complex than those found in Philo's *Questions and Answers on Genesis and on Exodus*.[4]

On the Giants

The treatises *On the Giants* and *On the Unchangeableness of God* are chosen for more detailed examination because they are a pair and illustrate how some of the treatises are woven together. *On the Giants* covers Gen 6:1–4a, and concludes with a transitional sentence: "Having for the present said sufficiently about the Giants, let us turn to the words which follow in the text". This transition leads in a direct way into *On the Unchangeableness of God* which contains an exposition of Gen 6:4b–12. Together these two treatises give a commentary on Gen 6:1–12.

Gig. 1–5: Question and answer on Gen 6:1

The text is Gen 6:1: Καὶ δὴ ἐγένετο, ἡνίκα ἤρξαντο οἱ ἄνθρωποι πολλοὶ γίνεσθαι ἐπὶ τῆς γῆς, καὶ θυγατέρες ἐγεννήθησαν αὐτοῖς ("And it came to pass when men began to wax many on the earth and daughters were born unto them").

Philo's exposition of the text centers in *Gig.* 1–3 on the words οἱ ἄνθρωποι πολλοί, "many humans", referred to in § 1b by πολυανθρωπίαν (multitude) and πάμπολυ (abundantly), and in § 3 πολλούς (many). In *Gig.* 4–5 the same words are repeated (οἱ ἄνθρωποι and πολλούς) together with other words from the text, θυγατέρας . . . γεννῆσαι (begat . . . daughters). Thus the theme is the meaning of "many" and "daughters".

---

[4] Cf. Cohn (1899) 392, in the translation by Goodenough (1962) 47: "Philo attaches his lucubrations to the biblical text, which he for the most part follows verse by verse; yet he never confines himself to the passages he is explaining, but wanders off, adduces related passages, and spreads himself out in the greatest detail over these and everything else connected with them, so that he seems in the process to have lost his thread".

The section has the form of question and answer and the context of Gen 6:1 is drawn into the exposition. Noah and his sons are mentioned in Gen 5:32, and the question is why humans grew numerous after the birth of Noah and his sons. In the subsequent context, Gen 6:5ff., there is a contrast pictured between the iniquity of men and Noah as a just man. This specific situation from biblical history is to Philo an example of a general principle in human life and in the cosmos: "when the rarity appears, the opposite always is found in abundance". This contrast is further specified as the contrast between the just and the unjust, the male ("sons") and the female ("daughters").

The question is introduced with a phrase which has διαπορεῖν as verb: ἄξιον . . . διαπορῆσαι, διὰ τί ("it is worth to examine, why) and the answer with a phrase in which the word αἰτία, reason, is central: ἀλλ' ἴσως οὐ χαλεπὸν ἀποδοῦναι τὴν αἰτίαν ("but perhaps it is not too difficult to render the reason"). It is common to introduce an exegetical question by phrases which have (δι)απορεῖν as verb, Opif. 72–75; Leg. all. 1:85–87, 101–104 and Dec. 36–43. The phrase used in the introduction of the answer, αἰτία, is also used in Opif. 79, 82, 83. The question in Gig. 1 is a long form for the corresponding use of διὰ τί, which occurs frequently in Questions and Answers, as can be seen from the Greek fragments to QG 1:1, 2:13, 62; 4:144, 145; QE 2:64, 65, as well as in Greek exegesis, for example in the Theaetetus Commentary 34:22 and Porphyry's De antro nympharum 15, as also the equivalent למה in rabbinic exegesis, for example in t. Sanh. 8:7 (Tosefta, ed. Zuckermandel).[5]

It is worth noting that the expositor refers to himself in 1. person singular, "I think" (οἶμαι), Gig. 1, and to his audience in 2. person singular, "Do you not see that . . ." (οὐχ ὁρᾷς ὅτι), Gig. 3.

Also in QG 1:89 Philo has a corresponding question and answer on Gen 6:1. In both places the question is why the race grew so numerous. In QG 1:89 this question is related to the approaching of the great Flood, and the answer is that God's favours always precede His judgments. In Gig. 1–5, on the other hand, it is related to the preceding birth of Noah and his sons, and the main point of the answer is that when something rare appears, its opposite always is found in abundance. Thus we here have two independent parallels

---

[5] See Borgen and Skarsten (1976–77) 10–12; Sterling (1991) 101; Lieberman (1950) 48; Runia (1987) 114 and 116; Bacher (1899) 1:96–97 and 2:100–01.

of the form of question and answer applied to the same text, *in casu*
Gen 6:1.

Gig. 6–18: a possible misunderstanding and its removal, Gen 6:2

Gen 6:2 reads: Ἰδόντες δὲ οἱ ἄγγελοι τοῦ θεοῦ τὰς θυγατέρας τῶν
ἀνθρώπων, ὅτι καλαί εἰσιν, ἔλαβον ἑαυτοῖς γυναῖκας ἀπὸ πασῶν, ὧν
ἐξελέξαντο. "And when the angels of God saw the daughters of men
that they were fair, they took to themselves wives from all, those
whom they chose". The exposition of this text in *Gig.* 6–18 is as
follows: The word "angels" (οἱ ἄγγελοι) in Gen 6:2 is repeated in the
exposition in *Gig.* 6b), 16, 17 and 18. In §§ 17–18 most of the words
from Gen 6:2 are used in the expository paraphrase. Thus, the interpretation of Gen 6:2 as a whole is given in *Gig.* 17–18.

Gig. 6: Text and a brief expository comment.
Subsequent to the quotation of Gen 6:2 the topic of "the angels" is
taken up in the form of a brief comment of direct exegesis: "angels"
are "demons"/"spirits".[6]

Gig. 7–15: Possible misunderstanding formulated and removed.
A possible misunderstanding is rejected: "And let no one suppose
that what is here said is a myth" (*Gig.* 7). Such removal of a possible
misunderstanding comes close to the form question and answer. The
problem in the present passage is seen as the misconception on the
side of some persons.[7]

The presentation of the proper understanding has the form of a
lesson or an excursus on the place and role of life and living beings
in cosmos with emphasis on angels, demons and souls, *Gig. 7–15*.
Souls are the forms of life which exists in the air. A parallel section
is found in *Somn.* 1:133–45.[8] Philo explicitly refers to the views of
"other philosophers" and their use of the term "demons", *Leg. all.*
1:6. In his interpretation of angels as demons/souls in the air Philo
generally follows Platonic tradition.[9]

---

[6] Also Josephus, *Ant.* 1:73, reads ἄγγελοι, as Philo, while the LXX reads υἱοί. See
Winston and Dillon (1983) 236–37.

[7] As for the point made by Philo it may be mentioned that a removal of a misunderstanding is also formulated in 1 Cor 9:9–10 where Deut 25:4 is quoted: "'You
shall not muzzle an ox when it is treading out the grain'. Is it for oxen that God
is concerned? Does he not speak entirely for our sake? It was written for our sake...."
Paul presents his comment in the form of question and answer.

[8] See further *Plant.* 14; *Conf.* 174 concerning the angels as demons/souls that
exist in the air.

[9] See Winston and Dillon (1983) 197–200.

Gig. 16–18: Consequences drawn from the excursus.
On the basis of this interpretation the question of evil angels/demons is taken up in *Gig.* 16–18: the demons are not to be feared, and the use of the word angel about bad angels is just a form of speech, since bad angels are no angels at all. As a witness to this form of speech Philo in *Gig.* 17 cites LXXPs 77:49:

> "He sent upon them the anger of his wrath, wrath and anger and affliction, a mission by evil angels". These are the evil ones who, cloaking themselves under the name of 'angels', know not 'the daughters' (Gen 6:2) of right reason, the sciences and virtues, but court the pleasures which are born 'of men' (Gen 6:2) (*Gig.* 17–18).

The view that the evil angels/demons are actually the souls of the wicked is also found in Josephus, *Ant.* 7:185.

Gig. 6–18 should not as a whole be classified as a question and answer exposition, as is suggested by Nikiprowetzky. The section consists of brief direct exegesis in § 6, a critical exhoration with a removal of a possible misunderstanding ("And let no one suppose . . .") in § 7a, which is argued for by a lengthy lesson ("For the universe must needs be . . .") in §§ 7–15, and consequences drawn ("So if you realize that . . .") in §§ 16–17, and then a final witness to the argument ("I have as witness to my argument . . ."). In § 18 Philo repeats words (λαμβάνουσι . . . τὰς θυγατέρας . . . ἐπελέξαντο ἑαυτοῖς . . .) from the text (Gen 6:2). Thus *Gig.* 6, where the text is quoted, and § 18 serve as an *inclusio*. The formulation of a possible misunderstanding and its rebuttal may be classified as a question and answer form.

Gen 6:2 is not interpreted in *QG*.

Gig. *19–57: Gen 6:3: Direct paraphrasing commentary*

Philo introduces in *Gig.* 19 the next text, Gen 6:3a, by a transitional sentence: "Among such as these then it is impossible that the Spirit of God should dwell and make for ever its habitation, as also the Lawgiver himself shows clearly. For he says, "The Lord God said, My Spirit shall not abide for ever among men, because they are flesh" ("εἶπε", γάρ φησι "κύριος ὁ θεός· οὐ καταμενεῖ τὸ πνεῦμά μου ἐν τοῖς ἀνθρώποις εἰς τὸν αἰῶνα διὰ τὸ εἶναι αὐτοὺς σάρκας").

The words οὐκ καταμενεῖ τὸ πνεῦμά μου, "my Spirit shall not abide" are rendered with variations in *Gig.* 20 μένει . . . καταμένει . . . οὐκ, in § 28 πνεῦμα θεῖον μένειν . . . διαμένειν, in § 29 τὸ θεῖον πνεῦμα καταμεῖναι, in § 47 τὸ . . . πνεῦμα θεῖον . . . καταμείνῃ, and in § 53 οὐ καταμένει τὸ θεῖον πνεῦμα. Thus the abiding of the Spirit is an over-riding theme of the exposition.

From § 28 to § 45 the word "flesh", σάρξ from Gen 6:3 is added to this theme as an explanation why the spirit cannot abide.

Gig. 19–27: Direct paraphrasing commentary; different meanings of a word.

Immediately after the cited text, Philo states the main theme by para-phrasing the words about the spirit not abiding for ever among 'us', the mass of men (*Gig.* 19–21). In the unit §§ 22–31 the theme is in-terpreted, first in §§ 22–27 by comments made on the word "spirit of God", each exemplified by a quotation from the Pentateuch: 1) God's spirit is air which rides upon the water. Gen 1:2 is cited in *Gig.* 22. 2) It is pure knowledge. An example is Bezaleel whom God filled with the divine spirit, with wisdom . . . (Exod 31:2f.; *Gig.* 23).

An example is also (*Gig.* 24: τοιοῦτόν ἐστι καί) that of Moses, whose spirit was transferred to the seventy elders, Num 11:17, *Gig.* 24–27. Philo's comment is: "But think not that this taking of the spirit comes to pass as when men cut away a piece and sever it. Rather it is, as when they take fire from fire, for though the fire should kindle a thousand torches, it is still as it was and is dimin-ished not a whit. Of such a sort also is the nature of knowledge" (*Gig.* 25). The same view is found in *Siphre Zuta* 163 and 200–01; *Siphre Numbers* 93; *Tanchuma B.* 4:57–58 and 61; *Num. Rab.* 15:19 and 25; *Cant. Rab.* 3:10; *Targ. Jer. Num.* 11:23. It is therefore probable that Philo draws on a widespread Jewish tradition about Moses at this point.[10] This Jewish tradition about Moses reflects in turn com-mon ideas in the Hellenistic world.[11]

Gig. 28–31: Direct paraphrasing commentary.

In *Gig.* 28–30 the focus is on the words "not abide" in the text, and an interpretation of the word "flesh" from Gen 6:3 is added. The spirit cannot abide because of the tie which binds us closely to the fleshly life.

---

[10] Ginzberg (1968) 3:251: "God was so pleased with the appointment of the elders that, just as on the day of the revelation, He descended from heaven and permitted the spirit of prophecy to come upon the elders, so that they received the prophetic gift to the end of their days, as God had put on them of the spirit of Moses. But Moses' spirit was not diminished by this, he was like a burning candle from which many others are lighted, but which not therefore diminished; and so likewise was the wisdom of Moses unimpaired".

[11] See Winston and Dillon (1983) 249.

There is a close parallel to *Gig.* 22–31 in *QG* 1:90 where the question reads: "What is the meaning of the words, "My spirit shall not remain in men forever, because they are flesh". Also in *QG* 1:90 the two meanings of "spirit" are given, 'movement of air' and 'wisdom', although with different emphases. Both places Bezaleel is mentioned as example of the "spirit" meaning wisdom, and both places it is said that the spirit does not remain because of the "flesh". The main differences are the lack of a reference to Gen 1:2 and to Moses as an example in *QG* 1:90.

Philo may have had *QG* 1:90 as a preliminary exposition for his more developed treatment of the same points in *Gig.* 22–31. It is as probable, however, that Philo writes two versions of known exegesis, one in the form of question and answer (*QG*), and one in the form of direct exegesis (*Gig.*).[12] In support of this view it may be mentioned that Philo, as shown above, in *Gig.* 24–27 probably draws on a tradition about Moses sharing his spirit with others without it being diminished.

Gig. 32–47: Direct paraphrasing exegesis: A parallel exposition of Lev 18:6.

A transitional statement in *Gig.* 32 leads into an extensive exposition of LXXLev 18:6: "a man, a man shall not go near to any that is akin to his flesh to uncover their shame. I (am) the Lord". The link between this quote and the text, Gen 6:3 is the term "flesh", σάρξ, which occurs both places.

In the exposition of Lev 18:6 in *Gig.* 32–47 phrases in the quote are treated separately: § 34a: the phrase "a man, a man" (ἄνθρωπος ἄνθρωπος) means the true man; in §§ 34b–38 the words in the quote, "flesh . . . not go near to" (σαρκὸς . . . οὐ προσελεύσεται) mean that while many earthly advantages such as riches, though akin to "the flesh", are to be accepted if they come to us and are used for the best, we must not seek them; in § 39 the phrase "uncover shame" (ἀποκαλύψαι τὴν ἀσχημοσύνην) means that he who makes money, glory and bodily strength his quest infects philosophy with the baseness of mere opinion; the phrase in §§ 40–47, "I (am) the Lord" (ἐγὼ κύριος), means that one is to take the stand with God against pleasure, and the word "Lord" stresses His sovereignty.

This exposition of Lev 18:6 stands on its own and is not woven together with words from Gen 6:3a, apart from the parallel term

---

[12] A similar conclusion is reached by Runia (1991) 71.

"flesh". It receives a treatment parallel to that of the main text, Gen 6:3a. There are no subordinate scriptural texts in this exposition of Lev 18:6 in *Gig.* 32–47.

Gig. 48–54: List of biblical references and conclusion.

A reference in § 47 to the theme of the abiding of the spirit (Gen 6:3a) builds the bridge to a list of Pentateuchal quotations which are centered around the notion of firm foundation without change and its contrast, instability, *Gig.* 48–52. The quotations are Num 14:44; Deut 5:31; Exod 18:14; and Lev 16:2, 34. Apart from the "bridge" in *Gig.* 47b, the list of quotations and their interpretation may have been an independent unit.

As a conclusion (ὥστε) the contrast is applied to the theme from Gen 6:3a, the abiding of the spirit, *Gig.* 53–54: In those who have set before them many ends in life the divine spirit does not abide. As contrast Philo refers to Moses pitching his tent outside the camp, Exod 33:7, and alluding to Moses' ascent at Sinai into the presence of God, Exod 20:21. Since this conclusion by the words οὐ καταμένει τὸ θεῖον πνεῦμα refers back to the text in *Gig.* 19, οὐ καταμενεῖ τὸ πνεῦμά, it serves the function of an overall *inclusio* for §§ 19–54.

The section *Gig.* 19–54 has not the form of question and answer. This is admitted by Nikiprowetzky, but he says it is implicitly present.[13] The section has direct paraphrasing exegesis, largely so that words and phrases from cited scriptural verses are interpreted in sequence, framed in by the overarching theme that the spirit will not abide forever. In *Gig.* 22 Gen 1:2, in *Gig.* 23, Exod 31:2f., and in *Gig.* 24, Num 11:17, are subordinate quotations relative to the main text, Gen 6:3a cited in *Gig.* 19.

Gig. 55–57: Question and answer form.

In *Gig.* 55–57 the exposition moves on to Gen 6:3b which was not included in the quote of Gen 6:3 in *Gig.* 19. According to Gen 6:3b the days of bad humans shall be a hundred and twenty years. According to Deut 34:7, however, Moses passed away just at the age of one hundred and twenty. The question is then: "How then can it be reasonable that the years of the guilty should match those of the sage and prophet"? The answer is that the bad and the good may be equally matched in times and numbers, and yet their powers may be widely different. The exegetical terminology is: πῶς οὖν εἰκὸς ...

---

[13] Nikiprowetzky (1983) 14.

εἶναι ("How then can it be reasonable that") and εἰς μὲν οὖν τὸ παρὸν ἀρκέσει τοῦτο εἰπεῖν, ὅτι . . . ("For the present it will be enough to say that"). It is probable that Philo composed this question and answer at the time of his writing of *Gig.* since he only gives a temporary answer and tells that he will discuss it further in a future inquiry.[14] He probably relies on tradition, however, since the age limit of one hundred and twenty years mentioned in Gen 6:3b is connected with Moses also in other Jewish sources. See *b. Hul.* 139b, and cf. *Gen. Rab.* 26:6.[15]

In the discussion of Gen 6:3b in *QG* 1:91 Philo has a detailed speculation on numbers, only loosely applied to the text: "But perhaps a hundred and twenty years are not the universal limit of human life, but only of the men living at that time, who were later to perish in the flood. . . ." It should be added that *Gig.* 55–57 is not dependent upon *QG* 1:91.

Gig. 58–67: Gen 6:4. Possible misunderstanding and its removal

In *Gig.* 58 Philo moves on to the next verse, Gen 6:4: "Now the giants were on the earth in those days". As in *Gig.* 7 the aim is to remove the possible misconception that what is said in this verse is a myth: "Some may think that the Lawgiver is alluding to the myths of the poets about the giants . . ." (ἴσως τις τὰ παρὰ τοῖς ποιηταῖς μεμυθευμένα περὶ τῶν γιγάντων). The answer is: ". . . he wishes to show you that" (βούλεται δὲ ἐκεῖνό σοι παραστῆσαι, ὅτι). This form may be classified as a question and answer form.

Philo gives his answer a threefold heading which he deals with successively:

a   some men are earth-born,
b   some heaven-born
c   and some God-born.

Then the characterization of each type follows in the same sequence (§§ 61–62):

a   "The earth-born are those who take the pleasure of the body for their quarry. . . ."

---

[14] Moses' age at the time of his death is not discussed in Philo's treatises on the life of Moses.
[15] Winston and Dillon (1983) 265.

b "The heaven-born are the votaries of the arts and of knowledge, the lovers of learning. . . ."

c "The men of God are priests and prophets who have refused to accept membership in the *politeia* of the cosmos . . . but . . . have been translated into the *noetic* cosmos and dwell there registered as freemen of the *politeia* of Ideas. . . ."[16]

Abraham and Nimrod serve as biblical .examples, and now the sequence is b), c), a). Abraham covers the types b) and c): b) While he sojourned in the land of the Chaldeans and his name was Abram (= the uplifted father) he was a man of heaven, searching into the nature of supra-terrestial and ethereal region. c) When his name was changed to Abraham, "the elect father of sound", he became a man of God, according to the oracle received by him, Gen 17:1: "I am your God. . . ."

a) Nimrod, the 'desertion', exemplifies the earth-born man, as seen from LXXGen 10:8: "he began to be a giant (γίγας) on the earth". Similarly, in rabbinic writings Nimrod is pictured as a rebel, *Siphra, Behuqqotay* 2:2, cf. *b. Pesah* 94b, and targum *Ps.-Jonath.*, ad loc.[17]

Abraham and Nimrod represents opposite movements across a 'borderline'. Abraham moved from the land of the Chaldeans and became a man of God, while Nimrod deserted, went over to the enemy and took up arms against his friends.

On the Unchangeableness of God

The last sentence in *Gig.* 67, "Let us turn to the words which follow in the text", serves as transition to the exposition of Gen 6:4b in the next treatise, *On the Unchangeableness of God*. In this treatise the sections can be characterized in the following way:

Immut. 1–19: Gen 6:4b. Various expository forms used

Immut. 1–19 is an exegesis of Gen 6:4b: "Καὶ μετ᾽ ἐκεῖνο" φησίν "ὡς ἂν εἰσεπορεύοντο οἱ ἄγγελοι τοῦ θεοῦ πρὸς τὰς θυγατέρας τῶν ἀνθρώπων, καὶ ἐγέννων αὐτοῖς". "And after that", he says, "when the angels of God went unto the daughters of men and begat for themselves".

---

[16] The translation in *PLCL* is modified.
[17] Winston and Dillon (1983) 272.

Immut. 1–4: Question and answer.

In *Immut.* 1–4 there is a question and answer form, with reference to the prepositional phrase μετ' ἐκεῖνο, but most of the other words from the text are built into the paraphrase. The prepositional phrase "after that" is understood to refer back to Gen 6:3, that the spirit shall not abide forever among men, because they are flesh. Gen 6:3 has been interpreted by Philo in *Gig.* 19–55. "It is after that spirit [had gone] that the angels or messengers go into the daughters of men" (*Immut.* 2).

In the exegetical question the verb σκέπτομαι is used (§ 1): οὐκοῦν ἄξιον σκέψασθαι, τίνα ἔχει λόγον τό . . . ("It is then worth to consider what is meant by the word . . ."). Similar use of this verb is found in *Leg. all.* 2:42; *Sacr.* 128; *Post.* 49; *Sobr.* 33; *Conf.* 168; *Migr.* 216; *Heres* 227 and 277. The answer is introduced by the words ἔστι τοίνυν . . . ("Thus it is. . . ."); cf. the use of (νῦν) ἐστι, *Leg. all.* 2:42.

Immut. 4–19: A list of examples to illustrate a point in the answer. The answer given concludes with the contrast between the offspring of God and the family of evil, i.e. those who "beget offspring for themselves", Gen 6:4a (*Immut.* 4a). Philo adds a list of biblical examples to illustrate this point. He introduces the list by addressing his own mind: "If you will know, mind, what it is to beget not for thyself, learn from. . . ." The examples are: Abraham (*Immut.* 4b), Hannah (§§ 5–15), and as a contrast, Onan (§§ 16–18), and a repetition of the phrase "begat for themselves" as an *inclusio* in § 19.

A question and answer form is built into the elaboration of the example of Hannah, §§ 11–13. The problem is the contradiction between the word in 1 Sam 2:5 that "the barren has borne seven", while Hannah had one child.

The question is introduced by the words πῶς οὖν . . . φησίν, ("How then . . ."), similar to πῶς γὰρ in *Leg. all.* 2:19. . . . ("For how . . ."). The answer is built into the formulation of the question: εἰ μή. . . . νομίζει, "if she does not mean. . . ."

Immut. 20–73: Gen 6:5–7. Question and answer

A transitional statement leads into the next point: "Enough on this point; let us extend our discussion to embrace the words that follow" (§ 20). *Immut.* 20–73 contains an exposition of Gen 6:5–7 about God seeing the wickedness of men and deciding to blot out man, whom he had made. The text reads: "ἰδὼν" οὖν φησι "κύριος

ὁ θεὸς ὅτι ἐπληθύνθησαν αἱ κακίαι τῶν ἀνθρώπων ἐπὶ τῆς γῆς, καί
πᾶς τις διανοεῖται ἐν τῇ καρδίᾳ ἐπιμελῶς τὰ πονερὰ πάσας τὰς ἡμέρας,
ἐνεθυμήθη ὁ θεός, ὅτι ἐποίησε τὸν ἄνθρωπον ἐπὶ τῆς γῆς, καὶ διενοήθη.
καὶ εἶπεν ὁ θεός· ἀπαλείψω τὸν ἄνθρωπον ὃν ἐποίησα ἀπὸ προσώπου
τῆς γῆς". ("The Lord God", says Moses, "seeing that the wickednesses
of men were multiplied upon the earth and that every man intended
evil in his heart diligently all his days, God had it in His mind that
He had made man upon the earth, and He bethought Him. And
God said, I will blot out man, whom I made, from the face of the
earth" (Gen 6:5–7).

Immut. 21–32: Question and answer.

A question is asked and an answer is given on the implicit problem
which might be raised by careless inquirers, whether God repented
(*Immut.* 21–32). Philo accuses the questioners of impiety: "For what
greater impiety could there be than to suppose that the Unchange-
able changes"?

Built into the answer is an elaboration which exemplifies God's
stability in His dealing with Moses (Deut 5:31) as a contrast to the
instability and changes in human life, in the cosmos and in time.
Hardly any word from Gen 6:5–7 is explicitly used in this problem-
solving exposition (an exception: τῶν ἀνθρώπων, § 21), in which the
theme of stability and change is in focus.

The question is introduced by the words ἴσως τινὲς ... ὑποτοπή-
σουσι ... αἰνίττεσθαι, ὅτι ... ("Perhaps some ... will suppose that ...
hinting that ..." For this use of ὑποτοπέω, cf. *Conf.* 162 and *Somn.* 1:118).

Immut. 33–50: Direct commentary and an excursus on everything's
place and role in creation.

Philo marks the transition: "Having now discoursed sufficiently on
the theme that the Existent does not experience repentance, we will
explain in sequence the words ...", and then Gen 6:6 is cited again:
ἐνεθυμήθη ὁ θεός, ὅτι ἐποίησε τὸν ἄνθρωπον ἐπὶ τῆς γῆς, καὶ διενοήθη
("God had it in His mind that He had made man upon the earth,
and He bethought Him"). A brief direct commentary in *Immut.* 33–
34 on the ideas "having in one's mind" and "bethinking" in the quoted
text from Gen 6:6, leads into an excursus on the topic that everything in creation has its appointed place, lifeless bodies, plants, animals
and human beings as the superior ones among animals §§ 35–48.
From the characterization of human beings Philo in §§ 49–50 turns
back to a direct paraphrasing commentary on sentences from the
text, Gen 6:6: "had in His mind and bethought Him" and "that He

had made man". By the connecting word παρό, "therefore" a subordinate quotation Deut 30:15, 19 is cited as an oracle in *Immut.* 50.

Immut. 51–69: Question and answer. The transition reads: "Having made this point sufficiently clear, let us consider the next words, which are as follows . . ." and then Gen 6:7 is quoted ἀπαλείψω τὸν ἄνθρωπον ὃν ἐποίησα ἀπὸ προσώπου τῆς γῆς, ἀπὸ ἀνθρώπου ἕως κτήνους, ἀπὸ ἑρπετῶν ἕως πετεινῶν τοῦ οὐρανοῦ, ὅτι ἐθυμώθην, ὅτι ἐποίησα αὐτόν. ("I will blot out man whom I made from the face of the earth, from man to beast, from creeping things to fowls of heaven, because I was wroth in that I made him", § 51.) Just as with the problem of God relative to repentance, so Philo here introduces a question which might be raised from Gen 6:7 by "some", that God feels wrath. In his answer Philo elaborates on a contradiction which expresses a truth, but on different levels: "'God is not as a man' (Num 23:19); . . . He is as a man" (Deut 8:5) (*Immut.* 53). The anthropomorphic concepts, like wrath, are used by Moses for training and admonition, not because God's nature is such. The question is repeated twice in *Immut.* 60–61: "Why then does Moses speak of feet and hands . . ."? (§ 60). "Why again does he speak of His jealousy, His wrath . . ."? (§ 60). Philo places the answer in Moses' mouth: "But to those who ask these questions Moses answers thus: . . ." (§ 61). In a lengthy answer Philo refers as a parallel example the physician, who may withhold the truth and deceive a sick in order to relieve him from the disease (*Immut.* 63–67). For this interpretation of Num 23:19, see *Sacr.* 94–96; *Conf.* 98; *Somn.* 1:234–37.

The exegetical terminology used is:
One question is formulated as πάλιν τινὲς. . . . ὑπολανβάνουσι . . . (*Immut.* 52). "Again, some . . . suppose (that . . .)". For this exegetical use of ὑπολαμβάνω, see *Leg. all.* 1:43; *Gig.* 7, etc. The answer is introduced by λέγεται δὲ. . . . . (§ 52). "But he [Moses] says . . ." The other question reads τίνος οὖν ἕνεκα . . . φησίν . . . (§ 60). "Why then does. . . . speak of . . ." And the answer follows as ἀλλὰ τοῖς πυνθανομένοις ἀποκρίνεται . . . (§ 61). "But to those who ask these questions he [Moses] answers. . . ."

Immut. 70–85: Gen 6:7–8. Question and answer. A list of scriptural references from the Psalms

Immut. 70–73(74): Question and answer.
The discussion above on Moses' use of anthropomorphisms about God is regarded by Philo as preliminaries: "Such are the points which

needed to be established as preliminaries to the inquiry" (*Immut.* 70).
Again Philo employs the form of question and answer. The question
is what the meaning is of the words "I was wroth in that I made
them", (ἐθυμώθην ὅτι ἐποίησα αὐτούς), Gen 6:7. Philo's answer leads
into a reference forward to Gen 6:8 (*Immut.* 70).

The exegetical terminology used in the question and the answer is:
The question is introduced by a phrase which has ἀπορεῖν, § 70: ἐπα-
νιτέον δὲ ἐπὶ τὴν ἐξ ἀρχῆς σκέψιν, καθ᾽ ἣν ἠποροῦμεν, τίνα ὑπογράφει
νοῦν τὸ "..." ("One must return to the original question which caused
us difficulty, namely, what thought is suggested by the words...").
The answer begins cautiously with the word ἴσως, "perhaps": ἴσως
οὖν τοιοῦτόν τι βούλεται παραστῆσαι, ὅτι... ("Perhaps then he wishes
to show, that...").

Immut. 74–84: A list of subordinate quotations from the Book of
the Psalms, Ps 100 (101):1 (*Immut.* 74), Ps 74 (75):8 (*Immut.* 77), and
Ps 61 (62):11 (*Immut.* 82). The quotations from the Psalms form a
list of references which illustrate the same theme. The introductory
phrases are:

"And so the Psalmist said somewhere" (καθάπερ καὶ ὁ ὑμνῳδὸς εἶπέ
που), *Immut.* 74.
"And therefore it is said in another place" (διὰ τοῦτο ἐν ἑτέροις εἴρη-
ται), *Immut.* 77.
"There is something similar to the above-mentioned words in another passage" (τοῖς δ᾽ εἰρημένοις ὅμοιόν ἐστι καὶ τὸ ἑτέρωθι λεχθέν),
Immut. 82.

Immut. 85: Conclusion of the section §§ 70–85.

*Immut. 86–121: Gen 6:8–9. Question and answer. Scriptural examples
illustrate the answer*

Immut. 86: A simple form of question and answer is used. The text
is Gen 6:8, "Noah found grace before the Lord God" (Νῶε εὗρε
χάριν ἐναντίον κυρίου τοῦ Θεοῦ). The question is introduced by Τί δέ
ἐστι τὸ ... συνεπισκεψώμεθα ("Let us consider what is the meaning").
The answer lacks introductory words. This form is close to some of
the forms found in the *Questions and Answers* commentary, as exemplified
in the Greek fragments of *QG* 1:70; 2:15, 59; *QE* 2:1, 67, 68 where
the questions (with slight variations) are introduced by the words Τί
δέ ἐστι. Without a formula-phrase being used to introduce the answer,

a word from the text is repeated and interpreted, which also is the case in several answers in the *Questions and Answers* commentary. In *Immut.* 86 the verb εὖρε ("found") in the text of Gen 6:8 is taken up in the answer, τῶν εὑρισκόντων ("of the finders . . ."). Similarly in *QG* 3:19 "Hagar" is mentioned in the text, Gen 16:1, and is repeated at the outset in the commentary. Cf. *QG* 3:9.

Immut. 87–103: In the answer two different contexts of 'finding' is given and in *Immut.* 87–103 Philo attaches a series of examples to the two contexts which are indicated:

Example 1: Num 6:2, 5, 9, 12 the "great vow".
Example 2a): Gen 27:20, what God delivers to us without toil;
   b) Deut 6:10–11, cities which they built not.
Example 3: Deut 1:43–44, those who use force.

The examples give a needed specification of the contexts indicated in the answer.

Immut. 104–16: Another question raised and answer given on Gen 6:8. Also here the question and answer form is used in the exposition of the sentence in Gen 6:8, Νῶε εὖρε χάριν παρὰ κυρίῳ τῷ θεῷ ("Noah found grace with the Lord God"). In the question two alternatives are given: "Is the meaning that he obtained grace or that he was thought worthy of grace"? The answer refers to these alternatives by the words "The former (τὸ μὲν πρότερον . . .) The latter (τὸ δ' ὕστερον). . . ." The former alternative is said not to be reasonable, because then he was not given more than practically all creatures receive. The second alternative seems to be reasonable, but is perhaps not true (ἴσως δὲ οὐκ ἀληθῆ), for who shall be judged worthy of grace with God?

The solution of the dilemma is a combination of both alternatives: "Perhaps then it would be better to accept this explanation, that (μήποτ' οὖν ἄμεινον ἂν εἴη ἐκδέχεσθαι τοῦτο, ὅτι) the man of worth, being zealous in inquiring and eager to learn, in all his inquiries found this to be the highest truth, that all things are the grace or gift of God. . . ."

In § 109 the words "One must observe . . ." (παρατηρητέον δ' ὅτι . . .) leads to an elaboration of a point in the answer given, the point about being worthy. Different degrees of worthiness are pictured against the background of unworthiness (§§ 109–16). Noah, Gen 6:8, represents a lower worthiness, while Moses, Exod 33:17, represents the higher form. As a contrast Philo in *Immut.* 111–16 characterizes the mind which loves the body and the passions. The biblical references here are Gen 39:1 and Deut 23:1.

Immut. 117–21: Direct paraphrasing commentary of Gen 6:9. The last sentence of § 116 introduces the theme of generation, "...Noah, of whose descendant Mose has given a genealogy of a truly strange and novel sort". The words "for he says" (φησὶ γάρ) is followed by a quotation of Gen 6:9, αὗται αἱ γενέσεις Νῶε· Νῶε ἄνθρωπος δίκαιος, τέλειος ὢν ἐν τῇ γενεᾷ αὐτοῦ· τῷ θεῷ εὐηρέστησε Νῶε ("these are the generations of Noah. Noah was a just man, perfect in his generation, Noah was well pleasing to God"). The exposition has the form of direct commentary in which the words ἄνθρωπος ("man"), δίκαιος ("righteous"), τέλειος ("perfect"), τῷ θεῷ εὐηρέστησε ("pleasing to God"), and γένεσις ("generation") are repeated in the exposition. The exegesis is built upon contrasts. One contrast (τὰ μὲν γὰρ ... γεννήματα ... οὐ τὰ τοιαῦτα) is the difference between "creatures compounded of soul and body" and "the offspring proper to a good mind". A parallel exposition of Gen 6:9 is given in *QG* 1:97, but in the form of question and answer. Although there are similarities as to content in the two versions, there is no basis for classifying *Immut.* 117–21 as question and answer form, as done by Nikiprowetzky.[18]

The other contrast (ἡ μὲν ... ἑτέρα δ᾽ ἐστὶν ἡ ...) is between two forms of "generation", the one as a change from the lower to the higher and the other from the higher to the lower. As example of the latter Joseph, the son of Jacob, is mentioned, Gen 37:2. Joseph was keeping sheep with the baseborn, the sons of concubines Bilhah and Zilpah.

Immut. 122–39: Gen 6:(9 and) 11. Question and answer. Supporting scriptural references and examples

Immut. 122–23a. The section consists of a question and answer based on the contrast between Gen 6:9 and 6:11: "One may properly ask, why ..." (Ζητήσαι δ᾽ ἄν τις προσηκόντως, τίνος ἕνεκα ...) is a question which refers to the surprising contrast between Noah's perfection in virtues (Gen 6:9) and the corruption of the earth, Gen 6:11, ἐφθάρη ἡ γῆ ἐναντίον τοῦ θεοῦ καὶ ἐπλήσθη ἀδικίας ("the earth was corrupt before God and filled with iniquity") (*Immut.* 122). The answer is given in § 123a, introduced by the words "One should

18 Nikiprowtzky (1983) 43–45.

say then that . . ." (λεκτέον οὖν ὅτι . . .): "It should be said then that when the incorruptible element takes its rise in the soul, the mortal is forthwith corrupted".

Immut. 123b–35. The answer is undergirded by three laws on leprosy, Lev 13:14–15 in *Immut.* 123b–26, Lev 13:11–13 in *Immut.* 127–30, and Lev 14:34–36 in *Immut.* 131–35. The undergirding is in § 123b introduced by "And therefore . . .", διὰ τοῦτο. . . ." The law in Lev 13:14–15 is seen by Philo as being contrary to the natural and ordinary view (ἀντιτατόμενος τῷ εἰκότι καὶ συνήθει) held by "all men", but the "lawgiver" has laid down something distinctly his own: "For all men hold that things healthy are corrupted by things diseased, and living things by dead things, but they do not hold the converse . . . But the lawgiver . . . has here laid down something distinctly his own". The formulation here is akin to that of question and answer form, since the problem of a statement contrary to the ordinary view is formulated and a solution is given. This undergirding given in *Immut.* 123a is continued (διὸ καί, § 127, and τούτῳ δ' ὅμοιόν ἐστι καί, § 131) in §§ 127–30 and in §§ 131–35.

Immut. 136–39. Undergirding examples, from 1 Kings 17:10 (the widow); Gen 38:11 (Tamar); 1 Kings 17:18 (the widow and the prophet as a man of God); 1 Sam 9:9 (seers).

The discussion of Gen 6:9 and 11 in *Immut.* 122–39 is summed up (οὖν) in Philo's transitional statement in *Immut.* 140a: "Thus apt indeed are these words of Moses, the holiest of men, when he tells us that the earth was being corrupted at the time when the virtues of just Noah shone forth".

Immut. 140–83: Gen 6:12. Question and answer. Direct paraphrasing exegesis of Num 20:17–20

Immut. 140–43. The text is from Gen 6:12: "ἦν δὲ" φησί "κατεφθαρμένη, ὅτι κατέφθειρε πᾶσα σὰρξ τὴν ὁδὸν αὐτοῦ ἐπὶ τῆς γῆς". ("it was destroyed" he says, "because all flesh destroyed his way upon the earth"). The problem discussed is a grammatical mistake in the text. The outline is as follows:

    a   the quoted text from Gen 6:12 introduced by φησί.
    b   the problem: some will think (δόξει μέν τισιν ἡ λέξις ἡμαρτῆθαι . . .) that there is a grammatical mistake when it reads πᾶσα σὰρξ τὴν ὁδὸν αὐτοῦ because a masculine form αὐτοῦ cannot be used with reference to the feminine word σάρξ.
    c   the solution: "But perhaps the word is not only about (μήποτε

δὲ οὐ περὶ . . . ἐστιν ὁ λόγος . . .) "the flesh which corrupts" its own 'way', but of (ἀλλὰ περὶ . . .) two things, the 'flesh which is being corrupted', and Another, whose way that 'flesh' seeks to mar and 'corrupt'". Thus Philo paraphrases Gen 6:12 in this way: "all flesh destroyed the perfect way (ὁδόν) of the Eternal and Indestructible, the way which leads to God".

Addressed (ἴσθι) to the reader or listener. Philo identifies the term way, ὁδός, in the text. It means Wisdom, σοφία, the high road along which the mind reaches the goal, the recognition and knowledge of God. As a contrast Philo gives a paraphrase of Gen 6:12: "Every comrade of the flesh (σαρκῶν) hates and rejects this path and seeks to corrupt (φθείρειν) it". Behind this exegetical answer a dualistic principle is seen: "For there are no two things so utterly opposed as knowledge (ἐπιστήμη) and pleasure of the flesh (σαρκὸς ἡδονή)".

Immut. 144–80. Against the background of this dualistic principle Philo gives a lengthy exposition of Num 20:17–20 in *Immut.* 144–80, but without the terms ἐπιστήμη and σάρξ being used. Thus this exposition is rather independent of the preceding exegesis of Gen 6:12, in which the term σάρξ was interpreted.

In *Immut.* 145 Num 20:17–20 is quoted:

a "παρελευσόμεθα διὰ τῆς γῆς σου

b οὐ διελευσόμεθα δι᾽ ἀγρῶν, οὐ δι᾽ ἀμπελώνων,

c οὐ πιόμεθα ὕδωρ λάκκου σου.

d ὁδῷ βασιλικῇ πορευσόμεθα. οὐκ ἐκκλινοῦμεν δεξιὰ οὐδὲ εὐώ-νυμα, ἕως ἂν παρέλθωμέν σου τὰ ὅρια".

e ὁ δὲ Ἐδὼμ ἀποκρίνεται φάσκων· "οὐ διελεύσῃ δι᾽ ἐμοῦ· εἰ δὲ μή, ἐν πολέμῳ ἐξελεύσομαί σοι εἰς συνάντησιν". καὶ λέγουσιν αὐτῷ οἱ υἱοὶ Ἰσραήλ· "παρὰ τὸ ὄρος παρελευσόμεθα.

f ἐὰν δὲ τοῦ ὕδατός σου πίω ἐγώ τε καὶ τὰ κτήνη, δώσω σοι τιμήν·

g ἀλλὰ τὸ πρᾶγμα οὐδέν ἐστι, παρὰ τὸ ὄρος παρελευσόμεθα". ὁ δὲ εἶπεν· "οὐ διελεύσῃ δι᾽ ἐμοῦ".

The quotation is interpreted in a systematic way. Words from a) are paraphrased in *Immut.* 148–53; from b) are paraphrased in § 154, from c) in §§ 155–58, from d) in §§ 159–65, from e) in §§ 166–67, from f) in §§ 168–71, and from g) in §§ 172–80. In the exegesis of point c) Deut 28:12 and Gen 48:15 are subordinate quotations.

In the introduction in *Immut.* 144 of the quotation of Num 20:17–20 in *Immut.* 145, the theme of the exposition is introduced: how the earthly Edom threatens to bar Israel from travelling on the royal road. Also here words from the quotation are paraphrased. Moreover, the closing statement in § 180b) refers back to this opening statement both by dealing with the same theme of barring the road, and by some of the same words used (underscored in the quotations below). The closing statement serves at the same time as a conclusion, as indicated by the use of μὲν οὖν, 'so then' in § 180b).

There are points of agreements between the opening statement and the closure of the exposition. The agreements are underscored: The opening statement, § 144:

> Thus those who are members of that race endowed with vision, which is called "Israel" ('Ισραήλ), when they wish to "journey along that *royal road*" (πορεύεσθαι τὴν ὁδὸν βασιλικὴν), find their way contested by *"Edom"* – ('Εδώμ) *the earthly one* – for such is the interpretation of his name – who, all alert and prepared at every point, threatens to bar them from *"the road"* (τῆς ὁδοῦ) and to render it such that none at all shall tread or travel on it.

The closing statement, § 180b):

> So then (μὲν οὖν) *the earthly "Edom"* ('Εδώμ) purposes to bar the heavenly and *"royal road"* (βασιλικὴν – ὁδόν) of virtue, but the divine Logos on the other hand would bar the [road of Edom] and his associates.

Immut. 181–83. Among these "associates", § 180b), the example of Balaam is added as a warning, §§ 181ff. A sentence from Num 22:31 is included in the description of Balaam, and the word "angel" (ἄγγελος) from the biblical reference is interpreted to mean ἔλεγχος, "conviction", "conscience". The warning is: "Therefore he who listens not, who is not turned from his course by the 'conviction' which stands in his path, will in time receive destruction 'with the wounded' (Num 31:8) whom their passions stabbed and wounded with a fatal stroke".

Summary

Nikiprowetzky thinks that *On the Giants* and *On the Unchangeableness of God* is a collection of exegetical questions and answers:[19]

---

[19] Nikiprowetzky (1983) 5–75.

Gig. 1–5: Question and answer 1.
Gig. 6–18: Question and answer 2.
Gig. 19–55: Question and answer 3.
Gig. 55–57: Question and answer 4.
Gig. 58–67: Question and answer 5.
Immut. 1–19: Question and answer 6.
Immut. 20–50: Question and answer 7.
Immut. 51–69: Question and answer 8.
Immut. 70–85: Question and answer 9.
Immut. 86–103: Question and answer 10.
Immut. 104–16: Question and answer 11.
Immut. 117–21: Question and answer 12.
Immut. 122–39: Question and answer 13.
Immut. 140–83: Question and answer 14.

The present analysis has demonstrated that these treatises have a more complex expository structure:

Gig. 1–5: Gen 6:1. Question and answer.
Gig. 6–18: Gen 6:2. A possible misunderstanding and its removal. The formulation of a possible misunderstanding and its rebuttal is a form akin to the question and answer form.
Gig. 19–57: Gen 6:3. Direct paraphrase. Parallel exposition of Lev 18:6. List of biblical references. Question and answer.

> *Gig.* 19–27: Direct paraphrasing commentary; different meanings of a word.
> *Gig.* 28–31: Direct paraphrasing commentary.
> *Gig.* 32–47: Direct paraphrasing exegesis. A parallel exposition of Lev 18:6.
> *Gig.* 48–54. List of biblical references and conclusion.
> *Gig.* 55–57: Question and answer form.

Gig. 58–67: Gen 6:4a. Possible misunderstanding and its removal.
The structure of *On the Unchangeableness of God* follows:
Immut. 1–19: Gen 6:4b.

> *Immut.* 1–4: Question and answer.
> *Immut.* 4–19: A list of examples to illustrate a point in the answer.

Immut. 20–73: Gen 6:5–7.

> *Immut.* 20: Text cited.
> *Immut.* 21–32: Question and answer.

Immut. 33–50: Direct commentary and an excursus on the place and role of living beings in creation.

Immut. 51–69: Question and answer.

Immut. 70–85: Gen 6:7–8. Question and answer.

Immut. 70–73(74): Question and answer.

Immut. 74–84: A list of scriptural references from the Psalms.

Immut. 85: Conclusion.

Immut. 86–121: Gen 6:8–9. Question and answer. Scriptural examples illustrate the answer.

Immut. 86: Question and answer.

Immut. 87–103: A series of examples.

Immut. 104–16: Question and answer.

Immut. 117–21: Direct paraphrasing commentary on Gen 6:9.

Immut. 122–39: Gen 6:11. Question and answer. Supporting scriptural references.

Immut. 122–23a. Question and answer.

Immut. 123b–35: Subordinate references to biblical laws.

Immut. 136–39: Biblical examples.

Immut. 140–83: Gen 6:12. Question and answer. Direct paraphrasing exegesis of Num 20:17–20.

Immut. 140–43. Question and answer.

Immut. 144–80. Direct paraphrasing and systematic exposition of Num 20:17–20.

Immut. 180–83. Added biblical example as a warning.

CHAPTER SEVEN

THE ALLEGORICAL LAWS, BOOK 1

Introduction

According to the manuscripts the treatises *Leg. all.* 1 and 2 are but parts of a single treatise interpreting Gen 2:1–3:1a.[1] Treatise 3 is called number two in the manuscripts.[2] This treatise contains an exposition of Gen 3:8b–19. Philo may also have written commentaries on Gen 3:1b–8a and 3:20–23, but it is not possible to be certain of this.[3]

Philo has built up these treatises in such a way that the expositions in *Leg. all.* 3 are more complex than those in *Leg. all.* 1, while *Leg. all.* 2 has an intermediate place. The exposition of seventeen verses (Gen 2:1–17) in *Leg. all.* 1 fills 28 pages in the Cohn-Wendland edition, the exposition of eight verses (Gen 2:18–3:1) in *Leg. all.* 2 covers 22 pages, and the exposition of eleven verses (Gen 3:8b–19) in *Leg. all.* 3 fills 56 pages.[4]

In *Leg. all.* 3, and to a lesser degree also in *Leg. all.* 1 and 2, Philo has used the running commentary on the verses from Genesis as headings for related expositions on other parts of the Pentateuch. Thus, the commentary on Gen 2:8 in *Leg. all.* 3:1–48, (Adam hiding himself), leads into a lengthy exposition of other Pentateuchal verses dealing with the theme of hiding and flight. Similarly, God's cursing of the serpent, Gen 3:14, is quoted in *Leg. all.* 3:65 and 107 and this leads into a broad exposition of the contrast between lives of pleasure and of virtue based on a list of examples taken from various parts of the Pentateuch. Such extensive expositions of interrelated passages are quite common in the other treatises of the *Allegorical Commentary* as well.

---

[1] See Cohn and Wendland (1897) 1:LXXXVI.
[2] *Ibid.*, 113, note; Morris (1987) 3:2, 832.
[3] See the discussion in Schürer (1909) 3:650–51, with references to *Sacra parallela*, and *Sacr.* 51: "But what is meant by a tiller of the soil I have shown in earlier books". Morris (1987) 3:2, 832, note 65, believes that *Sacr.* 51 refers to a lost treatise on Gen 3:23.
[4] Cf. Adler (1929) 8–24.

Leg. all., Books 1–3, do not serve one main theme, but is rather a running commentary on man and Paradise, which expresses various topics and concerns. In his exposition Philo deduces cosmic and religious/ethical principles from the Laws of Moses in such a way that they can be applied to the situation of Philo and the other Jews in Alexandria. Among the areas reflected are the dangers of luxurious living (1:75–76; 2:17), specified as temptations at banquets (2:29; 3:155–56; 3:220–21) and from wealth, honours and offices (2:107); furthermore, the temptation to use education only for making a political career in governmental positions regardless of the Jewish values and commitments (3:167).

The Allegorical Laws, *Book 1*

In *Leg. all.* 1:1–30 Philo interprets Gen 2:1–6 primarily within the framework of the microcosm by relating 'heaven' and 'earth' largely to mind and senseperception. The text from Genesis is cited sentence by sentence, each line interpreted by means of paraphrase. Apart from an arithmological excursus which is included in *Leg. all.* 1:8–15, these paragraphs consist of brief units of direct paraphrasing exegesis with only one brief use of a secondary biblical reference (Num 6:2 in *Leg. all.* 1:17). There is an explicit quotation from Euripides in 1:7. This section has a structure parallel to that of the commentary *Questions and Answers on Genesis and Exodus* in this respect that they are running commentaries with brief units of expositions. The main difference is the use of the form of questions and answers in *QG* and *QE*, while the expositions in *Leg. all.* 1:1–30 have the form of direct exegesis. These brief units of exposition in *Leg. all.* 1:1–30 are on the whole longer than the exegetical comments made in the running commentaries, the *Habakkuk Commentary* (*1QpHab*), the *Nahum Commentary* (*4Q169*), and *the Commentary on Psalm 37* (*4Q171, 173*) in the *Dead Sea Scrolls*.

Leg. all. *1:1: A direct brief paraphrasing commentary*

Although the first exposition in *Leg. all.* 1:1 is brief, it may exemplify the approach used:

The quoted text is taken from Gen 2:1: καὶ συνετελέσθησαν ὁ οὐρανὸς καὶ ἡ γῆ καὶ πᾶς ὁ κόσμος αὐτῶν. ("And the heaven and the earth and their whole cosmos were completed".)

The theme of the present text is set against the background of the creation story in Gen 1:

"Having formerly (πάλαι) told of the creation of mind (νοῦς) and sense-perception (αἴσθησις), he [Moses] now (νῦν) fully sets forth the 'consummation' (τελείωσις) of both". Also in the treatise *On Abraham* 2 there is a reference back to the story of creation: "The way in which the making of the cosmos was arranged, we set forth in detail (ἠκρι-βώσαμεν) . . . in the preceding treatise (ἡ σύνταξις)".[5] In *Leg. all.* 1:1 Philo refers back in a direct way to Moses' creation story in Genesis, while in *Abr.* 2 he refers to the composition written by himself, as expressed in the first person plural "we" in ἠκριβώσαμεν. Thus it is justified to include the treatise *On the Creation of the World* together with *On Abraham* in the *Exposition of the Laws of Moses* and maintain that *On the Creation* is not part of the *Allegorical Commentary* series.[6]

In his exposition of Gen 2:1 in *Leg. all.* 1:1 Philo clarifies the right meaning in contrast to an alternative meanings: "He [Moses] does not say that either the specific mind (οὔτε δὲ νοῦν ἄτομον) or the particular sense-perception (οὔτε αἴσθησιν τὴν ἐν μέρει) has reached completion, but (ἀλλ᾽) that the forms have done so, that of mind and that of sense-perception". The motivating basis for the interpretation follows: "For symbolically he calls (συμβολικῶς . . . καλεῖ) the mind (νοῦς) 'heaven' (οὐρανός), since the noetic natures are in 'heaven', but sense-perception (αἴσθησις) he calls 'earth' (γῆ), because sense-perception (αἴσθησις) possesses a composition of a bodylike and more 'earthly' (γεωδεστέραν) sort".

The word "cosmos" (κόσμος) is interpreted: "Cosmos", in the case of mind (νοῦς), means all incorporeal and noetic things, and in the case of sense-perception means things in bodily form and generally whatever are sense-perceived things.

The quotation marks indicate how words from the text are re-peated in the exposition. The distinction between the particular (ἐν μέρει) and the general (expressed by the term "forms", ἰδέαι) deter-mines the interpretation.[7] Here the words "heaven" and "earth" in Gen 2:1, with its reference back to Gen 1:1–2, are both seen as belonging to the level of the general forms.

The cosmic concepts of "heaven" and "earth" are here applied to the anthropo-

---

[5] The translation in *PLCL* has been modified.
[6] See further Morris (1987) 3:2,844–45.
[7] Cf. the use of ἐν μέρει in *Mos.* 2:52.

logical ideas of mind (νοῦς) and sense-perception (αἴ σθησις). The presupposition for this application is that humans are seen as a microcosm. Thus, instead of calling this interpretation an allegory of the soul, it is more adequate to call it a microcosmic application of the cosmic concepts of 'heaven', 'earth' and 'cosmos'.[8]

Leg. all. *1:2–20: Direct paraphrasing running commentaries on* Gen 2:2–4a, with an arithmological excursus

Leg. all. 1:2–20 covers Gen 2:2–4 and the section is framed by Gen 2:2a, "And God finished on the sixth day His works which he had made", cited in *Leg. all.* 1:2, and in the *inclusio* in 1:20: "Accordingly the notion that the universe came into being in six days is done away with".

In 1:2–7 Philo has a paraphrasing commentary where words from Gen 2:2 are interpreted together with points from arithmology. The emphasis is placed on the view that the number '6' represents things mortal and the happy and blessed things are parallel with the number seven. Here Philo paraphrases words from Gen 2:2b: ". . . the seventh day . . . He rested . . . from what He had begun". Philo interprets the verb κατεπαύσατο to mean "caused to rest" as distinct from ἐπαύσατο, "rested", since God never leaves off making.

The numerological exposition of the numbers 6 and 7 leads to an excursus on the number '7', *Leg. all.* 1:8–15 and then in § 16 Philo returns to a paraphrasing commentary on Gen 2:2. In the arithmological excursus, *Leg. all.* 1:8–15, the number '7' represents things heavenly. This number ties heaven and humankind together: "mortal things, having had their divine origin drawn from heaven, are moved for preservation in accordance with the number 7" (1:9). On the one hand the heavenly bodies move on the basis of '7', and on the other hand human life, grammar and music are determined by the same number of '7'. An even longer excursus on the number seven occurs in *Opif.* 89–128.

In *Leg. all.* 1:16a Philo gives a brief paraphrasing commentary of Gen 2:2b: "He caused to rest therefore on the seventh day". The direct exegesis is introduced by the exegetical phrase "this is as much as to say" (τοῦτο δ᾽ ἐστὶ τοιοῦτο), and the words κατέπαυσεν . . . ἑβδόμῃ

---

[8] Concerning macrocosm and microcosm, see *Opif.* 82; *Plant.* 28; *Heres* 155; *Migr.* 220; *Abr.* 71–75; *Mos.* 2:135. Cf. Plato, *Timaeus* 30D; 41D–44C. See Wolfson (1948) 1:424–25; Nikiprowetzky (1965) 271–306, esp. 289–302; Runia (1986) 262–66. See further below in the chapter "Reaching Out and Coming In".

are in various renderings brought into the paraphrase. Gen 2:3a is quoted in *Leg. all.* 1:16b and receives a brief direct paraphrasing commentary in § 17, while Gen 2:3b is quoted and words from the text are briefly paraphrased in *Leg. all.* 1:18. The words drawn on from the texts are ὁ Θεός, εὐλόγησεν, ἑβδόμην, ἡγίασεν, εὐλόγησέ τε, κατέπαυσεν, ποιεῖν. In the exposition of Gen 2:3a in *Leg. all.* 1:17 Num 6:2 is referred to, but is not explicitly cited. Philo refers back to the earlier exposition given in *Leg. all.* 1:5–6 when he in *Leg. all.* 1:18 writes: "But we pointed out (ἐδηλώσαμεν) that God when ceasing or rather caused to cease, does not cease making. . . ."

A brief paraphrasing commentary is given on Gen 2:4 in *Leg. all.* 1:19–20. The words βίβλιος γενέσεως, ὅτε ἐγένετο from the text are used in the paraphrase. In the *inclusio* at the end of § 20 Philo refers back to the exposition of Gen 2:2 in *Leg. all.* 1:2: "There is an end, then, of the notion that the universe came into being in 'six days'".

Leg. all. *1:21–27: Direct and systematic exposition of Gen 2:4b–5*

In a systematic way Gen 2:4b–5 is interpreted by means of expository paraphrase in *Leg. all.* 1:21–27. The text is divided as follows:

a ᾗ ἡμέρᾳ ἐποίησεν ὁ Θεὸς τὸν οὐρανὸν καὶ τὴν γῆν (In the day in which God made the heaven and earth)

b καὶ πᾶν χλωρὸν ἀγροῦ πρὸ τοῦ γενέσθαι ἐπὶ τῆς γῆς (and every green thing of the field before it appeared upon the earth)

c καὶ πάντα χόρτον ἀγροῦ πρὸ τοῦ ἀνατεῖλαι (and all grass of the field before it sprang up;)

d οὐ γὰρ ἔβρεξεν ὁ Θεὸς ἐπὶ τὴν γῆν, καὶ ἄνθρωπος οὐκ ἦν ἐργάζεσθαι τὴν γῆν (for God had not sent rain on the earth, and there was no man to till the earth.)

Words from a) are paraphrased in a direct commentary in *Leg. all.* 1:21, words from b) in §§ 22–23, words from c) in § 24, words from d) in §§ 25–27. Philo connects this exposition of Gen 2:4b–5 to the preceding exposition of Gen 2:4a: "Above he [Moses] has called this 'day' a 'book'. . ." (*Leg. all.* 1:21).

Leg. all. *1:28–30 is a paraphrasing commentary on Gen 2:6*

Πηγὴ δὲ ἀνέβαινεν ἐκ τῆς γῆς καὶ ἐπότιζε πᾶν τὸ πρόσωπον τῆς γῆς, "'And a spring went up out of the earth and watered all the face of it'. He calls the mind a 'spring of the earth', and the senses its 'face'".

Here the words "spring", "earth" and "face" are repeated in the paraphrase.

Leg. all. 1:31–42: Direct exegesis and questions and answers on Gen 2:7

Leg. all. 1:31–32 is part of the larger section of 1:31–42 in which Gen 2:7 is interpreted. Gen 2:7 is quoted in *Leg. all.* 1:31: "And God formed the man by taking clay from the earth, and breathed into his face a breath of life, and the man became a living soul". (Καὶ ἔπλασεν ὁ θεὸς τὸν ἄνθρωπον χοῦν λαβὼν ἀπὸ τῆς γῆς, καὶ ἐνεφύσησεν εἰς τὸ πρόσωπον αὐτοῦ πνοὴν ζωῆς, καὶ ἐγένετο ὁ ἄνθρωπος εἰς ψυχὴν ζῶσαν.) In *Leg. all.* 1:31–32 most of the words from the text are repeated in the form of direct and paraphrasing exegesis. Here the creation of man according to Gen 2:7 is compared with the creation of man according to Gen 1:27. In *Leg. all.* 1:33–42 points in the same text, Gen 2:7, are discussed by means of four questions and answers. The exegetical terminology used is:
Questions, 1:33:
"One might ask" (ζητήσαι δ᾽ ἄν τις,)

1 "why (διὰ τί) God deemed the earthly and body-loving man worthy . . ." (Here Gen 2:7 is compared with 1:27).
2 "in the second place, what 'breathed in' is (δεύτερον δέ, τί ἐστι τό)
3 thirdly, why (τρίτον, διὰ τί) . . . 'into the face'
4 fourthly, why (τέταρτον, διὰ τί) . . . 'breath' not 'spirit'". (Here Gen 2:7 is compared with 1:2).

The answers are also quite organized. *Leg. all.* 1:34–35 have the answer to the first question:

1a *Leg. all.* 1:34 reads: "it is firstly to be said that" (πρὸς μὲν οὖν τὸ πρῶτον λεκτέον ἓν μέν, ὅτι).
1b *Leg. all.* 1:35 reads: "A second thing to be said is this" (ἕτερον δὲ λεκτέον ἐκεῖνο).
2 In *Leg. all.* 1:36–38 the second question is answered (here Exod 7:1 and Gen 2:8 are quoted as part of the answer): "the phrase 'breathed into' is equivalent to" (τό γε μὴν . . . ἴσον ἐστί . . .).
3 The third question is answered in *Leg. all.* 1:39–41: "'into the face' is to be understood both physically and ethically" ('. . .' καὶ φυσικῶς καὶ ἠθικῶς).

4   The fourth question is answered in *Leg. all.* 1:42 (here words both from Gen 1:2 and 27 are drawn into the answer): "He said 'breath' not 'spirit' implying a difference between them" ('. .' δέ, ἀλλ' οὐ "." εἴρηκεν, ὡς διαφορᾶς οὔσης).

Leg. all. *1:43–55: Gen 2:8: Direct exegesis. Questions and answers*

Leg. all. 1:43–47 have direct and paraphrasing exegesis. The text is quoted in 1:43:
"And God planted a garden in Eden toward the sun-rising, and placed there the man whom he had formed" (Καὶ ἐφύτευσεν ὁ θεὸς παράδεισον ἐν Ἐδὲμ κατὰ ἀνατολάς· καὶ ἔθετο ἐκεῖ τὸν ἄνθρωπον ὃν ἔπλασε).

In 1:43–47 words from the text are paraphrased in the form of direct commentary. In the paraphrase words from other biblical passages are drawn into the exposition, such as "beginning" from Gen 1:1, "image" from 1:27, and "vision of God", which is an etymological interpretation of Israel, Gen 32:28. The term "wisdom" may come from Prov 8:22. The concrete understanding, that "God tills the soil and plants pleasaunces" is pointedly rejected. Rather, God plants earthly excellence, as a copy of the heavenly one, of virtue, right reason, etc.

In *Leg. all. 1:48–55*: two questions and answers are listed. In *Leg. all.* 1:48–52 a seeming contradiction between the text, Gen 2:8 (God planted a garden), and Deut 16:21 ("Thou shalt not plant thyself a grove") is discussed. In *Leg. all.* 1:53–55 the question raised is the difference between Gen 2:7–8 (man whom God moulded) and 2:15 (the man made after the image and archetype, cf. Gen 1:26–27).

The exegetical terminology used is:

> *Question*:
> *Leg. all.* 1:48: "Now one might ask, why (ζητήσειε δ' ἄν τις, διὰ τί) . . . am I forbidden to plant a grove" (Deut 16:21).
> *Answer*:
> *Leg. all.* 1:48–52: "What is then to be said? That it becomes God to plant . . ." (τί οὖν λεκτέον; ὅτι). Here Exod 20:23 and Lev 19:23 are drawn into the exposition.
> *Question*:
> *Leg. all.* 1:53: "Who then is it of whom it says later on that (τίς οὖν ἐστιν, ἐφ' οὗ ὕστερόν φησιν ὅτι) 'The Lord God took the man whom he had made, and placed him in the garden. . . .'"

Answer:

Leg. all. 1:53–55: "It would seem then that (μήποτ' οὖν) this is a different man. . . ."

Leg. all. *1:56–62, Gen 2:9: Direct exegesis. Question and answer*

In *Leg. all.* *1:56–59* the text, Gen 2:9, is quoted in *Leg. all.* 1:56, followed by direct paraphrasing exegesis in 1:56–59. The text reads (1:56):

a And God caused to spring out of the ground every tree fair to behold and good for food, (Καὶ ἐξανέτειλεν ὁ Θεὸς ἐκ τῆς γῆς πᾶν ξύλον ὡραῖον εἰς ὅρασιν καὶ καλὸν εἰς βρῶσιν)

b and the tree of life in the midst of garden (καὶ τὸ ξύλον τῆς ζωῆς ἐν μέσῳ τῷ παραδείσῳ),

c and the tree of knowledge of good and evil (καὶ τὸ ξύλον τοῦ εἰδέναι γνωστὸν καλοῦ καὶ πονεροῦ).

In 1:56–58 sentence a) is interpreted, and in 1:59 sentence b), both in the form of a direct commentary. Philo distinguishes in 1:59 between two groups of interpreters: "But some say that (οἱ δὲ λέγουσι)" and "but we, as it has been said, maintain (ἡμεῖς δέ, ὡς καὶ πρότερον ἐλέχθη, . . . λέγομεν)". The two interpretations are said to belong to two different contexts. Those who say that the heart is called "the tree of life" are setting forth a view in the field of medicine, while "we" identify the tree of life with generic virtue.

Leg. all. 1:60–62 interprets the sentence c), "the tree of the knowledge of good and evil", in the quoted text, Gen 2:9, but it is seen as a problem when compared with b), "the tree of life". The problem is that the location is given of the latter tree, "in the midst of the garden", but not the location of the former tree. *The problem* is formulated and the question raised in *Leg. all.* 1:60–61: "Of this he expressly says that (τοῦτο μὲν οὖν ῥητῶς φησιν ὅτι . . .) it is 'in the midst' but as to the other . . . he has not made it clear (τὸ δὲ ἕτερον . . . οὐ δεδήλωκεν . . .) whether it is within or without. . . . What then ought one to say?" (τί οὖν χρὴ λέγειν;)

The answer is introduced by ὅτι (*Leg. all.* 1:61): "that this tree is both in the garden and outside it, in literal fact in it, virtually outside it". Philo applies the trees to the soul: "Whenever, then, it shall have received the stamp of perfect virtue, it straightway becomes 'the tree of life', but when it receives that of wickedness, it straightway becomes 'the tree of knowledge of good and evil' . . . Thus wickedness neither *is* in the garden, nor is it *not* in it, for it can be there actually, but virtually it cannot.

In the answer Gen 42:36 is cited.

Leg. all. 1:63-87, Gen. 2:10-14: Direct exegesis. Question and answer

Gen 2:10-14 serves as an umbrella text for the section, *Leg. all.* 1:63-87, with direct paraphrasing exegesis in §§ 63-69 and question and answer in §§ 70.

Leg. all. 1:63-73 displays direct exposition and question and answer. The text, quoted in 1:63, reads:

    a A river goes forth from Eden to water the garden: thence it is separated into four heads (Ποταμὸς δὲ ἐκπορεύεται ἐξ Ἐδὲμ ποτίζειν τὸν παράδεισον· ἐκεῖθεν ἀφορίζεται εἰς τέσσαρας ἀρχάς);

    b the name of the one is Pheison; this is that which encircles all the land of Evilat, there where the gold is; and the gold of that land is good; and there is the ruby and the emerald (ὄνομα τῷ ἑνὶ Φεισών· οὗτος ὁ κυκλῶν πᾶσαν τὴν γῆν Εὐιλάτ, ἐκεῖ οὗ ἐστι τὸ χρυσίον· τὸ δὲ χρυσίον τῆς γῆς ἐκείνης καλόν· καὶ ἐκεῖ ἐστιν ὁ ἄνθραξ καὶ ὁ λίθος ὁ πράσινος).

    c And the name of the second river is Geon; this encompasses all the land of Aethiopia (καὶ ὄνομα τῷ ποταμῷ τῷ δευτέρῳ Γηών· οὗτος κυκλοῖ πᾶσαν τὴν γῆν Αἰθιοπίας).

    d And the third river is Tigris; this is that whose course is in front of Assyria (καὶ ὁ ποταμὸς ὁ τρίτος Τίγρις· οὗτος ὁ πορευόμενος κατέναντι Ἀσσυρίων).

    e And the fourth river is Euphrates (ὁ δὲ ποταμὸς ὁ τέταρτος Εὐφράτης).

After a brief introduction in 1:63-64, particular phrases and words are interpreted in two sequences, one in 1:65-73 and the other in 1:74-87. The first sequence begins with the words: "Let us look too at the phrases (ἴδωμεν δὲ καὶ τὰς λέξεις)". Words from sentence a), "A river goes forth from Eden . . .", in the text are interpreted in 1:65, from sentence b), "the name of the one is Pheison . . .", in 1:66-67, from sentence c), "And the name of the second river is Geon . . .", in 1:68, from sentence d), "And the third river is Tigris . . .", in 1:69-71, from sentence e), "And the fourth river is Euphrates", in 1:72-73.

Philo develops an exposition in the form of direct paraphrasing commentary, except in §§ 70-71, where a question about the interpretation of the three rivers is raised and the answer given: The question is introduced by the words "It is worth inquiring why" (ἄξιον μέντοι ἀπορῆσαι, διὰ τί ...), and the answer follows: "One must observe, then, that" (νοητέον οὖν ὅτι ...). The problem formulated is the unusual order of the three rivers, Pheison, Geon, and Tigris, when interpreted as virtues: 1. prudence, 2. courage, 3. self-mastery.

Leg. all. 1:74–87: Direct exegesis and question and answer.

The second expository sequence is introduced by an editorial transition: "Now let us go on to look at our subject in this way", 1:74. It runs from 1:74 to 87 with exegesis of sentence b) about the river Pheison in 1:74–84. Parts from the text are interpreted in sequence. In §§ 74–76 the words Φεισών (= "alteration of mouth"), Εὐιλάτ (= "in travail") and κύκλος ("encircling") are interpreted relative to the virtue prudence. Num 12:12 is referred to as a subordinate quotation. The words ἐκεῖ οὗ ἐστι τὸ χρυσίον ("where [whose] the gold is") in the text, Gen 2:11, are paraphrased in *Leg. all.* 1:77, and the words τὸ δὲ χρυσίον τῆς γῆς ἐκείνης καλόν ("Now the gold of that land is good", Gen 2:12) are interpreted in § 78. The next phrase from Gen 2:12, καὶ ἐκεῖ ἐστιν ὁ ἄνθραξ καὶ ὁ λίθος ὁ πράσινος ("And there is the ruby and the greenstone") is repeated and interpreted in §§ 79–81. Several subordinate biblical examples and texts are woven into the exegesis, Gen 29:35, 30:16, 49:15, and Exod 28:17ff. The theme of stone is illuminated by these references, and some of the patriarchs and Lea, and the high-priestly garment, are woven into the exposition.

In *Leg. all. 1:82–84* a question is raised and an answer is given. In § 82 the question is raised of a point of unevenness in the main text, Gen 2:12, sentence b): "Why then, while saying 'a green stone', does he not also say, 'a ruby stone'"? The terminology used to introduce the question is the simple "why" (διὰ τί) and the answer follows with the simple "because" (ὅτι), just as found in the Greek fragments of *QG* 1:1, 94; 2:62; 4:144, 145, and *QE* 2:64 and 65.

Leg. all. 1:85–87 also has the exegetical form of question and answer. The second sequence (§§ 74–87) of the exposition of the main text, Gen 2:10–14, ends in *Leg. all.* 1:85–87 with the question and answer on an unevenness in the presentation of the rivers: all the rivers are explicitly related to countries, with the exception of one, the Euphrates.

In the introductory phrase to the question the frequently used verb διαπορεῖν occurs:

"It is worth inquiring why" (ἄξιον δὲ διαπορῆσαι, διὰ τί ..., *Leg. all.* 1:85). Also a frequently used phrase brings in the answer: "It must be said, then, that" (λεκτέον οὖν ὅτι ..., 1:86). Philo states explicitly the hermeneutical key: "But the subject of the passage is not the river, but amendment of character" (1:85).

Leg. all. *1:88–89: Direct and brief exegesis of Gen 2:15*

After the long exposition of Gen 2:10–14, Gen 2:15 is quoted in *Leg. all.* 1:88: "And the Lord God took the man whom He had made, and placed him in the garden to till and to guard it" (Καὶ ἔλαβε κύριος ὁ θεὸς τὸν ἄνθρωπον ὃν ἐποίησε καί ἔθετο αὐτὸν ἐν τῷ παραδείσῳ, ἐργάζεσθαι αὐτὸν καὶ φυλάσσειν). Most of the words in the text are repeated in the exposition and interpreted by means of an expository paraphrase. The text is applied to the area of virtues.

Leg. all. *1:90–108. Direct exegesis and questions and answers on Gen 2:16–17*

Leg. all. 1:90–91: Question and answer.
The quotation from Gen 2:16–17 serves as an umbrella for the remaining part of *Leg. all.*, Book 1, comprising paragraphs 90–108:

a   And the Lord commanded Adam saying (Καί ἐνετείλατο κύριος ὁ θεὸς τῷ Ἀδὰμ λέγων):
b   From every tree that is in the garden you shall feedingly eat (ἀπὸ παντὸς ξύλου τοῦ ἐν τῷ παραδείσῳ βρώσει φάγῃ),
c   but of the tree of knowing good and evil you shall not eat of it (ἀπὸ δὲ τοῦ ξύλου τοῦ γινώσκειν καλὸν καὶ πονηρὸν οὐ φάγεσθε ἀπ' αὐτοῦ):
d   and the day that you eat of it you shall surely die (ᾗ δ' ἂν ἡμέρᾳ φάγητε ἀπ' αὐτοῦ, θανάτῳ ἀποθανεῖσθε).

Two questions and answers related to sentence a) in the text begin the exposition. The first question is introduced by a formula in which the verb διαπορεῖν is used: "One must raise the question *what* 'Adam He commands' and who he is" (ποίῳ . . . καὶ τίς . . ., διαπορητέον). Also the answer has a common formula word: "Perchance, then . . ." (μήποτ' οὖν). The answer is that Adam is the earthly and perishable mind.

Another commonly used verb introduces the second question, ζητεῖν: "And one must inquire, why (ζητητέον δέ, διὰ τί) when assigning their names to all the other creatures 'Adam' did not assign one to himself?" The answer has the commonly used λεκτέον, but here formulated as a question: "What, then, is to be said" (τί οὖν λεκτέον)? Here the difference between the quoted text, Gen 2:16–17, and the subsequent verses in Gen 2:19–20 about Adam naming all the other creatures, but not himself, is the problem.

Leg. all. 1:92–96: Two elaborations introduced by "naturally, then" (εἰκότως οὖν).

From the last answer two conclusions are drawn and elaborated upon, in *Leg. all.* 1:92–94 and 1:95–96, each exposition introduced by the words "naturally, then" (εἰκότως οὖν): "Quite naturally, therefore, Adam, that is, the Mind, . . . gives no name to himself. . ." (1:92–94); "Quite naturally, then, does God give the commandments . . . to the earthly man . . ." (1:95–96). Various points about Adam in Gen 1–3 are drawn into the two elaborations.

Leg. all. 1:97–100: Direct exegesis.

The exposition of sentence b) ("From every tree . . .") of the text, Gen 2:16, is given as direct paraphrasing exegesis in *Leg. all.* 1:97–99, and of sentence c), ("but of the tree of knowing good and evil", Gen 2:17) in *Leg. all.* 1:100. In the exposition of sentence b) in §§ 97–99 the words ἀπὸ παντὸς ξύλου . . . βρώσει φάγῃ are repeated in a direct paraphrasing exposition. By using analogous examples from athletics and from family life Philo explains his application of the text to soul-nourishment.

The paraphrasing exposition in *Leg. all.* 1:100 of sentence c) repeats the words ἀπὸ δὲ τοῦ ξύλου . . . οὐ φάγεσθε ("of the tree . . . you shall not eat") and from sentence b) the words ἀπὸ παντὸς ξύλου τοῦ ἐν τῷ παραδείσῳ . . . φάγῃ (from every tree that is in the garden you shall eat . . ."). In the form of direct exegesis Philo here refers back (ὡς ἔφην) to his earlier discussion of the location of the tree of the knowledge of good and evil in the form of question and answer, *Leg. all.* 1:60–62.

Leg. all. 1:101–04: Question and answer.

A difference between plural and singular in the umbrella text, Gen 2:16–17 cited in *Leg. all.* 1:60, is discussed in the form of question and answer in *Leg. all.* 1:101–04. The question is again introduced by the verb διαπορεῖν (1:101): "Next there is this further question to be raised (ἑξῆς κἀκεῖνο διαπορητέον). 'When He is giving the charge to eat of every tree of the garden, He addresses the command to a single person, but when He issues the prohibition. . . . He speaks to more than one'". Likewise the answer is introduced by the commonly used λεκτέον (1:102): "it must be said this, that firstly" (λεκτέον οὖν τάδε, ὅτι πρῶτον) . . . secondly, . . ." (δεύτερον, 1:103:).

Leg. all. 1:105–08: Question and answer.

Also words from sentence d), "the day that you eat of it", are referred to in the question and the answer above, but in 1:105 this sentence is cited and in itself interpreted in the form of another example of question and answer, in *Leg. all.* 1:105–08. The question is stated in 1:105:

> And further he says 'In the day that ye eat thereof, ye shall die the death' (Gen 2:17d). And yet after they have eaten, not merely do they *not* die, but they beget children and become authors of life to others. What, then is to be said to this (τί οὖν λεκτέον)?

The answer is introduced by "that", ὅτι, also in 1:105: "that (ὅτι) death is of two kinds. . . ."

Summary

Leg. all. 1:1: A direct brief paraphrasing commentary on Gen 2:1.

Leg. all. 1:2–20: Direct paraphrasing running commentaries on Gen 2:2–4a, with an arithmological excursus. *Leg. all.* 1:2 and 1:20 are framed by an *inclusio*.

Leg. all. 1:21–27: Direct paraphrasing and systematic exposition of Gen 2:4b–5.

Leg. all. 1:28–30: Direct paraphrasing commentary on Gen 2:6.

Leg. all. 1:31–42: Direct paraphrasing exegesis and questions and answers on Gen 2:7.

Leg. all. 1:43–55, Gen 2:8: Direct paraphrasing exegesis. Questions and answers.

Leg. all. 1:56–62, Gen 2:9: Direct paraphrasing exegesis. Question and answer.

Leg. all. 1:63–87, Gen 2:10–14 is umbrella text. Direct paraphrasing exegesis and question and answer.

    Leg. all. 1:63–73: Direct exposition and question and answer.

    Leg. all. 1:74–87: Direct exposition and question and answer.

Leg. all. 1:88–89: Direct and brief paraphrasing exegesis of Gen 2:15.

Leg. all. 1:90–108, Gen 2:16–17 is umbrella text. Direct paraphrasing exegesis and questions and answers.

    Leg. all. 1:90–91: Question and answer.

    Leg. all. 1:92–96: Two elaborations introduced by "naturally, then" (εἰκότως οὖν).

    Leg. all. 1:97–100: Direct exegesis.

    Leg. all. 1:101–04: Question and answer.

    Leg. all. 1:105–08: Question and answer.

Concluding remarks

In the preceding chapter reference was made to a question asked by David Runia concerning Philo's expositions: "Is there a uniform method (e.g. the *quaestio* and *solutio*) that is repeated over and over again, or does Philo exhibit a diversity of approaches"?[9]

Our examination of material from Philo's expository works has shown that the form of question and answer is one among several expository forms used by him. A variety of forms may be grouped under the designation 'direct exegesis', in which the meaning of the biblical text is explained without a question being formulated. Some such forms are brief or more extensive commentary on a cited text, the detailed explanation of words in a quoted text, units with cited text, paraphrase and *inclusio*, a lesson on a topic presented as an excursus, the reviewing of a series of biblical stories and/or cited texts as documentation of a theme, the rewritten Bible form, etc.

More specifically in the *Allegorical Commentary*, as exemplified in the present study by the treatises *On the Giants, On the Unchangeableness of God*, and *The Allegorical Laws*, Book 1, the structure of a running commentary is basic, and in the expositions the form of question and answer and various forms of direct exegesis are found.

In the direct exegesis the simple format of text and comment may be used, as for example seen above in *Leg. all.* 1:1. Here a quoted text is followed by an explaining comment with no subordinate Penta-teuchal quotation added. This simple form also occurs elsewhere in Philo's writings, such as in *Leg. all.* 3:177 where Gen 48:15–15 is interpreted, and also in the *Exposition*, in *Spec.* 4:149–50 where Deut 19:14 is interpreted.[10]

In *Immut.* 144–80 there is a direct paraphrasing and systematic exposition of Num 20:17–20 and the closing words in *Immut.* 180 refers back to the opening formulations in § 144. Such a form may be used independently of its present context. Examples of similar

---

[9] Runia (1987) 112.

[10] In *Spec.* 4:149–50 exposition gives a comment upon the text in a general way without words from it being paraphrased. It is of importance to note that the pericope does not fit well into its context and thus stands out as a unit of its own. Accordingly F.H. Colson remarked: "It is difficult to see why this passage is introduced here. The text is clearly quoted not for its literal meaning, but for its application to the customs which are unwritten laws. But the laws which have been and are still to be discussed are not unwritten". *PLCL* 8:100 n. a.

forms are found in *Leg. all.* 3:162–68, 169–73, and *Sacr.* 76–87.[11]

Our study so far has demonstrated the relevance of another question asked by Runia: "The role of the secondary biblical texts which Philo habitually introduces is also controversial . . . do these secondary texts merely function as illustratory material, or do they take on a life of their own"?[12] One observation may be mentioned here. Some of the added biblical examples and/or scriptural quotations exemplify the answer given to an exegetical question raised. They may illuminate further the point in the answer, positively or by contrasting examples. Thus, in *Leg. all.* 3:65–106 the question and answer based on Gen 3:14–15 (God cursing the serpent) in *Leg. all.* 65–68 leads to a list of examples from biblical history to illustrate the theme of predestination, §§ 69–106.

In *Immut.* 70–73 a question is raised about the wrath of God, Gen 6:7. The answer is: "Perhaps then he wishes to show that the bad have become what they are through the wrath of God and the good through his grace". The grace is expressed in Gen 6:8 "Noah found grace with Him [God]". Then tied to the answer, in *Immut.* 74–84 a list of subordinate quotations from the Book of the Psalms, Ps 100 (101):1 (*Immut.* 74), Ps 74 (75):8 (*Immut.* 77), and Ps 61 (62):11 (*Immut.* 82) illustrate and deepen the understanding of the theme of grace.

In *Immut.* 86 the question is raised what it means that "Noah *found* grace before the Lord God" (Νῶε εὗρε χάριν ἐναντίον κυρίου τοῦ Θεοῦ, Gen 6:8). In the answer two different contexts of 'finding' are given in *Immut.* 87–103: a) to find again what they possessed and have lost, and b) find for the first time. Philo attaches a series of examples to make concrete the two contexts which are indicated: The examples which demonstrate the two contexts are taken from Num 6:2, 5, 9, 12 (the "great vow"), Gen 27:20 (what God delivers to us without toil), Deut 6:10–11 (cities which they built not), and Deut 1:43–44 (those who use force).

In *Immut.* 122–23a a question is raised about the contrast between Noah's perfection (Gen 6:9) and the corruption of the earth (Gen

---

[11] See Borgen (1965) 28–58, Borgen (1983) 32–46; Borgen (1993A) 268–291. Such a form is also found in the *midrashim*. See Lehrman (1961) VII: "The first chapters form a running commentary on each verse of Exodus I–XI, keeping at the same time the continuity of the narrative steadily in view. The rest of the book (XV–LII) cites only selected verses. . . . The result is a medley of heterogenous homilies with the first verse only as their text".

[12] Runia (1987) 112.

6:11). The answer is: "It should be said then that when the incorruptible element takes its rise in the soul, the mortal is forthwith corrupted". Then in *Immut.* 123b–35 the answer is undergirded by three laws on leprosy, Lev 13:11–13, 14–5, and 14:34–36.

In *Immut.* 140–80 the question about the words in Gen 6:12 that "all flesh destroyed his ways . . ." receives the answer that it means "all flesh destroyed the perfect way of the eternal and Indestructible, the way which leads to God". Attached to this notion of the way and of dualistic conflict, Philo adds a systematic exposition of Num 20:17–20, about the "royal road". This biblical passage and its interpretation seems to be an independent expository unit which have been attached because of the term "road" and the general dualistic perspective.

Thus Philo has a differentiated use of secondary texts and/or biblical examples. In his *Allegorical Commentary* Philo has as basic structure the form of a running commentary. Within this framework he uses a variety of expository forms. In his *Exposition of the Laws of Moses* Philo has as basic structure the form of 'rewritten Bible'. Within this framework, likewise, he includes a variety of expository forms.

His *Questions and Answers on Genesis and Exodus Philo* are more uniform. The basic structure has the form of a running commentary. Within this framework Philo presents a collection of questions and answers. It is important that the form of question and answer is used in the *Allegorical Commentary* and in the *Exposition* as well.

Philo employs formula-like exegetical terminology, which is especially rather stereotyped in the question and answer form. Philo's use of formula-like exegetical terminology supports the view that, although he is an independent and inspired exegete, he at the same time has his place within a traditional exegetical activity. He is to be understood as an exegete among other exegetes.

CHAPTER EIGHT

PROCLAMATIO GRAECA – HERMENEUTICAL KEY

Having analysed and characterized examples of expository forms, structures and terminology we shall examine aspects of the ideas expressed and applications made by Philo in his exegesis. The question to be asked is: How far is it possible to identify some of the hermeneutical principles which guide Philo in his expository enterprise? Some clues may be found in *Mos.* 2:1–65.

God's Laws proclaimed to the Greek-speaking world

In the Diaspora setting of the Alexandrian Jews the translation of the Laws of Moses into Greek was a major revelatory event. Philo testifies to such an understanding in his interpretation of this event in *Mos.* 2:25–44. The context of this story is as follows:

Moses was the paradigmatic person of king, lawgiver, high priest and prophet (*Mos.* 2:1–11). In *Mos.* 2:12–65 Philo praises Moses as lawgiver. Surprisingly enough he does not here tell about the giving of the Laws on Mt Sinai but extols Moses on the basis of the Laws' qualities as made evident in their history after they were received. The glory of Moses as lawgiver is seen in the permanence of the Laws (*Mos.* 2:12–16), in the respect paid to them by other nations (*Mos.* 2:17–44), especially by Ptolemy Philadelphus when he arranged for the Septuagint translation (*Mos.* 2:25–44), and in the content of the Laws themselves (*Mos.* 2:45–65).

Philo develops here a perspective of national and universal revelatory history. In contrast to the laws of other nations the Laws of the Jewish nation were

> firm, unshaken, immovable, stamped, as it were, with the seals of nature herself, [they] remain secure from the day when they were first enacted to now, and we may hope they will remain for all future ages as though immortal, so long as the sun and moon and the whole heaven and universe exist (*Mos.* 2:14).

On this basis Philo interprets the history of the Jewish people: "Thus, though the nation has undergone so many changes, both to increased prosperity and the reverse, nothing – not even the smallest part of the ordinances – has been disturbed" (*Mos.* 2:15).

Philo expresses here a common view held by Jews in the Diaspora as well as in Palestine.[1] Even his formulation in *Mos.* 2:14 seems to be based on widespread phraseology, as can be seen from similar statements like the one in Matth 5:18: ". . . till heaven and earth pass away, not an iota, not a dot, will pass from the law until all is accomplished".

This revelatory history has its goal in the time when the Laws of Moses, being also the divine Laws of nature, will be acknowledged by all nations:

> Thus the laws are shewn to be desirable and precious in the eyes of all, ordinary citizens and rulers alike, and that too though our nation has not prospered for many years. It is but natural that when people are not flourishing their belongings to some degree are under a cloud. But if a fresh start should be made to brighter prospects, how great a change for the better might we expect to see! I believe that each nation would abandon its peculiar ways, and, throwing overboard their ancestral customs, turn to honouring our laws alone. For, when the brightness of their shining is accompanied by national prosperity, it will darken the light of the others as the risen sun darkens the stars (*Mos.* 2:43–44).

From this it is seen that Philo looked forward to the time when all nations will become Jewish proselytes.

Philo interprets this revelatory history of the Laws of Moses within the Greek distinction which divided the world's population into two parts, the Greeks and the barbarians.[2] Within this context two events have basic significance: 1. the giving of the Laws at Mt Sinai in the Hebrew language for the barbarian half of the human race, and 2. the translation of these Laws into Greek on the island Pharos at Alexandria to make them known to the Greek half of the world:

> In ancient times the laws were written in the Chaldean tongue, and remained in that form for many years, . . . so long as they had not yet revealed their beauty to the rest of mankind. . . . Then it was that some people, thinking it a shame that the laws should be found in one half

---

[1] See Josephus, *Ag.Ap.* 2:277, Matth 5:19 and Luke 16:17.

[2] See *Immut.* 136; *Mos.* 2:18, 20; *Jos.* 134; *Praem.* 165; *Legat.* 141; *Quod Omn.* 73, 94, 98, 138; *Prov.* 2:15. This distinction is also applied to the classification of languages: Greek is the language of the Greek half of the world, while Hebrew serves as the main language of the barbarian world, *Mos.* 2:27ff.; cf. *Conf.* 68. – Cf. Paul's use of the distinction Greek and barbarians in Rom 1:14.

only of the human race, the barbarians, and denied altogether to the
Greeks, took steps to have them translated. (*Mos.* 2:26–27).

This second event took place in the Ptolemaic period in Egypt, under
Ptolemy Philadelphus, the third in succession to Alexander, the con-
queror of Egypt. (*Mos.* 2:25–40).[3]

In *Mos.* 2:25–40 Philo gives a summary of the traditional account
of the origin of the Greek translation. His version is in basic agreement with the story of the translation given in the *Letter of Aristeas*.
There are also important differences, however.[4] Philo connects his
story about the translation of the Laws of Moses into Greek with the
annual celebration of this event on the island of Pharos. He then
probably recounts the traditional aetiological story which was part of
this festival. Thus, Philo is hardly in a direct way dependent upon
the *Letter of Aristeas*, but both of these versions may draw on Alexandrian traditions about the translation.[5]

To Philo, therefore, the Septuagint translation has a theological
and ideological importance. When it was translated under king Ptolemy II Philadelphus, that is, more than two centuries before the time
of Philo, it was the event in revelatory history when the Laws of
Moses revealed their beauty to the Greek half of the world (*Mos.*
2:26–27). This universal aim is also expressed in Philo's description
of the work of the translators on the island of Pharos:

> . . . taking the sacred books, [they] stretched them out towards heaven
> with the hands that held them, asking of God that they might not fail
> in their purpose. And He assented to their prayers, to the end that the
> greater part, or even the whole, of the human race might be profited
> and led to a better life by continuing to observe such wise and truly
> admirable ordinances (*Mos.* 2:36).

In their worship and in their work as translators they were priests
and prophets and went hand in hand with the purest of spirits, the

---

[3] Philo's eulogy of this Ptolemaic king is mainly due to him being associated with
the translation of the Laws of Moses into Greek, but also to his many other accom-
plishments. A similar praise of Ptolemy II Philadelphus is given by Tertullian in his
Apologia 18, and Epiphanius in his *On Weights and Measures* 9 calls him "a lover of the
beautiful and of literature". See Meecham (1932) 329.

[4] Meecham (1932) 121–124, points to several dissimilarities between Philo's version and that of the *Letter of Aristeas*, such as parts in the *Letter of Aristeas* which are
not mentioned by Philo, and additions found in Philo.

[5] See the similar conclusion drawn by Swete in Swete (1902) 12; cf. Meecham
(1932) 123–24.

spirit of Moses. Thus the Greek words used correspond literally with the Hebrew (Chaldean) words, and both versions are one and the same (*Mos.* 2:37–40).

To Philo, the reason for the translation was not the lack of knowledge of Hebrew among Alexandrian Jews, but the need for the Laws of the Jewish nation, which at the same time were the One God's cosmic and universal Laws, to be made known to all nations, so that in the end all nations should make them their own and become proselytes. In his works, then, Philo continues this *proclamatio Graeca* with the same aim in mind. For theological reasons Philo based his presentation of the Laws of Moses on the event in revelatory history which brought them from the Hebrew/barbarian half to the Greek half of the world, whether he himself knew Hebrew or not.[6]

The glimpse given by Philo of the Septuagint festival on the island Pharos shows that there were a large number of non-Jews in Alexandria who were sympathizers with Judaism and took part in at least one Jewish festival, by implication probably in several of the activities in the Jewish community. These sympathizers, together with the Alexandrian Jews, celebrated the Greek translation of the Laws of Moses. Thus, there is reason for working on the hypothesis that Philo had in mind the kind of people present at these Septuagint festivals when he writes. Thus one important setting for his writings is the borderline between the Jews and the surrounding world, especially the non-Jewish sympathizers.

The conclusion is: Philo spells out the meaning the Laws of Moses, accurately translated into Greek, has for the Greek-speaking half of the world. The translation which took place on the island Pharos at Alexandria in the time of Ptolemy Philadelphus was a decisive event in revelatory history, the goal of which is the recognition of these Laws of Moses by all nations. Philo's presentation of the Laws of Moses continues this presentation of the Laws of Moses to the Greek half of the world, and when he writes, he probably primarily has in mind his fellow Jews and the non-Jewish sympathizers, as exemplified by the combined group of people who took part in the annual

---

[6] Concerning the much debated question whether Philo knew Hebrew or not, see Borgen (1984A) 123. The question whether Philo knew Hebrew is not of decisive importance for an assessment of his possible use of Hebrew traditions. The basic fact is that he renders etymological interpretations based on Hebrew, and that he employs some. traditions which were common to Greek-speaking and Hebrew-speaking Jews.

Septuagint festival. Those sympathizers valued the Jewish Laws highly
since they joined them in the celebration of the event at which they
were translated into Greek.

The Mosaic Law and cosmic law

The question to be asked is whether or not it is possible to find a
thought-model or some basic principles which might provide a hermeneutical clue to Philo's expositions of the Laws of Moses. In a recent
article Y. Amir stresses the following points as premise for Philo's
exegesis:[7] To Philo the biblical word has authority. This authority is
founded on its character as a collection of oracles. "Moses himself
learnt it by an oracle and has taught us how it was" (*Det.* 86). Moses
is both receiver and transmitter of the Divine teaching. Philo uncritic-
ally accepted the Septuagint text before him as identical with the
Hebrew Bible. Although Philo on the whole recognizes a dual meaning in Scripture, i.e. both a literal and an allegorical meaning, his
view is that Moses' deepest concern was his religious-philosophical
doctrine, which may be arrived at by allegorical interpretation.

According to F. Siegert the theological basis for Philo's interpretation of Scripture is his strong accent on the transcendence of God.[8]
Basically God cannot be spoken of. As 'the Being One' He is beyond motion and emotion, beyond evil, and beyond any contact with
matter. The two powers 'God' (Θεός) and 'Lord' (Κύριος) bridge the
gap between God's simultaneous transcendence and immanence.
Philo's "eclecticism consists in being *a Platonist about transcendence, and
a Stoic about immanence*".[9]

Siegert agrees with Amir that to Philo Moses was the author of
the Laws. Amir stresses here that Philo's view is alien to the rabbis.[10]
Siegert also sees the difference between Philo's understanding and the
rabbinic view that God speaks immediately in the Torah. Both Amir
and Siegert recognize that according to Philo Moses was in a trance
when God spoke through him in the first person. To Siegert the Philonic concept of inspiration excluded any intellectual activity on the
side of humans. On this basis Siegert maintains that in some contexts

---

[7] For the following, see Amir (1988) 421–53.
[8] Siegert (1996) 168–72.
[9] Siegert (1996) 170.
[10] Amir (1988) 434–36.

Philo's supernaturalism is in no way inferior to that of the rabbis.[11]

These analyses made by Amir and Siegert give insights into Philo's ideas about the Pentateuch as an inspired and authoritative text. Amir mentions in passing that according to Philo Moses also receives from within a share of the Divine being. He again stresses the contrast between Philo and the rabbis: "Even the fact that in two passages [Exod 4:6 and 7:1] the Tora conditionally refers to Moses as 'God' – a fact that the rabbis did their best to explain away – is enthusiastically welcomed by Philo".[12] Amir here overlooks the fact that in *Tanchuma*, ed. Buber, IV, 51f. it says: "... he [God] called Moses 'God', as it is said, 'See, I have made you a god to Pharaoh' (Exod 7:1)".[13]

Although Amir and Siegert touch questions about the relationship between the literal and the allegorical as well as between the particular and the cosmic-universal aspects of Philo's expositions, further examination needs be made of the central hermeneutical function of these features.

In several passages Philo deals with the relationship between God, the eternal law, the cosmic law and the Laws of Moses, as for example in *Mos.* 2:48–53; *Opif.* 3 and 142–44; *Spec.* 1:13–14; *QE* 2:42; *Ebr.* 142; *Somn.* 2:174.

The presupposition of these ideas is the biblical tradition that the God of Israel is at the same time the Creator and that the books of the Mosaic Law begin with the story of creation. There was a broad Jewish tradition which built upon this biblical idea. In the Book of Sirach the concept of Wisdom was thought to pervade the cosmos and to have made her home in Israel, in Jerusalem, Sir 24:3–12. Sirach identified Wisdom with Torah, 24:23.

Also in rabbinic writings creation and the revealed Torah are connected in such a way that the Torah also is cosmic law. Heaven and earth cannot exist without Torah, *b. Nedarim* 32a; God consulted the Torah when He created the world, *Gen. Rab.* 1:2. Of special interest is Josephus' statement in *Ant.* 1:24 that everything in the Mosaic Law is set forth in keeping with the nature of the universe.

This relationship between the Law and the cosmos is a central theme in Philo's works.[14] One of the places where he deals with this

---

[11] Siegert (1996) 171.
[12] Amir (1988) 436.
[13] See Meeks (1967) 193. Cf. *Num. Rab.* 15:13.
[14] See Wolfson (1948) 2:189–92; Nikiprowetzky (1977) 117–55; Winston (1984) 386–88. See also Barraclough (1984) 507–08. See esp. *QE* 2:42 and also *Abr.* 1–6.

theme in a principal way, is *Mos.* 2:45–52. In §§ 45–47a he gives an outline of the Laws of Moses as basis for an expository elaboration in the form of question and answer. Philo's summary runs as follows:[15]

> They [the sacred books] consist of two parts, one the historical, the other concerned with commands and prohibitions. . . . One division of the historical side deals with the creation of the world, the other with genealogies, and this last partly with the punishment of the impious, partly with the honouring of the just.[16]

In § 47b Philo considers the question why Moses began his lawbook (νομοθεσία) with history. Part of his answer is:

> in relating the history of early times, and going for its beginning right to the creation of the universe, he [Moses] wished to shew two most essential things:
>
> first that the Father and Maker of the cosmos was in the truest sense also Lawgiver,
>
> secondly that he who would observe the laws will accept gladly the duty of following nature and live in accordance with the ordering of the universe, so that his deeds are attuned to harmony with his words and his words with his deeds (§ 2:48).

Against this background Philo formulates statements of harmony, such as in *Opif.* 3 and *Mos.* 2:52 where the term συνᾴδω, 'sing together', 'be in harmony with', 'agree with' is used as also is the term ἁρμονία, 'harmony':

> "It consists of an account of the creation of the cosmos, implying that the cosmos is in harmony with (συνᾴδω) the Law, and the Law with the cosmos" (*Opif.* 3).[17]
>
> Thus whoever will carefully examine the nature of the particular enactments (τὰ διατεταγμένα) will find that they seek to attain to the harmony (ἁρμονία) of the universe (τὸ πᾶν) and are in agreement with (συνᾴδω) the principles of eternal nature (*Mos.* 2:52).

The plural participle used as noun, τὰ διατεταγμένα, means 'enactments', 'ordinances' of a code of law. In *Mos.* 1:2 it is used about ordinances of the legislators of non-Jewish states, ordinances which in many cases were opposite to those of Moses. In *Mos.* 2:15 Philo states that in the laws of Moses not even the smallest part of the ordinances has been disturbed. In *Dec.* 174 the phrase refers to ordinances related

---

[15] A parallel summary is given in *Praem.* 1–3.
[16] The translation in *PLCL* is modified.
[17] The translation in *PLCL* is modified.

to the tenth commandment against desire, ordinances intended for admonition or punishment.[18] In *Mos.* 2:138 and *Dec.* 158 the plural form of the participle is used about the appointed rites in the temple, such as purifications, etc.

Of special interest is the formulation "of the particular enactments" (τῶν κατὰ μέρος διατεταγμένων) in *Spec.* 2:1, since here the prepositional phrase κατὰ μέρος is used in a way similar to the use of ἐν μέρει in *Mos.* 2:52. Other examples are ordinances for the Sabbath (§ 2:250) and ordinances about the Great vow (Num 6:2; *Immut.* 87). In the context of *Mos.* 2:52 the ordinances comprise ethical virtues in contrast with vices. Those who follow injustice and vices are enemies not of men, but of the whole of heaven and the universe, as were those who were punished by the deluge – with Noah and his family as exceptions – and the cities destroyed by fire (§§ 2:53–65).

The phrase τὰ διατεταγμένα may also be used with reference to the Mosaic Laws by persons from outside of Judaism, such as by a scoffer in *Conf.* 2, and by the sympathetic governor Petronius who refers to the fact that the Jews were trained in the Laws and carry the likeness of the ordinances enshrined in their souls (*Legat.* 210).

The conclusion is that the particular enactments referred to in *Mos.* 2:52 are the specific laws and regulations in the Laws of Moses. This conclusion is in accordance with *Abr.* 3 where the Patriarchs are understood to be the more general archetypes as distinct from the particular (ἐπὶ μέρους) laws which follow in the treatises *On the Decalogue*, and *On the Special Laws*.

From this analysis a hermeneutical key can be formulated:
The particular ordinances of the Jewish Law coincide with the universal cosmic principles. Thus to Philo universal and general principles do not undercut or cancel the specific ordinances or events of the Mosaic Law.

Philo furthermore applies the Stoic idea of cosmos as a city to the biblical story of the creation:[19] Moses

> considered that to begin his writings with the foundation of a man-made city was below the dignity of the laws, and surveying the greatness and the beauty of the whole code with the accurate discernment of his mind's eye, and thinking it too good an godlike to be confined within any earthly walls, he inserted the story of the genesis of the "Great

---

[18] In Philo's numbering the tenth commandment is the fifth head of the second set of the ten commandments.

[19] *SVF* 1:262; Cicero, *De natura deorum* 154.

City" (μεγαλόπολις), holding that the laws were the most faithful picture (ἐμφερεστάτην εἰκόνα) of the world-polity (πολιτεία) (*Mos.* 2:51).

The idea of the cosmic city or commonwealth is also found in *Spec.* 1:13–14 and 34; *QE* 2:14, and in *Opif.* 142–44. It should be noted that according to *Opif.* 143 this cosmic commonwealth consists both of noetic beings and visible stars.

By calling the Laws of Moses the most faithful picture (ἐμφερεστάτην εἰκόνα) of the cosmic *politeia*, Philo makes an exclusive claim for these Laws. They are both the picture of and the revelatory means by which one can perceive the cosmic commonwealth and its law, and live accordingly. The Laws of Moses are "stamped with the seals of nature itself", *Mos.* 2:14.[20]

Goodenough believes that when Philo says the Laws of Moses are a picture, or copy, he gives them a secondary status relative to the higher law. Thus the man of higher experience will go beyond the Mosaic code in order to be in himself a living law, like the patriarchs.[21] Some observations speak against this view: 1. When Philo in *Opif.* 3 writes that the cosmos is in harmony with the Law and the Law with the world, then the Law is not just an imitation which can be surpassed, as maintained by Goodenough.[22] 2. Philo does not regard the Laws of Moses as parallel to the laws of the cities established by human legislators, *Mos.* 2:48–51. The Mosaic Laws come from the One God who is the Lawgiver. 3. As will be shown below in the chapter on heavenly ascent, the mystical ascent may reach above creation, but then to the God who is also Creator and Lawgiver.

What is then the role of Israel in this context? It is a chosen people that has a universal role, just as its Law is modelled on the cosmic law.[23] This understanding is formulated in *QE* 2:42 where Exod 24:12c ("the law and the commandment which I have written . . .") is interpreted:

---

[20] These perspectives have especially been placed in focus in Nikiprowetzky (1977) 117–55.
    The concept of 'the law of nature' has Stoic background, but Philo subordinates this law under the transcendent God, who created the world and governs it. For the discussion of the concept, see Köster (1968) 521–41; Horsley (1978) 35–59; Runia (1986) 466, n. 333, and Martens (1991) 309–22.
[21] Goodenough (1935) 88–94.
[22] *Ibid.*, 89–90.
[23] Scholars have often regarded particularistic nationalism and universalism (and individualism) as mutually exclusive alternatives and, accordingly, they find an inner conflict running through Philo's works between his Jewish nationalism and his indi-

> And rightly does He legislate for this race [the contemplative race, i.e. Israel], also prescribing (its Law) as a law for the world, for the chosen race is a likeness of the world, and its Law (is a likeness of the laws) of the world.[24]

In this role the people function as the priesthood of all mankind and the Temple and the sacrifices have cosmic significance.[25]

The hermeneutical insights drawn from these observations are that Philo can in different ways interpret one and the same biblical text basically on two, sometimes on three levels, such as for example on the concrete and specific level, the level of the cosmic and general principles, and the level of the divine realm of the beyond.

Although the study of I. Christiansen on Philo's allegory was too schematic in its approach, she reached a general conclusion similar to the one suggested here: "Die Allegorese ist eine Interpretations form, mit der eine Ideeneinheit entfaltet wird, die das Schriftwort unentfaltet enthält, indem neben das Schriftwort ein gleichartiger Begriff gestellt wird, der allgemeiner ist als das entfaltete Schriftwort".[26]

It should be mentioned that a two level exegesis is also present in other Jewish writings, for example in such a way that both levels may be pictured in concrete and specific terms. Thus, in the *Book of Jubilees*, Noah, Abraham and others observed and enjoined the laws *on earth*, but the laws are the ones inscribed on *heavenly* tablets, which were later given to Moses (*Jubilees* 6:17; 15:1; 16:28, etc).[27]

In general support of the understanding of Philo's two-level exegesis outlined above one might refer to the hermeneutical function of Philo's ascents according to *Spec.* 3:1–6. Philo states that his soul ascended to the heavenly sphere. This and successive more moderate ascents enable him to unfold and reveal in the Laws of Moses what is not known to the multitude:

> So behold me daring, not only to read the sacred messages of Moses, but also in my love of knowledge to peer (διακύπτω) into each of them

---

vidualistic universalism. As an example, see Fischer (1978) 184–213, and the criticism of his work by Müller (1980) 238–40, and by Hengel (1983) 657–58.

[24] See Nikiprowetzky (1977) 118.

[25] Cf. *Abr.* 56 and 98; *Mos.* 1:149; *Spec.* 1:66–67, 76 and 82–97; 2:163–67 and 167; *Fug.* 108–09; *Heres* 84; *Somn.* 2:188, 231. See further Josephus' cosmic interpretation of the Temple in *Ant.* 3:179–87. See Laporte (1972) 75–190.

[26] Christiansen (1969) 134.

[27] Confer Philo's reference to the view of others in *Abr.* 276. See further Bousset (1926) 125, n. 3 and 126, n. 1. The idea that the Patriarchs kept the commandments of the Torah is familiar in rabbinic dicta as well. See Urbach (1975) 1:335ff.

and unfold (διαπτύσσω) and reveal (ἀναφαίνω) what is not known to the many (*Spec.* 3:6).[28]

Philo has a varied use of the term διακύπτω. In most cases it means to stoop or peer so as to get a view of the inside (*Migr.* 222; *Heres* 111), through a curtain (*Ebr.* 167); to look into the inner realities, heaven (*Jos.* 146), or to look down from the realm of the stars (*Spec.* 3:2). Here in *Spec.* 3:6 the word then means that Philo peers into the inner meaning of the Laws of Moses.

The verb διαπτύσσω is used rather infrequently by Philo. In two places it characterizes exegetical activity, however: 1) in *Somn.* 2:127 where the general exegetical activity of the Jews on the Sabbath is pictured: "Will you sit in your conventicles . . . and read in security your holy books, expounding (διαπτύσσω) any obscure point. . . ." In *Cont.* 78 Philo characterizes the exegetical work of the Therapeutai. He says that they employ allegorical interpretation. The literal ordinances are the body of the Scriptures and the soul is the invisible meaning ("mind") of their wording:

> It is in this mind especially that the rational soul begins to contemplate the things akin to itself and looking through the words as through a mirror beholds the marvellous beauty of the concepts, unfolds (διαπτύσσω) and removes the symbolic coverings and brings forth the thoughts. . . .

Thus the word may mean allegorical interpretation, but can also have the more general meaning of unfolding what is not clear in the Laws of Moses.

The verb ἀναφαίνω, cause to give light, display, bring to light, shows that Philo's interpretations are not esoteric, but are displayed to others. This point is evident when Philo in *Mos.* 2:26 says that as long as the Laws of Moses only existed in the Chaldean (= Hebrew) language they had not yet displayed/revealed (ἀναφαίνω) their beauty to the rest of mankind. This revelation took place when the Laws were translated into Greek.

Philo's use of these terms together with the context of *Spec.* 3:1–6 indicates that Philo's hermeneutical statement in § 6 refers to the inner and higher insight which his "stays" in the ethereal and aerial spheres gave into earthly matters and into the Sacred writings. This interpretation includes allegory, but is not limited to it, as is evident from Philo's *Exposition of the Laws of Moses* of which *Spec.* 3:1–6 is a

---

[28] The translation in *PLCL* is modified.

part. In this comprehensive work of Philo allegorical interpretations as such are not prominent. The general (ethical) meaning behind the specific commandments and regulations are, however, brought out by Philo. Thus the higher inner meaning referred to in *Spec.* 3:6 is this broader unfolding of expository insight done by Philo in his exegesis.

Philo was an exegete among other exegetes, and he refers to many others, although not by name.[29] Here only two examples will be mentioned in order to indicate different hermeneutical approaches. In *Migr.* 89–93 Philo criticizes some who in their interpretation of the Sabbath, the Feast and circumcision were in danger of separating the specific and concrete level from the higher level of general ideas and convictions. Philo keeps both levels together just as soul and body belong together. It is then interesting to note that the specific and concrete level does not just refer to biblical texts, but to biblical and traditional laws as they were to be practised in Jewish community life.

Philo also refers to exegetes who did not look for a higher general and cosmic meaning if that is not stated in the text itself. Some examples of this approach are: in Deut 34:4 God humiliates Moses by not permitting him to enter the promised land (*Migr.* 44–45); in Gen 11:7–8 the confusion of tongues refers to the origin of the Greek and barbarian languages (*Conf.* 190); Gen 26:19–32 tells about the actual digging of wells (*Somn.* 1:39), and in Exod 22:26f. the material return of the garment is meant (*Somn.* 1:92–102).

Moreover, Philo may deal with concrete and specific human experiences and events, at times seen together with biblical examples. Thus in *Praem.* 11–14 the idea of hope is illustrated by examples from various professions, such as the meaning of hope in the life of a tradesman, a skipper, a politician, an athlete, etc. Then the biblical figure of Enos expresses every man's need for setting his hope in God.

The relationship between the historical treatises *Against Flaccus* and *On the Embassy to Gaius* and Philo's other writings poses a problem. For example Siegert rightly recognizes that Philo was one of several Sages of the Jewish community of Alexandria. Among them he was chosen to be the head of their embassy sent to the Emperor Gaius Caligula.[30]

---

[29] See Shroyer (1936) 261–84; Hay (1979–80) 41–75; Hay (1991A) 81–97; Borgen (1984) 259–62; Borgen (1984A) 126–28.
[30] Siegert (1996) 163–64.

Referring to the treatises *Against Flaccus* and *On the Embassy to Gaius* Siegert writes: "His [Philo's] *historical writings* bear witness to the fact that the situation dramatically changed for the worse. This is theologically important because it made Philo think of history, of politics and of concrete troubles. He did so in a prolific way. . . . Thus the moralizing generalities which make the bulk of Philo's preserved exegeses reflect 'normal' circumstances. They should not make us forget that the same author is able to be à theologian of history".[31]

Although Siegert rightly has seen the important problem about the relationship between Philo's expository writings and his historical wrings, *Against Flaccus* and *On the Embassy to Gaius*, the explanation suggested by him is not convincing. There must have been deep tension between the Jews and other groups in Alexandria even prior to the persecution and pogrom, in the period before the dramatic events of violence took place. Thus the earlier 'normal' circumstances were hardly without elements of conflict. In addition, the fact that Philo was trusted by his fellow Jews so that he became the head of the delegation sent to Gaius Caligula is difficult to account for had he not previously been actively engaged in rivalry and troubles between the Jewish community and non-Jews in Alexandria.

Thus in principle Goodenough was right when he attempted to identify political attitudes, ideas and ideology also in Philo's biblical expositions, although he did it too schematically.[32] Thus two important questions should be raised: 1. is there evidence which speaks in favour of the understanding that Philo was involved in politics also before the tragic events which took place in 38–41? 2. Are there passages in his *Exposition* and his exegetical commentary which reflect tensions and an emerging conflict, which then culminated in the pogrom? These questions are relevant in a study which aims at understanding Philo as an exegete for his time.

Within Philo's two- or three-level hermeneutical perspective there is room for various emphases. Thus the focus may be set on the level of specific historical events, interpreted by ideas from the higher level of the Laws, the cosmic principles and the divine guidance. The treatises *Against Flaccus* and *On the Legation to Gaius* belong to this kind of writing. The focus may also primarily be placed upon the higher level of general cosmic principles and God's realm above the

---

[31] *Ibid.*, 182.
[32] Goodenough (1938).

created world. *The Allegorical Commentary* qualifies for this classification. Another possibility is to place both levels together in immediate sequence, as especially is the case in several entries in the *Questions and Answers on Genesis and Exodus* and parts of *On Abraham* and *On Joseph*.[33] Various aspects of both levels may be woven together as is largely the case in Philo's rewriting of the Laws of Moses in *On the Life of Moses, On the Decalogue, On the Special Laws, On the Virtues* and *On Rewards and Punishments*.

Some exegetical approaches and terms

The section *Mos.* 2:12–65 discussed above, provides glimpses into some of the various approaches and forms employed by Philo in his expository activity. Philo's characterization of Moses as Legislator leads into a characterization of the Laws and their function in the life of the Hebrew/Jewish people seen in comparison with the laws of other peoples. Within this broader context some more specific forms of exposition are illustrated. One example is the form of question and answer quoted above from *Mos.* 2:46ff. After having stated that the Laws consist of two parts, one the historical and the other concerned with commands and prohibitions (*Mos.* 2:46–47a), Philo raised a problem (2:47b): "it must be told why he began his lawbook with the history, and put the commands and prohibitions in the second place". Then the answer follows in § 48, where Philo formulates aspects of his hermeneutical key. The phrase οὗ χάρις, "for what reason" introduces the problem here, as similarly τοῦ χάρις does in *Dec.* 36. The answer is introduced by the word λεκτέον, "it must be said/told", as also is the case in *Dec.* 37, *Leg. all.* 1:85–87, 91–92, 101–04, etc. Above this expository form of question and answer has been analysed.

In *Mos.* 2:53–65 Philo gave a report on biblical stories, presented in a rewritten form. Philo stated this explicitly by referring back to the stories: ὡς μηνύει τὰ λόγια, "as the oracles declare" (*Mos.* 2:56) and ὡς αἱ ἱεραὶ βίβλοι περιέχουσιν, "as the sacred books relate" (*Mos.* 2:59). In this way the biblical story of the destruction of Sodom and Gomorrah and the story of the Deluge were told (*Mos.* 2:53–65) to illustrate and substantiate Philo's hermeneutical statement in § 52:

---

[33] See Borgen (1987) 22–23 and 53–54; Wan (1993) 35 and 39.

Thus whoever will carefully examine the nature of the particular enactments will find that they seek to attain to the harmony of the universe
and are in agreement of the principles of eternal nature.

As already shown above in our examination of expository forms, Philo
interpreted the Laws of Moses extensively by rendering biblical material in rewritten form. It is of importance to note, however, that Philo
in this way related his hermeneutical formulations even in *Mos.* 2:48,
51–52 to expository forms, approaches and terminology. Thus it is
evident that Philo's hermeneutical principles were at work in Philo's
expository activities.

A central element in all kinds of exegesis is the wish to explicate
and explain the text. As already seen, such activities produce in turn
a certain exegetical terminology and expository forms, which in spite
of freedom develop into flexible conventions. Such examples of expository forms and structures were given in the preceding chapters. In
the present chapter some further samples of exegetical terminology
will be given to strengthen the understanding that Philo's expository
activity was part of an exegetical tradition.

A typical exegetical term used is τουτέστιν, 'this is' or 'this means'.[34]
By means of this phrase a word or a phrase is explained by another
word, phrase or sentence. As an example *Leg. all.* 1:24 may be cited:
"'And all the grass of the field' he says, 'before it sprang up' (Gen
2:5), that is to say (τουτέστι), 'before' the particular objects of sense
'sprang up'". Some other examples are found in *Leg. all.* 1:45, 65,
98; 2:38, 41, 45, 59, 62, 77, 92; 3:11, 16, 20, 28, 46, 52, 95, 142,
143, 145, 153, 154, 176, 230, 232, 242, 244; *Cher.* 17; *Sacr.* 62, 86,
119; *Deter.* 10, 59, 119; *Post.* 53, 150, 168, 182; *Gig.* 53, 54; *Plant.* 42,
116; *Ebr.* 40, 53, 95, 70, 125; *Heres* 304; *Congr.* 49; *Fuga* 135, 192,
201; *Somn.* 1:112; 2:76; (*Spec.* 1:306).

Other exegetical terms used by Philo within various forms of contexts are phrases built on the word ἴσον, 'equal (to)', as for example
in *Leg. all.* 1:36: "'Breathed into' (Gen 2:7), we note, is equivalent to
(ἴσον ἐστί) inspired".[35] Other examples are: *Leg. all.* 1:65, 76; 2:16,
21; 3:51, 119, 189, 219, 246, 247, 253; *Cher.* 7, 119; *Sacr.* 12, 112;
Deter. 38, 70, 96, 169; *Agr.* 166; *Plant.* 90, 114; *Sobr.* 15; *Conf.* 72, 84,
111, 150, 160, 189; *Migr.* 5, 7, 27, 42, 80, 101, 160; *Congr.* 158, 172;
(*Spec.* 3:133); (*Aet.* 46).

---

[34] Cf. Adler (1929) 23.
[35] *Ibid.*

Also many other exegetical terms and methods are used: One meaning may be discarded in contrast to the proper meaning, for example by the contrast 'not' – 'but', which is exemplified in *Leg. all.* 1:1. In *Leg. all.* 1:1 Gen 2:1 is cited: "And the heaven and the earth and all their world were completed". In the exposition the contrast rejects one interpretation over against another: "He [Moses] does not (οὔτε δὲ) say (φησίν) that either the individual mind or the particular sense-perception have reached completion, but (ἀλλ᾽) that the originals have done so".

A contrast may be used either to confirm a reading of the text or to correct a certain reading against an alternative one.[36] In *Migr. 1 and 43* the contrast offers a confirmation of the reading of the text of Gen 12:1: "'Into the land which I shall shew (δείξω) thee'. He says not (εἰπὼν οὐχ) 'which I am shewing (δείκνυμι)', but (ἀλλ᾽) 'which I will shew (δείξω) thee'. Thus he testifies to the trust. . . ."

Such philological confirmation of the reading of a text is used in rabbinic exegesis, as in *Mek. on Exod.* 15:11 and also in the New Testament, in Gal 3:16.

Mek. on Exod. 15:11 reads: "'Doing עושה wonders'. It is not written here (אין כתיב כאן) 'Who did (עשה) wonders', but (עושה) 'who does (עושה) wonders', that is, in the future".

Gal 3:16 reads: "'and to his offspring (καὶ τῷ σπέρματι)'. It does not say (οὐ λέγει) 'and to offsprings' (καὶ τοῖς σπέρμασιν), as referring to many; but (ἀλλ᾽), referring to one, 'and to your offspring (καὶ τῷ σπέρματι σου)', which is Christ".

The contrast may correct a certain reading, as is the case in *Deter. 47–48* with parallels in rabbinics, as in *Mek. on Exod.* 16:15, and in the New Testament, in John 6:31–32.

Deter. 47–48 reads: "'Cain rose up against Abel his brother and slew him (αὐτόν)' (Gen 4:8). . . . It must be read in this way (ὥσθ᾽ οὕτως ἀναγνωστέον), 'Cain rose up and slew himself (ἑαυτόν)', not (ἀλλ᾽ οὐχ) someone else".

Correspondingly *Mek. on Exod.* 16:15 reads: "'Man did eat the bread of strong horses' (Ps. 78:25). Do not read (אל תקרי) 'of strong horses' (אבירים), but (אלא) 'of the limbs' (איברים), that is, 'bread' that is absorbed by the 'limbs'".

John 6:31–32, with the Greek verb translated back into Hebrew, is a parallel: "'Bread from heaven he gave (ἔδωκεν/נתן) them to eat'

---

[36] For the following, see Borgen (1965) 62–65.

(Exod 16:4,15? Ps. 78:24?)[37] Truly, truly I say to you, 'not (οὐ) Moses
gave (δέδωκεν [ἔδωκεν]/נתן) you the bread from heaven, but (ἀλλ')
my Father gives (δίδωσιν/נותן) you the true bread from heaven'".

In accordance with his two or three level exegesis Philo often moves
from one level of meaning to another one. He may do so by using
a modified form of contrast which indicates that he accepts both
levels of meaning, such as 'not only' – 'but', οὐ μόνον . . . ἀλλὰ καί . . .
as seen in *Spec.* 4:149–50:

> 'Thou shalt not remove thy neighbour's landmarks which thy fore-
> runners have set up'. Now this law, we may consider, applies not
> (οὐ) merely (μόνον) to allotments and boundaries of land . . . but also
> (ἀλλὰ καί) to the safeguarding of ancient customs.

By this sample selection it has been demonstrated that Philo in a
flexible way utilizes exegetical terminology and approaches in the
direct exposition of the text on the basis of the principles 'this is/
means' or 'this is not/does not mean'. Another expository technique
is used in the forms of question and answer. Samples of the exegetical terminology used in this approach to the text was given in the
chapter on the question and answer form.

It is then probable that Philo in his interpretative activity in a
flexible way relies on conventional exegetical terminology.

Conclusion

*According to Philo the translation of the Septuagint, which took place on the
island Pharos at Alexandria in the time of Ptolemy Philadelphus, was a decisive
event in revelatory history, the goal of which is the recognition of these Laws of
Moses by all nations. Philo's interpretation of the Laws of Moses continues this
presentation of these Laws to the Greek half of the world.*

*The hermeneutical insights gained are: In his exposition of the Laws of Moses
Philo can in different ways interpret one and the same biblical text within the
context of two, sometimes on three level exegesis. These levels can be characterized
as 1) the specific, 2) the general and 3) the beyond or 1) the particular, 2) the
universal, and 3) the beyond, or again 1) the concrete, 2) the abstract and 3) the
beyond, and finally as 1) the earthly, 2) the cosmic or heavenly or the created
cosmos and 3) the beyond. The general terminology of literal and allegorical
exegesis does not give an adequate characterization of all these aspects of Philo's*

---

[37] Borgen (1965) 40–41; Menken (1996) 47–65.

two- or three-levels exegesis. Philo's use of conventional exegetical terminology, although in a flexible way, demonstrates that he is to be seen as an exegete among other exegetes.

Against the background of this discussion of some of Philo's hermeneutical principles, the task is to analyse further aspects of Philo's biblical interpretations with his one, two or three level exegesis in view. Here it seems fruitfull to examine his use of the Laws of Moses in the context of the interrelationship between the Jews and their non-Jewish surroundings. Since the treatises *In Flaccum* and *De Legatione ad Gaium* give evidence of the fact that this relationship was tense, the question should be asked: Are there passages in Philo's *Exposition of the Laws of Moses* and his exegetical commentaries which also reflect tensions and an emerging conflict which then culminated in the tragic pogrom in A.D. 38?

CHAPTER NINE

TENSION AND INFLUENCE

Tension

Both Philo and Josephus testify to the fact that the long tradition of tension between the Jewish community and some of the non-Jews were still alive in the first century A.D. Philo writes explicitly that there were circles in Alexandria where anti-Jewish traditions were nurtured and taught, as exemplified by Gaius Caligula's slave Helicon who had learned them during his upbringing in that city (*Legat.* 170).[1]

Some of the areas of criticism and tension are built into Philo's exegesis and can be specified. In the *Exposition's* section on the virtues common to all commandments, *Spec.* 4:133–238 and *On the Virtues*, Philo in *Virt.* 51–174 rewrites the Laws to exemplify the virtue of *philanthropia.* In § 141 he refutes charges of misanthropy by stating that the Jews are told to be humane to fellow-human beings, also to enemies (§§ 102–24), and to show compassion even to flocks and herds (§§ 125–47, drawing on Exod 22:29; 23:19; 34:26; Lev 22:27–28; Deut 14:21; 22:10, and 25:4).

In the section *On the Special Laws* Philo counters the same accusation in his rewriting of the Mosaic laws about the ten feasts (*Spec.* 2:39–222) by claiming that even the universal call and role of the Jewish nation express this care of the Jews for all men:

> ... it astonishes me to see that some people venture to accuse of inhumanity the nation which has shewn so profound a sense of fellowship and goodwill to all men everywhere, by using its prayers and festivals and first-fruit offerings as a means of supplication for the human race in general and of making its homage to the truly existent God in the name of those who have evaded the service which it was their duty to give, as well as of itself (*Spec.* 2:167).

In his exposition of the observance of the Sabbath, Philo writes: "On this day we are commanded to abstain from all work, not because the law inculcates slackness ..." (*Spec.* 2:60). Likewise in *Hypoth.* 7:10–14

---

[1] Smallwood (1970) ad loc.

he tells about the Sabbath gatherings with reading from the Laws of Moses and exposition, and asks: "Do you think that this marks them as idlers . . ."? (7:14). There is a broad documentation for the criticism of the Jews for laziness because they abstained from work on the sabbath. See Juvenal's *Satire* 14:96–106 and confer Josephus' *Ag.Ap.* 1:209 and Augustine, *De Civitate Dei* 6:11.

In his review of biblical history in the *Hypothetica*, Philo defends Moses against the accusation of being an impostor and mountebank (cf. Molon, *Ag.Ap.* 2:145) by referring to his success at the exodus in bringing the whole people in complete safety amid drought and hunger and ignorance of the way and lack of everything as well as if they had abundance of everything (*Hypoth.* 6:3–4).

Both Josephus and Philo tell that the commandment and observance of circumcision was ridiculed by non-Jews. According to Josephus, *Ag.Ap.* 2:137.142–43, the Alexandrian Apion derided the practice of circumcision. In his *Exposition* Philo even opens his four books *On the Special Laws* with a defense of the commandment and practice of circumcision (*Spec.* 1:1–11): "I will begin with that which is an object of ridicule among many people . . ., namely the circumcision of the genital organs" (1:1–2). Both counter this criticism by referring to the fact that circumcision was also practised among the Egyptians (Philo in *Spec.* 1:2, and also in *QG* 3:47–48 and Josephus in *Ag.Ap.* 2:140ff.). The practice of circumcision among Egyptians is documented in *Herodotus* 2:36–37 and 104, *Diodorus* 1:28; 3:32. *Herodotus* 2:104 is quoted by Josephus in *Ag.Ap.* 1:169–70.

R.D. Hecht finds it surprising that Philo did not follow the outline of the Decalogue, but opens the first book *On the Special Laws* with this discussion of circumcision. He rightly understands this statement to deal with a preliminary issue and once treated, Philo feels it was appropriate to begin with the First Commandment and the special laws arranged under it. Hecht says that if *On the Special Laws* were some form of halakhic text or digest of laws enacted by Jewish courts in Egypt or were intended to synthesize Graeco-Roman law and philosophy, as suggested by Belkin, Goodenough and Heinemann, one should expect Philo to spend some time with the details of the observance of circumcision. The passage is devoid, however of anything which might be construed as halakhic distinction, court practice or synthesis between Jewish piety and Graeco-Roman law. Instead, Philo lists various reasons for keeping the observance of circumcision and interprets its meaning. On the one hand, circumcision is seen as the destruction of the arrogance and conceit which stand as a major impediment to a proper understanding of the *nomos*. Circumcision becomes the symbolic vestibule to the Law and the entrance for the ascension of the soul within the Law or in conformity with it. In this way Hecht rightly suggests that the biblical observance of circumcision, rightly understood, has a hermeneutical function.

Hecht's view needs to be modified at one point, however. Philo does not primarily see circumcision among the Jews as a symbol of the ascent of the soul. It is a figure of the excision of excessive pleasure, and the excision of the evil belief of some that they can assume godship and close their eyes to the Cause of all that come into being. Among the Jews circumcision and the belief in God the Creator are closely connected.

According to Hecht, the implication is that *On the Special Laws* is an apology. Philo is exclusively engaged in deducing the reasonableness of the Law.[2] He is right in seeing an apologetic motif in *Spec.* 1:1–11 when Philo defends circumcision against those who ridicule the practice. This is one way in which Philo is an exegete for his time.[3] It is then evident that the opening section of *On the Special Laws* 1 places the whole work within the context of the borderline between the Jewish nation and the other nations, but the apologetic motif is only one among the perspectives which are at work in Philo's exposition.

In Philo's report on the persecution of the Alexandrian Jews in A.D. 38–41 he mentions another controversial law and practice, the abstention from eating pork. The observance of this commandment was criticized by Gaius Caligula, *Legat.* 361–62. Philo answers the emperor in a diplomatic way: "Different people have different cus-

---

[2] Hecht (1984) 52–79.

[3] Hecht is also right when he states that Philo's aim is not to discuss the specifics of the observance as such, but it should be emphasized much more than Hecht does, that Philo in some or many cases presupposes this observance and that he deals also with 'halakhic' questions as for example when the practice of the Laws on the borderline between Jews and Gentiles become an issue. Such details may even at times be given in Philo's allegorical commentaries. "For example, in *Migr.* 91 Philo criticises some who tend to abrogate the laws for the observation of the sabbath, and light fires or till the ground or carry loads or institute proceedings in court or act as jurors or demand the restoration of deposits or recover loans. . . ." Thus, *On the Special Laws* and Philo's other writings are neither to be understood as ideal laws, nor as a report on the laws which are practiced in Alexandria. Rather, according to Philo the Laws of Moses comprise at the same time what we would call religion, philosophy and ordinances at the same time. And many of the ordinances were actually being observed.

toms and the use of some things is forbidden to us as others are to our opponents" (*Legat.* 362). Likewise Apion denounced the Jews for not eating pork (Josephus, *Ag.Ap.* 2:137). In his comment Josephus refers to the circumstance that all the Egyptian priests abstain from swine's flesh (2:141).

These observations made in Philo's interpretation of the Mosaic Laws demonstrate that the practice of the Laws caused frictions in the relationship between Jews and their surroundings.

To worship the gods of the many

When Philo in *On the Special Laws* 1:315–16 paraphrases Deut 13:1– 11 about the false prophet, he presupposes that there were Jews who, on the basis of inspired prophetic oracles, were encouraged to worship the gods recognized in the different cities.[4] Philo also refers to the possibility that someone's family members or friends might urge Jews to fraternize with the multitude, frequent their temples, and join them in their libations and sacrifices (*Spec.* 1:315–16). Among the modifications of the biblical text made in Philo's rewriting are: LXXDeut 13:7b: "... let us worship foreign gods ..." (λατρεύσωμεν θεοῖς ἑτέροις), and Philo, *Spec.* 1:316: "... fraternize with the many (συνασμενίζειν τοῖς πολλοῖς) and resort to the same temples and join in their libations and sacrifices...." LXXDeut 13:10 implies that the seducer is to be reported to the authorities, while Philo, *Spec.* 1:316, rephrases this to mean that the report on the seducers is to be sent to all lovers of piety.[5]

It is of interest to note that a similar problem is pictured in Rev 2:20 in the New Testament. In Thyatira Jezebel claimed to be a prophetess while teaching the people in the *ekklesia* to participate in pagan cults: "But I have this against you, that you tolerate the woman Jezebel, who calls herself a prophetess and is teaching and beguiling my servants to practice immorality and to eat food sacrificed to idols".

Neither John in the edict to Thyatira, nor Philo in his paraphrase of Deut 13:1–11, elaborated upon the exact content of the prophetic

---

[4] For the following, cf. Borgen (1994) 38–39.

[5] See Seland (1995) 136–60. It should be added that in another passage Philo tells of how Jews felt the attraction of pagan cults with their poetry and music, beautiful sculptures and paintings (*Spec.* 1:28–29). A broader discussion of Philonic material is given Sandelin (1991) 109–50.

messages favouring participation in the polytheistic cults of the many. Philo mentioned the ("inspired") oracles and pronouncements (λόγια καὶ χρησμοί) of the false prophet (*Spec.* 1:315), and John referred to (false) prophetic teaching (διδαχή) (Rev 2:24, cf. 2:20).

According to Philo those who follow the false prophet are to suffer the death penalty. In *Spec.* 1:54–56 he referred to the action of Phinehas, Num 25, and advocated execution on the spot of Israelites who take part in idolatrous worship. Scholars have discussed whether this was a theoretical or practical law in Philo's time.[6] The possibility of applying this biblical case to Philo's own time was at least latent, as can be seen from the fact that the author of 1 Maccabees, who wrote towards the close of the 2nd century B.C., used the Phinehas story to legitimate the action of self-redress of Mattathias who killed one who stepped forward to sacrifice on a heathen altar in Modein, 1 Macc 2:23–27.[7]

In another passage in his *Exposition, Praem.* 162–64, Philo suggests a milder approach which offers apostates the possibility of conversion. Josephus (*Ant.* 4:141–44) entertains the latter view in his interpretation of the Phinehas story: Moses did not order the trespassers to be killed, but tried to win them back by way of conversion (μετάνοια). When this failed, Phinehas and other zealous Jews killed many of the transgressors. Correspondingly, in Rev 2:16 Jesus Christ gives the congregation in Pergamum the alternative of repentance or the sword, where the latter is understood by John as being the sword of his mouth.

Philo and Josephus, as also Paul (1 Cor 10:14) and John of Patmos (Rev 2:14 and 20), say no to participation in pagan cults. In everyday life, the negative attitude of refusal led to the question: 'where is the boundary line to be drawn'? As already shown, Philo's 'no' did not prevent him from watching boxing, wrestling and horse-racing (*Prob.* 26 and *Prov.* 58), etc.

Participation in non-Jewish traditions and society

One area which receives much attention by Philo in his works is the encyclical education. Philo makes clear that this education may serve

---

[6] See Seland (1995) 17–181.
[7] Seland (1995) 50–51.

Jewish aims, if used properly. His attitude towards the encyclica as well as to a political career in society at large, is therefore ambiguous.

He has a concentrated discussion of the encyclical education in his exegetical commentary *On Mating with the Preliminary Studies* and deals with the topic time and again in many of his other writings.[8] Within this broad topic a few points may be lifted up in the present study so as to indicate its place on the borderline between the Jewish and non-Jewish communities. Primary attention will be paid to points from the expositions in *On the Mating*. In §§ 1–70 words and phrases from Gen 16:1–2 are paraphrased: 1. "Now Sarai, Abrams wife, bore him no children. She had an Egyptian maid whose name was Hagar; 2. and Sarai said to Abram, 'Behold now, the Lord has prevented me from bearing children; go into my maid; it may be that I shall obtain children by her'. And Abram hearkened to the voice of Sarah". In §§ 71–120 Philo moves on to an exposition of Gen 16:3: "And Sarai the wife of Abram, after Abram had dwelt ten years in the land of Canaan, took Hagar, the Egyptian, her handmaid, and gave her to Abram her husband as a wife".

When Philo interprets Abraham's relationship in terms of educational ideas, he is dependent upon the interpretation of the figure of Penelope in Homer. For example, Ps.-Plutarch says that those who, being unable to attain philosophy, wear themselves out in the encyclical disciplines, like the suitors of Penelope, who when they could not win the mistress, contended themselves with her maids (Ps.-Plutarch, *De liberis educandis* 7D). Correspondingly, when Abraham did not, at first conceive a child with Sarah, Wisdom, he took the maid, Hagar, encyclical education, in her place.

This transformation of Penelope and her maids into Sarah and Hagar meant that Philo produced a parallel interpretation within a Jewish context, to express a Jewish point of view regarding encyclical education: the encyclical education is the school which the Jews have in common with their pagan surroundings. When Philo in *Congr.* 20 interprets the words "Hagar, the Egyptian", Gen 16:3, he expresses this understanding: "The votary of the encyclical studies, the friend of wide learning, must necessarily be associated with the earthly and Egyptian body; since he needs eyes to see and read. . . ." At the same

---

[8] A thorough study of Philo's educational ideas with emphasis on the encyclica has been made by Mendelson (1982). See also Wuellner (1975), Borgen (1965) 100–11 and Colson (1917) 151–62.

a distinction is drawn between foreigners and citizens: The Egyptian Hagar, meaning encyclical education, is "on the borderline between foreigners and citizens", *Congr.* 22.

Thus, the encyclical education, Hagar, is a sojourner and servant to knowledge, and wisdom and every virtue (Sarah = virtue), which are native born, indigenous, citizens in the truest sense, *Congr.* 22–23. Thus, the encyclical education may be used to serve Jewish ideals and wisdom (*Congr.* 74–76), or can be misused to lead persons away from them (cf. *Leg. all.* 3:167).

Accordingly, Abraham receives education from two schools: the encyclical education is the school which the Jews have in common with the pagan surroundings; the other school is the genuine, Jewish philosophy. Philo expresses this situation in his interpretation of Abraham, Sarah and Hagar in *Congr.* 35: ". . . the virtue that comes through teaching, which Abraham pursues, needs the fruits of several studies, both those born in wedlock, which deal with wisdom, and the base born, those of the preliminary lore of the schools".

In the commentary on Gen 17:1–5, 15–22, *On the Change of Names*, Gen 17:19, "Yes, Sarah thy wife shall bear a son", is quoted and interpreted in *Mut.* 252ff.: Sarah also, that is virtue, shall bear a son, as well as Hagar, the lower instruction. Then in *Mut.* 259–60 the biblical idea of the manna, Exod 16:4, is brought into the exposition and interpreted as virtue and wisdom. This manna is contrasted with 'the lower instruction', ἡ μέση παιδεία, a synonym for 'the encyclical training', ἡ ἐγκύκλιος παιδεία.[9] This distinction reflects a general understanding of the difference between philosophy and encyclical training. In his *Ad Lucilium Epistulae Morales* 88, Seneca defends a position which shows many similarities to that of Philo in *Mut.* 253–63.[10] Like Philo, Seneca also closely associates the terms, 'virtue' (*virtus*) and 'wisdom' (*sapientia*), with philosophy in contrast to encyclical education (*artes liberales*). Although Seneca admits that this encyclical training can prepare the soul for the reception of the philosophical virtue, he attacks it rather sharply, because, in his opinion, it contributes nothing at all so far as 'virtue' itself is concerned.[11]

---

[9] See Borgen (1965) 102–03.

[10] Gummere (1920) 2:348–77.

[11] See especially *ibid.*, 2:360f. (§ 20). For a discussion of Seneca's critical viewpoints, see Lechner (1933) 210f.; Colson (1917) 153; Seneca links his discussion to the viewpoints of Poseidonios, who regarded the encyclical subjects as auxiliary to philosophy. See especially Gummere (1920) 2:362–67 (*Epistle* 88:21–28). Cf. Apelt (1907) 118ff.; Pohlenz (1942) 429ff.

Philo shows a somewhat more moderate attitude, since in *Mut.* 263 he also allows the encyclical education to be characterised by the term 'virtue', although its 'virtue' is of a lower quality than that of revealed wisdom.

In general scholars have been reluctant to consider Philo's discussion of the encyclia against the background of the relationship between Judaism and paganism. Ignoring the concrete case of Philo and the other Jews in Alexandria, such scholars as E. Bréhier and W. Völker interpret the encyclia as a preliminary stage in the moral and religious progress of individuals, although their interpretations give very different emphases to details.[12] E.R. Goodenough considers the encyclia a preliminary stage in the ascent towards the vision of the mystery.[13] H.A. Wolfson discusses the relationship among the encyclia, philosophy and Scripture from the viewpoint of the philosophical question of cognition, and concludes that Philo regards Scripture to be superior to the others.[14] Finally, A. Mendelson sees the encyclia as a stage in the ascent of the heaven-born man to the life of the Sage.[15]

A more adequate understanding of Philo's ideas in this respect is set forth by I. Heinemann and by M. Pohlenz who have seen that the issue of Judaism and paganism is involved in Philo's evaluation of the encyclia.[16] Philo even indicates that Jews sent their children to the gymnasium for their education. He tells that the parents benefit the children physically by means of it and by the training given there, and they receive mental training by means of letters, arithmetic, geometry, music, and philosophy (*Spec.* 2:230). Against this background it is fitting that Hagar, i.e. encyclical education, was a non-Jewish Egyptian woman (*Congr.* 20ff.; *QG* 3:19.21; *Abr.* 251).

Another area about which Philo's writings provide much material, is the area of sports. Philo even betrays such an expert knowledge of Greek sports that he himself probably was active in athletics during his youth.[17] If so, he could hardly have avoided practicing within a polytheistic setting. In the gymnasia there were numerous statues of deities, and the games in which the students participated were religious festivals. In Cyrene there is even found an inscription from

---

[12] Bréhier (1908) 279–95; Völker (1938) 158–98.
[13] Goodenough (1935) 247–48.
[14] Wolfson (1948) 1:145–51.
[15] Mendelson (1982) 69–76.
[16] See *PCH* 6:4 and Pohlenz (1942) 428.
[17] Harris (1976) 90–91; Mendelson (1982) 26; Feldmann (1968) 224–26; Chambers (1980) 129–44; Hengel (1974) 1:70–74.

A.D. 3–4 dedicated to Hermes and Heracles with a list of ephebes in which five of the names are obviously Jewish.[18]

Philo oscillates between sport in the concrete sense and sport in the ethical and spiritual sense. One example is found in his commentary *On Husbandry* where he interprets the words "Noah was the first tiller (γεωργός) of the soil" (Gen 9:20). Philo then describes professional gardening in the literal sense and goes on to soul-gardening. Contrasting the professional tiller (= Noah) and the mere worker on the soil (= Cain), Philo elaborates on two other pairs of opposites in the Laws, the shephard and the rearer of cattle (*Agr.* 26–66) and a horseman in contrast to a rider (§§ 67–119). In the blessing spoken to Dan (Gen 49:17–18) it is said that the horseman shall fall backwards. Philo interprets this positively: it implies victory, not defeat because if Mind finds itself mounted on Passion, the only course is to jump or fall off. If one cannot escape from fighting in a bad cause, court defeat.

At this point Philo brings in sport contest on two levels, both in its literal sense and in its ethical sense. A Jew should try to run away and avoid taking part, but if compelled to do so, should not hesitate to be defeated in the unholy contests, but bind upon ones head the wreaths won in the holy ones (*Agr.* 110–21). As for the sport contest in its literal sense, R. Simeon ben Lakish, correspondingly, is said to have once been a professional gladiator, which he justified on the ground of grim necessity (*b. Git.* 47a).[19]

Thus, among those Jews who said no to participating in pagan cults, Philo and others drew the boundary line in a way to enable them to participate in the areas of sports and cultural activities.

Food, meals, vices and virtues

The question of food and meals was a difficult issue in the relationship between Jews and non-Jews. Philo indicates a solution to the problem in rendering of LXXGen 43:31–32: ". . . he said: 'Set on bread. And they set on for him alone, and for them by themselves and them by themselves, and for the Egyptians dining with him by themselves, for

---

[18] See Applebaum (1979) 177 and 219. See further Borgen (1994) 41.

[19] Borgen (1984) 253 and n. 103. There was disagreement among rabbis on the question of whether a Jew might watch gladiator fights or not, *t. Abod. Zar.* 2:7.

the Egyptians could not eat bread with the Hebrews . . .'"[20] Philo's paraphrase in *Jos.* 202–03 reads:

> The method of entertainment followed for all and each severally according to ancestral practice (κατὰ τὰ πάτρια ἑκάστοις – trans. mine), since he strongly disapproved of neglecting old customs, particularly at a festivity where the pleasures outnumber the disagreeables. "When the guests were seated, arranged by his commands in order of age, as at that date it was not the custom to recline at convivial gatherings, they were surprised to find that the Egyptians affected the same fashions as the Hebrews, and were careful of order of preference, and knew how to discriminate between younger and older in the honours which they paid them. . . ."

Thus it seems that the Hebrews and the Egyptians sat in two separate groups, but nevertheless dined together with Joseph as their host, and that he entertained each group in accordance with their ancestral customs. If so, this passage about Joseph's practice of table-fellowship between Hebrews and Egyptians may have a parallel in the case reported by Paul in Gal 2:11–14. Although details are not given, Paul makes it clear that 'some who came from James' stressed separation during the meals so that Jews could follow their own customs. They might have advocated that Jews and gentiles were to have different meals, but in the same room, similar to Philo's picture of the banquet arranged by Joseph.[21]

Philo himself probably adopted the practice of selective eating. In his commentary, *On the Allegorical Laws* 3:107–99 he interprets Gen 3:14–15 about then curse on the serpent, meaning pleasure. When it is said that the serpent shall go on the belly, this means that bodily necessities compels us to go forth from the house of wisdom – girded with Logos – putting out of sight all that is unreasonable. Philo illustrates this point with his own experience. He recounts that he had taken part in ill-regulated meals at which he had to fight by means of *logos* (as learned from the Laws of Moses) in order to win the noble victory of self-mastery (*Leg. all.* 3:156).

---

[20] The translation in *PLCL* is modified.

[21] Betz (1979) 108, comes close to this understanding: "If Cephas' shift of position resulted in 'separation', this must have been the demand made by the 'men from James'. If they made this demand, it was made because of their understanding of the Jerusalem agreement (cf. 2:7–9). The separation of the mission to the Jews from that to the Gentiles would imply that Peter would retain his Jewish way of life, and this included first of all the dietary and purity laws. As a result, cultic separation would have to be observed also during table fellowship with Gentile Christians".

Since the purpose of the dietary laws of Moses, according to Philo's *Exposition*, is to control the unruly (pagan-like) desires and to get rid of extravagance (*Spec.* 4:100–31),[22] such "ill-regulated (ἀδιάγωγος) and extravagant meals" as mentioned in *Leg. all.* 3:156, probably meant that forbidden food was served, possibly also in a pagan cultic setting.

In rabbinic writings there are numerous warnings against Jews eating with gentiles.[23] There are passages, however, such as *Mishna Aboda Zara* 5:5 and *Mishna Berakot* 7:1, which deal with questions arising from gentile guests sharing tables in the home of Jews.

As for pagan meals, in his account in *On the Embassy to Gaius* of the events which took place under Gaius Caligula, Philo tells about some pagans who when sacrificing to the emperor poured the blood upon the altar and took the flesh home and feasted on it (*Legat.* 356). Although Philo mentions pagan temples and pagan worship in several places, his information about sacrifice and things connected with it is difficult to analyze because he largely interprets them in ethical thought-categories. Thus pagan sacrifice represents vices, such as the consumption of strong drink and gross eating accompanied by wine-bibbing. While the participants in pagan festivals in this way awaken the insatiable lusts of the belly, they inflame also the lusts seated below it. Moses observed this and therefore did not permit his people to conduct their festivities like other nations. He bade them in the very hour of their joy make themselves pure by curbing their appetites for pleasure (*Spec.* 1:192–93). Philo makes this point in his exposition of the Mosaic prescriptions about burnt offering, preservation-offering and sin-offering in *Spec.* 1:190–246.

In the *Exposition* Philo's interpretation of the last commandment against covetousness (*Spec.* 4:78–131) is largely a treatment of the Jewish dietary laws. Moses discarded passion in general and detested it as most vile in itself and in its effects (*Spec.* 4:95), and especially passion in the form of gluttony (*Spec.* 4:100ff.). Philo compares the Jewish legislation with the laws of the Spartans, the Ionians and the Sybarites. Moses "approved neither of rigorous austerity like the Spartan legislator, nor of dainty living, like him who introduced the Ionians and Sybarites to luxurious and voluptuous practices" (*Spec* 4:102).

In his ethical interpretation of the clean and unclean animals in Lev 11 and Deut 14 Philo is dependent upon exegetical traditions,

---

[22] Concerning ethical interpretation of the dietary laws, see Stein (1957) 146–48.
[23] See Str.-B. (1961) 4:1, 374–78.

as can be seen from agreements with the *Letter of Aristeas*. Both say that the clean animals, the ones with parted hoof, teach men that they must distinguish between virtuous and bad ways of life (*Spec.* 4:106–9 and *Aristeas* 150). The other criterion is animals which chew the cud, which means the using of memory to call up what has been learned (*Spec.* 4:106–09 and *Aristeas* 153). Both disqualify all birds which are carnivorous and use their strength to attack others (*Spec.* 4:116–18 and *Aristeas* 145–47).

According to Deut 14:4f. ten animals are clean. Philo elaborates on the number 10. Ten is the perfect number and is basic to all that exists. With this number Moses seals his list of the clean animals when he wishes to appoint them for the use of the members of his *politeia* (*Spec.* 4:105).

The creeping reptiles, with some exceptions, are forbidden. They represent the passions and cravings of the belly. To keep the dietary laws means then to ascend to heaven:

> Blessed are they to whom it is given to resist with superior strength the weight that would pull them down, taught by the guiding lines of right instruction to leap upward from earth and earth-bound things into the ether and the revolving heavens . . . (*Spec.* 4:115).

Philo here indicates that the keeping of the dietary laws among the members of the Jewish *politeia* makes it possible for the Jews to realize their heavenly citizenship. Moreover, the animals with the parted hoof and the chewing of the cud symbolize the teaching aspect of the *politeia* founded by Moses, where a teacher teaches the pupil the principles and lore of wisdom and the distinction between the way of virtue and the way of vice (*Spec.* 4:105–08).

The specifics in connection with the practicing of these observances are hardly touched here, since Philo presents an interpretation of the dietary laws with gentiles in mind, just as was the case in the *Letter of Aristeas*.[24] The keeping of observances and their specific applications are at least to some extent presupposed, as can be seen from the fact that the refusal to eat swine's flesh was used as a test to force women to reveal whether they were Jewish or not (*Flac.* 95–96).

---

[24] See Hecht (1979–80) 112–14; Tcherikover (1958) 59–85.

Clubs and pagan worship

Philo's commentary *On Drunkenness* is founded on Gen 9:20–21, particularly on the words "And he [Noah] drank of the vine and was
drunk". In the treatise he presents Moses' view that drunkenness is
a symbol for foolishness or foolish talking, insensibility, greediness,
cheerfulness and nakedness. Foolishness or foolish talking occupies
Ebr. 11–153. Its chief cause is want or defiance of education. How
abhorrent this is to Moses is shown by the law in Deut 21 that the
parents of a rebellious and profligate son must bring him for judge-
ment before the elders. In *Ebr.* 14–15, 20–29 and 95 some specifics
can be traced as to participation in non-Jewish social clubs.[25] The
Scriptural reference is Deut 21:18–21 concerning the disobedient son
who does not listen to his father and mother (*Ebr.* 14). The accusations brought against the son are listed as "disobedience, contentiousness, paying of contributions and drunkenness" (*Ebr.* 15). Philo
applies the biblical reference to his own time. The "paying of contributions" (συμβολῶν εἰσφορά) means that the person joined a social
association or club. Religious activities always played a role at such
gatherings. Philo's criticism of persons who joined such clubs probably presupposes that some Jews did join. He argues that the lifestyle
in the club is characterized by gluttony and indulgence, so that by
paying their contributions they are actually mulcting themselves in
money, body and soul (*Ebr.* 20–22). The disobedient son made a
god of the body, worshipping the vanity most honored by the Egyptians, i.e. Apis, whose symbol is the golden bull of Exod 32. Philo
gives a vivid picture of this worship:

> Round it the frenzied worshippers make their dances and raise and
> join in the song, but that song was not the sweet wine-song of merry
> revellers as in a feast or banquet, but a veritable dirge, their own fune-
> ral chant, a chant as of men maddened by wine, who have loosened
> and destroyed the tone and vigor which nerved their souls (*Ebr.* 95).

The disobedient one learns from others, joins "the many" and also
consents to initiate evil himself, *Ebr.* 23–26.

From this it is seen that Philo ties drunkenness and the excessive
indulgence in food and the pagan god together as a worship of the

---

[25] See Borgen (1987) 227–28; concerning club life in Alexandria, see Borgen (1965)
124–25, with reference to Heinemann (1962) 431; Seland (1996).

body as god. Here as in *Leg. all.* 3:156 he calls such a life-style a be-haviour of "irregularity" (ἐκδιαί τησις) (*Ebr.* 21). Philo uses this term and the corresponding verb to mean acting against the Laws of Moses and to subvert the Jewish customs and abandon the old Jewish ways of communal life (*Somn.* 2:123; *Jos.* 254; *Mos.* 1:31, 241, 278, 298, 2:167, 270; *Spec.* 3:126; *Praem.* 98; *Flac.* 14 and 50). To Philo partici-pation in the religious meals in an association would most probably lead both to a breaking of the Jewish dietary laws and also at the same time to eating forbidden and idolatrous food.

Philo seems here to exclude the possibility that Jews could enter the social clubs of the non-Jews. He does not exclude this possibility completely, however, since in *Ebr.* 20 he says: "As for contributions and club subscriptions, when the object is to share the best of pos-sessions, prudence, such payments are praiseworthy and profitable". To Philo prudence, φρόνησις, means wisdom which guides and regu-lates human life in accordance with the divine Laws of Moses (*Praem.* 79–81; see also *Mos.* 1:25; 2:189, 216; *Spec.* 1:191–93, 277; 2:18, 62, 257–259; *Virt.* 180). So Philo is of the opinion that Jews may join non-Jewish social clubs and be permitted to keep their own customs and standards of behaviour. He does not specify how this could be done, however. As to the problem of the cultic aspects (sacrifices, etc.) in club activities, Philo does not specify how a Jew should behave in order to avoid taking part in idolatrous worship. Such specifica-tion is also lacking when he reports on experiences he has had when attending performances in the theater and the hippodrome (*Prob.* 26 and *Prov.* 58).

Tension and conflict

Philo did not only tell about the ascents of biblical persons as can be seen from an unexpected autobiographical paragraph in *On the Spe-cial Laws*, Book 3. In this book Philo is moving on to the exposition of laws which he organizes under the headings of the second table of the Ten Commandments. Before he begins this exposition, he reports on his own ascents in *Spec.* 3:1–6. In this opening section Philo tells about his own ascent to the heavenly bodies and his descent because of envy and cares connected with the (Jewish) *politeia* (*Spec.* 3:1–6). The section consists of two main parts: A) Philo's ascent to an ethe-real sphere, at a distance from the plagues of mortal life on earth,

Spec. 3:1–2. B) Philo descending to the cares of the *politeia*, and experiencing lower ascents while struggling with civil cares and turmoil.

In this passage, *Spec.* 3:1–6, Philo has a report on his own ascents as he experienced them in two different situations. In one situation he felt himself to be at a distance from earthly troubles, *Spec.* 3:1–2. In the other situation he was deeply involved in the cares and troubles of the Jewish *politeia* (3:3–6a).

Among the many questions which may be raised, one is of primary interest for the present discussion, namely the nature of the civil cares and their historical context.[26] It has been suggested that this descent because of envy refers to the pogrom against the Alexandrian Jews in A.D. 38 and Philo's role as head of the Jewish delegation which was sent to Rome. Several observations speak in favour of such an understanding. Of special importance are the many parallel points which exist between on the one hand *On the Special Laws*, Books 3–4, *On the Virtues* and *On Rewards and Punishments* and on the other hand *Against Flaccus* and *On the Embassy to Gaius*. These parallels will be discussed in the next chapter. The results of this comparative analysis may be indicated already at this point in beforehand.

In spite of the many agreements with *Against Flaccus* and *On the Embassy to Gaius* the reflections of tension and conflicts in *On the Special Laws* 3–4, *On the Virtues* and *On Rewards and Punishments* are not strong enough to prove that Philo in *Spec.* 3:3 has the pogrom under Gaius Caligula in mind.[27] More probably these features suggest that Philo in *Spec.* 3:3, etc. refers to situations which took place at an earlier time, and probably were preludes to these critical events of A.D. 38–41. In spite of the privileges granted the Jews by Augustus and Tiberius, the Alexandrian Jewish community had a struggle for full civil rights during the Roman period, and they lived in tension in between the native Egyptians and the Greek full citizens of the city.[28] The circumstance that there was no direct persecution or oppression in respect of the Jews of Alexandria during the reign of Tiberius, is therefore no argument for not seeing that period as background for *Spec.* 3:1–6, as maintained by Morris.[29]

---

[26] *PAPM* 25:52–59.
[27] So also Cohn (1899) 433ff. and Morris (1987) 3:2, 844.
[28] See Tcherikover (1963) 1–32.
[29] Morris (1987) 3:2, 843–44. See the same reference for Morris' comments upon the views of E.R. Goodenough and A. Moses.

Some observations support the view that Philo's involvements with troublesome civil matters in *Spec.* 3:1–6 reflects the period prior to this pogrom in A.D. 38. First, he is here reporting on his experiences over a period of time during which he, struggling in the ocean of civil cares and turmoil, nevertheless managed several times to lift his head above the water. Second, in reviewing Pentateuchal history in *Virt.* 187–227 on whether nobility is to be based on family relationship or on a virtuous life, Philo clearly applies his argument to a situation of enmity between Jews and non-Jews. He writes in *Virt.* 226: ". . . enemies of the Jewish nation (τὸ τῶν Ἰουδαίων ἔθνος) . . ., because they give their compatriots licence to put their trust in the virtue of their ancestors and despise the thought of living a sound and steadfast life". Earlier in § 213 he has stated that polytheism is evidence for the absence of nobility: "What could be more grievous or more capable of proving the total absence of nobility in the soul than this, that its knowledge of the many, the secondary, the created, only leads it to ignore the One, the Primal, the Uncreated and Maker of all. . . ." Accordingly, the polytheists can gain nobility and a virtuous life by becoming proselytes like Abraham, and by joining the Jewish *politeia* (§§ 212–19).

The situation reflected in this discussion of nobility is one of tension and enmity in which Jews made claims of superiority from their ancestry, and non-Jews, correspondingly, claimed superiority due to their ancestry. Philo then stressed that a virtuous life was the criterion of nobility, and that polytheists may meet this criterion by becoming proselytes, like Abraham, and by joining the Jewish community. Thus *Virt.* 187–227 reflects a situation of rivalry and tension between Jews and non-Jews, but not cruel events such as happened in the pogrom of A.D. 38.

Thirdly, there are examples of ill-treatments of Jews. Philo reports a case where a Jew and his family were ill-treated by a tax-collector (*Spec.* 3:159–66). In *Spec.* 3:153 he begins his exposition of Deut 24:16, that "fathers should not die for their sons nor sons for their parents, but each person who has committed deeds worthy of death should suffer it alone and in his own person". In § 158 Philo sharply criticises those who openly threaten to inflict the most grievous sufferings on one set of persons in substitution for another under the pretext of their friendship, or kinship, or partnership, or some similar connection with the culprits.

Philo then reports on a case which happened in the Jewish community (παρ' ἡμῖν), §§ 159–62:

> An example of this was given a little time ago in our own district by a person who was appointed to serve as a collector of taxes. When some of his debtors whose default was due to poverty took flight in fear of the fatal consequences of his vengeance, he carried off by force their womenfolk and children and parents and their other relatives and beat and subjected them to every kind of outrage and contumely in order to make them either tell him the whereabouts of the fugitive or discharge his debt themselves. As they could do neither, the first for want of knowledge, nor the second because they were as penniless as the fugitive, he continued this treatment until while wringing their bodies with racks and instruments of torture he finally dispatched them by newly invented methods of execution. He filled a large basket with sand and having hung this enormous weight by ropes round their necks set them in the middle of the market-place in the open air, in order that while they themselves sank under the cruel stress of the accumulated punishments, the wind, the sun, the shame of being seen by the passers-by and the weight suspended on them, the spectators of their punishments might suffer by anticipation ... and when there were no kinsmen left, the maltreatment was passed on to their neighbours and sometimes even to villages and cities which quickly became desolate and stripped of their inhabitants who left their homes and dispersed to places where they expected to remain unobserved.

Not only uncivilized persons do this, but, according to Philo, in the past there were legislators themselves who acted in this way to the greatest injustice (*Spec.* 3:166).[30] Moses, "our legislator", observing the errors current among other nations regarded them with aversion as ruinous to the best *politeia* (§§ 167–68).

An example from the *Allegorical Commentary* also show the precarious situation of the Jews in Alexandria. In *Somn.* 2:110–54 Philo interprets Joseph's dream that the sun, moon and stars bowed down to him (Gen 37:9–11). He explains that the dream from one point of view describes the arrogance of those who regard themselves as superior not only to men but to nature. As one example of such a leader of vainglory Philo tells the story of a recent governor over Egypt who exalted himself to such an extent that he attempted to disturb the ancestral customs of the Jews and tried to interfere with their celebration of the Sabbath (*Somn.* 2:123ff.):

---

[30] Concerning the problem of finding definitive evidence for such a law put into practice, see *PLCL* 7:639–40.

Not long ago I knew of one of the ruling class who when he had Egypt in his charge and under his authority purposed to disturb our customs and especially to do away with the laws of the Seventh Day which we regard with most reverence and awe. He tried to compel men to do service to him on it and perform other actions which contravene our established custom, thinking that if he could destroy the ancestral rule of the Sabbath it would lead the way to irregularity in all other matters, and a general backsliding. . . .

After this survey of various forms of interactions, tensions and conflict between the Jews and their surroundings reflected in *On the Special Laws, On the Virtues*, and *On Rewards and Punishments*, and also in *On the Dreams*, Philo's accounts and interpretations of the pogrom under Emperor Gaius Caligula are to be examined. The emphasis will be placed on Philo's interpretation and how he applies scriptural and expository ideas to the events.

CHAPTER TEN

THE CONFLICT

Introduction

The situation of tension examined in the preceding chapter, grew into conflict in A.D. 38 at the time when Flaccus was governor and Gaius Caligula emperor. The conflict resulted in a cruel pogrom.

The aim of the present study of *On the Embassy to Gaius* and *Against Flaccus* is not to discuss chronological questions and the historical events as such, but to analyse the way in which the Laws of Moses played a role in the conflict and examine points of contact with Philo's *Exposition of the Laws*.[1]

In such an investigation it is important to remember the fact that the Jewish Laws did not only provide ideas and guidelines for a person's way of life. They were woven into the very fabric of Jewish society and institutions.[2] Thus, one might speak about the practised Laws. B. Gerhardsson clarifies the varied settings of the Torah within the Jewish community. He sees the Laws as part of the Jews' sacred authoritative tradition and teaching in its entirety. He distinguishes between 1) verbal tradition in written and oral forms, and

> 2) behavioural tradition. 'The life in the Torah' was eminently an inherited, characteristic way of life, conscious patterns for the way in which the people and different groups and individuals should live: rites, customs, ethos, halacha. Here we meet Torah as practice. 3) Institutional tradition. The faithful Jews also maintained a rich inheritance of institutions and establishments, social structures, hierarchy, official divisions of role and more of the same. Even this was ordered by God; this was Torah as institution. 4) Material tradition. The Torah-tradition finally included sacred localities, clothes, tools and other outward things: the Temple, the synagogues, scrolls, phylacteries, tassels on cloaks etc.,

---

[1] See the brief surveys in Borgen (1987) 48–49; Borgen (1984) 250–51; Borgen (1984A) 120–21; cf. Borgen (1996) 196–97. Concerning historical and chronological questions, see Smallwood (1970) 14–50.

[2] Borgen (1976) 67–75.

things of importance for life in the Torah. If the expression can be allowed, I would like to call it 'Torah as things'.[3]

The Laws were at work in the sacrificial rites in the Temple, in the observance of the cultic calender and the festivals, in the expectation that people conform to boundary markers between Jews and gentiles, in the dietary laws, the rite of circumcision etc. Moreover, the legal system functioned in the interplay between conventions, power dynamics and politics, and scriptural norms and texts. Insofar as the Jews lived within the confine of the Roman empire, their practice of the Laws of Moses had to stay within the limits set by the Roman authorities.

Seen within this perspective, the conflict in Alexandria and Jerusalem was a struggle for the way in which the Laws of Moses should be interpreted and practised in society, as civil rights, a way of life and as institutional life centered around the synagogues and the Temple. Philo's two treatises *Against Flaccus* and *On the Embassy to Gaius* give ample support for this understanding: the Alexandrian Jews experienced an attack on their Laws, their synagogues, their Temple and their ancestral customs. References to these points are found all through these two treatises, as in *Flac.* 41, 47, 50, 53 and *Legat.* 6–7, 115, 117, 152–53, 156–57, 161, 170, 200, 210, 232, 236, 240, 249, 256. Examples are:

> He [Flaccus] knew that both Alexandria and the whole of Egypt had two kinds of inhabitants, us and them, and that there were no less than a million Jews resident in Alexandria and the country from the slope into Lydia to the boundaries of Ethiopia; also that this was an attack against them all, and that ancestral customs (ἔθη πάτρια) cannot be disturbed without harm, yet he disregarded all these facts and permitted the installation of the images.... (*Flac.* 43)
>
> ...Gaius had no right to be likened to any of the gods or demi-gods.... For he looked with disfavour on the Jews alone because they alone opposed him on principle, trained as they were we may say even from the cradle, by parents and tutors and instructors and by the far higher authority of the sacred laws and also the unwritten customs (ἐξ ... τῶν ἱερῶν νόμων καὶ ἔτι τῶν ἀγράφων ἐθῶν), to acknowledge one God who is the Father and Maker of the world. (*Legat.* 114–15). Was our temple the first to accept sacrifices in behalf of Gaius' reign only that it should be the first or even the only one to be robbed of its ancestral tradition of worship (ἵνα ... ἀφαιρεθῇ τῆς θρησκείας τὸ πάτριον)? (*Legat.* 232).

---

[3] Gerhardsson (1990) 507–08; Borgen (1996A) 196–97.

> When we are dead let the prescript [i.e. Gaius' order that a statue of himself as a god was to be erected in the Temple] be carried out; not God himself could blame us who had a twofold motive, respectful fear of the emperor and loyalty to the consecrated laws (. . . τῆς πρὸς τοὺς καθωσιωμένους νόμους ἀποδοχῆς) (*Legat.* 236).

These and other formulations demonstrate that the treatises *Against Flaccus* and *On the Embassy to Gaius* report on conflicting views on the role of the Laws of Moses in society and conflicting views on the interpretations of these Laws in practice.

In *On the Embassy to Gaius* and *Against Flaccus* Pentateuchal laws, ideas and principles – as understood by Philo – are used as interpretative keys. The historical events and persons are recorded by Philo as an eyewitness, and thus the treatises are at the same time important historical sources.

Philo has similarly applied Pentateuchal principles to historical events and persons already in his various expositions on the Laws. In the commentary *On the Unchangeableness of God* Philo interprets Gen 6:4–12 about the increasing wickedness upon earth and about Noah who was well pleasing to God. In *Immut.* 144–80 there is a direct paraphrasing and systematic exposition of LXXNum 20:17–20 which is cited in *Immut.* 145:

> We will pass by thy land. We will not go through the cornfields nor through the vineyards. We will not drink the water of any well of thine. We will journey by the king's way. We will not turn aside to the right or the left, till we have passed thy boundaries.
>
> But Edom answers, saying, "Thou shalt not pass through me, else I will come out in war to meet thee". And the sons of Israel say to him, "We will pass through the mountain country. But if I and my cattle drink of thy water, I will give thee value. But the matter is nothing (τὸ πρᾶγμα οὐδέν), we will pass along the mountain country".

Interpreting the words "matter" (τὸ πρᾶγμα) and "nothing" (οὐδέν) in LXXNum 20:17–20 Philo drew the conclusion that mortal matters have no real being. They swing suspended, and fortunes change. Examples are the regions and nations which are tossed up and down, like Greece, Macedonia, Persia, Parthia, Egypt, Ethiopia, Carthage, Libya and Pontus, Europe and Asia (§§ 172–78).

Above in the preceding chapter points from Philo's interpretation of the dream of Joseph, Gen 37:9–11, cited in *Somn.* 2:111, were mentioned. In this dream the sun, moon and stars bowed down for Joseph. It was a dream about human arrogance, according to Philo.

Philo lists in §§ 117–22 Xerxes and the Germans as examples of persons who exalt themselves above men and the world of nature. Xerxes was punished by insanity, and the Germans deserve detestation and ridicule. Another example was the governor over Egypt referred to earlier. He attempted to disturb the ancestral customs of the Jews and tried to interfere with their celebration of the Sabbath, *Somn.* 2:123ff. Philo understands the governor's action in principle to mean that he went beyond the limits of a human being:

> ... he will ... scarce refrain from demanding that honour and homage be paid by the things of heaven to the things of earth, and to himself more abundantly inasmuch as being a man he conceives himself to have been made superior to other living creatures (*Somn.* 2:132).

In the *Exposition of the Laws of Moses*, examples of interpreted history are also given in *Jos.* 131–36. After referring to Joseph's interpretation of the dreams of the chief butler, the chief baker and the king (§§ 80–124 based on Gen 40:5–46) Philo states that all life is a dream and the task of a true statesman is to discover the truths which lie behind this dream (§ 125). Life passes by like a dream. Likewise the dream-like uncertainty of external goods are exemplified by the fates of the tyrant of Sicily, Dionysius, Croesus, the king of Lydia, by nations, such as Egypt, Macedonia, Persia and Parthia, the royal house of the Ptolemies, and the Successors of Alexander.

In *On the Embassy to Gaius* and *Against Flaccus* the same approach is followed, in such a way that the Pentateuchal ideas and principles at work in Jewish community life and interpreted by Philo, are used as interpretative keys.

Jewish virtues and Egyptian evil:
On the Virtues, *that is*, On the Embassy to Gaius

Before *On the Embassy to Gaius* is analysed, a brief survey of the content should be given. In *Legat.* 1–7 the central party in the conflict is characterized. This party is the Jewish nation, "who sees God" and is under His providential care. The other party is the great Emperor Gaius (*Legat.* 8–119), who had become an evil despot and claimed to be god (*Legat.* 113). In Gaius' inner circle Egyptians in Alexandria played a central role (*Legat.* 120–71). Moreover, in Rome the Jewish embassy negotiated with Gaius' Egyptian adviser and met with the Emperor (*Legat.* 172–83/84). The crisis in Palestine occupies then a large section of the treatise, *Legat.* 184–348. Finally, the embassy met with Gaius again, *Legat.* 349–72. The treatise breaks off with the promise of the Palinode, *Legat.* 373. As seen from this outline, the actual report on the embassy only covers a small part of the book, mainly §§ 172–83/84 and 349–72.

Since *On the Embassy to Gaius* tells about events which, according to Philo, happened to the Jewish nation and not just to one individual person (*Legat.* 370–71), this treatise gives decisive support to our understanding that Philo's works are to a large extent to be seen within the context of the relationship between the Jewish community and the gentiles.

F.H. Colson finds the title *On the Virtues* to be mysterious. Eusebius, *Historia Ecclesiastica* II:18, 8, misunderstood the title and thought that Philo gave the treatise this heading 'in mockery and irony'. Most scholars do not think that this interpretation is correct.[4] Scholars such as H. Box and others suggest that the concept of 'virtue' here refers to the virtues of God, the manifestation of God's power in the defence of His people. His providence works in history (*Legat.* 220, 336–37). Moreover, Philo may speak of the virtues of God, ἀρεταὶ θεοῦ, even coupled with the powers, δυνάμεις (*Contempl.* 26; *Somn.* 1:256; *Mos.* 2:239). Old Testament basis for this view is seen in Isa 42:8 and 12; 43:21; 63:7, etc.[5]

F.H. Colson and F.W. Kohnke hesitate to accept this view, since the basis in the book itself for this understanding is weak, and it is difficult to see why the important word θεοῦ is not found in the title. Moreover, the phrase θεῖαι ἀρεταί refers to God's attributes, not to His interventions in history.[6]

On this background the conclusion is that the title is *On the Virtues*, and it should basically be understood in the same way as the term 'virtue' in Philo's expository treatise called *On the Virtues*. The key to the interpretation is then found in the understanding of the Jewish Laws expressed in *Legat.* 195–96: "The truly noble are always hopeful, and the laws create good hopes for those who take more than a mere sip of their study. Perhaps these things are sent to try the present generation, to test the state of their virtue (ἀρετή) and whether they [the present generation] are schooled (πεπαίδευται) to bear dire misfortunes with a resolution which is fortified by reason and does not

---

[4] See Smallwood (1970) 39.
[5] Box (1939) XXXVIII; Smallwood (1970) 39–40 and 272.
[6] *PLCL* 10: XIV–XVI; *PCH* 7:167.

collapse (προκαταπίπτουσα) at once". The virtues of the Jews were made manifest in the way their training in the Laws gave them courage to stand up even against the Emperor Gaius, and to persuade Petronius to champion their cause (*Legat.* 192–96, 233–38, 327–29, 369).[7]

The idea here is the same as that in another expository treatise, *On Rewards and Punishments*. In *Praem.* 4–5 Philo states that those who have been schooled by Moses are asked to make a practical exhibit of what they have learned (ἐπαιδεύθησαν). . . . "Then it was found that the true athletes of virtue did not disappoint the high hopes of the laws which had trained them, but the unmanly whose souls were degenerate through inbred weakness . . . collapsed (προκαταπίπτοντες). . . ." In both passages the idea is that those trained in the laws of Moses are tested whether they can take the hardships of life on the basis of the standards they have learned and not to collapse. As can be seen, two of the words quoted are the same both places.

The conclusion is that the treatises *On the Virtues* and *On Rewards and Punishments* refer to persons of virtue or vice in events in the biblical past and picture the lives of virtue and vice in the (eschatological) future, while *On the Virtues: On the Embassy to Gaius* tells about the effect of the Laws in the present enabling the Jews in the present to pass the test of the life of virtue in critical events. Correspondingly, the treatise *Against Flaccus* deals primarily with punishment of the vicious person in the present. Thus Philo in these treatises show that the principles of the Laws of Moses were at work in the passion story of the Jews in A.D. 38–41.

In the preceding chapter of the present study it was suggested that *On the Virtues: On the Embassy to Gaius* is a treatise to be seen together with the treatises *On the Virtues* and *On Rewards and Punishments*, and also with the treatises *On the Special Laws* 3–4, which Philo wrote after his ascent to heaven was interrupted when he was drawn into the troubles in the *politeia* (*Spec.* 3:1–6). Thus, when Philo in *Spec.* 3:3 speaks of a great sea of cares in the *politeia*, this indicates that he had to face a serious and major problem situation. The suggestion was made that *On the Special Laws*, Book 3, and also the subsequent treatises, Book 4, *On the Virtues* and *On Rewards and Punishments*, probably were written in a situation of tension and conflict in the Jewish community of Alexandria, possibly in the trying period before the pogrom in A.D. 38.

[7] *PLCL* 10: XIV–XVI; Smallwood (1970) 39–40; *PCH* 7:167–68.

Some of the points of agreement should be listed to show that in their sufferings the Jews gave evidence for a life in accordance with the Laws of Moses, as interpreted by Philo in the *Exposition*. Both in *On the Special Laws* 3 and in *On the Embassy to Gaius* Philo uses the metaphor of being pulled down into turbulent streams of water: "... the great sea ... in which I am swept away ... though submerged I am not sucked down into the depths ..." (*Spec.* 3:3 and 6); "... we were able to lift our head above water. ... Waterlogged by such considerations we were dragged down and submerged into the depths ..." (*Legat.* 370 and 372). The Emperor Gaius' claim to be god fits the interpretation of Num 15:30 ("... the person who does anything with a high hand ... reviles the Lord") in *Virt.* 171-74. Here it is said that the arrogant sinner who oversteps human nature by holding himself wholly divine (cf. *Legat.* 75) will have God as accuser and revenger. It may refer in general to any ruler who "exalts himself not only above men, but above the world of nature". Elsewhere Philo gives Xerxes as an example, *Somn.* 115-20.

Philo in *Legat.* 122 (cf. § 363) tells about the Alexandrians pillaging the Jews. He says that they jeered and reviled (κατακερτομοῦντες καὶ ἐπιχλευάζοντες) them. The same Greek term is used by him in *Praem.* 169 to characterize the attitude and action of the enemies who cursed and reviled the Jews, before the eschatological reversal will take place. Philo alludes in *Praem.* 169 to LXXDeut 30:7: "And the Lord your God will put these curses upon your enemies, and upon those that hate you, who have persecuted you". The enemies rejoiced in the misfortunes of the nation (*Legat.* 137 and 353f.), as also said in *Praem.* 169). The term lamentation (ὀλοφύρσις) is used in *Praem.* 171 and the verb lament (ὀλοφύρομαι) occurs in *Legat.* 197 and 225.

The characterization of the Jewish nation in *Legat.* 3-7 is in accordance with ideas found in *On the Special Laws*, Books 3 and 4, *On the Virtues* and *On Rewards and Punishments* and also to some degree elsewhere in Philo's expositions. Some of the common phraseology is:

1   "the Father and King of the Universe and the cause of all things (πάντων αἴτιον) has taken for His portion" (προσκεκλήρωται), *Legat.* 3, and compare *Spec.* 4:180: "the Ruler of the Universe who has taken it for His portion" (προσκεκλήρωται) and *Virt.* 34: "the Hebrews ... who having been made the portion (προσκεκληρωμένοι) of the Maker and Father of the Universe ... pay reverence ... to the supreme and

primal cause" (αἴτιον). The phrase the suppliants' race (τὸ ἱκετικὸν γένος), *Legat.* 3, has a parallel in the characterization of Jacob as suppliant (ἱκέτης), *Praem.* 44.

2   The term Israel, interpreted as "seeing God" (ὁρῶν θεόν), *Legat.* 4, is one of Philo's commonly used etymological interpretations of the designation Israel.[8] In *Praem.* 36ff. Philo tells that the name Israel, meaning "he that sees God", was given to Jacob.

3   the thought in *Legat.* 5 of "souls who have been schooled to soar above (ὑπερκύπτω) all created things..." is similar to that in *Praem.* 30 of "he to whom it is given to soar above (ὑπερκύπτω) not only material... things...."

4   The ideas of powers, and especially the Creative Power and the Ruling Power mentioned in *Legat.* 6 are frequently mentioned by Philo, as for example in *Plant.* 86 and *Abr.* 124.[9]

5   The question of God's providential care for men, and in particular for the Jewish nation, is a central theme in Philo's works (*Legat.* 3; *Virt.* 215–16 and *Praem.* 42; 104; cf. *Spec.* 4:180).

The conclusion is: The treatise *On the Virtues: On the Embassy to Gaius* shows how the Jews were tested in their life by the misfortunes which happened to them during the pogrom A.D. 38–41. In this way they in the present gave evidence for a life in accordance with the virtues formulated in the Laws of Moses, as they were called to do in the treatises *On the Virtues, On Rewards and Punishment,* and *Spec.* 4:132–238. The several similarities between these treatises and the treatise *On the Virtues: On the Embassy to Gaius* support this understanding.

On this basis, Philo's interpretation of the conflict in *On the Embassy* should be sketched. As already stated, Philo and the Alexandrian embassy in Rome understood themselves to carry responsibility for the whole Jewish nation, a nation who as a whole was involved in a world-wide encounter with the enemy, *Legat.* 193–94.[10] The largest

---

[8] See Borgen (1965) 115–18; Delling (1984) 27–41. Cf. Birnbaum (1993) 54–69; Birnbaum (1992).

[9] See Wolfson (1948) 1:217–94, especially pp. 224–25; 325ff.; 2:138–49.

[10] Smallwood (1970) 258, finds it puzzling that Philo in *Legat.* 194 refers to the universal *politeia* (ἡ καθολικώτερα πολιτεία) of the Jews, since there was no single and universal *politeia* embracing all the Jews in the empire. Smallwood has overlooked that the term may be used about the commonwealth of Moses in general, such as in *Spec.* 1:51, etc. Thus from the view point of Philo, the Jews were one commonwealth, one *politeia*, with varying degrees of civil and political rights at the various places.

parts of the treatise tell about the Roman emperors Gaius, Augustus and Tiberius (*Legat.* 22–113, 143–58 and 309–18), and about the conflict in Jerusalem and Palestine where the King of the Jews, Agrippa, showed loyalty to the Laws, the Temple and to God's people (*Legat.* 184–348). This Jewish nation largely faced two different forces in the gentile world, the Egyptian evil force, based on the polytheistic worship of ferocious wild beasts as gods, and the Greek and Hellenizing force which accepted the rights of the Jewish monotheists and even positively served as tools of the One God.

The dualism between the Jews and the Egyptians gives the interpretative category for understanding the conflict in Alexandria and the conflict with Gaius Caligula. The evil Egyptians operated in the attack on the Jews in Alexandria, as seen in *Legat.* 162–66:

> § 162: But Gaius grew beside himself with vanity, not only saying but thinking that he was God. He then found among the Greeks or the outside world no people fitted better than the Alexandrians to confirm the unmeasured passion which craves for more than is natural to mankind. For the Alexandrians are adepts at flattery and imposture and hypocrisy, ready enough with fawning words but causing universal disaster with their loose and unbridled lips. § 163: How much reverence is paid by them to the title of God is shown by their having allowed it to be shared by the indigenous ibises and venomous snakes and many other ferocious wild beasts. It naturally followed that by this unrestricted use of names appertaining to God, while they deceived the littlewits who do not see through Egyptian godlessness (atheism), they stand condemned by those who understand their great folly or rather impiety. § 164: Failing to understand this Gaius supposed that he was really regarded by the Alexandrians as a god, since they incessantly used plainly and without any indirection terms which other people employ when speaking of God.

Also in Rome the Egyptians were active, and they were in majority among Gaius' domestics:
Legat. 166:

> The majority of these [Gaius' domestics] were Egyptians, a seed bed of evil in whose souls both the venom and the temper of the native crocodiles and asps were reproduced. The one who played the part of chorus leader to the whole Egyptian troupe was Helicon, an abominable execrable slave. . . .

Helicon turned Gaius against the Jews. Philo tells that he had enough material. He had right from his cradle in Egypt been taught anti-Jewish traditions, *Legat.* 170.[11]

The conflict between the Jews and the Egyptians was a dualism of principle. It was a sharp form of dualism between the Jews worshipping the one true God and the Egyptians being atheists in their worship of the many animal gods. This conflict is spelled out on a principle level in Philo's rewriting of biblical material under the first and second commandments of the Decalogue in *Dec.* 52, 58, 65–66 and 76–81.

Since "the Egyptian character is atheistical in its preference for earth above heaven, for the things which live on the ground above those that dwell on high, and the body above the soul" (*Fug.* 180), the dualism between Jews and Egyptians is at the same time a theological and cosmic dualism. Thus it is a dualism between the people whose "vision has soared above all created things" (*Legat.* 5) and the Egyptians who worship created beings and even put the world upside down by preferring earth above heaven. Gaius' claim to be worshipped as god belongs also to this earthly and atheistical form of religion. In this way the Alexandrian Greeks as well as Gaius are to be ranked among the Egyptians. It is therefore inadequate when E.M. Smallwood in her comments on *Legat.* 166 says that Philo there uses the term "Egyptians" contemptuously to denote people who were in fact Greeks. To Philo the term Egyptians here expresses a basic theological dualism. This interpretation was made all the more easy by the fact that Egyptian religious traditions and practice were mixed into the syncretism of the Alexandrian Greeks.[12]

The evil Egyptian enemy, with whom the Emperor Gaius Caligula sided, attacked the Jewish nation, the people of God. But there was a third force at work in the pagan world, namely those who recognized the rights of the Jews and in different degrees followed values which coincided with ideals and virtues in the Laws of Moses. On this basis Philo writes an encomium of the Emperor Augustus, so that his scornful description of the Emperor Caligula largely is a contrasting characterization. In contrast to Gaius' Egyptian character Augustus was a promoter of Greek culture: he "enlarged Hellas

---

[11] See the chapter above on tension and influence and the chapter on historical survey. See also Smallwood (1970) 247–48.

[12] Smallwood (1970) ad loc.; *PAPM* 32:45–46, 165, n. 6, 187.

by many a new Hellas and hellenized the outside world in its most
important regions" (*Legat.* 147). He recognized the rights of the Jews
to worship and live in accordance with their ancestral laws and customs (§§ 153–61), and he adorned the Jerusalem Temple and ordered
that continuous sacrifices should be carried out every day at his own
expense as a tribute to the most high God (§ 157). As for himself, he
never wished anyone to address him as a god (§ 154).

In his encomium of Augustus Philo employs a phraseology which
is similar to formulations used by him in his various expository treatises. These parallels even indicate that Augustus was a tool used by
the One God. Augustus led disorder into order (ὁ τὴν ἀταξίαν εἰς
τάξιν ἀγαγών), *Legat.* 147, a phrase which Philo elsewhere applies to
God, especially in the creation, and of the work of the good ruler
(see *Plant.* 3; *Spec.* 4:187, 210). Augustus was the guardian of peace
(ὁ εἰρηνοφύλαξ) (*Legat.* 147). Augustus seems here to be understood
as God's instrument, because God is the one who brings peace and
is the guardian of peace, according to Philo (*Heres* 206; *Dec.* 178;
Spec. 2:192). Augustus is one who gave each man his due (*Legat.* 147),
a principle which is in accordance with the Laws of Moses (*Spec.* 4:57).
Augustus distributed his favours (αἱ χάριται) without stint to be common property (*Legat.* 147), which also is what God does (*Opif.* 23;
Spec. 4:22; *Praem.* 101). Augustus' generous rule may even here point
to the eschatological time, when God's gifts (αἱ χάριται) will be
received abundantly (*Praem.* 168). Finally, Augustus was the great benefactor (εὐεργέτης) (*Legat.* 148). The same term is used in *Flac.* 74,
where Philo even calls Augustus "the saviour and benefactor Augustus".
Again he uses a terminology that elsewhere frequently refers to God
(*Spec.* 1:209; *Sobr* 55; *Legat.* 118). In his study on the encomium of
Augustus (*Legat.* 143–47) G. Delling shows that Philo has composed
the section by combining "Jewish" features with terminology commonly used in such praises of rulers.[13]

Philo interprets the conflict in Palestine along the same lines. Besides
Gaius the adversaries of the Jews were Capito, the collector of revenue
in Judaea, who cherished a spite against the population (*Legat.* 199),[14]
persons of alien races, intruders for mischief who lived in Jamnia,
where the Jews were in the majority (*Legat.* 200), and in Rome again

---

[13] See Delling (1972) 171–192.
[14] It is hardly correct that Capito was collector of revenue in Judaea. He was
rather in charge of imperial properties. See Smallwood (1970) 261.

the Egyptian Helicon, and together with him one Apelles who came from Ascalon (*Legat.* 203–05). "So then Helicon, scorpion in form of a slave, vented his Egyptian venom on the Jews and so too Apelles with the venom of Ascalon. For that was the place he came from, and the Ascalonites have a truceless and irreconcilable hostility to the Jewish inhabitants of the Holy Land on whose borders they live" (*Legat.* 205).

Emphasizing the fundamental importance of the Laws of Moses, Philo outlines the policy of the Jewish nation in this way:

> For all men guard their own customs, but this is especially true of the Jewish nation. Holding that the laws are oracles vouchsafed by God and having been trained in this doctrine from their earliest years, they carry the likeness of the commandments enshrined in their souls. Then as they contemplate their forms thus clearly represented they always think of them with awe. And those of other races who pay homage to them they welcome no less than their own countrymen, while those who either break them down or mock at them they hate as their bitterest foes (*Legat.* 210–11).

Here Philo indicates that among the pagans there are persons who are symphathizers of the Jews and their laws, and others who mock and attack them. Among this positive group of pagans between the Jews and their adversaries, Philo includes Petronius, the Roman legate to Syria[15] who himself appears to have acquired some rudiments of Jewish philosophy and religion (*Legat.* 245).

To sum up: In Alexandria, Palestine and other places the Jewish nation, who belonged to the One God above all of creation, was attacked by the Egyptians who were atheists and worshipped things on earth which they preferred to the high heavenly spheres and the beyond. The Alexandrians, Gaius, pagans in Jamnia and Ascalon followed this evil Egyptian idolatry by worshipping the Emperor as god and attempting to force the Jews to do the same.

In contrast to this Egyptian evil there were persons in the middle who recognized the rights of the Jews to live in accordance with their ancestral customs and who in various ways and in varying degree showed respect for the divine Laws of the Jews, and were even positively influenced by them or followed principles and virtues which coincided with them. Among these Philo included the emperor Augustus and the legate Petronius.

---

[15] See the chapter entitled "Reaching Out and Coming In".

In this struggle the Jewish nation, who was God's own portion, was under His providential care in spite of all misfortunes and sufferings. They were in this way put to the test whether they would collapse or live up to the virtues revealed in the Laws of Moses and base their hopes on these Laws and the God to whom they belong. In this way the treatise rightly carries the title *On the Virtues* and is to be seen as a contemporary and applied parallel to Philo's other treatise named *On the Virtues*.

Justice and punishment: Against Flaccus

Also for the treatise *Against Flaccus* the Pentateuchal principles and practices, as interpreted by Philo, serve as interpretative key. The main point of this treatise shows special kinship to Philo's book *On Rewards and Punishments*, and it may be characterized as *Against Flaccus*, or *On Punishment*.

The content of the book may be summarized in this way:
A characterization of Flaccus, his greatness as governor and his endangered position after the death of Tiberius and the accession of Gaius in A.D. 37 is given in *Flac.* 1–15. Then the account of the persecutions of the Alexandrian Jews follows, *Flac.* 16–96. Flaccus lost control and was subject to pressures from the sedetious Egyptians (*Flac.* 17–24). The ancient and innate hostility of the Egyptians against the Jews led to envious resentment against the fact that a Jew, Agrippa, had been made a king. They stirred up Flaccus and made him as envious as themselves. He did not interfere when the Egyptians insulted the Jewish King Agrippa when he passed through Alexandria on his journey home (*Flac.* 25–40). They asked for images of the Emperor Gaius to be installed in the synagogues. Flaccus worked together with the Egyptian mob and attempted to fill the whole world with hatred against the Jews (*Flac.* 41–52). Flaccus denounced the Jews as foreigners and aliens (*Flac.* 53–54). He permitted the mob to plunder the houses of the Jews, and a pogrom followed, including the attack on the Jewish council of elders (*Flac.* 55–85). The Jews were accused for having stocks of arms. Their houses were searched, but no arms were found. The Jewish women were ill-treated (*Flac.* 86–96).

The reversal is presented in *Flac.* 97–191: Flaccus is punished corresponding to his misdeeds against the people under God's care, the Jewish nation. Flaccus had suppressed the resolution of congratulation passed by the Jewish council upon Gaius' accession to the throne. King Agrippa rectified the matter by passing on the resolution to Rome, placing the blame on Flaccus. Divine justice began then to hit Flaccus, and the reversal began (*Flac.* 97–103). Flaccus is arrested, the Jews offer thanks to God for having taken pity on His people (*Flac.* 98–124): "At this point justice (δίκη), the champion and defender of the wronged, the avenger of unholy men and deeds, began to enter the lists against him" (*Flac.* 104). The punishments of Flaccus correspond to his crimes against God's people. Flaccus' fate shows that God's help to the nation of the Jews was not withdrawn (*Flac.* 125–91).

There are significant similarities between features in this treatise and points in other writings of Philo, especially in *On the Special Laws*, Books 3 and 4, *On the Virtues* and *On Rewards and Punishments*. Flaccus was filled with windy pride (μέγα πνέοντα) (*Flac.* 124), just as said in *Virt.* 171 about the person who provokes God. In *Virt.* 171 Philo cites Num 15:30: "Whosoever sets his hand to do anything with presumptuousness provokes God".

The Jews suffered cruelty (*Flac.* 59–66) as is also said in *Praem.* 171. In the treatise *Against Flaccus*, just as in *On the Embassy to Gaius*, the adversaries are on the one hand the Jews as God's people in Alexandria and all over the world and on the other hand the evil and envious Egyptians who had an ancient and innate hostility to the Jews (*Flac.* 17ff. and 29ff.; 121–24, etc.). Although Philo on the level of civil rights draws a distinction between the Greek Alexandrians and the Egyptians (*Flac.* 78–80), there is in Alexandria and Egypt only one basic distinction, the distinction between Jews and the others, "us and them" (*Flac.* 43).

Within the non-Jewish side the Egyptians represent the evil enmity against God and His people, an enmity which manifested itself through the acts of the Alexandrian mob and the leaders of the gymnasium and the clubs and spread to the governor Flaccus and throughout the whole world. Thus, the dualistic force is characterized as Egyptian, here centered around the idea of envy and hostility against the Jews: envy is part of the Egyptian nature (*Flac.* 29).[16] "Envy" (φθόνος) is one of the key terms which characterizes the evil nature

---

[16] Here, as well as in *On the Embassy to Gaius*, it is inadequate to state that Philo calls the anti-Jewish inhabitants of Alexandria Egyptians to insult them, as said by Box (1939) 79. To Philo Egyptians represent the evil within a "theologically" understood dualism, and the concept includes the evil Egyptians and others who show enmity against God and His people.

of the Egyptians (*Flac.* 29–30), and "envy" was the reason that Philo
had to interrupt his ascent and journey in the heavenly sphere
and enter into the turbulent waters of cares in the *politeia* (*Spec.* 3:3).
"Envy" was also seen by Philo as that which hampered the positive
impact made by the law-abiding Jews upon their pagan surroundings (*Mos.* 2:27).

According to *Flac.* 121 the Alexandrian Jews offer thanks to God
because he has shown pity and compassion upon them, and in *Flac.*
123 they refer to their desolate and deprived state as a result of the
pogrom. In *Spec.* 4:179–80 Philo tells that God shows compassion
and pity on the Jewish nation, as on an 'orphan', when misfortunes
fall upon it.[17]

Finally, in *Flac.* 121–4 the Jews, when Flaccus was arrested, offered
thanks to God because He had taken pity and compassion (οἶκτος
καὶ ἔλεος) on them. They had deplored their desolate situation,
deprived as they were of everything. Likewise, in *Spec.* 4:179–180,
interpreting Deut 10:17–18 (". . . he executes justice for the father-
less . . ."), Philo says that the whole Jewish race is in the position
of an orphan. When misfortunes fall upon them they have none to
take their part. Nevertheless, the Jewish people is always an object of
pity and compassion (ἔλεος καὶ οἶκτος) to the Ruler of the Universe
whose portion it is.

The punishments of Flaccus were meted to him in accordance
with the biblical principle that good lives receive rewards and bad
lives punishments (*Praem.* 2 and 3). As also shown in the preceding
chapter Flaccus suffered punishment for his evil deeds against the
Jews on the basis of justice and the principle of reversal. Flaccus in
his exile on the island Andros exclaimed that ". . . all the acts which
I madly committed against the Jews I have suffered myself" (*Flac.*
170ff., cf. *Praem.* 169). In both treatises the same terms are used, justice (δίκη, *Praem.* 136; *Flac.* 104; 115 and 189), and reversal (μεταβολή,
Flac. 153; 154 and 159 and *Praem.* 169). This principle of justice was
at work when Flaccus was cut into pieces: "For it was the will of justice (δίκη) that the butcheries which she wrought on his single body
should be as numerous as the number of Jews whom he unlawfully
put to death" (*Flac.* 189). The principle of reversal is central in the
eschatological outlook of *Praem.* 169–71: "Everything will suddenly
be reversed, God will turn the curses against the enemies of these

---

[17] See Fischer (1978) 203–04, and Borgen (1992) 341–61.

penitents . . ." (*Praem.* 169). Flaccus suffered punishment on the basis of this rule of reversal (*Flac.* 146–91). In *Flac.* 167 it is told how Flaccus had restless nights:

> Then when the night had quite closed in he would go indoors, praying in his endless and boundless sorrow that the evening might be morning, so much did he dread the darkness and the weird visions which it gave him, if he chanced to fall asleep. So in the morning again he prayed for evening, for to the gloom that surrounded him everything bright was repugnant.

F.H. Colson has pointed out that this passage is a reminiscence of the curse in Deut 28:67 "In the morning thou shalt say, Would God it were even! and at even thou shalt say, Would God it were morning"! The very same Old Testament word is paraphrased as a curse in *Praem.* 151. In both places Philo takes the words which follow "for the sight of thine eyes which thou shalt see" to refer to the awful dreams seen by the accursed.[18]

In his understanding that justice and providence are at work in history, Philo entertained ideas which had Jewish roots, although penetrated also by Greek ideas. As parallel one might mention the Wisdom of Solomon where correspondingly biblical and Stoic ideas are brought together in the interpretation of biblical history.[19]

In conclusion: As is the case with *On Virtues: On the Embassy to Gaius*, so also with the treatise *Against Flaccus*, the points of agreement with the books *On the Special Laws 3–4*, *On the Virtues* and *On Rewards and Punishments* show that it is to be regarded as an application of the biblical interpretations outlined in these books of the *Exposition of the Laws of Moses*. Since the emphasis is on crimes done against God and His people and the reversal of his misdeeds meted out as punishments, the treatise *Against Flaccus* is especially to be seen as a contemporary parallel to the treatise *On Rewards and Punishments*.

Interpreted history

What kind of writings then are *Against Flaccus* and *On Virtues: On the Embassy to Gaius*? Philo here narrates theologically interpreted history

---

[18] See *PLCL* 8:408, n. a, and 9:393, n. b.
[19] See Sowers (1967) 20–24. Concerning rabbinic polemic against Epicurean denial of providence and justice, see Fischel (1973) 35.

based on ideas related to the Laws of Moses. In this respect these
treatises show a similarity to history writing in the Old Testament,
in Judaism and in the New Testament.

As for Philo's specific point about rulers being punished for their
blasphemous arrogance, both Josephus, *Ant.* 19:20–23 and Acts 12:20–
23, exemplify this kind of interpretation of history. Acts 12:21–23
reads:

> On an appointed day Herod put on his royal robes, took his seat upon
> the throne, and made an oration to them. And the people shouted,
> "The voice of a god, and not of man"! Immediately an angel of the
> Lord smote him, because he did not give God the glory; and he was
> eaten by worms and died.

At the same time Hellenistic ideas and motifs have been worked into
Philo's interpretation of the events, as for example the use of the
concept of justice, δίκη, as shown by S. Sowers in his essay "On the
Reinterpretation of Biblical History in Hellenistic Judaism".[20]

Contemporary literary forms have also had their influence. An encomium on the Emperor Augustus is included in *Legat.* 143–51, and
the characterization of the Emperor Gaius is partly formulated as a
contrast. According to *Legat.* 373 the story reveals Gaius' character,
a standard motif in moral tales which offer examples. And in *Against
Flaccus*, the story of Flaccus' journey into exile on the island of Andros
is in the pattern of Greek historical essay-writing. So it may be largely
imaginative in details, since he in Alexandria probably only had general
knowledge of Flaccus' fate. Elements such as the lament of the central figure, his recall of past fortunes changed into misfortunes, his
despair, repentance, and fear of approaching death are common topics
in such literature, especially where it includes in travels.[21] This Greek
literary form serves Philo's theological purpose, however, since it shows
how God's punishment is based upon justice, so that Flaccus now is
punished in accordance with the crimes he committed against God
and His people.

The ending of *On the Virtues: On the Embassy to Gaius*, ". . . one must
tell the palinode", raises problems. This indicates a recantation to
follow. If so, it presumably told of Gaius' death and his successor
Claudius' new policy, which was more favourable to the Jews, al-

---

[20] Sowers (1967).
[21] See *PCH* 7:125–26 and 168–69.

though within marked limits. But if, as is more probable, Philo means that history itself brought about the change, no additional writing needs be supposed.[22] This last viewpoint is supported by Philo's main aim in writing the treatise *On the Virtues: On the Embassy to Gaius*: Philo wants to demonstrate the virtues of the Jewish people. They rely upon God and His Laws even when they are severely tested by attacks from evil enemies. With this aim in mind it was sufficient for Philo just to indicate God's punishment of Gaius, without developing it into another treatise.

---

[22] See *PLCL* 10:187, n. a., and *PCH* 7:169.

CHAPTER ELEVEN

ILLEGITIMATE AND LEGITIMATE ASCENTS

Illegitimate ascents

In the treatise *On the Embassy to Gaius* a distinction is made between the legitimate ascent of the Jewish people, whose souls soar above all created things (*Legat.* 5) and the illegitimate invasions to the divine realm by the Emperor Gaius (§§ 78.93 and 114–16). The notion of legitimate and illegitimate ascents are here applied to a specific and historical situation. The question is then to be asked: Does Philo in his expositions develop the idea of ascent in a way that may give a broader biblical and ideological background of his use of the idea in the treatise *On the Embassy?*

The story about the tower of Babel seems to provide such a background. It is understood by Philo to be an illegitimate ascent, as can be seen in *Somn.* 2:283ff. In the context which begins at *Somn.* 2:215, Philo interprets the two parallel dreams of Pharaoh in which the seven lean devour the seven fat kine, Gen 41:17–24. He focuses his exposition on the phrase in Gen 41:17: "I thought I stood upon the edge of the river". "The river" is understood to mean speech, which may be either good or bad (*Somn.* 2:238–40). Examples of good speech and of silence from speech are given in §§ 241–73. Then in *Somn.* 2:274–299 Philo lists three kinds of wrong speaking: 1. the speaking of the pleasure lovers, represented by Pharaoh (§§ 276–78); 2. of the sophists, represented by the people of Egypt (§§ 279–82); 3. and the third kind, which consists of those who deny the existence of God and providence, such as those who built the tower of Babel (Gen 11):

> . . . those who extended their activities of their word-cleverness to heaven itself. . . . They declared that nothing exists beyond this world of our sight and senses, that it neither was created nor will perish, but is un-created, imperishable, without guardian, helmsman or protector. Then piling enterprises one upon another they raised on high like a tower their edifice of unedifying doctrines. . . . And therefore when they hoped to soar to heaven in mind and thought to overthrow (trans. mine) the eternal kingship, the mighty undestroyable hand cast them down and

overturned their edifice and their doctrine. And the place is called 'confusion' . . . (*Somn.* 2:283–86).

With regard to this somewhat sketchy reference to philosophical ideas, Philo would in his criticism primarily have in mind the denial of providence by the Sceptics and the Epicureans and the uncertainty expressed by the Sceptics as to the existence of the gods.[1] Philo understands such views to be an attack on God's eternal cosmic government. The passage calls the attempt an ascent, a running up, to heaven in the realm of thoughts (εἰς οὐρανὸν ταῖς ἐπινοίαις ἀναδραμεῖσθαι, cf. *Opif.* 36; *Cher.* 41; *Plant.* 22; *Spec.* 2:6), and the invasion is described in drastic terms, as a running up "for the overthrow, ἐπὶ καθαιρέσει, of the eternal kingship". As punishment "the mighty undestroyable hand casts them down (καταβάλλει)".

This invasion takes place in the realm of thinking, and the reference to the eternal kingship leads in the subsequent context to ideas about the political realm of rulers and government (*Somn.* 2:286–91). This oscillation between philosophy and politics is seen in *Somn.* 2:290–91:

> But so long as they remain unpunished . . . they deal out destruction to the government of the universe with their unholy words, enroll themselves as rulers and kings (ἄρχοντας καὶ βασιλέας), and make over the undestroyable sovereignty of God to creation which passes away and perishes and never continues in one stay. Thus it is their way to talk bombastic, boastful absurdities such as 'We are the rulers (ἡγεμόνες), we are those who reign (trans. mine); all things are based on us. Who can cause good or its opposite, save we? With whom does it really and truly rest to benefit or harm, save us? They are but idle babblers who say that things are linked to an invisible power, and think that this power presides over everything in the world whether human or divine'.

In a footnote in *PLCL* a comment is made at this point: "The description of the third class, though primarily an attack on philosophical creeds, passes in this and the subsequent sections into a general denunciation of human pride".[2] Although the political terms ἄρχων, βασιλεύς, ἡγεμών, οἱ δυναστεύοντες, may be used figuratively about human pride in general, it seems more probable to state that the description passes into a denunciation which has its main focus on the pride of political rulers who do not recognize God as the ruler of the universe. Thus, Philo has in this interpretation of the tower of Babel

---

[1] See Wolfson (1948) 1:164–167, 299; 2:382; *PLCL* 5:610.
[2] *PLCL* 5:573, n. b.

primarily in mind non-Jewish philosophies and godless governments.

Also in *Conf.* 111–14 the invasion into heaven by the building of the tower of Babel is interpreted by means of a language which fuses together (non-Jewish) philosophical ideas, terms about man-centered government and human vices:

> 'Let us build ourselves a city' (Gen 11:4), which is like. . . . Let us enact laws which shall eject from our community the justice whose product is poverty and disrepute – laws which shall assure the emoluments of the stronger to the succession of those whose powers of acquisition are greater than others. And let a 'tower' (Gen 11:4) be built as an acropolis, as a royal and impregnable castle for the tyrannic evil, whose feet shall walk upon the earth, and whose head reach to 'heaven' (Gen 11:4), carried by our arrogance to that vast height. For in fact that tower not only has human misdeeds for its base, but it seeks to rise to the region of celestial ('olympic') things, with the argument of impiety and godlessness in its van. Such are its pronouncements, either that the Deity does not exist, or that it exists but does not exert providence, or that the world has no beginning in which it was created, or that though created its course is under the sway of varying and random causation. . . .[3]

In support of the view that the passages quoted above includes the claims of political rulers, Philo's interpretation of Deut 10:9 (". . . the Lord is their [the tribe of Levi's] portion") and Num 18:20 ("I am thy portion and inheritance") in *Plant.* 67–68 may be mentioned. In this passage Philo makes the distinction between on the one hand boasting persons who have acquired kingship and supremacy and made themselves masters, some even of all earth's regions, all nations, Greek and barbarian alike, all rivers, and seas, and also extended their rule to the high realm of unlimitless freedom, and on the other hand great kings who receive God as their portion.

As already demonstrated, Gaius Caligula was a historical manifestation of a ruler who illegitimately went beyond the limits of human beings and invaded the divine realm,[4] as stated in the phrase already cited above (*Legat.* 75): ". . . he no longer considered it worthy of him to abide within the bounds of human nature but overstepped (put one's head over: ὑπερέκυπτε) them in his eagerness to be thought a

---

[3] The translation in *PLCL* is modified. Concerning tyrannic rule, etc. see Goodenough (1938) 86, 93, etc. Concerning Philo's rejection of views found in Greek philosophical traditions, see Wolfson (1948) 1:108ff., 165ff., 295ff., and *PLCL* 3:508, n. on § 199.

[4] Cf. Halperin (1988) 47–67.

god". It is to be noticed that the verb used here is the same as in *Legat.* 5, where it refers to the proper ascent of the souls of Israel. In the case of Gaius "the created and corruptible nature of man was made to appear uncreated and incorruptible by a deification which our nation judged to be the most grievous impiety" (§ 118). According to Philo, Gaius' viceroy in Syria, Petronius, characterized his superior in this way: "...a despot who is young and judges that whatever he wishes is beneficial and that what he has once decreed is as good as accomplished, be it ever so unprofitable and charged with contentiousness and arrogance. For having soared above (leap over: ὑπερπηδάω) man, he is already enrolling (γράφει) himself among gods" (§ 218).

This description of Gaius has much in common with Philo's interpretation of the builders of the tower of Babel in *Somn.* 2:283–95, part of which has been cited above:

"... they hoped to soar up (run up: ἀνατρέχω) to heaven in the realm of thoughts for the overthrow of the eternal kingship" (§ 285); "... they enroll (ἀναγράφουσι) themselves as rulers and kings (ἄρχοντας καὶ βασιλέας), and make over the undestroyable sovereignty of God to creation which passes away and perishes. . . ." Thus it is their way to talk bombastic, boastful absurdities such as "We are the rulers, we are those who reign; all things are based on us. Who can cause good or its opposite, save we? With whom does it really and truly rest to benefit or harm, save us"? (§§ 290–91).

Thus criticism like that expressed in *Somn.* 2:283–95 could readily be applied to the criticism of Gaius.

The conclusion is: In these passages about illegitimate invasion Philo oscillates between spiritual ideas and concrete social and political phenomena. The passages have an ideological perspective which fits well together with the interpretation of history found in *Against Flaccus* and *On the Embassy to Gaius*, and add support to the view that these two treatises are to be understood and interpreted within the context of Philo's other writings.

The legitimate ascent of Moses, god and king

In the opening section of the treatise *On the Embassy to Gaius* the focus is given to the legitimate ascent of the Jewish people, whose souls soar above all created things (*Legat.* 5). Likewise, the legitimate ascents pictured in Philo's expositions are of primary importance, especially the ascents of Moses.[5] For example, Philo interprets LXXExod 20:21: ". . . Moses went into the darkness where God was" to be a reference to an ascent by Moses into the presence of God. This verse is used by Philo in *Mos.* 1:158; *Post* 14; *Gig.* 54; *Mut.* 7; and in *QE* 2:28. Both in *Post.* 14 and *Mut.* 7; Exod 20:21 occurs together with Exod 33:13 where Moses prays that he might be granted to see God. In both places the passages are understood to mean Moses' wish to see the true existence of God, by entering "into the darkness where God was". This wish of his is denied him, but he is granted to see what is below God. Compare the similar points made in *Spec.* 1:41–50, a section which was discussed above in the preceding chapter. The interpretation of Exod 20:21 in *Gig.* 54 is different. In the terminology of mysteries, Moses' entry "into the darkness where God was" is understood to mean that Moses learned the secrets of the most holy mysteries: There he becomes not only one initiated, but also the hierophant of secret rites and teacher of divine things, which he will impart to those whose ears are purified.

Of special interest is *Mos.* 1:149–162 where Moses' ascent means his transformation into being divine king and a model for those who will follow him. Philo's two treatises, *On the Life of Moses* 1 and 2, cover most of the story of Moses in the Pentateuch. In *Mos.* 1:1–148 Philo gives a narrative account of Moses' life from his birth, to God's use of Moses as agent in the punishments of the Egyptians and subsequently to the departure of the Hebrew immigrants from Egypt. The whole section of §§ 149–162 is an excursus which breaks off from the Pentateuchal narrative. It gives a characterization of the nature of Moses' kingship in relation to God, the Hebrew nation and cosmos. In the transitional words of § 163 Philo refers back to a main point in this preceding section on Moses' kingship: "So, having received the authority (τὴν ἀρχήν) which they willingly gave him, with the sanction and assent of God (βραβεύοντος καὶ ἐπινεύοντος θεοῦ). . . ."

The section *Mos.* 1:149–162 reports on Moses becoming a divine king. At the outset, Philo states that Moses had the status of a king to be as the adopted son of the daughter of the then reigning king of Egypt. Moses gave up his political leadership and renounced completely his expected inheritance from the kinsfolk of his adoption (*Mos.*

---

[5] Philo's place within the context of Jewish traditions is quite evident in the legitimate ascents of Enoch, Moses and Elijah mentioned in *QG* 1:86. See Borgen (1993).

1:148–49). The iniquities committed in Egypt lead to Moses' renouncement because of his inborn hatred for evil.

Moses' royal career is seen against the background of the contrasting careers of "some" rulers. Moses became king in a different way than those who thrust themselves into positions of power by military conquest (*Mos.* 1:148).

> In solitary contrast to those who had hitherto held the same authority, he did not treasure up gold and silver, did not levy tributes, did not possess houses or chattels or livestock or a staff of slaves or revenues or any other accompaniment of costly and opulent living, though he might have had all in abundance (1:152). . . . In dress and food and the other sides of life, he made no arrogant parade to increase his pomp and grandeur . . . he was liberal in the truly royal expenditure . . . (1:153) . . . He abjured the accumulation of lucre, and the wealth whose influence is mighty among men . . . (1:155).

This picture of Moses' way to kingship reads like a 'mirror for kings'. Parallels are found in a fragment of the treatise *On Kingship* by the Pythagorean Diotogenes and in Dio Chrysostom's *Discourses on Kingship*.[6] According to Diotogenes, the king

> . . . must excel the rest in virtue and on that account be judged worthy to rule, but not on account of his wealth, or power, or military strength. For the first of these qualities he has in common with all sorts of people, the second with irrational animals, and the third with tyrants, while virtue alone is peculiar to good men. So that what king is self-controlled in pleasure, given to sharing his possessions, and is prudent and powerful in virtue, that man will be a king in very truth (*Stobaeus* IV:7.26, translated by E.R. Goodenough)[7]

From Dio the following lines apply:[8]

> . . . [the king] is not to become licentious or profligate, stuffing and gorging with folly, insolence, arrogance, and all manner of lawlessness . . . (*The first Discourse on Kingship* 12–13). . . . Blessings he dispenses with the most lavish hand, as though the supply were inexhaustible . . . (§ 24). And when he [Zeus] saw that the lad [Heracles] wished to be a ruler, not through the desire for pleasure and personal gain, which leads most men to love power . . . (§ 65).

---

[6] *Stobaeus* IV:7.26. See Goodenough (1928) 70; Meeks (1967) 109–10. On Dio Chrysostom, see *Oration* 1:12–13.24.65.

[7] Goodenough (1928) 70; Meeks (1967) 109–10.

[8] Cohoon (1961) ad loc.

Due to his virtuous performance, this royal 'prince', Moses, became
worthy of being given the status as friend of God, and of receiving
a greater mandate due to this special status. Accordingly terms for
reward and worthiness have a prominent place. As worthy privilege
given, God has handed over (παρέχω) to Moses a worthy privilege
(γέρας ἄξιον) (Mos. 1:148). His performance and personal quality was
evident because he gave up the lordship of Egypt and because of his
own nobility of soul and magnanimity of ˙spirit and hatred of evil.
Then the reward/charge is explicated: to Him who presides (τῷ πρυτα-
νεύοντι) . . . over all things it seemed good to requite him (ἔδοξεν αὐτὸν
ἀμείψασθαι) with the kingship . . . (§ 149).

In Mos. 1:149 Philo states that God thought good to requite Moses
with the kingship of a nation (ἔθνος) more populous and mightier, a
nation destined more than all others to act as priests (ἱερᾶσθαι), who
should offer prayers (τὰς . . . εὐχὰς ποιησόμενον) for ever on behalf of
the human race (ὑπὲρ τοῦ γένους τῶν ἀνθρώπων), for the avoidance
of evil and for the participation in what is good. When Philo writes
about the establishment of this priestly call of this priestly and royal
nation he refers to Exod 19:6. In Abr. 56 and Sobr. 66, where Exod
19:6 is cited, he applies this verse to the patriarchs, Abraham, Isaac
and Jacob.[9] The idea of the Jews as a priestly nation was widespread
in Judaism, as can be seen from 2 Macc 2:17; Mek. Exod. 19:6; Jub.
16:18. Also in the Book of Revelation the people are characterized
as a priestly people, Rev 5:9–10. Here a difference is seen.[10]

In Mos. 1:156 Philo elaborates on the word "friend" in LXXExod
33:11 where Moses is seen as a friend of God: "And the Lord spoke
to Moses face to face, as if one should speak to a friend . . ." Philo
says in Mos. 1:156 that "the Prophet is called the friend of God".

In his elaborations on the idea of friendship (Exod 33:11) in Mos.
1:155–157, Philo used terms and phrases which were parallel to the
language he utilized in direct political contexts. In Legat. 285 Philo
relates the term "worthy" to receiving benefits from the emperor
Gaius as his "friends".[11] King Agrippa wrote to emperor Gaius: "You
have deemed some of your friends' homelands as a whole worthy
(ἠξίωσας) of Roman citizenship". Agrippa was one of Gaius' dearest

---

[9] See Fiorenza (1972) 91–92.

[10] To Philo the priestly people is the Jewish people, while John the Seer referred
to a people drawn from all nations. See Fiorenza (1972) 91–92 and 282–90.

[11] See Neumann (1894); Bammel (1952) 205–210; Stählin (1973) 145–146, 164,
n. 171.

friends (*Legat.* 268). The emperor had granted him a kingdom and later added other areas to it (*Legat.* 326). Agrippa was king and friend of Caesar (φίλος Καίσαρος) (*Flac.* 40). In another example, Flaccus had been chosen by Tiberius Caesar to be among his foremost friends and had for six years been entrusted with Egypt, the greatest of his possessions (ἡ κτῆμα) (*Flac.* 158). Correspondingly, Moses was God's friend and shared in his possession (ἡ κτῆσις) (*Mos.* 1:156).

Philo's description of the area under Moses' sovereignty coincides partly with his manner of describing the area under the Roman emperor's control. Philo states that God granted Moses the whole earth and sea and rivers (*Mos.* 1:155); the Roman emperors held the sovereignty of the whole earth and sea (*Legat.* 8; 43; 49). Moses' sovereignty was even greater. As *cosmopolites* he received the whole cosmos as his portion (κλῆρον). In a corresponding way this last term is applied by Philo to king Agrippa: He received countries from Gaius as his portion (κλῆρον) (*Legat.* 326).

In specifying what "the whole cosmos" meant, Philo in *Mos.* 1:155–56 relates the terms earth, sea and rivers to the context of the Greek scientific idea of the elements, τὰ στοιχεῖα: ". . . the whole earth and sea and rivers, and of all the other elements and the combinations which they form" (*Mos.* 155). Moses was partner of God's possessions, and therefore each element obeyed him (1:155–56), as seen in the miraculous events which took place when the Israelites left Egypt (*Mos.* 1:96–97 and 216).

It is worth noting that the term "partner" (κοινωνός), which in *Mos.* 1:155 characterizes the relationship between Moses and God, is also used for persons who are (to be) partners as emperors, such as was the case with Gaius and his cousin, Tiberius Gemellus, *Legat.* 23; 25; 28, cf. *Flac.* 10.[12]

Named God

In *Mos.* 1:158 Philo gives a further definition of Moses' partnership with God. As "God's friend" Moses was deemed worthy of bearing God's title, and he was named "god":

> For he was named god and king of the whole nation, and entered, it is told (Exod. 20:21), into the darkness where God was, that is into the unseen, invisible, incorporeal and archetypal essence of existing things.

---

[12] Concerning Tiberius Gemellus, see Smallwood (1961) 169–72.

Here Philo draws on Exod. 7:1 and 20:21. LXXExod 7:1 reads:
". . . Behold, I have given you as god to Pharao . . .", and LXX 20:21
reads: "And the people stood afar off, and Moses went into the
darkness where God was".

It is important to notice that although Philo in *Mos.* 1:158 uses
Platonizing language about the archetypal reality in his interpretation
of the darkness where God was, LXXExod 20:21, he in *QE* 2:28 has
a more Jewish elaboration of the same Biblical phrase: ". . . to enter
the darkness and to dwell in the forecourt of the palace of the Father".
Ralph Marcus suggests that, behind the Armenian word translated
as "forecourt", the Greek word used was αὐλή or a similar word.[13]
The picture of God's heavenly court and palace was a well known
idea in Judaism, especially in apocalyptic literature and in the later
hekhalot literature.[14] Thus Philo's Platonizing words in *Mos.* 1:158 have
as background the royal picture of God's palace/temple.

There are different interpretations of Philo's designation of Moses
as "god". Wayne Meeks argues that Moses' kingship gives him an
intermediary status between God and the rest of men. Moses was
made God's vice-regent.[15] In support of this understanding Meeks
refers to rabbinic and Samaritan parallels. Similarly, Martha Himmelfarb refers to *Mos.* 1:158 in the chapter "Transformation and
the Righteous Dead". According to her, Philo, in his description of
the ascent of Moses, gives perhaps the most extended treatment in
Jewish or Christian literature of the divination of a human being.[16]

David Runia argues in favour of almost the opposite understanding: Moses is not being exalted to a position as God's cosmic vice-
regent, but is a philosopher-ruler and cosmopolite (κοσμοπολίτης) who
receives the cosmos as portion. Runia refers to the philosopher-king
envisaged by Plato (*Rep.* 473c–d) and to the Stoic ideas about the
good (ὁ σπουδαῖος) man, one of whose characteristics is that he is a
cosmopolite (κοσμοπολίτης), *Mos.* 1:157. Runia refers to *Deter.* 161–62
where Philo draws a distinction between God and Moses as 'god'.[17]

The present analysis leads to a conclusion closer to those of Meeks
and Himmelfarb than to that of Runia. There are several observa-

---

[13] *PLCL Supplement* 2:69.
[14] Concerning heaven as a royal court and palace, see Himmelfarb (1993) 14.
[15] Meeks (1967) 110–11; Meeks (1968) 354–359. Cf. Goodenough (1928) 55–102;
Goodenough (1938) 86–120.
[16] Himmelfarb (1993) 48–49, 70–71.
[17] Runia (1988) 49–75.

tions which speak in favor of Himmelfarb's understanding of Moses' ascent in *Mos.* 1:158 as a parallel to apocalyptic ascent stories which tell about Biblical persons entering the heavenly temple or palace.

1   As shown above, Philo himself states in *QE* 2:28 that Moses' entry into the darkness where God was, was an ascent to the forecourt of the Father's palace/temple. Thus Philo's exegesis of Moses' ascent, Exod 20:21, cannot adequately be understood solely on the basis of Moses as the philosopher-king envisaged by Plato in *Rep.* 473c–d.

2   The similarities between the ascent of Moses and Gaius' claim to divinity suggest that the title "god" given to Moses is meant to give him a status that transcends that of a human king. In relation to God in the absolute sense, Moses is not God in reality, since he has been *given* this role by Him: God is the only One who is active and not passive. From the view-point of his relationship to man, however, Moses was 'god' (*Deter.* 161–62). Thus, this passage does not, as Runia thinks, speak in any basic way against the view that divinity is attributed to Moses in passages such as *Mos.* 1:158; *Sacr.* 9, etc. where Moses, as "god", is seen in a place *next* to God.[18] Philo even goes so far as to say that God sent Moses as a loan to the earthly region and appointed him as god, placing all the bodily region and the mind which rules it in subjec-tion and slavery to him (*Sacr.* 9).

3   When Philo in *Mos.* 1:158 says that Moses saw what is hid-den from the sight of mortal nature and became a model and godlike picture for men to imitate, then he means that Moses had been transformed in accordance with his title "god". Moses as god and king was the model for the He-brew nation to follow in their exodus as they faced the at-tacks from the king of Egypt and other enemies as told in *Mos.* 1:163–180.

It is seemingly a problem that Philo in *Mos.* 1:158 interprets Exod. 7:1 "Behold I send you as *god* to *Pharaoh*" to mean Moses is "*god* . . . of the whole *nation*", that is, of the Hebrew nation. The explanation is

---

[18] Runia (1988) 60–61. By making the distinction between God in the absolute sense and Moses as god in a relative sense, i.e. in dependence on Him, Philo solves the problem of ditheism.

that Moses, as god and king, is the model, παράδειγμα, to be imitated
by the Hebrew nation as they face Pharaoh and other antagonists.

Having perceived the "invisible and incorporeal archetypal essence
of existing things", Moses, being god and king, so models his life
after it that he becomes a paradigm for those who are willing to
copy it (*Mos.* 1:158). As king destined also to be legislator, he was a
living and articulate law (*Mos.* 1:162).

In an essay Meeks also made a brief comparison between Moses
as the legitimate divine king and the Emperor Gaius as the counterfeit God.[19] Such a comparison between Moses as the legitimate divine
king and the emperor Gaius as the counterfeit should be explored
further. As shown above the whole section of §§ 149–162 is an
excursus which breaks off from the Pentateuchal narrative. It gives a
characterization of the nature of Moses' kingship in relation to God,
the Hebrew nation and cosmos. Wayne Meeks has shown that traditions about Moses as a divine and heavenly king are found in various
Jewish writings, such as in Philo's writings, in Ezekiel the Tragedian's
The Exodus, in rabbinic and also in Samaritan writings. The traditions
cut a cross the conventional classifications of sources as 'normative'
and 'Hellenistic', 'apocalyptic', 'philosophical', 'mystical', and even
Jewish and Samaritan.[20]

Philo expresses the view that Moses, as a result of his entry before
God, was a living and reasonable law (νόμος ἔμψυχός τε καὶ λογικός)
in anticipation of his coming role as the legislator appointed by God,
Mos. 1:162. Moses' counterfeit, Gaius, regarded himself as a law (νόμος),
and broke the laws of the lawgivers of every country, *Legat.* 119. In
this way Philo gives two contrasting applications of the topos of Hellenistic kingship that the king's business was to articulate the divine
realm and will into which he could penetrate: Moses was an authentic personification of the divine law, while Gaius illegitimately claimed
that he was a law in himself.[21]

Moses saw what is hidden for mortal nature and became a godlike work (θεοειδὲς ἔργον), like a well-wrought picture (γραφή), a model
(παράδειγμα) for those who are willing to copy it, *Mos.* 1:158. Gaius,
the counterfeit, went further in his claim of being god and regarded
himself as a divine manifestation. He even "introduced into Italy the

---

[19] Meeks (1976) 43–67.
[20] Meeks (1968) 354.
[21] See Goodenough (1935) 186, n. 36, with reference to Cicero, *De legibus*, III:1.2.

barbarian practice of *proskynesis* of Gaius as god", *Legat.* 116.[22] Although Philo applies God's title to Moses, he does not see him as object of *proskynesis* or sacrifice.

Conclusion

At the beginning of this chapter a question was asked: Does Philo in his expositions develop the idea of ascent in a way that may give a biblical and ideological background of his use of the idea in the treatise *On the Embassy*? Philo's expositions of the tower of Babel and of Moses as god and king give basis for answering this question in the affirmative. His interpretations of the tower of Babel have an ideological perspective which serves well as an ideological background for the illegitimate deification of the Emperor Gaius pictured in *Against Flaccus* and *On the Embassy to Gaius*.

Philo pictures Moses' ascent as his legitimate transformation into being god and king. Thus the illegitimate ascent of the Emperor Gaius to the divine realm is by Philo seen as making him into a counterfeit god.

In the treatise *On the Embassy to Gaius* the distinction is drawn between the illegitimate invasion of Gaius and the legitimate ascent of the Jewish people, and not the ascent of Moses. The explanation of this difference is Philo's understanding of Moses ascent as the paradigmatic model of the ascent of the people.

---

[22] See Smallwood (1970) 209–11.

CHAPTER TWELVE

REACHING OUT AND COMING IN

The impact on other peoples

In spite of the fact that there were tensions and at times open conflicts between the Jewish community and its non-Jewish surroundings, there were also times and periods with degrees of positive intercourse. In such times the Jews would to some extent make a positive impact on segments of their surroundings. It should then be remembered that Philo's conviction was that the particular Laws of Moses were in harmony with the universal cosmic law. This view implied that the Jewish people had a universal role to play.

In his account of the pogrom under Gaius Caligula Philo indicates that where the Jews are very numerous in a city they may influence their surroundings to the extent that they might make an impact upon the Roman governor. Philo points to this possibility in his explanation of the mild and positive reaction of the Roman legate to Syria, Petronius, when he received the order that a statue of the Emperor was to be transported to Jerusalem. Philo brings the Roman legate Petronius close to Judaism:

> Indeed it appears that he himself had some rudiments of Jewish philosophy and religion acquired either in early lessons in the past through his zeal for culture or after his appointment as governor in the countries where the Jews are very numerous in every city, Asia and Syria, or else because his soul was so disposed, being drawn to things worthy of serious effort by a nature which listened to no voice nor dictation nor teaching by its own. But we find that to good men God whispers good decisions by which they will give and receive benefits, and this was true in his case (*Legat.* 245).

In Alexandria and Egypt the Jews were numerous, numbering not less than a million, according to Philo (*Flac.* 43). Thus, in spite of tensions and conflict, the Jews would influence non-Jewish groups also in positive ways. Moreover, Philo explicitly states that during the reign of the Ptolemaic kings and of the Roman emperors Augustus and Tiberius the Jews were allowed to live in accordance with their own Laws. Thus Philo praises Augustus and Tiberius for their personal qualities and their favourable attitude toward the Jews. They recognized the rights of the Jews to worship and live in accordance with their ancestral laws and customs (*Legat.* 153–58). Nevertheless, also during the reign of Augustus and Tiberius there were persons who were not well disposed to the Jews and made accusations against them (*Legat.* 159–60).

In *On the Life of Moses*, Book 2, Philo paints such a positive picture: The Laws of Moses ". . . attract and win the attention of all, of barbarians, of Greeks, of dwellers on the mainland and islands, of nations of the east and the west, of Europe and Asia, of the whole inhabited world from end to end" (*Mos.* 2:20). That the Laws were precious in the eyes of rulers, was documented by the initiative taken by Ptolemy II Philadelphus (284–46 B.C.) to have them translated from Hebrew into Greek (*Mos.* 2:25–43).

Although the Jews had not prospered for many a year and the people were to some degree under a cloud, their Laws and observance made an impact:

> But, in course of time, the daily, unbroken regularity of practice exercised by those who observed them brought them to the knowledge of others, and their fame began to spread on every side. For things excellent, even if they are beclouded for a short time through envy, shine out again under the benign operation of nature when their time comes (*Mos.* 2:27).

The celebration of the Sabbath made a strong impact upon the Greek and barbarian peoples:

> For, who has not shewn his high respect for that sacred seventh day, by giving rest and relaxation from labour to himself and his neighbours, freemen and slaves alike, and beyond these to his beasts? (*Mos.* 2:21).

Josephus, in *Ag.Ap.* 2:282–83, describes in a similar way the broad influence of Judaism on the gentile world: Among the observances kept by non-Jews, Josephus lists the abstaining from work on the seventh day, the fasts, the lighting of lamps and many of the prohibitions in the matter of food.

Both Philo and Josephus exaggerate the impact of the Sabbath and other observances on other peoples, but there are data which indicate that there was some basis for the statements. Tcherikover points to the fact that personal names such as 'Sambathion', etc. were used also by non-Jews from the first century A.D. and onwards in Egypt and in other areas of the Mediterranean world. Tcherikover and others draw the conlusion that such names attest the adoption of Sabbath observance by numbers of non-Jews.[1]

Correspondingly Seneca wrote: ". . . the customs of this accursed race have gained such influence that they are now received throughout all the world. The vanquished have given laws to their victors".[2] Along the same line Philo tells that the annual Septuagint festival on the island of Pharos was an event in which also non-Jews participated:

> Therefore, even to the present day, there is held every year a feast and general assembly in the island of Pharos, whither not only Jews but multitudes of others cross the water, both to do honour to the place in which the light of that version first shone out, and also to thank God for the good gift so old yet ever young. But after the prayers and thanksgivings, some fixing tents on the seaside and others reclining on the sandy beach in the open air feast with their relations and friends, counting that shore for the time a more magnificent lodging than the fine mansions in the royal precincts. Thus the laws are shewn to be desirable in the eyes of all, ordinary citizens and rulers alike . . . (*Mos.* 2:41–43).[3]

As seen from these passages in *Mos.* 2, there was some degree of positive intercourse between the Jewish community and their surroundings, as it seems, in a situation with less tension and conflict than during the reign of Gaius Caligula.

Proselytes 'coming in'

A comprehensive body of material in Philo of Alexandria's expository writings deals with proselytes who become Jews. In most of these passages the focus is on individual persons. According to Philo the conversion of gentiles to Judaism consists of three aspects:

---

[1] *CPJ* 1:94–96; 3:43–87; Goldenberg (1979); Cohen (1989) 20–21.
[2] Stern (1976–84) § 186.
[3] In a corresponding way synagogal communities at a later time attracted many gentile Christians. Thus John Chrysostom of Antioch preached in 386–87 A.D. against the Jews and against Christians who go to the synagogue on the Sabbath, who receive circumcision, celebrate the Jewish Pesach, keep the Jewish dietary laws and other observances, such as fasting. Moreover, in canon 29 of the council of Laodicea held in the second half of the fourth century, the following formulation occurs: "It is forbidden that Christians live like Jews and rest on Sabbath; they should work on that day. They should prefer the Lord's day to rest on, if possible, since they are Christians. If they turn out to be judaizers, let them be accursed by Christ". See Sheppard (1979); Horst (1989).

1) The religious conversion: the central theme is the change from worshipping many gods to the worship of the One True God.[4] On the whole the specific conversion passages do not name the various gods, but refer to them in a general way. For example, in his rewriting of the Mosaic Laws to illustrate the virtue of *philanthropia*, Philo in *Virt.* 102–04 tells how the proselytes have abandoned the images of their gods, and the tributes and honours paid to them, and thus turned away from idle fables to the clear vision of truth and the worship of the one and truly existing God within the context of the Jewish Law.[5]

This is a necessary aspect of conversion because of the Jews' rejection of the many gods. Philo's rejection of the many gods is in agreement with his hermeneutical key stated in *Mos.* 2:48–52, where he outlined three levels: God, the created cosmos, and the level of human life and of the particular laws and enactments. Basically polytheism is to make the second point, the cosmos, to take the place of God the Creator.

Accordingly, Philo offers sharp criticism of the various forms of polytheism. In the rewriting of the Bible in *On the Decalogue* and *On the Special Laws* the polemic against polytheism plays a central role, and various gods are specified.[6] The two first commandments of the Decalogue serve as basis for such criticism in *Dec.* 52–57 and *Spec.* 1:13–31. Philo pictures a hierarchy of polytheistic cults, a) the worship of the heavenly bodies, b) worse is the worship of lifeless images, and c) the worst and most ridiculous form of polytheism is the Egyptian worship of the fiercest and most savage of animals.[7]

a) As for the worship of heavenly bodies Philo mentions several Greek and Roman gods: "... some call the earth Kore or Demeter

---

[4] Also in Christian missionary outreach the religious conversion meant a change from many gods to the one God: Gal 4:8–9 and 1 Thess 1:9 illustrate the theme "from many gods to one God": "Formerly, when you did not know God, you were in bondage to beings that by nature are no god; but you have come to know God. ..." (Gal 4:8–9); "... how you turned to God from idols, to serve a living and true God ..." (1 Thess 1:9–10). A corresponding formulation in Philo is found in *Virt.* 102–104: "the proselytes ... abandoning ... the temples and images of their gods ... to the worship of the one and truly existing God. ..." See further Borgen (1987) 212–13.

[5] See also *Joseph and Aseneth* 13:11–12.

[6] See Wolfson (1948) 1:27–32; Sandelin (1991) 113–15.

[7] See Mendelson (1988), 34–35, who outlines a more detailed hierarchical order: "astral worship, deification of the entire universe (pantheism), deification of certain elements within the universe, idol worship, worship of domesticated animals, and finally worship of savage animals".

or Pluto, and the sea Poseidon. . . . They call air Hera and fire Hephaestus, the sun Apollo, the moon Artemis, the morning star Aphrodite
and the glitterer Hermes. . . . So too . . . two hemispheres . . ., they
call them the Dioscuri . . ." (*Dec.* 54–56).[8] Philo reflects here Stoic
theology in which the Greek gods are interpreted as cosmic and physical phenomena.[9]

In his polemic he builds on a central Jewish attitude and view,
and he can at the same time follow inner Greek polemic against the
worship and the popular understanding of gods.[10] As for the Jewish
attitude, in the historical survey of Alexandrian Judaism above, it
was demonstrated that in his polemic against polytheism Philo represents a long tradition. The polemic given in Wisd 13:2 is in particular close to Philo's criticism of the deification of the created:

> For all men are foolish by nature, and had no perception of God. And
> from the good things that were visible they had not the power to know
> him who is. Nor through the paying attention to his works did they re-
> cognize the workman, but either fire, or wind, or swift air, or the circle
> of the stars, or rushing water, or the heavenly luminaries, the rulers of
> the world, they considered gods. And if through delight in their beauty
> they supposed that these were gods, let them know how far superior is
> the Lord of these, for the originator of the beauty created them.[11]

According to Philo (*Spec.* 1:19–20) the heavenly bodies are not gods,
but are subordinate rulers. The honour should be reserved for the
Immaterial and the Invisible who is the Maker of all. "And if anyone renders the worship due to the Eternal, the Creator, to a created
being and one later in time, he must stand recorded as infatuated
and guilty of impiety in the highest degree" (§ 20).

b) As for the worship of lifeless images, Philo at several places
moves into a criticism of sculptoral presentations of deities. So also
in *Spec.* 1:21:

> There are some who put gold and silver in the hands of sculptors as
> though they were competent to fashion gods; and the sculptors taking
> the crude material and furthermore using mortal form for their model,

---

[8] For the same and similar identification of gods with the elements, see Plato,
Cratylus 404C; Diog Laert 7:147; Cornutus 4 and 19; Sextus Empiricus, *Adv Mathem*
9:37 with reference to Homer, *Odysee* 11:303. See *PLCL* 7:610 and 9:519, and *PCH*
1:383, nn. 1 and 2.
[9] See Diels (1899) 45ff.
[10] Philo's points are similar to the criticism of the Stoics by the Sceptics. See *PCH*
1:383, n. 1.
[11] Translation by Goodspeed (1959) 202–03.

and to crown the absurdity shape gods, as they are supposed to be. And after erecting and establishing temples they have built altars and in their honour hold sacrifices and processions. . . . Such idolators are warned by the Ruler of All in these words: 'Ye shall not make with Me gods of silver and gold' (Exod 20:23).[12]

c) Philo is especially sharp and scornful in his criticism of the Egyptian polytheistic worship:

> . . . they have advanced to divine honours irrational animals, bulls and rams and goats. . . . And with these perhaps there might be some reason, for they are thoroughly domesticated and useful for our livelihood.[13] . . . But actually the Egyptians have gone to a further excess and chosen the fiercest and most savage of wild animals, lions and crocodiles and among reptiles the venomous asp, all of which they dignify with temples, sacred precincts, sacrifices, assemblies, processions and the like. . . . Many other animals too they have deified, dogs, cats, wolves and among the birds, ibises and hawks; fishes too, either their whole bodies or particular parts. What could be more ridiculous than all this? Indeed strangers on their first arrival in Egypt . . . are like to die with laughing at it, while anyone who knows the flavour of right instruction, horrified at this veneration of things so much the reverse of venerable, pities those who render it and regards them with good reason as more miserable than the creatures they honour, as men with souls transformed into the nature of those creatures, so that as they pass before him, they seem beasts in human shape (Dec. 76–80).[14]

It is important to note that Philo here identifies the Egyptians with the deities which they worship. Thus the dualism between monotheism and polytheism is in particular a dualism between the Hebrew people and the Egyptians. Thus the circumstance that Philo placed Greek and Roman gods highest in the hierarchy also indicates a higher ranking of the Greeks and the Romans in Philo's world view.

In contrast to the pagan peoples the Laws of the Hebrew nation do not permit men to worship the many gods, but they call on the human race to honour the only God, the Creator. How can this universal God be uniquely the God of the particular Jewish nation? The reason is that all mankind went wrong except the Jewish nation.

---

[12] See further Dec. 66; Mos. 2:205; Cont. 7; Spec. 1:28–29.

[13] See the defence of Egyptian animal worship by Hecataeus, referred to above in the survey chapter on the history of Alexandrian Judaism.

[14] For Philo's surveys of Egyptian animal worship, see Spec. 1:79; Spec. 2:146; Mos. 1:23; Cont. 8–9; Prov. 2:65; Legat. 139 and 163; QE 1:8. For the broad criticism of Egyptian animal worship by Jews, Greeks and others, see Smelik and Hemelrijk (1984) 1852–2000.

Philo makes this point in his rewriting of the feast of the 'Sheaf' (*Spec.* 2:162–76), referring to Lev 23:10ff. The sheaf is a first-fruit, both of the land given to the Jewish nation and of the whole earth. Thus it is a first fruit both of this nation and for the whole human race. "The reason of this is that the Jewish nation (τὸ Ἰουδαίων ἔθνος) is to the whole inhabited world what the priest is to the state" (*Spec.* 2:163).

> When they [the other peoples] went wrong in what was the most vital matter of all [by worshipping many gods instead of the One true God], it is the literal truth that the error which the rest committed was corrected by the Jewish nation (τὸ Ἰουδαίων ἔθνος) which passed over all created objects because they were created and naturally liable to destruction and chose the service only of the Uncreated and Eternal . . . (*Spec.* 2:166).

Accordingly, the Jews are the true men, a point made by Philo in *Spec.* 1:302–03 against the background of the idea expressed in Deut 10:14–15 that God is the owner of all of creation: ". . . out of the whole human race He chose as of special merit and judged worthy of pre-eminence over all, those who are in true sense men (οἱ πρὸς ἀλήθειαν ἄνθρωποι) and called them to the service of Himself" (*Spec.* 1:303).

Against this background it is obvious that the change from polytheism to the Jewish form of monotheism was central when gentiles joined the Jewish people and became proselytes.

2) The second aspect related to becoming a proselyte is the ethical conversion seen as the change from a pagan way of life to the Jewish virtuous life, which has the worship of the One God a source.[15] Referring to the biblical doctrine about God as Creator, Philo writes (*Virt.* 181–82):

---

[15] The transition from pagan immorality to a moral way of life is pictured in Christian sources in a way similar to ideas found in Philo: The lists of vices in 1 Cor 6:9–10 and Gal 5:19–21, have points in common with Philo's descriptions of pagan life. For example, without using the form of catalogue, Philo in *On the Contemplative Life* describes the life of the gentiles as does Paul, as a life of idolatry, immorality and excessive banqueting.

In 1 Cor 6:11 and Gal 5:22–3 the new life of the converts is seen in contrast to the gentile life of vices. In Gal 5:22–33 Paul even renders a list of virtues similar to the list given by Philo in *Virt.* 182. Paul writes: "But the fruit of the spirit is love, joy, peace, patience, kindness, goodness, faithfulness, gentleness, self-control". Also elsewhere in Christian literature the new life is characterized in a similar way, such as for example in Justin, *Dialogue* 110:3: ". . . we cultivate piety, justice, brotherly charity, faith and hope. . . ." See Borgen (1983A) 81–82.

For it is excellent and profitable to desert without backward glance to the ranks of virtue and abandon vice that malignant mistress; and where honour is rendered to the God who is, the whole company of the other virtues must follow in its train as surely as in the sunshine the shadow follows the body. The proselytes become at once temperate, continent, modest, gentle, kind, humane, serious, just, high-minded, truth-lovers, superior to the desire for money and pleasure. . . .

The theme of immorality and morality receives much attention from Philo. In *Virt.* 181–82 the focus is on the ethical aspect of human life and of virtues, and the foundation is seen to be the worship of the God who is. Conversely, there is a close relationship between polytheistic worship and immoral behaviour.[16]

Philo may at times see the gods or statues of gods as representations of immoral behaviour. For example, to Philo the Egyptians in particular represent body, pleasure and vices, as in the expository commentaries *On the Sacrifices of Abel and Cain* (*Sacr.* 48) and *On the Posterity and Exile of Cain* (*Post.* 96 and 155). As persons who worship animals the Egyptians and others have an evil way. Thus when Philo applies the biblical description of the disobedient son (Deut 21:18–21) to the joining of clubs in his own time, he states that the son made a god of the body, a god of the vanity most honoured among the Egyptians, i.e. the bull Apis (*Ebr.* 95; cf. *Spec.* 3:124–27).

In the *Exposition, Spec.* 1:21–27, Philo similarly draws the line from his criticism of the sculptural presentations of deities to person's immoral worship of wealth. His biblical reference is God's word in Exod 20:23: "Ye shall not make with Me gods of silver and gold". In the interpretation of these words Philo takes two steps. He argues from the greater to the lesser to the effect that this verse comprises gods made of *any* kind of material: "'Neither shall ye make gods the work of your hands from any material if you are prevented from using the best', for silver and gold hold first place among the sculptor's materials" (*Spec.* 1:22).

Philo draws in § 23 the distinction between the literal prohibition and the deeper meaning hinted at. The 'literal prohibition' (ἡ ῥητὴ ἀπαγόρευσις) refers both to the word spoken by God, cited from Exod 20:23, and Philo's application of the word to mean gods made from any kind of material. Thus ῥητός means here the spoken and obvious meaning which at the same time hints at (αἰνίττομαι, speak darkly or

---

[16] Sandelin (1991) 115–19.

in riddles, hint a thing, suggest) another meaning and application. This deeper meaning is not an abstract cosmic principle, but has to do with ethical values and conduct, even conduct relative to externals, wealth: The prohibition suggests that "the money-lovers who procure gold and silver coins from every side and treasure their hoard like a divine image in a sanctuary . . ." (*Spec.* 1:23) are strongly condemned. Thus, the criticism of the making of gods of silver and gold leads to criticism of the worshippers of wealth and of those who have abundance of it.

Having dealt with some of Philo's expositions of the two first of the Mosaic Ten Commandments, we shall give examples from his criticism of the immorality which according to him is present in the laws of other nations. Thus in his treatment of the Sixth Commandment, "Thou shalt not commit adultery" (*Spec.* 3:7–82), he draws sharp contrasts between the legislation of Moses and other chief legislations. The Laws of Moses show aversion and abhorrence to the Persian custom, according to which Persian magnates may marry their mothers. In the case of Oedipus the son of Laius this also was done in old days among the Greeks. Those nations receive punishment in the form of wars (*Spec.* 3:13–19). Moses' prohibition against espousing a sister (Lev 18:9; 20:17), is seen in contrast to the various laws of the Athenians, the Lacedaemonians and the Egyptians. The Egyptians bestowed on bodies and souls the poisonous bane of incontinence and gave full liberty to marry sisters whether they belonged to one of the brother's parents or to both (*Spec.* 3:22–23).

Sharp criticism is levied against the practice of pederasty, and the transformation of the male nature to the female, which has ramped its way into the cities. Here Philo criticizes the feast in the mysteries of Demeter. See *Spec.* 3:40–42. Heavy criticism is levelled against those who live a licentious life in dainty feeding, wine-bibbing and the other pleasures of the belly and the parts below it. Loosing their senses they conceive a frantic passion even for intercourse with animals, illustrated by Philo with the story of Pasiphae, the wife of King Minos long ago in Crete. She was mounted by a bull, and bore a half-beast called the minotaur (*Spec.* 3:43–45). In Philo's presentation of the Seventh Commandment, against murder, Moses' prohibition of the exposure of infants is contrasted with the evil practice among many other nations (*Spec.* 3:110ff.).

Thus Philo combines ethical dualism between virtue and vices with the dualism of the Hebrew/Jewish people and the pagan world. A

life dominated by the search for bodily pleasure is a life typical of
the Egyptians, who have made a god of the body, exemplified by
their worship of the god Apis. The money-lovers whose passion is
wealth are like pagans who use precious and expensive material in
making sculptural presentations of the gods. Against the background
of these and other immoral views and practices Philo advocates that
to become a proselyte meant a change from pagan to Jewish life-
style and ethics.

3) The social conversion: Passages in the *Exposition* and in *On the
Life of Moses* illustrate this point. Assuming biblical passages like
Deut 10:18, that God loves the proselyte, Philo in *Virt.* 102–4 tells
that the proselytes have left their family, their country, their customs. Abraham is the prototype of the proselyte who leaves his
home in this way (*Virt.* 214). Citing and paraphrasing Deut 10:17–18
Philo states that the proselytes have made their kinsfolk into mortal
enemies (*Spec.* 4:178). The proselytes have entered a "new and godly
commonwealth, *politeia*" (*Spec.* 1:51, alluding to passages like Lev
19:33–34 and Deut 10:17–18); in *Virt.* 180 it is explicitly stated that
the proselytes enter "the government of the best law", that is, the
Laws of Moses. Abraham is the standard of nobility for all proselytes who, abandoning strange laws, monstrous customs which assign
divine honours to stocks and stones, have joined "a commonwealth,
politeia, full of true life and vitality" (*Virt.* 219).

Although these passages on proselytes deal primarily with individuals who enter the new community, it is pertinent to ask if this
concept also can be applied to collectives, such as ethnic groups and
nations. *Mos.* 2:43–44 shows that at least in one of the scenarios for
the future Philo looks forward to the time when all nations will become
Jewish proselytes:

> It is but natural that when people are not flourishing their belongings
> to some degree are under a cloud. But, if a fresh start should be made
> to brighter prospects, how great a change for the better might we ex-
> pect to see! I believe that each nation would abandon its peculiar ways,
> and, throwing overboard their ancestral customs, turn to honouring
> our laws alone. For, when the brightness of their shining is accompa-
> nied by national prosperity, it will darken the light of the others as the
> risen sun darkens the stars.

He uses here several phrases which also are used in passages about
proselytes: *Mos.* 2:44 καταλιπόντας . . . τὰ ἴδια, with parallel about
the proselyte in *Spec.* 1:309, κ. τὰ πάτρια. Another phrase with almost

the same meaning is used in *Mos.* 2:44 πολλὰ χαίρειν φράσαντας τοῖς πατρίοις. *Mos.* 2:44 μεταβαλεῖν ἐπὶ τὴν τούτων μόνων τιμήν, with parallel about the proselyte in *Virt.* 177, μ. πρὸς ἀνυπαίτιον ζωήν. As for the phrase ἂν οἶμαι . . . . ἑκάστους μεταβαλεῖν it refers to the optative form of a sentence with the predicate changed into infinitive. The optative with ἂν denotes a future action that is qualified by or dependent upon, some circumstances or condition, whether expressed or implied.[17] Here the condition for the future action in the form of collective conversion is the impact made by the Laws of Moses together with the glorious and prosperous times of the Jewish people.

The universal acceptance of the Laws of Moses is also the future hope expressed in *Sib.* 3:702–30. When the peoples see how well God guards and cares for His Elect, then they will say: "Come, let us all fall on the ground and entreat the immortal king, the great eternal God. Let us send to the Temple, since he alone is sovereign and let us all ponder the Law of the Most High God . . ." (*Sib.* 3:716–19).[18] Such parrallel ideas support the understanding that Philo in *Mos.* 2:43–44 envisions the time when all nations will become Jewish proselytes by abandoning their own laws and accept the Laws of Moses.

EXCURSUS

Christian sources draw on similar traditions in their characterization of how the the Christian 'proselytes' form a cross-national community, a people among many peoples. The best example is found in Eph 2:11–22. As gentiles they were uncircumcised and alienated from the commonwealth of Israel, ἡ πολιτεία τοῦ Ἰσραήλ. The border-line was marked by "the law of commandment and ordinances" (v. 15). As converts they are not strangers nor foreigners, but fellow-citizens, συμπολῖται, and members of the household of God. In Eph 2:12 the term πολιτεία is used, the very term which also is central to the Jewish people/nation in Philo's passages on proselytes. The conclusion of this analysis of Eph 2:11–22 seems then at first to be that Christian mission and Jewish proselytism are identical entities. The passage seems to tell how the gentile converts were brought into the commonwealth of Israel, i.e. to be members and citizens of the Jewish nation, within the limits set by the political circumstances.

---

[17] Reik (1907) 107.
[18] Charlesworth (1983) 1:378, cf. 741–59; cf. Volz (1934) 172 and 390.

In spite of this use of legal and technical terminology from the realm of state and ethnic communities, the passage in Eph 2:11–22 breaks away from this context. According to Eph 2:11–22 the Christian proselytes are not to make an ethnic and judicial break away from their families, country and nation. Thus the gentile converts are not to become citizens of the Jewish nation of the Torah. The law of commandments is abolished. In this way the Jewish idea of the people of God has been reshaped to mean the church of Christ into which both gentiles and Jews are to enter. The atonement in Christ has made this new cross-national and inclusive community possible.[19]

Abraham, the proselyte and the founder of the nation

The concept of proselytism is so fundamental to Philo that he time and again stresses that the very founder of the Hebrew nation, Abraham, was a proselyte. In addition to the extensive exposition of the migration of Abraham from the Chaldeans in the treatise *On Abraham* other occurences in the *Exposition* are found in *Virt.* 212–14 and *Praem.* 58. In the *Allegorical Commentary* the migration is interpreted in *Leg. all.* 3:244, 2:59; *Cher.* 4; *Deter.* 159; *Gig.* 62; *Migr.* 1–12, 176–92, 195; *Heres* 287–89; *Congr.* 45–49; *Mut.* 16, 67–76; *Somn.* 1:53–60 and 161. In the *Questions and Answers* the theme of migration is found in *QG* 3:1 and 4:88.

The treatise *On Abraham* gives a good point of departure for a study of this role of Abraham. Philo interprets the biblical story on all three levels suggested by the hermeneutical clue given in *Mos.* 2:48 and 51–52. The concrete biblical story about Abraham's migration is applied to the Jewish community of Philo's own time, and is also brought up on the cosmic level, and even beyond, to God's level.

In *Abr.* 60–67 Philo rewrites the biblical story about Abraham's migration: Under the force of an oracle Abraham left home for a strange land (Gen 12:1–7) – or rather returned "from amid strangers to his home".[20] Philo places this story of Abraham's migration within his own time by seeing it as a contrast not only to the penalty of

---

[19] See Borgen (1983A) 81.

[20] Philo seems to assume that this command was given to Abraham in Chaldaea and not in Haran. His interpretation may be based on Gen 11:31: ". . . they went forth together from Ur of the Chaldeaens to go into the land of the Canaans; but when they came to Haran. . . ."

banishment formulated by legislators in their laws, but also to persons who travel for business, politics or leisure.

In *Abr.* 68–84 Philo interprets Abraham's migration on the macrocosmic and micro-cosmic level and on the level beyond the created order. In this way Philo makes the connection between the concrete biblical history of Abraham and cosmic ideas related to his expositions in *On the Creation*. Abraham's migration meant the search for the true God by a virtue-loving soul. Seen within a macrocosmic context for the patriarch to become a proselyte meant to migrate from his Chaldean search for God within the created order, in astrology, to the recognition that the world is not sovereign but dependent, not governing but governed by its maker and First Cause.[21]

From a microcosmic point of view Abraham's ascent went via Haran (Gen 11:31; cf. 12:4), i.e. via a microcosmic apprehension of a person's invisible mind as the ruler of the senses. Etymologically Haran means "holes", a symbol for the seat of our senses, *Abr.* 72–76. Philo's reasoning is that "it cannot be that while in yourself there is a mind appointed as your ruler which all the community of the body obeys, the cosmos . . . is without a king who holds it together and directs it with justice" (§ 74).

Excursus

In different ways the correspondence between macrocosm and microcosm is pictured in Philo's works: both may be seen as consisting of body and reasonable soul (ψυχὴ λογική). Man is a small microcosm (βραχὺς κόσμος), the world a great man, 'mega-anthropos' (μέγας ἄνθρωπος) (*Heres* 155, section on equality as an elaboration on Gen 15:10 "he divided them in the middle"). As mentioned above, Philo sees the mind as the ruler which all the community of the body obeys and God rules cosmos as king (*Abr.* 74–75). The sun shines in the cosmos and the mind in man (*Post.* 58, an interpretation of Exod 1:11 about "Heliopolis", Sun City). God planted a tree in the macro-

---

[21] Insofar as the Chaldean study of the cosmos expresses positive search for the beyond, Philo's view of Abraham's Chaldean background is favourable, such as is the case in *Cher.* 4; *Migr.* 178–81, and *Mut.* 67–68. Insofar as the Chaldeans think that the cosmos itself is god, Philo levels sharp criticism against their astrological studies, as he does in *Abr.* 69–70, 84, 88; *Virt.* 212–13; *Praem.* 58; *Migr.* 179, 194, *Congr.* 48–49; and *Somn.* 1:161. Cf. Sandelin (1991) 113–15.

cosm and a tree in man as a microcosm (*Plant.* 1–31, an interpretation of Gen 9:20 about Noah as the tiller of the soil): Heaven is made as the most perfect of imperishable objects of sense, and man the noblest of things earthborn and perishable, a micro heaven (βραχὺς οὐρανός) (*Opif.* 82, an interpretation of the creation of heaven and earth and of man, Gen 1:1 and 27). The High Priest of the Israelites, who is consecrated to the Father of cosmos, is to be transformed into cosmic nature and himself to be a microcosm. As symbolized in his cosmic vesture, the (nation's) High Priest has a universal role to play (*Mos.* 2:134–35, an interpretation of Exod 28).

Philo's ideas about macrocosm and microcosm should not be seen as ideas which are alien to rabbinic traditions, since the correspondence between man as microcosm and the world as macrocosm is also expressed by rabbis.[22] A brief formulation of the correspondence between the creation of the world and the creation of man is found in *Tanch. Pequde* § 3, where it is said that as God created the world he also created man, and as man was created from the navel as center, so God began the creation of the world by laying down its foundation stone. In *Aboth RN* 31:3 there is a detailed catalogue of agreements between macrocosm and microcosm. Some samples from among the agreements are:

> In the world He created forests, and in man He created forests: the hairs on the head. . . . Walls in the world, walls in man: his lips. Doors in the world, doors in man: his teeth. . . . A King in the world, a king in man: his head. . . .

After this excursus on macrocosom and microcosm we return to the section on Abraham's migration in *Abr.* 60–67. In *Abr.* 61 ("for anyone who contemplates the order in nature and the *politeia* . . .") Jewish and Stoic ideas are fused. The idea of a cosmic *politeia* (city) is Stoic. See *Opif.* 142–44; *Mos.* 2:51, and *SVF* 1:262 and Cicero, *De natura deorum* 154. The view that anyone who contemplates nature and the cosmic city needs no speaker to teach him to practise a law-abiding and peaceful life, is also present in Josephus, *Ant.* 1:155–56, but Josephus goes even further than Philo does when he states that Abraham conceived the creator behind the universe:

> He was thus the first boldly to declare that God, the creator of the universe, is one, and that if any other being contributed aught to man's

---

[22] See Meyer (1937) 39–40, 43–44, 116–17, 149–49.

welfare, each did so by His command and not in virtue of its own inherent power. This he inferred from the changes to which land and sea are subject, from the course of sun and moon, and from all the celestial phenomena.

To Philo search for the beyond by the mind could not bring about the encounter with God. God had to reveal Himself, as is said in Gen 12:7: "God was seen by Abraham" (*Abr.* 77). "For it were impossible that anyone should by himself apprehend the truly Existent, did not He reveal and manifest Himself" (*Abr.* 80). On this basis Abraham became friend of God and God was seen by him (*Abr.* 68–71).

Similarly, as seen in our analysis in the chapter about the expository commentaries *On the Giants* and *On the Unchangeableness of God*, Philo in *Gig.* 62–64, interpreting Gen 6:4 about the giants, had an interpretation of Abraham according to which his migration went from the land of the Chaldeans, meaning mere opinion, to the cosmic level where he was a man of heaven, and then finally, he became a man of God.

Two points need to be discussed further: a) how far does Philo rely on expository traditions about Abraham, and b) does Abraham to Philo just represent a(ny) wise man and sage, or does he represent proselytes who join the Jewish nation?

As for the question of tradition, a central point in Philo's deeper interpretation (allegory) shows close kinship with ideas in Jewish traditions. When Philo tells that Abraham had been reared in Chaldean astrology with its deification of the world (*Abr.* 69–70), the same picture of him is given both in Josephus' *Jewish Antiquities* and in rabbinic writings.[23] According to Josephus (*Ant.* 1:158), already Berosus (3. cent. B.C.), saw Abraham as an astrologer: "Berosus mentions our father Abraham, without naming him, in these terms: 'In the tenth generation after the flood there lived among the Chaldeans a just man and great and versed in celestial lore'". The view that Abraham was an astrologer is presupposed in *Gen. Rab.* 44:12: "You are a prophet, not an astrologer".

b) When Abraham's migration is interpreted as the ascent of the soul/the mind of the sage, one might think that Philo discards the particular and specific reference to biblical history and regards Abraham only as a symbol of the ascent of a sage and the human

---

[23] Stein (1931) 28. Further sources about Abraham as an astrologer is referred to by Gundel and Gundel (1966) 52–53.

soul in general. If so, an exclusive application of Abraham's migration to the particular Jewish people would be excluded.

Three observations speak against drawing such a conclusion: (1) Philo states in his hermeneutical key that there is harmony between particulars in the Mosaic laws and the universe, since God, the Creator is the Lawgiver (*Mos.* 2:48–52). (2) In the *Exposition* Philo does not only interpret Abraham's migration as a cosmic ascent, as in *Abr.* 68–87, but applies it explicitly to the Jewish people and to proselytism, as in *Virt.* 212–19. In *Virt.* 212 it is said that the oldest member of the Jewish nation (τοῦ τῶν Ἰουδαίων ἔθνους ὁ πρεσβύτατος) was a Chaldean by birth. He left his family and home.

Here there are agreements between *Abr.* 67 and *Virt.* 214. Philo's elaboration in *Abr.* 67 reads:

> And so taking no thought for anything,
> either for his fellow clansmen,
> or wardsmen,
> or schoolmates,
> or comrades,
> or blood relations on father's or mother's side,
> or country,
> or ancestral customs,
> or community of nurture
> or home life,
> – all of them ties possessing a power to allure and attract which is hard to throw off –
> he followed a free and unfettered and unfettered impulse and departed (μετανίσταται). . . .

Briefly the same picture of Abraham's departure is given in *Virt.* 214:

> [Abraham] leaves (καταλείπει)
> his country,
> his kinsfolk,
> his paternal home. . . .

According to *Virt.* 213–16 his migration meant that he left polytheism and grasped the truth that there is one Cause above all, and that it provides for the world. Cf. *Opif.* 170–72. Thus Abraham "is the standard (κανών) of nobility for all proselytes (ἐπηλύταις), who, abandoning the ignobility of strange laws and monstrous customs which assigned divine honours to stocks and stones and soulless things in general, have come to settle in a better land, in a *politeia* full of true life and vitality, with truth as its director and president" (*Virt.* 219).

Similarly, in Virt 102–104 Philo writes that the proselyte, having abandoned (ἀπολελοιπότας)
their kinsfolk by blood,
their country,
their customs,
and the temples and the images of their gods,
set forth to a better home. . . .

Thus, Philo keeps together both the external action of becoming a
Jewish proselyte and the spiritual migration when the soul ascends to
the cosmic realm and beyond.

(3) In the concluding statement in *Abr.* 88 Philo himself ties together the particular man Abraham and the general idea of the ascent
of the soul:

> So in both expositions, the literal (τήν τε ρητήν ὡς ἐπ' ἀνδρός) and the
> allegorical as applied to the soul (τὴν δι' ὑπονοιῶν ὡς ἐπὶ ψυχῆς), we
> have shown both man and soul to be worthy of our affection. We
> have shown how the man in obedience to divine commands was drawn
> away from the stubborn hold of his associations and how the mind did
> not remain for ever deceived nor stand rooted in the realm of sense,
> nor suppose that the visible world was the Almighty and Primal God,
> but using its reason sped upwards and turned its gaze upon the intel-
> ligible order which is superior to the visible and upon Him who is
> maker and ruler of both alike.

Correspondingly, at the close of the treatise *On Abraham*, Abraham is
called "the founder of the nation" (ἀρχηγέτης τοῦ ἔθνους) (*Abr.* 276).
This designation is in *Dec.* 1 further specified. Here Philo calls Abraham and the other patriarchs "founders of *our* nation (ἀρχηγέται τοῦ
ἡμετέρου ἔθνους)", i.e. founders of the Jewish nation of which Philo
and his contemporarians are members. Even Moses is seen in this
perspective by Philo. Moses was seventh in descent from the first set-
tler who became the founder of the whole Jewish nation (*Mos.* 1:7;
cf. Exod. 6:16ff.).

The conclusion is: Philo interprets the founder of the Jewish nation,
the proselyte Abraham, on all three hermeneutical levels, on the concrete biblical level where he left Chaldaea and on Philo's contemporary level, where Abraham is seen as the founder of the Jewish nation,
on the level of macrocosm and microcosm, where he is searching in
the heavenly region and in the mind, and on the trans-cosmic, divine
level, where God revealed Himself to Abraham and Abraham became
God's friend. Seen from this perspective the Jewish people is basic-

ally the proselyte people that have the proselyte Abraham as their
founding father.

Active methods of recruitment?

There are sources which suggest that Jews actively reached out in
order to recruit proselytes. In *Virt.* 211–19 Philo pictures Abraham
as a proselyte who approached his pagan surrounding by himself
being a model that called for respect and by his persuasive prophetic
speech. He is a model presented by Philo to the gentiles for them to
imitate when becoming proselytes.

According to *Virt.* 177 Moses actively reached out to the gentiles.
He invites polytheists and offers them instruction, exhorting them to
turn away from the many gods to God, the Creator and Father of
all. Correspondingly, Philo encourages those whose actions serve the
common weal to use

> "freedom of speech and walk in daylight through the midst of the *agora*,
> ready to converse with crowded gatherings . . . and . . . feast on the fresh
> sweet draught of words which are wont to gladden the minds of such
> as are not wholly averse to learning" (*Spec.* 1:321). ". . . we [the Jews)
> should follow her [nature's] intentions and display in public (προτιθέναι)
> all that is profitable and necessary for the benefit of those who are
> worthy to use it" (1:323).[24]

It may also be repeated in this context that Philo reckons with the
possibility that Petronius had some rudiments of Jewish philosophy
and religion which might have been acquired in lessons in the past
through his zeal for culture (*Legat.* 245). Whether or not these lessons
were thought to have been given by Jews or not Philo does not tell.

These indications of actively reaching out reflected in Philo's writing receive more plausability from the active proselytizing documented
in Rome. Cn. Cornelius Scipio Hispanus (ca. 139 B.C.) "banished
the Jews from Rome, because they attempted to transmit their sacred
rites to the Romans".[25] In A.D. 19 Jews were even expelled from
Rome by the Emperor Tiberius, and at least one of the reasons was
related to proselytes (Josephus, *Ant.* 18:81–84; Tacitus, *Annales* 2:85:4;

---

[24] See McKnight (1991) 55. Cf. the preaching by the prophet Jonah according to
Josephus, *Ant.* 9:208–14.

[25] Stern (1976–84) § 147a; cf. § 147b).

Dio Cassius, *Historia Romana* 57:18:5a). McKnight, who generally tries to minimize the importance of these data, admits that here active Jewish proselytizing has been at work.[26]

In this chapter it has been shown that Philo is much occupied with the movements back and forth across the visible and invisible borderline between the Hebrew people and other peoples. The various movements of reaching out and coming in are reflected in passages in several of his writings. The founder of the Jewish nation, Abraham, was a proselyte and a model for proselytes, and Moses is the seventh generation after the proselyte founder. In the hope for future one facet is the idea that all nations may leave their own laws, become proselytes and accept the Law of Moses.

Thus, although Philo's treatises *Against Flaccus* and *On the Embassy to Gaius* demonstrate that there was so severe tension between the Jewish community and their surroundings that it climaxed in a terrible pogrom, his praise in *On the Embassy to Gaius* of Augustus, Tiberius and others give evidence for the fact that at times the tension was kept under control and more positive intercourse could take place.

According to the Laws of Moses God is not just the God of the Jewish nation. God is the Creator of cosmos. This aspect will receive further attention in the next chapter.

---

[26] McKnight (1991) 73–74.

CHAPTER THIRTEEN

MAN AND GOD'S PEOPLE WITHIN
A COSMIC CONTEXT

Animals and nature

In the preceding chapters aspects of the complex relationships and movements on the borderline between Jews and non-Jews have been examined, with focus upon influence, proselytism and apostasy, tension and conflict. The task now is to develop further Philo's interpretation of the role of God's people seen within its context. This time the context is not just other peoples, but animals, nature and the cosmos.

The main sources for examining the relationship of humans to animals and nature are in Philo's *Exposition of the Laws of Moses*. The startingpoint for our study is found in *Opif.* 77–88. This passage has the form of question and answer. In the chapter about this question and answer form much attention was paid to *Opif.* 77–88. The observation was made that the problem of an unexpected order and rank in the Pentateuchal story is raised, and that close parallels exist in rabbinic writings. In the present chapter the focus will be on ideas expressed in the passage.

Gen 1:28 deals in a direct way with human beings' rule over the animals and over nature in general. In the index of the Loeb-edition, volume 10, only two references are given to this biblical verse, namely *Opif.* 84 and 88. One might then think that the topic is peripheral to Philo. This is David Runia's understanding when he writes: "Man has a special place in the cosmos not because of his dominance over the creation, nor because of his cleverness in practical matters, but because he contemplates the worlds of thought and sense and so can reflect on his own nature and situation." In a footnote Runia adds: "Note how Philo plays down this central theme of Gen 1:26–30 in his interpretation in *Opif*".[1] The present analysis will provide support

---

[1] Runia (1986) 472, and note 372. It should be added that Runia elsewhere states that his comprehensive study on Philo and the *Timaeus* of Plato is necessarily

for the understanding that the topic has a firm place in Philo's exegesis.[2]

Opif. 77–88:
Question:
(*Opif.* 77): One should inquire the reason why man comes last in the world's creation; for, as the sacred writings show, he was the last whom the Father and Maker fashioned. Four answers are given, and a further comment is attached. The outline goes as follows:

1   *Opif.* 77–78: God provided first for man's means of living, so that man would find a banquet ready for him when he came.
2   *Opif.* 79–81: Just as man found all provisions needed for life, those who strive for righteousness will experience peace, order and all good things in readiness. Man gave himself to pleasure, however, and so now must work.
3   *Opif.* 82: Man as miniature heaven ties the end of creation to the beginning, heaven.
4   *Opif.* 83–86: Man came after all created things, as king and master.
5   *Opif.* 87–88: Added comment: Man is not inferior because he was created last.

For our analysis it is natural to start with point 4, *Opif.* 83–84, because Philo here paraphrases parts of Gen 1:26/28. The first sentence in paragraph 84 ties the paragraphs 83 and 84 together:

> for which reason too the Father, having brought him [man] into existence as a living being by nature capable of sovereignty, appointed him, not only in fact but also by verbal election, king of all living beings under the moon . . . (trans. mine).

In *Opif.* 83 man's actual sovereignty over the other living beings is demonstrated: "for they were sure, as soon as they saw him, to be amazed and do homage to him as to one who by nature is ruler and despot" (trans. mine). Then in paragraph 84a God's explicit and verbal appointment of man as king is referred to, by means of a paraphrase of parts of Gen 1:26/28. In the paragraphs 84b–86 Philo provides proofs of man's rule from experience, that is, from "what is to be seen" (τὰ φαινόμενα).

---

onesided and needs to be supplemented by the study of other aspects of Philo's works, *ibid.*, 6.
    [2] For the following, see Borgen (1995) 371–81.

As already stated, Gen 1:26 and 28 are paraphrased in *Opif.* 84a.[3] Man's nature:

γεννήσας αὐτὸν ὁ πατὴρ ἡγεμονικὸν φύσει ζῷον, the Father, after having brought him into existence as a living being naturally adapted for sovereignty

Appointed as king:

οὐκ ἔργῳ μόνον ἀλλὰ καὶ τῇ διὰ λόγου χειροτονίᾳ καθίστη τῶν ὑπὸ σελήνην ἁπάντων βασιλέα not only in fact but by express mandate appointed him king of all creatures under the moon

The charge area in detail:

χερσαίων καὶ ἐνύδρων καὶ ἀεροπόρων· ὅσα γὰρ θνητὰ ἐν τοῖς τρισὶ στοιχείοις, γῇ, ὕδατι, ἀέρι, πάντα ὑπέταττεν αὐτῷ those that move on land and swim in the sea and fly in the air, for all things mortal in the three elements of land and water and air He made subject to men

The region not included in the charge:

τὰ κατ᾽ οὐρανὸν ὑπεξελόμενος, ἅτε θειοτέρας μοίρας ἐπιλαχόντα but exempted the heavenly beings as having obtained a portion more divine.

Philo's phrasing reflects both Gen 1:26 and 28. It draws specifically on Gen 1:28 in the respect that it refers to the creation of man as an event that has taken place. Gen 1:26 on the other hand reports on God's decision to create man. It draws also specifically on Gen 1:28 in the respect that it refers to the actual charge given man by God, while Gen 1:26 again reports on the background for the giving of this charge. On the other hand, Philo's paraphrase is closer to Gen 1:26 insofar as man's dominion over animals and creation in general is seen against the background of a statement about man's nature. It is to be noticed that the point in Gen 1:28 about man and woman multiplying and filling the earth is not cited by Philo.

Philo draws on a widespread Jewish exegetical tradition when he refers to man's role as ruler as an answer to the question why man was created last. Thus *Gen. Rab.* 19:4 reads, "Yet you were created after everything else, so you should rule over everything that came before".[4] The same point is also made in *4 Ezra* 6:53: "On the sixth day you commanded the earth to bring forth before you cattle, beasts

---

[3] The translation in *PLCL* is modified.
[4] Neusner (1985) 1:202.

and creeping things; and over these you placed Adam as ruler over
all the works which you had made".[5]

It is also in agreement with Jewish traditions when Philo specifies
the words MT כבש and רדה, LXX: κατακυριεύω and ἄρχω in Gen
1:28 to mean the rule by a king. A close parallel is found in *Pesiqta
Rabbati*, Supplement 21: "And God had in mind to appoint him ruler
over His world, and king over all of His creatures, as He said: I am
the King of the upper world and man is the king of the lower world".[6]

Philo uses a technical phrase for the appointment of a king: καθί-
στημι βασιλέα. Both in Philo and in *Pesiqta Rabbati* the same limita-
tion is made for man's rule: He does not rule over heaven, but only
over the lower world. Philo (*Opif.* 84) states that God "made him
king of creatures under the moon" and God "exempted the heavenly beings" from being subject to man. Correspondingly it is said in
Pesiqta Rabbati that God is the king of the upper world, and man is
the king of the lower world.

In spite of the fact that Philo in *Opif.* 84a draws on Jewish traditions, he formulates these traditions within the context of a Greek
world view and categories. Thus the list in Gen 1:28 "the fish of the
seas and flying creatures of heaven, and all the cattle and all the
earth and all the reptiles that creep on the earth" is systematized
by him into three of the four elements which in Greek philosophy
denoted the four basic components which constituted the physical
world. Philo writes: "those living on land (χερσαίων), those living in
the sea (ἐνύδρων) and those traversing the air (ἀεροπόρων), for as
many mortal beings as are in the three elements, earth, water, air
(ἐν τοῖς τρισὶ στοιχείοις, γῇ, ὕδατι, ἀέρι) . . ." (trans. mine). The Greek
ideas of the four elements had influenced Jewish views quite broadly,
as can be seen from Wisdom of Solomon 7:17 (". . . the constitution
of the world and the working of the elements . . .") and 19:18–21
("For the elements changed in order with one another . . ."); *Num.
Rab.* 14:12 end (the four elements, earth, water, air and fire); *Tanhuma
Pequde* 3 end (man was made out of the combination of the elements), cf. *4 Maccabees* 12:13 (about man).[7]

Philo applies Greek thought categories already formulated by
Aristotle, when he in *Opif.* 84a draws the distinction between the

[5] Metzger (1983) 536.
[6] Cf. *PCH* 1:58, n. 1.
[7] Borgen (1965) 133; Diels (1899) 46, n. 1; Ginzberg (1968) 5:72.

sublunar (ὑπὸ σελήνην) air, earth and sea and the supralunar heaven.[8]

In *Opif.* 88 Philo has an elaboration of the theme of the mandate given human beings by God according to Gen 1:28. Philo gives examples from experience, with reference to charioteers and pilots without drawing on words from Gen 1:28:

> ...And so the Creator has made man after all things, as a sort of charioteer and driver in order that he may hold the reins and steer the things on earth, having charged him with the care of animals and plants, like a viceroy (ὕπαρχος) of the chief and Great King (trans. mine).

Philo's use elsewhere of the term ὕπαρχος emphasizes the aspects of subordination and obedience, but includes also the idea of participation in the functions of the superiors. The aspect of subordination is in focus in *Legat.* 161 where it is told that Tiberius gave orders to the procurators about what to tell the Jews, and in § 207 where it is reported that Gaius gave orders to Petronius, the governor of Syria, to guard the passage of the statue of the emperor on its way to Jerusalem. In *Virt.* 55 the emphasis is placed on the aspect of participation. Here it is told that Joshua was distinguished from the multitude and was almost a viceroy to Moses and working together with him in the duties of government. According to *Spec.* 1:19 the heavenly bodies are not gods, but are subordinate under God as his viceroys. Thus, in principle they may be subject to criticism from their superior.

The actual sovereignty

Philo's interpretation of man's rule in Gen 1:26 and 28 in *Opif.* 84 as a god-given charge to him as king, is elaborated upon in *Opif.* 83 where man's actual royal function is described. Here the phrase ἡγεμὼν φύσει ("ruler by nature") is used, similar to the phrase ἡγεμονικὸν φύσει ζῷον in *Opif.* 84a. Instead of βασιλεύς ("king") the term δεσπότης, master, lord, despot, is used in § 83. Man's royal function is here seen by the way in which the animals acted towards him:

---

[8] See Zeller (1911) 198; Nilsson (1950) 674; Pohlenz (1948) 322 (Seneca); 350 (Plutarch and Marc Aurel). See further Cicero, *De natura deorum* II:17.56; *De re publica* 6:17 (end); *Tusculanae disputationes* 1:42ff., 60; Seneca, *De ira* III:6.1; *Ad Lucilium epistulae morales* 49:16, etc.

> Man had to come last after all created things, in order that, by ap-
> pearing suddenly as the last one he might produce consternation (cf.
> Gen 9:2, ὁ τρόμος, καὶ ὁ φόβος ὑμῶν) in the other living beings. For as
> soon as they saw him they were sure to be astonished (τεθηπέναι) and
> do *proskynesis* (προσκυνέω) to him as to a ruler by nature and a despot.
> Thus, the animals, by beholding him, were all tamed, also the most
> savaged ones. (trans. mine).

When Philo tells about the homage which the animals made to man,
he draws on a Jewish exegetical tradition. In polemical form this
tradition is evidenced in *Pirqe Rabbi Eliezer*, ch. 11:

> ... as the creatures saw him [Adam], standing as a representation of
> God's glory, then they believed that he had created them, and they
> came to worship him. Then Adam said: You want to prostrate your-
> selves before me? Not so! I and you, all of us will prostrate ourselves
> before Him, who has created us. ...[9]

In *Opif.* 84b–86 Philo refers to examples from experience as a proof
of man's rule: a vast number of cattle are led by an ordinary man;
a shepherd, a goatherd, and a cowherd lead flocks of sheep and
goats and herds of oxen. Bulls are yoked to the plough to plough the
land. Rams are laden with wool and give it to the shears. A horse
carries the rider on the back and brings him to his wanted destina-
tion. Correspondingly, in *Opif.* 148 Philo draws the line from from
present day experience back to the creation: men born many generations after the creation keep safe a torch of sovereignty passed
down from the first man. Philo uses here as metaphor the well known
picture of a torch race to illustrate the continuity between Adam
and the subsequent generations with regard to their dominion over
the animals.

Moreover, when Philo states that the animals were wild but sub-
missive to man already before the Fall, his view is akin with that of
some rabbis, although they are formulated differently. According to
Gen. Rab. 34:12 the animals' fear and terror of man, which existed
before the Fall, but ceased to exist after the Fall, came back after the
Flood, as seen from Gen 9:2. Correspondingly, in *QG* 1:56 it is said
that Noah represents creation number two, and he received then the
same honour as did Adam, and was accordingly appointed king of
the creatures of the earth.

---

[9] Cf. Grünbaum (1893) 56, and *PCH* 1:57, n. 3.

Jewish criteria in a "Greek" debate

In the passages discussed so far the presence of Jewish traditions have been evident, although also influenced by Hellenistic ideas of Greek background. A treatise that is not part of Philo's *Exposition of the Laws of Moses*, the dialogue *De animalibus* demonstrates how Philo expresses similar views on the basis of Greek terminology and thought categories. The treatise *De animalibus* is preserved in an Armenian translation and an English translation has been provided by Abraham Terian.[10] In the following we mainly draw on his translation and commentary.

Philo's opponent in the dialogue is his nephew Tiberius Iulius Alexander. Terian thinks that Alexander's views are on the whole genuine. Philo is the single author of the treatise, however, as can be seen in its composition, which is structured after the first part of Plato's *Phaedrus*. Alexander and Philo compare human beings and animals. Alexander argues for their similarity. Like human beings the animals have reason. Thus there is a moral and juridical relationship between them.

Philo claims that animals do not possess reason. Only rational beings have free will and can make ethical evaluations and actions. Since the animals are not rational, they do not act ethically (*De animalibus* 77–100). Philo concludes: "to elevate animals to the level of the human race and to grant equality (= ἰσότης) to unequals (= ἄνισοι) is the height of injustice (= ἀδικία)" (§ 100).

Although Alexander's view on the rationality of animals were anticipated by Plato (*Tht.* 189E; *La.* 196E; *Sph.* 263E) they were most probably taken over by Philo from the arguments used by the New Academy, such as Carneades of Cyrene (2nd century B.C.). Such ideas from the New Academy were reiterated by many writers and are well attested by Sextus Empiricus (*P.* 1:62–77). In his answers to Alexander Philo draws on arguments used by Stoic philosophers from Chrysippus to Posidonius.

As far as vocabulary is concerned there is in this treatise not a word that would suggest a Jewish context. Terian agrees with Leisegang's understanding, however: by arguing for the rationality of animals Alexander is opposing not only the Stoic, but also the Judaeo-biblical view that only man is endowed with the rational spirit. Terian states

---

[10] Terian (1981). See especially the introduction, pp. 25–64.

that by emphasizing the irrationality of animals in contrast to the rationality of human beings, Philo sanctions their use of animals. Thus Philo expresses a view that can be in agreement with the biblical idea of man's dominion over the animals, Gen 1:26–28.

Dominion over the created world in general

So far the present discussion has centered on human beings' dominion over animals. A further question needs to be taken up: How does Philo understand man's relationship to the created world in general? Also in this realm Philo draws on traditions which he has in common with sections found in rabbinic literature. Also here *Opif.* 77–88 can serve as point of departure. The close parallel in *Tosephta Sanhedrin* 8:7 and 9 to parts of this section, was analysed above in Chapter 5, about the question and answer form. The conclusion was that Philo in parts draws on traditions which were widespread in Jewish and Christian writings.

The problem is one of unexpected order in the scriptural account: why was Adam created last? The first of Philo's answers is basically the same as one of the answers given in *t. Sanh.* 8:9: he came last like a person who is invited to a banquet as a guest comes after the party has been prepared.

Also with regard to the second answer, *Opif.* 79, to the question why man was created last, Philo utilizes Jewish traditions, as in *Gen. Rab.* 8:6. Here the answer is that provisions for life were ready for man when he was created. This idea refers to Gen 1:28, where it is said that living beings exist for the sake of human beings.

The idea that the created world exists for the sake of human beings was widespread. Since the Jews understood themselves to be the true human beings, it can be said that the created world exists for the sake of Israel. See *4 Ezra* 6:54–59; 7:10f.; 9:13; *2 Bar.* 14:17–19; 15:7 (for the sake of the righteous ones); 21:24; *As. Mos.* 1:12; *Siphre Deut.* 48:85a; *Tanh.B Bereshit* 3ff.; *b. Sanh.* 98b; *b. Ros.Has.* 10b, 11a; *Gen. Rab.*, 1:4; *Lev. Rab.* 36:4; *Cant. Rab.* 5:11§ 4; *Tanh.B Bereshit* 10. The idea that the world existed for the sake of human beings existed among the Stoics, as can be seen in Cicero, *De natura deorum* 2:133; 154ff.; cf. *SVF* 2:527, 1041, 1152–1167; 3:369 and 658. Against this background the question is to be asked: Does Philo refer to human beings in general, or primarily to the Jews as true humanity?

Greed, idolatry and vices now

This point (that man found all provisions for life) in the second answer on the question why man was created last, stands together with other ideas in *Opif.* 79–81. The original ideal conditions of man are pictured, the bad situation of the present, and the possible future restoration of the ideal situation. The ideal is that human beings, like the first man, should spend their days without toil or trouble surrounded by lavish abundance of all that they needed. The present situation forms a contrast to this, however. Due to irrational pleasures (ἡδοναί) gluttony and lust (γαστριμαργία καὶ λαγνεία) desires for glory or wealth or power (αἱ δόξης ἢ χρημάτων ἢ ἀρχῆς ἐπιθυμίαι), sorrows (αἱ λῦπαι), fear (φόβος), folly, cowardice and injustice (ἀφροσύνη καὶ δειλία καὶ ἀδικία) and other vices, human beings now suffer penalty and punishments: they have difficulty in obtaining the necessaries of life, and they suffer all kinds of hardships and disasters.

A restoration is possible, however, if men's passions were calmed and brought under control by self-mastery, and the inclination to do wrong was corrected by justice, and life was determined by virtues. Then the warfare of the soul would have been abolished, peace would prevail, and God would provide for the human race good things all coming forth spontaneously and in all readiness.

At other places Philo says that idolatry destroys the cosmic harmony and corrupts man's situation. This point may be illustrated by Philo's interpretation of the First Commandment (*Dec.* 52–65). In this section several of the ideas in *Opif.* 77–88 reoccur: the four elements, cosmos seen as *megalopolis* and human beings' sovereignty over the animals. These agreements are in accordance with Philo's view that the specific written Laws were in harmony with the cosmic laws of creation, seen as the laws of cosmos as *megalopolis* (*Mos.* 2:48 and 51–52).

In *Dec.* 52–65 Philo then offers sharp criticism of those who have deified the four elements, earth, water, air and fire, and others deifying the sun, moon, planets and fixed stars. In contrast to these errors Philo pictures cosmos as a *megalopolis* with God as the Creator (ὁ γεννητής), the ruler (ὁ ἄρχων) of *megalopolis*, the commander-in-chief of the invincible host army (ὁ στρατάρχης τῆς ἀηττήτου στρατιᾶς), the pilot (ὁ κυβερνήτης) who steers all things in safety (*Dec.* 53). Since the stars are created, they are the brothers of human beings, since all have one Father, the Creator of the universe (ὁ ποιητὴς τῶν ὅλων) (*Dec.* 64).

As seen in previous chapters of the present study an even sharper criticism is directed to those who worship man-made images sculptures, paintings, etc. (*Dec.* 66–76) and the most horrible form of idolatry is the worship of the fiercest and most savage of wild animals, as done by the Egyptians (*Dec.* 76–80). Searching in the two elements given by God to man for his use, earth and water, they found on land no creature more savage than the lion nor in water than the crocodile, and these they worship (*Dec.* 78). When Philo in *Dec.* 78 writes that the two elements, earth and water, are given by God to man for his use, then he again alludes to Gen 1:26–29, where it says that God has given man the charge of being stewards over animals and plants and to use them for food.

Philo also internalizes man's conflict with the wild beasts and the warfare among the beasts themselves. As already seen, he applies this internalization to the Egyptians as a collective entity. A non-Egyptian who sees the Egyptians worshipping wild beasts "regards them with good reason as more miserable than the creatures they honour, as men with souls transformed into the nature of those creatures, so that as they pass before him, they seem beasts in human shape" (*Dec.* 80; cf. *Legat.* 166). This internalization of the experience of wild animals is given a general application by Philo when he talks about "the wild beasts within the soul" (*Praem.* 88, cf. § 91). Correspondingly Philo in *Opif.* 81 refers to the warfare in the soul.

One might expect that such an application of ideas from the animal world to man's inner life should lead to further internalization of the various species of the reference to animals in the creation story. Philo does this, but on a limited scale. The most elaborate example is found in *QG* 2:56 where Philo first gives a literal interpretation of Gen 9:1–2 and Gen 1:28 as referring to man's role as king over the animals, and he then presents the deeper meaning which deals with the inner struggle within human beings:

> But as for the deeper meaning, it is to be interpreted as follows: He desires that the souls of intelligent *men increase* in greatness and *multitude* (and) in the form of virtues, and fill the mind with its form, as though it were *the earth*, leaving no part empty and void for follies; and that they should *dominate and rule over the earthly* body and its senses, and *strike terror and fear into beasts*, which is the exercise of the will against evil, for evil is *untamed and savage*. And *over the birds*, (that is) those who are lightly lifted up in thought, those who are (filled) with vain and empty arrogance, (and) having been previously armed, cause great harm, not being restrained *by fear*. Moreover, (over) *the reptiles*, which are a symbol of

poisonous passions; for through every soul sense-pleasures and desires and grief and fear *creep*, stabbing and piercing and wounding. And by *the fish* I understand those who eagerly welcome a moist and fluid life but not one that is continent, healthy and lasting.[11]

The probable reason why Philo does not develop more of an internalization in his exposition of Gen 1:26/28 is that to him humankind's actual relationship to animals and nature was of importance as such. The more extensive and detailed microcosmic and macrocosmic aspects are then explicated by him from elsewhere in the creation story, as for example in his exposition of Gen 2:18–20 in *Leg. all.* 2:9–13, where the wild beasts symbolize the soul's passions, etc.

Heavenly ascents

Opif. *69–71*

After this analysis of aspects of human beings' relationship to animals and nature, points about their relationship to the higher regions of cosmos and even to the divine reality beyond the created cosmos should be examined. It then becomes evident that Philo does not only employ the notion of ascent in his interpretation of biblical persons and events, in his understanding of the Jewish people and of experiences in his own life, but also to anthropology as such.

In order to illustrate how Jewish and non-Jewish elements are woven together in a passage on heavenly journey in Philo, *On the Creation* 69–71 may serve as an example.[12] The passage is an exegetical interpretation of the concepts of "man", "the image of God" and "His likeness" in the quotation from Gen 1:26. These words are paraphrased in the opening exegesis in *Opif.* 69ab. Then a more independent elaboration about the earthly and heavenly journey by the mind follows in §§ 69c–71b. The structure of the exposition is as follows: 1. Scriptural quotation (Gen 1:26); 2. An affirmative paraphrasing interpretation; 3. Rejection of a possible misunderstanding, *in casu*, an anthropomorphic understanding; 4. An acceptable, non-anthropomorphic interpretation, with elaboration about the ascent of the mind.

---

[11] English translation in *PLCL Supplement* 1: ad loc. See further *Deter.* 25–26; *Agr.* 41; 57–58, and cf. the interpretation of Gen 2:20–23 in *Leg. all.* 2:9–13.
[12] For the following analysis of *Opif.* 69–71, see Borgen (1993) 251–54.

T.H. Tobin states that the conceptions of this non-anthropomorphic interpretation are drawn from the philosophical viewpoints of
the period, mainly from Plato.[13] Similarily, in the French translation
of *On the Creation* 69–71 there are only references to Platonic and
Stoic parallels.[14] More thorough investigations show that there are
several points which have parallels both in Jewish and non-Jewish
sources. When man's likeness with God is seen as the corresponding
role of the soul/the mind and God (*Opif.* 69), a widespread tradition
is utilized. This tradition is also found in the later rabbinic writings,
such as *Lev. Rab.* 4:8, *Midr. Ps.* 103:4–5 and *b. Berakoth* 10a, as well
as in the non-Jewish writings, such as in Seneca (1st Cent. A.D.)
Ep. 65:24 and Philodemus (1st Cent. B.C.), *De Pietate* 15:14–21, cf.
Josephus, *War* 7:346–347.[15]

The agreements are seen in the following quotations:

> *Philo, Opif.* 69: "It (the mind, the ruler of the soul) is in a fashion a god
> of him who carries and enshrines it. For the Great Ruler is related to
> the whole cosmos as also the human mind is to man. For it is invisible
> while itself seeing all things, and it has an invisible substance, while it
> is comprehending the substance of others".
>
> *b. Ber.* 10a: "Just as the Holy One, blessed be He, fills the whole
> world, so the soul fills the body. Just as the Holy One, blessed be He,
> sees, but is not seen, so the soul sees but is not itself seen".
>
> *Seneca, Ep.* 65:24: "God's place in the world corresponds to the soul's
> relation to man".

Thus, this word about the correspondence between soul/body and
God/world was a commonplace in the ancient world. Philo is closer
to the rabbinic version, however, since he does not share the Stoic
pantheistic understanding of God, and he moreover makes the same
point as that found in *b. Ber.* 10a, that God/the mind sees without
being seen.

A more general agreement exists when Philo presupposes a dicho-
tomic anthropology, where the soul is connected with heaven and
the body with earth. This anthropology is found in rabbinic and in
apocalyptic sources as well as in Greek Platonic/Stoic tradition.[16] In
Siphre Deut., Haazinu, 306.28 this view is stated in an explicit way:
man's body is earthly, but his soul is heavenly. Even the Platonic

---

[13] Tobin (1983) 37, 44–47.
[14] *PAPM* 1:186–187.
[15] See *PCH* 1:51; Ginzberg (1968) 1:60 and 5:80–81; Bergmann (1912) 151.
[16] See Meyer (1937).

idea of the pre-existence of the soul before it enters the body (cf. *Phaedrus* 248c; *Phaidon* 80B) had penetrated into Jewish anthropology, as can be seen from the late *3 Enoch* 43:3; and rabbinic writings such as *b. Yebam.* 62a; 63:b; *b. Abod. Zar.* 5a; *b. Nid.* 13b; *Gen. Rab.* 24:4; *Lev. Rab.* 15:1; moreover, in Philo, *Gig.* 12–15; *Somn.* 1:138–139; Josephus, *War* 7:342–348.

On the basis of such an anthropology, the idea of the heavenly ascent of the soul is a natural development. Philo draws in *Opif.* 70, as elsewhere, on the common picture of the soul as a winged bird, Plato, *Phaedon* 109E; *Phaedrus* 249C; *Theat.* 173E; *Gen. Rab.* 93:8; 100:7; *Lev. Rab.* 4:5; *Koh. Rab.* 12:4; *b. Sanh.* 92ab; *y. Moed Qatan* 3:82b; *y. Yebam.* 15:15c; *Midr. Ps.* 11:6–7; *3 Baruch* (Greek) 10.[17]

As for the ascent itself, Philo in *Opif.* 69–71 pictures it in five stages: (1) land and sea, (2) air, (3) ether and the stars, (4) the noetic world and (5) the Great King Himself. Philo here combines two kinds of travel, the search of the soul up to the spheres of air, stars and beyond, and the ecstatic longing, like those filled with Corybantic frenzy, to see God. A person's journey together with the stars, etc. occurs several places in Philo's writings, with close agreements of terminology. For example, the term συμπεριπολέω, "Go around together with", is used about the wandering together with the stars, etc. also in *Spec.* 1:37; 2:45; 3:1, and *Praem.* 121. This word is a term for heavenly journey in astrology, as can be seen from its use in Philodemus, D. 3:9 and *Catalogus Codicum Astrologorum* 1:136.[18] In *Spec.* 1:37 and 2:45 it is used together with another astrological term for a heavenly journey αἰθεροβατέω, "tread the ether". This latter verb also occurs in *Spec.* 1:207 and *Migr.* 184, cf. *Her.* 238 (birds). References to astrological sources are *Anthologia Palatina, Planudea* 4:328; Pseudo-Lucian *Philopatris* 25. The astrological background is also evident in the similar term οὐρανοβατέω, "tread the heaven", which is used by the astrologer *Vettius Valens* 6, *Introduction*.[19] Cf. also *QG*

[17] See Ginzberg (1968) 5:81; Malter (1911/12) 476; Aptowitzer (1925). Concerning 3 Baruch (Greek) 10, see Gaylord (1983) 673.
[18] See also Philo's use of μετεωροπολέω, *Leg. all.* 3:71.84; *Det.* 27; *Plant.* 145; *Her.* 128.230.237.239; *Somn.* 1:139; *Mos.* 1:190; *Spec.* 1:207.
[19] See Gundel and Gundel (1966) 29–30; 180–181; cf. Hartman (1985) 125; Völker (1938) 181–82; Cumont (1912) 81, about the astronomer Ptolemy: "Mortal as I am, I know that I am born for a day, but when I follow the serried multitude of the stars in their circular course, my feet no longer touch the earth; I ascend to Zeus himself to feast me on ambrosia, the food of the gods".

3:3. The idea of the dancing and singing of the stars, etc. occur also in apocalyptic and rabbinic writings.[20]

The distinction between the travel up to the ethereal region, and the next stage of the ascent, Philo marks by the Platonic category of the world of the senses and the noetic world (*Opif.* 70–71). The final stage, however, draws on Cybele-tradition ("filled with Corybantic frenzy") and on Jewish tradition (God seen as "the Great King"). Philo here sees the vision of God, the Great King, as the final aim of the ascent. God is called the Great King in several apocalyptic and other Jewish sources, such as *1 Enoch* 84:2.5; 91:13; *Sib. Or.* 3:499.560; *Ps. Sal.* 2:32.

In *Opif.* 69–71 Philo has an anthropological interpretation of the notion of ascent which as such applies to every person. This general anthropological understanding becomes more differentiated when applied to different persons and groups, however. For example in *Spec.* 1:37–50 Philo refers to the ascent of a certain group of persons, the philosophers, and gives at the same time a distinct picture of Moses.

Spec. *1:37–50*

When Philo in *Spec.* 1:37–50 deals with the ascent of philosophers, he probably does not think of Jews, but he gives, nevertheless, a positive evaluation up to a certain point of their search upwards. *On the Special Laws* 1 is an exposition of the first two of the Ten Commandments. In § 32 two questions are asked: "One is whether the Deity exists . . ., the other is what the Deity is in essence". The second question is answered in §§ 36–50. The outline of §§ 37–50 runs as follows:

A. The ascent
Who are ascending: those who have not taken a mere sip of philosophy but have feasted more abundantly on its reasonings and conclusions.
The journey: their reasoning power (ὁ λογισμός) soars through the ether and accompanies the revolutions of the sun and moon and the whole heaven.
The radiance: the soul's eye (τὸ τῆς ψυχῆς ὄμμα) is dizzied by the flashing of the rays.

---

[20] *3 Enoch* 46; Wertheimer (1967–68) 2:426. See Grözinger (1982) 265.271–72, etc.

B. Commentary

The analogy of the stars: we cannot know their essence, but persist in the search because of our love for learning.

Vision of God: the clear vision of God is denied us, but we ought not to relinquish the quest. Compare that the eye cannot see the sun in itself, but sees the emanations of its rays.

C. The hierophant, Moses, Exod 33:13–23

Prayer: "Reveal Yourself to me", Exod 33:13 LXX. God's answer is a polemic against illegitimate invasion: "Know yourself, then, and do not be led away by impulses and desires beyond your capacity, nor let yearning for the unattainable uplift and carry you off thy feet, for of the obtainable nothing shall be denied you" (*Spec.* 1:44). *Prayer*: "I beseech You that I may at least see the glory that surrounds You . . ." (§ 45, cf. Exod 33:18 LXX). The answer is that neither God nor His Powers can be apprehended in their essense. The imprint of the Powers in the order of the universe may be seen, however.

The ascent is in § 37 seen as a movement upwards away from earth to the sun and the moon (ἀπὸ γῆς ἄνω μετέωρος ἀρθείς). This philosophical search upwards leads to observations which may serve as an analogy to the understanding of God (*Spec.* 1:39–40), such as: it is impossible with certainty to know the essence of the stars, likewise it is impossible to have a vision of God as He really is, but one should not relinquish the quest. Moses is the hierophant, the sacred guide, to the right search for God, as seen from his prayers for God to reveal himself to him (Exod 33:13–23), and God answers that He will give him a share in what is attainable (*Spec.* 1:41–50). Thus, the true search and the reception of revelation as far as it is possible, have Moses as guide. The ascent motif has in these last paragraphs the form of being a dialogue between Moses who addresses God in prayers, and God who gives his replies.

Thus, in *Spec.* 1:37–50 the general search upwards through philosophical reasoning receives a positive evaluation. Philo seems in this way to look with favour on such search also outside of the Jewish nation. Nevertheless, the proper ascent is tied to Moses and the nation under the Laws of Moses. This conclusion receives support from the subsequent context in § 51, where it is said that the ones who are of the same sort (τοὺς ὁμοιοτρόπους) as Moses are those who are faithful to the nobility of their birth (i.e. Jews) and proselytes, who have joined the new and godly *politeia*. And the specifications given in *Spec.*

1:51–53 relative to the proselytes, prove that the concrete Jewish nation is meant. The proselytes have left their fatherland, kinsfolk and friends and are to receive citizenship and equal rights as the native born.

The ascent of the Jewish nation

Spec. *2:164–66*

The importance of *Spec.* 2:164–66 has already been emphasized. In that passage Philo states that when the multitude of humans went wrong and worshipped many gods, the Jews rectified the error. Now the aspect of ascent will be set in focus. Philo notes that both Greeks and barbarians recognize God the creator but combined with polytheism, and only *the Jews soar above all created objects and serve the Uncreated God*:

> When the others went wrong in what was the most vital matter of all, it is the literal truth that the error which the rest committed was corrected by the nation of the Jews (τὸ Ἰουδαίων ἔθνος), which soared above (ὑπερκύψαν = put one's head over) all created objects . . . and chose the service of the Uncreated and Eternal. . . .

Against this background one might ask: what is the relationship between the ascent of human beings as such (cf. *Opif.* 69–71) and the ascent of the particular Jewish people? The answer is here that the basic search for the vision of the true God, the Great King was hampered by polytheism. Thus the true humanity was realized in the Jewish nation who chose the service of the Uncreated and Eternal God.

The collective and national application of the notion of man's ascent in *Spec.* 2:164–66 supports the view that there is no basic gap between Philo's 'historical' treatise, *On the Embassy to Gaius,* and his other writings. Against this background one might take another look at details in the use of the idea of ascent in *Legat.* 5–6.

Legat. 5 reads:

> . . . in souls (ἐν ψυχαῖς) who have soared above (ὑπερκύψασαι, put one's head over) all that is created and has been schooled to see (ὁρᾶν πεπαίδευνται) the uncreated and
>> divine, the primal good,
>> more excellent than the excellent,
>> more blessed than blessedness,

more happy than happiness itself,
and any perfection there may be greater than these.[21]

Here the motif of ascent is both formulated as a movement upwards, as putting the head above, and as seeing. It is to be noted that they were schooled to see, probably meaning being trained in the Laws of Moses. It is important to notice that the ascent motif is here formulated in the same way as in *Spec.* 2:164–66, as putting one's head above all created things.

The proper ascent pictured in *Legat.* 5 is in *Legat.* 6 followed by a characterization of a kind of ascent that fails to reach its goal. In this latter paragraph Philo describes the inability of reason to ascend:

> . . . For reason (ὁ λόγος) cannot attain to ascend (προσαναβαίνειν) to the entirely sacred and impalpable God, but it sinks and falls back unable to find the proper words by which it may approach to describe – I do not say the Existent One – for even if the whole heaven should become an articulate voice, it would lack the apt and appropriate terms needed for this – but for his Powers, which are His body-guard, the creative, the kingly, the providential and others as many as are both beneficial and punitive. . . .[22]

In this statement Philo makes the point that reason is unable to ascend to, and find proper words for, God and for His Powers. Although the formulation as such is general, within its context it has a special application: "The argument in 4–7 is that what the unaided human intellect (λόγος) fails to attain, the Jew with his special insight (4) can attain through a mystical experience".[23]

The concrete Jewish nation is here in *Legat.* 5 at the same time seen from the spiritual side, as expressed by concepts like 'the souls'. One might object to this national interpretation and maintain that visionary souls might exist among human beings in general. The context of *On the Embassy to Gaius* makes this general interpretation impossible, however. Our analysis of the treatise makes evident that it relates the fundamental conflict between the Jews and their non-Jewish surroundings, including a conflict with the ideology and activity of the Emperor Gaius Caligula. And in *Legat.* 3–4 it is made clear that "the souls" refer to "the suppliants' race", which is the portion

[21] The translation in *PLCL* is modified.
[22] The translation in *PLCL* is modified.
[23] Smallwood (1970) 155. Cf. Goodenough (1935) 12.

of the Father and King of the universe. This race is called in the Hebrew tongue "seeing God". Thus the etymological interpretation of 'Israel' as 'the one who sees God' is here equated with all Jews even in a context of their conflict with other people.[24]

E. Birnbaum claims that this use of Israel and its etymological interpretation in *Legat.* 3–5 is an isolated case in Philo's writings.[25] Just two points should be mentioned to refute this understanding: 1) The basic idea of the ascent is here formulated in the same way as in *Spec.* 2:164–66, as putting one's head above all created things, and the idea both places is applied to the Jewish people. 2) Philo's use of the etymology of Israel in *Mos.* 2:196, where a halfbreed had a quarrel with someone of the nation/race who had vision and knowledge (ἀπὸ τοῦ ὁρατικοῦ καὶ ἐπιστημονικοῦ γένους). This halfbreed was urged by fondness for Egyptian atheism. Both here and in *Legat.* 4 the 'visionary race' is seen in contrast to and in conflict with the pagan surrounding. Thus it seems forced exegesis when Birnbaum in her comment on *Mos.* 2:196 states that since Philo refrains from calling the nation 'Israel' throughout the two treatises on Moses, the phrase "the race that has vision and knowledge" cannot mean Israel as such but only the biblical nation Israel.[26]

The study of the place of human beings in relation to animals and nature, and in relation to their ascent to the higher realms of cosmos and the trans-cosmic realm has led to the conclusion that Philo connects anthropology with his understanding of the Jewish people: the nation of Israel/Jews is the true humankind.

---

[24] Concerning "the suppliants race" and the etymological interpretation of Israel to mean "the one who sees God", see Smallwood (1970) 152–54. Among other studies in which the etymology "seeing God" is discussed, are Borgen (1965) 115–18; Delling (1984).

The etymological interpretation of 'Israel' as 'the one who sees God', 'the nation of vision' and similar phrases, is based upon Hebrew and is translated into Greek. The word Israel may have been read as איש ראה אל or in other ways which have allowed for this etymology.

[25] Birnbaum (1992) 184–87, 321–26, and (1993) 59–60.

[26] Birnbaum (1992) 181, cf. 184 and 208–09.

CHAPTER FOURTEEN

PHILANTHROPIA AND THE LAWS OF MOSES[1]

Main aspects

In the preceding chapters the analysis moved from the borderline between Jews and non-Jews as the context reflected in Philo's writings into the broader context of the understanding of human beings in relation to animals, nature, cosmos and God's realm beyond cosmos. Attention has been paid to the question of dualism in principle and in the inter-ethnic dynamic. It remains to examine aspects of ethics and observance within the perspectives of specific laws and ethical principles and of the relationship between God's people, other humans, animals and plants. Philo's interpretation of the Greek virtue *philanthropia* will illuminate these points, in particular since this virtue is in *Virt.* 51–174 applied to Moses' life and to a large body of Mosaic laws and is part of Philo's rewritten Bible, the *Exposition of the Laws of Moses*. Moreover, increasing attention seems to have been paid to this virtue in Philo's time.[2]

In Jewish sources the words φιλανθρωπία and φιλάνθρωπος occur in the apocryphal writings of the Septuagint, in the Aristeas Letter, in Josephus' and in Philo's writings.[3] In the New Testament it is found in Acts 27:3; 28:2 and Tit 3:4. Josephus employs the terms quite extensively, and in Philo the words are used spottedly in various treatises and appears, as stated above, in a concentrated manner in *Virt.* 51–174.

The essay "Philo's Ethical Theory" by D. Winston may serve as a convenient point of departure. He writes about Middle Stoa: "It was only the Middle Stoa, in the writings of Panaetius and Antiochus, through a fusion of the Stoic notion of *oikeioisis* and the Peripatetic doctrine of *oikeiotes*, that an all-embracing doctrine of human unity

---

[1] In this chapter the word φιλανθρωπία is rendered in various ways, such as by transliterating it as *philanthropia*, partly translating it as 'love of men', 'love of human beings', etc.

[2] For the following, see Borgen (1996B).

[3] Luck (1970) 109–10.

took shape".[4] He maintains that Philo's thoughts on *philanthropia* are based on the idea of man's kinship with God and correspondingly on a universalistic concept of man: "'All we men', writes Philo, 'are kinsmen and brothers, being related by the possession of an ancient kinship, since we receive the lot of the rational nature from one mother'. (*QG* 2:60; cf. *Dec.* 41; *Det.* 164; *Spec.* 4:14)".[5] Winston concludes his discussion of Philo's ideal of *philanthropia* by considering its implications for the biblical doctrine of election, and he states that Philo, at every possible opportunity, emphasizes the universal aspects of Jewish particularism.[6]

Against this background the following points serve as hypotheses for the present study:

1   In Philo's use of *philanthropia* two frames of reference are seen. a) To Philo the most important thought-category is: God, Moses, God's people, proselytes and settlers, irrational animals and plants; b) There is an interplay and partly a tension between this frame of reference and the thought-category of God, human beings, animals and plants.

In Philo's works the Greek concepts of the virtues, *in casu philanthropia*, have been made to interpret aspects of the Laws of Moses, and thereby of the Jewish religion.

2   Several concerns are at work in Philo's presentation of *philanthropia*, such as apologetic, systematic and theological motifs.

3   Although the distinction is drawn between God's people and others, and between men and animals, the concept of *philanthropia* may mean a reaching out across the boundaries, although without these boundaries being obliterated.

4   In Philo's writings the concept of *philanthropia* in some contexts means benevolence, but it often has the broader meaning of fellowship-feeling and related attitudes.

5   Although central aspects of the concept are associated with the nature of God and with the picture of kings, an influence from the understanding of man, as for example, human qualities in contrast to those of the beasts, can be seen. A universalistic perspective is in Philo's writings tied to the notion of the people of God being the center of mankind.

---

[4] Winston (1984) 392.
[5] Winston (1984) 393; cf. Geiger (1932) 7–9.
[6] Winston (1984) 398.

Although the analysis will be focused upon the section on *philanthropia* in *On the Virtues*, some passages where the term is used in other treatises, will also be included.

God – Moses – the people

Philanthropia characterizes God's relationship to human beings. This is seen

a   when He revealed himself to Abraham, the sage, who, as a proselyte, migrated from astrology and the Chaldean creed that the world itself was god, *Abr.* 77–84: When it is said in Gen 12:7 that "God was seen (ὤφθη) by Abraham", it meant that God was not manifested (ἐμφανής) to him before, but that He, in His love for human beings (φιλανθρωπία) and when the soul came into His presence, came and revealed His nature, so far as the beholder's power of sight would allow. As a result his name was changed from Abram to Abraham (Gen 17:5).[7]

b   when He, the King of kings, dwells in the soul as a palace-temple to show goodness to "our race" (*Cher.* 98–100): In Num 28:2 God gives regulations to Moses and the people about "bounties, and gifts and fruits which you shall observe and offer to me at My feasts". When Philo elaborates upon the word "feasts", he offers, as shown in an earlier chapter, sharp criticism of the festal assemblies among the different nations, whether Greek or barbarian. As a contrast to the external temples he speaks of the soul as a house of God: "What house shall be prepared for God the King of kings, the Lord of all, who in His tender mercy (δι' ἡμερότητα) and love of human beings (φιλανθρωπίαν) has deigned to come from the boundaries of heaven to the utmost ends of the earth, to show his goodness (ἐπ' εὐεργεσίᾳ) to our race (τοῦ γένους ἡμῶν)"? (*Cher.* 99). The answer is: the soul that is fitted to receive Him.[8]

---

[7] This view that God's *philanthropia* brings about the initial revelation of God to a proselyte and the change in the person's situation and identity, is an interesting parallel to the use of the term in Titus 3:3–7.

[8] Cf. the similar thought in *Virt.* 188.

c   when in *Virt.* 77 God's love of man is in particular directed
to the twelve tribes. Here it is told that Moses offered his
benedictions to the tribes of the nation (Deut 33), and Philo
adds his own comment: One ought to believe that these benedictions will be fulfilled, because Moses who gave them was
beloved of God, the lover of men (φιλάνθρωπος) and those
for whom he asked held the highest rank in the army led by
the Maker and Father of all.

d   when God's love meets the needs of human beings, corresponding to the behaviour of an ideal king (*Plant.* 90–92):
When Jacob said "And the Lord shall be to me for God"
(Gen 28:21), it meant that God as a King in His love for
human beings makes it His delight to supply what is lacking
(τὸ ἐνδεές) in each one.

e   when specific needs, such as hunger, are met by God (*Mos.*
1:191–208): Philo paraphrases and elaborates upon the giving of the manna (Exod 16), and writes in § 198 that God
was moved by the clemency and love to human beings which
belongs to His nature (διὰ τὴν σύμφυτον ἐπιείκειαν καὶ φιλανθρωπίαν), and took pity on them and healed their sufferings.

f   when the angels, as the 'words' of God, οἱ τοῦ θεοῦ λόγοι,
descend as helpers (*Somn.* 1:146–47): Here Philo internalizes
the Biblical story about Jacob's ladder (Gen 28), to mean
the 'logoi' which ascend and descend between the heavenly
mind and the earthly sense-perception. They descend out of
love for human beings and compassion (διὰ φιλανθρωπίαν καὶ
ἔλεον) for our race (τοῦ γένους ἡμῶν), to be helpers and com-
rades, in order that with the healing of their breath may
quicken into new life in the soul.

The background for the use of *philanthropia* in these passages is the
fact that already in Greek usage the term characterized the attitudes
and behaviour of the gods (for example Hermes, Eros and Demeter)
towards human beings (Aristophanes, *Peace*, 392–93; Plato, *Symposium*,
189C; Plutarch, *Moralia* 758AB; Apollonius of Tyana, *Epistle* 75:55K).[9]
When Philo in *Cher.* 98–100 and *Plant.* 90–92 pictures God as King,
and tells that as King He acts in His love of human beings, he had

[9] See Schmidt (1938) col. 2125; Hirzel (1912) 23–24; Luck (1970) 107–08; Le
Déaut (1964) 256–60; Betz (1978) 490–91.

as background Hellenistic ideas of kingship. Philo provides himself examples of this use when he in *Legat.* 67 and 73 tells about the *philanthropia* of the emperor Gaius Caligula and in *Legat.* 158 of the emperor Augustus.[10]

Moses and his laws

In *Virt.* 51–174 events in the life of Moses and a selection of his laws are seen as manifestations of *philanthropia*.

Picturing Moses as the paradigm of φιλανθρωπία, Philo first refers to his two treatises on the life of Moses in which he sets forth the actions which Moses performed from his earliest years to old age for the care of each single man and for them all (*Virt.* 52). Then Philo illustrates Moses' royal and paradigmatic role further by reporting on biblical events related to the end of his life, such as the appointment of his successor, Joshua (Num 27:16–23; Deut 33:7, 23), his hymnic song to God (Deut 32:1–43) and the benedictions offered on the twelve tribes (Deut 32), *Virt.* 55–79. Moses should give the election of his successor to God alone, especially since the person appointed would preside over the nation that is a suppliant of Him who truly exists, and is the most populous of all the nations upon earth (*Virt.* 64).

Philo makes the important statement that what the disciples of philosophy gain from its teaching, the Jews gain from their customs and laws:

> For just as successful navigation demands a pilot of good judgement and knowledge, so, too, a governor of all-round wisdom is needed to secure for his subjects in every place a happy and orderly life. Now wisdom's years are from of old, ere not only I [Moses], but the whole universe was born (Prov 8:22–30), and it is not lawful or possible that any other should judge her save God, and those who love her with a love that is guileless and pure and genuine. I [Moses] have learnt from my own history not to choose anyone else from among those who seem to be suitable and approve him for government (*Virt.* 61–62).
>
> ... the person appointed will preside not over some ordinary nation, but over the most populous of all the nations upon earth, one which makes the greatest of all professions that it is a suppliant of Him who

---

[10] See further Luck (1970) 108–10; Le Déaut (1964) 264, 267–68; Due (1989) 163–70.

truly exists and is the Maker and Father of all. For what the disciples
of the most excellent philosophy gain from its teaching, the Jews gain
from their customs and laws, that is to know the highest, the most
ancient Cause of all things and reject the delusion of created gods . . .
(*Virt.* 64–5).

Thus all future rulers would find a law to guide them right by looking to Moses as their archetype and model . . . (*Virt.* 70).

In these passages it is made evident how Philo stresses the distinctive nature of the Hebrew nation relative to other nations, and how
he defines this distinctiveness from this nation's divine and cosmic
foundation. Moses had grasped the thought that the nation was akin
to things divine (*Virt.* 79).

Philo characterizes Moses' unselfish and pious way of selecting his
successor, as "proof of the love of man and faithfulness which he
showed to his whole tribe (δεῖγμα τῆς πρὸς ἅπαν τὸ ὁμόφυλον αὐτοῦ
φολανθρωπίας καὶ πίστεως)" (*Virt.* 66).[11] Philo concludes his characterization of Moses as a paradigm in this way: "We have stated the
proofs of the legislator's *philanthropia* and fellowship-feeling (τὰ δείγματα
τῆς τοῦ νομοθέτου φιλανθρωπίας καὶ κοινωνίας) . . . (*Virt.* 80), a quality
which he possessed through a happy gift of natural goodness, and
also as the outcome of the lessons which he learnt from the holy
oracles." Thus Moses loved virtue, goodness and man, *Virt.* 175.[12] It
is worth noting that Moses is not called the sage and the wise man
(ὁ σοφός) in this section of *On the Virtues*, although that often is the
case elsewhere in Philo's writings.[13]

Philo can use the term *philanthropia* to characterize non-Jews. The
Emperor Gaius Caligula's performance in the initial stage of his reign
receives such a positive evaluation: "For as they [the multitude] had
hoped that kindness and love for men (χρηστότητα γὰρ καὶ φιλανθρωπίαν) were established in his soul . . ." (*Legat.* 73). The Emperor
Augustus was fair in his treatment of the Jews. When the doles
in Rome were distributed on the Sabbath, he ordered the dispensers
to reserve for the Jews till the morrow the charity (φιλανθρωπία),
Legat. 158.

---

[11] The idea of Moses' unselfishness when selecting his successor is also found in
rabbinic writings. See *Siphre Num.* 138; *Midrash Shir* 1:10b–11a: Moses, being a truly
pious man, thought when he saw his end approach, not of himself, but of the welfare
of the community, for whom he implored a good and worthy leader.

[12] See further on Moses in van Veldhuizen (1985) 215–24.

[13] *Leg. all.* 2:87, 93; 3:45, 131, 140f., 144, 147; *Spec.* 2:194; 4:69, 143, 157, 175, etc.

Seemingly Philo goes even further, when relating the concept to human beings in general as distinct from animals, when he in *Virt.* 81 writes that, before dealing with *philanthropia* in relationship to animals, he would begin with men. As it turns out, in *Virt.* 82 and subsequent paragraphs the boundary between God's people and others is still basic, however, since "the men" consist of the members of the same nation οἱ ὁμοεθνεῖς, incomers (proselytes, οἱ ἐπηλύται), and settlers (μέτοικοι, *Virt.* 102–05). Philo's characterization of οἱ ἐπηλύται, incomers, shows that proselytes are meant: ". . . abandoning their kinsfolk by blood, their country, their customs and the temple and images of their gods, . . . they have taken the journey to a better home . . . to the worship of the one and truly existing God" (*Virt.* 102). The acceptance of proselytes by the Jews is also by Josephus seen as a proof of the Jews' love for man and their magnanimity (*Ag.Ap.* 2:261). As for the settlers, they are, according to Philo, foreigners who, being unable to live in their own land, live in an alien state (*Virt.* 105).

In *Virt.* 106–08 Philo refers to a named non-Jewish people, the Egyptians. He quotes Deut 23:7 "you shall not abhor an Egyptian because you were a sojourner in Egypt," (*Virt.* 106) and in § 108 he paraphrases Deut 23:8 "The children of the third generation that are born to them may enter the assembly of the Lord" in this way: "And if any of them should wish to pass over into the community of the Jews, they must . . . be so far favoured that the third generation is invited to the congregation (εἰς ἐκκλησίαν)". It is evident that Philo does not only refer to the Laws of Moses as such, but that he also applies Deut 23:8 to the concrete Jewish community in his own time, since he writes "into the community of the Jews (πρὸς τὴν' Ἰουδαίων πολιτείαν)".

As for the relation to other non-Jews, Philo deals with them in specific situations, such as enemies in wartime (*Virt.* 109–15), based on Deut 20:10–13. Philo here probably had mainly non-Jewish enemies in mind. Analogous application of *philanthropia* to the treatment of enemies is found in Xenophon, *Cyropaedia* VII:5,73 and in Plutarch's *Lives, Cleomenes* 30:1; *Alexander* 44:3.[14]

In what ways are non-Jews in general included in the practice of *philanthropia* by Jews? In the section on *philanthropia*, Philo writes that "we should do no wrongs to men of other nations (οἱ ἑτεροεθνεῖς), if

[14] See Martin, Jr. (1961) 171 and 174.

we can accuse them of nothing save difference of race (τὸ ἀλλογενές)" (*Virt.* 147). In the treatise *On Joseph* Philo states that a guiding principle for Joseph, as viceroy of Egypt, was "the natural *philanthropia* (ἡ φυσικὴ φιλανθρωπία)" which he felt to all, and particularly to those of his blood (*Jos.* 240). When in *QG* 3:62 it is said that Abraham according to Gen 17:27 circumcised persons of foreign birth, Philo generalizes it to mean that the wise man is helpful and philanthropic (Marcus: φιλάνθρωπος). He saves and calls to himself also those of foreign birth and of different opinions (Marcus: ἑτεροδόξους), giving them of his own goods with patience and ascetic continence. Philo may here say that the wise man (i.e. the proper Jew) shares circumcision with non-Jews to make them become proselytes, or he may think of the spreading of the practice of circumcision even among some non-Jews.[15]

When Philo in *Virt.* 125–60 moves on to animals and plants, he holds to the proper meaning of φιλανθρωπία, as love to men, and does not identify Moses' regulations for man's treatment of animals (§§ 125–47) or man's handling of plants (§§ 148–60) as in themselves *philanthropia.* But man's attitude towards animals and plants should be of the same kind as the attitude of *philanthropia* in relationships among men, such as the attitudes of moderation and gentleness (ἐπιεικὲς καὶ ἥμερον, *Virt.* 125), etc. The interplay between human beings and animals is in *Virt.* 140 characterized in this way:

> . . . Moses rising to a further height extended the duty of fair treatment (τὸ ἐπιεικές) even to irrational animals, so that by practising on creatures of dissimilar kind we may show love to men (φιλανθρωπία), abstaining from strokes and counter-strokes to vex each other, and not hoarding our personal good things as treasures, but throwing them into the common stock for all in every place, as for kinsmen and brothers by nature.[16]

It should be noted here that Josephus as well as Plutarch can apply the term *philanthropia* to man's proper behaviour to animals (Josephus, *Ag.Ap.* 2:213 and Plutarch, *Cato Maior* 5:5; *De sollertia animalium* 6:964A, and 13:970A).

---

[15] See Mendelson (1988) 109–10.
[16] The translation in *PLCL* is modified.

Motifs

Philo defends his people against charges of misanthropy. The background was the widespread tensions between Jewish communities and some of the non-Jews.[17] Already the Egyptian priest Manetho (c. 300 B.C.) criticized the Laws of Moses in which Osarsiph (= Moses) ordained that the Jews should have no connection with any save members of their own confederacy.[18] Also Hecataeus of Abdera (c. 300 B.C.), who in general had a sympathetic attitude towards the Jews, states that "as a result of their own expulsion from Egypt he [Moses] introduced an unsocial and intolerant mode of life" (διὰ γὰρ τὴν ἰδίαν ξενηλασίαν ἀπάνθρωπόν τινα καὶ μισόξενον βίον εἰσηγήσατο.[19] Apollonius Molon (1st cent. B.C.) charged the Jews with xenophobia and exclusiveness. He reviled the Jews as atheists and misanthropes (ὡς ἀθέους καὶ μισανθρώπους).[20] Similarily Diodorus Siculus (1st cent. B.C.), writes:

> [The Jews] alone of all nations avoided dealings with any other people and looked upon them as their enemies. . . . They made their hatred of mankind into a tradition, and on this account had introduced utterly outlandish laws. . . .[21]

According to Tacitus (c. 56 A.D.–120 A.D.) hate and enmity towards other people are the counterpart to the strong solidarity which the Jews display towards one another: "toward every other people they feel only hate and enmity (*sed adversus omnes alios hostile odium*)".[22] "They sit apart at meals and they sleep apart, and . . . they abstain from intercourse with foreign women".[23]

Both Philo and Josephus defend the Jews against such criticism. They do it by stressing philanthropic aspects of the Jews as expressed in their specific laws and their role as God's people. Referring to the unjust attacks rendered against the lawgiver, Moses, by Apollonius Molon, Lysimachus, and others, Josephus gives a brief account of the Jewish constitution. In this way he will make apparent that the

---

[17] For the following, see Borgen (1992B) 125–27; Mendelson 1988.
[18] See Stern (1976–84) § 21, quoting Josephus, *Ag.Ap.* 1:228–52.
[19] Stern (1976–84) § 11.
[20] Stern (1976–84) § 49, citing Josephus, *Ag.Ap.* 2:145–48.
[21] Stern (1976–84) § 63 with reference to *Bibliotheca Historia*, Fragments of Book 34–35, 1:1–2.
[22] Stern (1976–84) § 281.
[23] Stern (1976–84) 26.

Jews possess a code designed to promote piety (πρὸς εὐσέβειαν), fellowship (πρὸς κοινωνίαν), and love to mankind towards the world at large (πρὸς τὴν καθόλου φιλανθρωπίαν), besides justice, hardihood, and contempt of death (*Ag.Ap.* 2:145–46). In contrast to the Spartans, who expelled foreigners, the Jews showed love to man (φιλανθρωπία) and magnanimity by welcoming others who wish to share their own customs (*Ag.Ap.* 2:261). Philo also relates the attitude of *philanthropia* to the proselytes, but instead of characterizing proselytism in general, as Josephus does, he, as shown above, characterizes the attitudes and actions of the Jews towards those who have become proselytes. Towards the proselytes the commandment of neighbourly love (Lev 19:33–34) applies: "He [Moses] commands the members of the nation to love the proselytes . . . as themselves both in body and soul" (*Virt.* 103).[24]

As a refutation of charges of misanthropy, Philo, in *Virt.* 141 maintains that the Jewish nation and their laws even go beyond the normal meaning of *philanthropia* by acting correspondingly even to creatures of dissimilar kind, to animals, and that through the instruction of the laws the Jews learn gentle behaviour:

> . . . let those clever libellers continue, if they can, to accuse the nation of misanthropy and charge the laws with enjoining unsociable and unfriendly practices, when these laws so clearly extend their compassion to flocks and herds, and our people through the instruction of the law learn from their earliest years to correct any wilfulness of souls in gentle behaviour.

Just in the exclusive role of the Jews, being those who worship the true God, they cared for all men, according to Philo (*Spec.* 2:167). Thus the particularistic and special worship of God by the Jews was interpreted by Philo as universal in its outreach, and in principle all men's duty.

A theological motif is present when Philo understands God to be the source of *philanthropia* on the human level. Thus in *Virt.* 51 Philo stresses that *philanthropia* is the virtue closest akin to piety (εὐσέβεια),

---

[24] Heinemann (1931) col. 308, rightly states that Philo does not refer to the commandment on the love of neighbour as found in Lev 19:18. Nissen (1974) 478, makes the general statement that "der Gedanke einer *Liebe* zum mitmenschen bei ihm nirgendwo begegnet; er scheint ihm so fremd und fern zu sein, dass er auch das biblische Gebot der Nächstenliebe weder zitiert noch paraphrasiert, weder auf es anspielt noch es auswertet". Nissen has here overlooked that Philo draws on the commandment of neighbourly love as it is rendered in Lev 19:33–34.

its sister and twin. Elsewhere he states that the one who is pious is also one who loves men (*Abr.* 208). Accordingly he criticises those who divides the two:

> Now we have known some who ... turning their backs upon all other concerns devoted their personal life wholly to the service of God. Others conceiving the idea that there is no good outside doing justice to men have no heart for anything but companionship with men.... These may be justly be called lovers of man, the former sort lovers of God. Both come but halfway in virtue; they only have it whole who win honour in both departments ... (*Dec.* 108–10).

As shown above, the concept of *philanthropia* is in Hellenistic sources often seen as an attribute of gods, as Philo correspondingly applies the concept to God. Philo characterizes the dual perspective of God's and man's *philanthropia* as *imitatio Dei*. In *On the Virtues* this idea is made explicit in §§ 168–69, with primary reference to the ideal behaviour of rich and prominent persons: "Especially does he give this lesson as most suitable to the rational nature that a man should imitate God (μιμεῖσθαι θεόν) as much as may be and leave nothing undone that may promote such likeness (ἐξομοίωσιν) as is possible".[25]

Here Jewish and Greek ideas are fused together to characterize the life based on the Laws of Moses. On Jewish grounds the concept of *imitatio Dei* is found among other places in *Mekilta, Beshallah* 3 on Exod 15:2; *b. Shabbat* 133b; *b. Sotah* 14a. According to *Mekilta* Abba Saul interpreted Exod 15:2 in this way: "I will imitate Him [God]. As He is merciful and gracious, be you also merciful and gracious". As for the idea of being like God (*Virt.* 168), Philo knows that the idea was Platonic since he in *Fug.* 63 cites Plato, *Theaetetus* 176AB: "... we ought to fly away from earth to heaven as quickly as we can; and to fly away is to become like (ὁμοίωσις) God, as far as possible. And to become like Him is to become holy, just, and wise". The idea of ascent to heaven, which is exploited by Philo in *Fug.* 62–63, is not utilized by him in *Virt.* 168–69, but both to Plato and Philo to imitate and become like God means living a virtuous life.

---

[25] See further Winston (1984) 398, with references also to *Spec.* 4:73; cf. *Spec.* 1:294; *Congr.* 171.

Inter-human relationships – benevolence

According to H. Bolkestein the term φιλανθρωπία in Philo essentially
means benevolence, i.e. care for the poor. Thus in general Philo
understands the concept in what Bolkestein calls its oriental usage.[26]
According to him *philanthropia* in *On the Virtues* largely refers to commandments and rules in favour of the poor: §§ 82–87: not to exact
interest on loans; § 88: wages of the poor man are to be paid on the
same day; § 89: the creditor is not to enter the debtor's house to
seize a pledge; §§ 90–94: the gleaning of the harvest is to be left to
the poor; §§ 121–24: the treatment of servants and slaves.[27]

Bolkestein's view is onesided, however, when he stresses so much
the aspect of benevolent favours towards the poor. Some of the references he made to *On the Virtues* do not deal only with the poor.
For example, the theme in *Virt.* 82–87 is that one shall not exact
interest on loans to brothers, including anyone of the same citizenship or nation. Although the prohibition is of special importance to
the poor, it has a broader address as well. For example, according to
§ 89 the debtor may or may not have money to pay back a pledge
or a surety. Similarily, hospitality has a broader connotation than
benevolent help to the poor. Drawing on Gen 18 Philo tells that
Abraham showed his *philanthropia* by being hospitable to three trav-
ellers, and Philo makes the following generalization, which does
not focus on the poor: "For in the wise man's house no one is slow
in showing *philanthropia*; but women and men, slaves and free, are
full of zeal to do service to their guests" (*Abr.* 109).[28] It may be
added that in Acts 28:2 hospitality and *philanthropia* were more of a
benevolent act, since the Maltesians showed hospitality to the ship-
wrecked ones.

Thus, a broader and more balanced understanding of the concept
philanthropia than that suggested by Bolkestein, is needed in order to
do justice to Philo's varied application of the term. To Philo it covered aspects of fellowship feelings and corresponding behaviour, and
not primarily benevolence to the poor.

There are even paragraphs in which the concept of *philanthropia* is

---

[26] Bolkestein (1967) 426–28.
[27] Bolkestein (1967) 427, fn. 1.
[28] Concerning the relationship between *philanthropia* and hospitality in Greek sources,
see Luck (1970) 107–08.

not primarily seen as the proper behaviour with an emphasis on the others to whom the virtue is addressed. Instead it may be used to characterize the acting person himself. Moses who "perhaps loved her [*philanthropia*] more than anyone else has done, since he knew that she was a high road leading to holiness . . ." (*Virt.* 51). He set before his subjects his own life as a model. As mentioned above, Philo tells that at the end of his life Moses did not choose anyone from his own family as his successor. He entreated God and asked Him to find the man and he blended his thankfulness to God with his affection to the nation. Here the term φιλανθρωπία, love for men, is used together with πίστις, faithfulness, and κοινωνία, fellowship feeling, primarily to characterize Moses himself (*Virt.* 51–80).

In a corresponding way Philo may focus the attention upon the attitude and practice of the persons themselves, those who display *philanthropia*. Thus, in *Virt.* 95, he says that according to the Laws of Moses they are not to regard the firstborn oxen and sheep and goats as their personal property, but as first fruit. In this way they honour God and demonstrate that they do not take all things as their personal gain. As a result they may have the ornament of those queens of the virtues, piety and *philanthropia*. Similarily, Moses in his laws did not give full liberty to food and drink, but bridled them with ordinances most conducive to self-restraint and love of man (πρὸς ἐγκράτειαν καὶ πρὸς φιλανθρωπίαν) and most of all to piety (πρὸς εὐσέβειαν) (*Spec.* 4:97).[29]

This combination of piety, self-restraint and *philanthropia* makes it understandable that Philo maintains that Moses with all the injunctions in *Virt.* 51–160 tamed and softened the minds of the citizens of his commonwealth and set them out of the reach of pride and arrogance (§§ 161–74). Thus,

> . . . he who has been carefully taught that his vigour and robustness is a gift of God, will take account of his own natural weakness, the weakness which was his before he enjoyed the gift of God, and will thrust aside the spirit of lofty arrogance and give thanks to Him who brought about the happy change (§ 165).

---

[29] In the picture of Cyrus as an ideal king, Xenophon pictures him as one who in his life displayed self-restraint, love of man and piety. As Moses is pictured as a model king by Philo, Cyrus is seen as a model king by Xenophon. See Due (1989) 147–84.

Robustness

Although the concept of *philanthropia* has to do with the feeling of fellowship and mercy, Philo makes clear that this is only one attitude among several, since this virtue belongs together with other virtues, such as justice and courage. Moreover, Philo's particularism and corresponding restrictions at times modify *philanthropia* to a large extent. For example, although board and hospitality are usually given to neighbours, the first fruits must be kept out of the hands of a dweller near the priest, because there is a danger that the consecrated meats may be profaned through an untimely generosity (*philanthropia*). Otherwise order will be destroyed (*Spec.* 1:120). As for the treatment of settlers, *philanthropia* means that they are allowed to stay in a country not their own on the condition that they pay some honour to the people who has accepted them (*Virt.* 105).

Philo demonstrates a restrictive attitude when he in *Spec.* 1:324 writes:

> But while the law stands pre-eminently in enjoining fellowship (κοινωνία) and love of men (φιλανθρωπία), it preserves the high position and dignity of both virtues by not allowing anyone whose state is incurable, to take refuge with them, but bidding him avaunt and keep his distance.

An elaborate exposition follows in *Spec.* 1:325–45, in which Philo explains that those who are to be kept away are sexual deviates (Deut 23:1–2), polytheists, and others. In conclusion Philo indicates clearly that he has his own contemporary situation in mind, since he characterizes the positive and contrasting group as "we, the pupils and disciples of Moses" (*Spec.* 1:345).

Correspondingly, in some of the Greek sources the concept of love of man, φιλανθρωπία, is modified by particularistic virtues. Thus, Isocrates (436–338 B.C.) in *To Nicocles*, 2:15 associates it with 'love for the city', φιλόπολις.[30] Similarily, Moses' φιλανθρωπία is focused upon his patriotic love for his people, τὸ φιλοεθνὲς πάθος (*Virt.* 69). Also Plutarch has a particularistic use of the concept of *philanthropia*, since he identifies it with Greeks and with Hellenic civilization, laws and way of life (*Pyrrh.* 3–4; *Phil.* 8:1–3, etc).[31] The difference between Philo and Plutarch is that Philo basically applies it to the Jewish

---

[30] See Le Déaut (1964) 267–68.
[31] See Martin, Jr. (1961) 167–68.

people, while Plutarch applies it to Hellenic civilization as it was practised by the Greek people and by other persons and peoples.[32]

The question of anthropology

The question of the universalistic concept of mankind needs be touched upon once more, since Philo, besides thinking in terms of God, the people and others, also uses the broader categories of human beings, animals and plants:

> He [Moses] did not set up consideration and gentleness as fundamental to the relation of men to their fellows only, but poured it out richly with a lavish hand on animals of irrational nature and the various kinds of cultivated trees (*Virt.* 81; cf. 125, 140 and 148).

How can Philo combine such universalistic categories with his focus on God's love towards the Jewish people and the mutual love of men within this one nation? As seen above, Greek usage at times limits the application of *philanthropia* to the polis, the people or to Hellenic civilization, while in Greek philosophical traditions the universalistic application of *philanthropia* might be derived from the idea of the kinship among all human beings.[33] A Jewish understanding was that one regarded the Jewish people of God to be the center of mankind. They were the true men (*Spec.* 1:303). As already stated above, the Jewish nation has received the gift of priesthood and prophecy on behalf of all mankind (*Abr.* 98). It is consecrated to offer prayers on behalf of the human race, and their worship is on behalf of all (*Mos.* 1:149; *Spec.* 2:167). So also the high priest of the Jews makes prayers and gives thanks not only on behalf of the whole human race, but also for nature (*Spec.* 1:97). The Jewish nation is to the whole inhabited world what the priest is to the *polis* (*Spec.* 2:163).

From the people of God the impact of *philanthropia* is to be spread to all. Cautiously Philo indicates that the whole human race ought

---

[32] Martin, Jr. (1961) 168 notices that since *philanthropia* may be identified with civilized way of life as such, bathing and anointing of one's body can be called *philanthropia* (Plutarch, *Lycurgus* 16:6). This is what a civilized man does. Philo has a similar statement in *Migr.* 217: "... merchants and traders for the sake of trifling profits cross the sea ... letting stand in their way ... neither the daily intercourse with friends ... nor the enjoyment of our fatherland and of all the gracious amenities of civic life (πατρίδος καὶ πολιτικῶν φιλανθρωπιῶν ἀπόλαυσιν). ..."

[33] Le Déaut (1964) 280–81, with references to Aristotle, *Nicomachean Ethics* 1155a.20; Stoa, *SVF* 1:262. See especially Winston (1984) 392.

to follow the Mosaic legislation. He hints at this perspective in *Virt.*
119:

> This (τοῦτο) is what our most holy prophet through all his regulations
> especially desires to create, unanimity, neighbourliness, fellowship, reci-
> procity of feeling, whereby houses and cities and nations and countries
> and the whole race of men may advance to supreme happiness.

This is a generalizing elaboration of the preceding paragraphs 116–
18 where Philo has interpreted Exod 23:5 about protecting and re-
storing animals to enemies and thereby bringing about reconciliation
and ending a feud among the persons involved. Together with his
fellow-men Philo carries this all-embracing hope in an existential way,
both in the form of prayer and as a trust in God (*Virt.* 120).

Summary

1 The hypothesis given at the beginning of this essay has been confirmed in the present analysis: Philo's concept of *philanthropia* is
   rooted in ideas about God, Moses and God's people. In this way
   the Greek concepts of the virtues have been made to interpret
   the Laws of Moses and to serve Jewish religious categories.
2 In Greek usage the application of *philanthropia* may be restricted
   to love of the polis, the people or of Hellenic civilization. In Greek
   philosophic traditions, however, the universalistic application of
   philanthropia might be derived from the idea of the kinship among
   all human beings. In a Jewish understanding the application of
   the concept of *philanthropia* to the particular people of God was
   central. The universalistic aspect then was understood to mean
   that this Jewish people of God with its laws and worship was the
   center of mankind. From the people of God the influence of
   philanthropia is to be spread to all. Philo specifies persons and groups
   such as proselytes, settlers and Egyptians.
3 *Philanthropia* characterizes God's relationship to human beings. The
   background for the use of *philanthropia* in these passages is the
   fact that already in Greek usage the term characterized the attitudes and behaviour of the gods. When God is pictured as the
   King who acts in His love of human beings, then the background
   is Hellenistic ideals of kingship.
4 Having pictured Moses as the paradigm of φιλανθρωπία, Philo
   gives in *On the Virtues* a survey of his laws and regulations which
   fit this model.

5   When Philo in *Virt.* 125–60 moves on to animals and plants, he holds to the proper meaning of φιλανθρωπία, as love to men, and does not identify Moses' regulations for man's treatment of animals or man's handling of plants as in themselves to be *philanthropia*. But man's attitude towards animals and plants should be one of moderation and gentleness. By practising on creatures of dissimilar kind one may learn to show love to men.

6   The Laws of Moses instruct the conquerors to treat enemies with generosity and mercy, *philanthropia*. The same attidude is advocated by Xenophon in *Cyropaedia* and by Plutarch in his *Lives*.

7   Several motifs are seen to be at work in Philo's interpretations, such as

     – an apologetic motif, where Philo defends the Jews against charges of misanthropy.

     – a systematic motif, where it can be seen that Philo deals with *philanthropia* within the large scheme of his 'Exposition of the Laws of Moses'. The virtues are common to all commandments and bind them together.

     – a theological motif, when Philo uses *philanthropia* to characterize God, whom he also understands to be the source of *philanthropia* on the human level. It is the virtue closest akin to piety (εὐσέβεια), its sister and twin.

     – a drive for fusing Jewish and Greek ideas together. For example, Philo combines the Jewish concept of *imitatio Dei* and the Platonic idea that man's goal is to be like God.

8   Bolkestein interpreted *philanthropia* in Philo's writings mainly to be benevolence to the poor. A broader and more balanced understanding of the concept is needed in order to do justice to Philo's varied application of the term. In Philo's writings it also covers aspects of fellowship feelings and proper behaviour in cases where the recipients are not poor or in need of mercy.

9   There are paragraphs in which the concept of *philanthropia* is not primarily seen as the proper behaviour to others, but is used to characterize the acting person himself, his self-restraint and his veneration of God.

10   Philo makes clear that love of man, *philanthropia*, does not lead to softness. This virtue is only one among several. It belongs together with other virtues, such as justice and courage. Moreover, Philo's particularism brings several restrictions to the application of *philanthropia*.

In conclusion: Philo's varied usages of the concept of *philanthropia* should be seen against the background of the varied usages in Greek sources. In different ways both general and particularistic applications of the concept are present in both areas. This approach seems to be more adequate than measuring Philo's interpretations and applications primarily against the background of universalistic ideas about the unity of man found in some developments of Greek philosophy.

CHAPTER FIFTEEN

A CONDITIONED FUTURE HOPE

Although Philo largely sees human beings in general and God's people in particular within a cosmic context, it has already been documented that he includes accounts of biblical and historical events in his expositions as well as elements of future hope. Accordingly he combines both aspects, the cosmic setting and the perspective of past, present and future in time.

Several of the thematic areas analysed meet in the picture of the future given by Philo in the treatise *On Rewards and Punishments*. In *Praem.* 79–126 the focus is placed on the future restoration, more specifically in §§ 79–91, centered on the relationship between animals and human beings, and in §§ 98–126, on man and creation in general, with emphasis on man's wealth and health. Within this context the question of the future role of the Jewish nation and other peoples is raised.

Points of similarities between this treatise and the treatises *Against Flaccus* and *On the Embassy to Gaius* have already been examined. It remains to compare some points from *On Rewards and Punishments* with points from others of Philo's treatises.

It should be repeated here that the treatise *On Rewards and Punishments* is an integral part of the *Exposition of the Laws of Moses*. Against the background of the story of the creation (*Opif.*), the stories of the patriarchs as living prototypes of the Laws (*Abr., Jos.*), the Laws themselves interpreted (*Dec., Spec.*), Philo has described their function relative to virtues and vices (*Virt.*), and proceeds now to the different attitudes and actions of men relative to the Laws, and the resulting consequences in on the one hand rewards and blessings and on the other hand in punishments and curses (*Praem.*).

In a summary fashion Philo in *Praem.* 9 even refers to the place of human beings in creation as previously stated in *Opif.* 77–86:[1]

---

[1] The translation in *PLCL* is modified.

> For from the beginning and simultaneously with the first creation of
> all things, God provided beforehand, raised from the earth, what was
> necessary for all living animals and particularly for the human race to
> which he granted sovereignty over all earthborn creatures (*Praem.* 9).

Moreover, the hermeneutical key is to be kept in mind, as it is outlined in *Mos.* 2:48–52, with its two or three levels, the concrete and
specific level, the general cosmic and ethical level, and the divine
level of the beyond. The task is to indicate the ways this key is of
help in the analysis of the treatise *On Rewards and Punishments*.

In *Praem.* 79–172 blessings and curses are listed.[2] This form is
biblical, and Philo draws here extensively on Lev 26 and 28 together
with Deut 28. The blessings are conditioned upon obedience to the
Laws: "If, he [Moses] says, you keep the divine commandments in
obedience to the ordinances and accept his precepts . . ., you shall
have as a first reward victory over your enemies", *Praem.* 79. In *Praem.*
85–98 Philo describes this victory. In §§ 85–91a the theme is man's
war with the wild beasts and the victory in the war within man
himself.

Since the treatise *On Rewards and Punishments* is part of the *Exposition*, it is relevant to refer back to *On the Decalogue*, and *On the Special
Laws* 1–4 with regard to terms used in *Praem.* 79. The term "commandment" (ἐντολή) is a Deuteronomic term, LXXDeut 28:1, and is
used in *Spec.* 1:300, alluding to LXXDeut 10:12–14. The word commandment (πρόσταγμα) refers in *Dec.* 132 to the second commandment on the second table of the Decalogue. The participle τὰ
διαγορευόμενα, translated as "precepts" comes from διαγορεύω, declare, give orders, forbid, a word which occurs in *Spec.* 1:249; 2:130;
3:150, 4:143 and 4:219. These references show that the laws which
are to be kept according to *Praem.* 79, are the commandmends and
precepts of the Laws of Moses, as exemplified in *On the Decalogue* and
On the Special Laws 1–4.

It is evident that Philo's description of the first victory, *Praem.* 85–
91a moves on two levels: on one level the theme is man's war with
the wild beasts, and on the more general and ethical level the theme
is that of keeping the commandments, i.e. the victory in the war,
meaning the war against the beasts within and among men. As shown
in the discussion of man's sovereignty over the animals, the motif of
the war in man himself was present in *Opif.* 79–81, where it was said

---

[2] For a general presentation of Philonic ideas about a Messianic age, with special
reference to *Praem.* 79–172, see Wolfson (1948) 2:407–26.

that if men's passions were brought under control, wrongs were checked by righteousness, etc, then the warfare in the soul would have been brought to an end, and ideal conditions would be restored.

As for man's conflict with the beasts as pictured in *Praem.* 85–91a, the line can also be drawn back to *On the Creation of the World*, as can be seen from agreements between *Praem.* 89b–90 and *Opif.* 83–84a. In *Praem.* 89b the words about the beasts' fear of man as their master, καταπλαγέντα δ' ὡς ἄρχοντα καὶ φύσει δεσπότην εὐλαβῶς ἕξει, are a close parallel to words in *Opif.* 83, κατάπληξιν . . . προσκυνεῖν ὡς ἂν ἡγεμόνα φύσει καὶ δεσπότην. Both *Praem.* 85–90 and *Opif.* 83–86 deal with land-animals and sea-animals.

When Philo in *Praem.* 85–90 pictures the future peace among the animals, he goes beyond his idea about the original situation after creation, however. According to *Opif.* 83, although the animals subordinate themselves to man, they still had fierce conflict among themselves. Philo's future hope, as stated in *Praem.* 85–90, is that even this conflict will end. Thus Philo does not here only draw on his interpretation of Gen 1:26/28, but also on Lev 26:6: "And I will give peace in the land . . . and I will remove evil beasts from the land. . . ."

This additional reference does not sufficiently cover Philo's ideas either, when he tells about peace both among the animals and between the animals and human beings. There must therefore be here an influence from Isa 11:6–9:

> The wolf shall dwell with the lamb, and the leopard shall lie down with the kid, and the calf and the lion and the fatling together, and a little child shall lead them. The cow and the bear shall feed; their young shall lie down together; and the lion shall eat straw like the ox. The sucking child shall play over the hole of the asp, and the weaned child shall put his hand on the adder's den. They shall not hurt or destroy in all my holy mountain; for the earth shall be full of the knowledge of the Lord as the waters cover the sea.

Similar ideas about future were also expressed elsewhere, such as in *Sib. Or.* 3:788–795; Isa 65:25; *2 Apoc. Bar.* 73:6; Virgil, *Ecloge* 4:18–25.

Just as in Isa 11:6–9 so also in *Praem.* 89–90 bears, lions and leopards are mentioned, but Philo adds elephants and tigers. He lists the snake, corresponding to the asp in Isa 11. He lacks the domestic animals, cows and bulls, which are mentioned in Isa 11. In Isa 11 it is said that the animals will graze together (LXX: βόσκω, feed, passive: eat, graze) and Philo expresses the same by the term σύννομος, feeding in herds together, τὸ σύννομον, being in a herd together. Thus Philo combines the idea from Gen 1:26/28 about man's sovereignty over the animals with ideas from Isa 11:6–9 (and other texts) about peace among the animals.

Philo has a longing and a hope for future which he expresses in this way: "Would that this good gift might shine upon our life and that we might be able to see that day . . ." *Praem.* 88. Philo ties this hope to "some" who are worthy of salvation (ὅταν κρίνῃ τινὰς σωτηρίας ἀξίους). Their personal blessing will then be brought to people in general for all to share, *Praem.* 87. Similarily, the blessings of abundance of food, safe residence, health, etc, will come as a reward to those who keep the Laws, *Praem.* 98–125. Those who practise frugality (ὀλιγόδεια, contentment with little) and practise self-restraint (ἐγκράτεια), will have abundance (*Praem.* 100).

Here in *Praem.* 98–125 Philo elaborates on the same expectations of abundance for those obedient to the Laws as he has sketched briefly in *Opif.* 79. In *Praem.* 98–125 the direct reference back to the ideal condition of the first human beings is less direct, however. Philo rather draws on various scriptural texts such as Lev 26:3–4: "If you walk in my statutes and observe my commandments and do them, then I will give you your rains in their seasons, and the land shall yield its increase, and the trees of the field shall yield their fruit". In *Praem.* 101 Philo paraphrases these Old Testament verses.

As for the curses, *Praem.* 127–152, they are correspondingly an elaboration of the idea that man's original estate was destroyed by greed and passion. The following two sentences demonstrate the parallelism: *Opif.* 80: ". . . penalty is difficulty in obtaining the necessaries of life". *Praem.* 127: "The first curse . . . is poverty . . . and lack of necessaries. . . ." The picture given forms a contrast to man's rule of the animals as pictured in *Opif.* 83–84 and in *Praem.* 89: The curse means that God, when he brought forth the universe, created the wild animals to warn those who were willing to be rectified and punish the incorrigible (*Praem.* 149). Philo here connects Gen 1:24–25, the creation of the animals, with Lev 26:22: "And I will let loose the wild beasts among you. . . ."

Cosmos, humanity and Israel

Within this perspective of protology and eschatology a further analysis of the place of human beings and of the Jewish nation is needed. When Philo in *Opif.* 77–88 discusses the relation between human beings and creation at large, it seems obvious that he speaks about humanity. This passage must be interpreted as part of the *Exposition* as a whole, however. Then one has to ask whether this conclusion is adequately formulated.

Again one must refer to *Spec.* 2:166:

> When they [the Greeks and the barbarians] went wrong in what was the most vital matter of all, it is the literal truth that the error which the rest committed was corrected by the nation of the Jews, which went beyond the created world . . . and chose the service only of the Uncreated and Eternal . . . (*Spec.* 2:166).

And again it should be repeated that the Jews are the true human beings: ". . . out of the whole human race He chose of special merit . . . those who are in a true sense men (οἱ πρὸς ἀλήθειαν ἄνθρωποι) and called them to the service of Himself . . ." (*Spec.* 1:303). Here Philo paraphrases the words addressed to Israel in Deut 10:15: ". . . and chose . . . you above all peoples. . . ." In accordance with this view, Moses, like the first man, was a cosmopolitan (*Opif.* 3 and *Mos.* 1:157).

Those referred to by Philo in the word "some" in *Praem.* 87 are then, accordingly, those who keep the Laws of Moses. This understanding is in accordance with the introduction which in *Praem.* 79–84 is given to the larger section on blessings. In this introduction Philo gives, as stated above, an exposition of Deut 28:1LXX when he in *Praem.* 79 writes: "If, he [Moses] says, you keep the divine commandments. . . ." The same view is expressed in *Praem.* 98 where Philo speaks about those who follow God and always cleave to His commandments. The possible future function of this people needs be explored more fully.

The central role of the people of God

In *Praem.* 91–97 Philo tells how the peoples will subjugate themselves under the divine people, either voluntarily or by the appearance of "a Man" (Num 24:7 LXX), that is, a commander in chief who shall conquer them.[3] The two passages most important for our discussion are *Praem.* 79.93–97 and 163–72. *Praem.* 79.93–97 belongs to the section on blessings:[4]

---

[3] See Borgen (1992) 341–61.
[4] The translation in *PLCL* is modified.

The Condition:
(79) If, he says, you keep the divine commandments . . .,
The Blessing:
the first boon you will have is victory over your enemies.
The Blessing Is specified as victory:
Alternative 1, the enemy will give in peacefully:
(93) Either, then, as he says, the war will not pass through the
land of the godly at all, but will dissolve and fall into pieces of
itself when the enemy perceives the nature of their opponents,
that they have in justice an irresistible ally. (For virtue is majes-
tic and august and can, unaided and silently, allay the onsets of
evils, however great.)
Alternative 2, futile attack:
(a. Victory by superior strength):
(94) Or if some fanatics whose lust for war defies restraint or
remonstrance come careering to attack, till they are actually
engaged, they will be full of arrogance and bluster, but when
they have come to a trial of blows, they will find that their talk
has been an idle boast, as they are unable to win.
Because, forced back by your superior strength, they will fly
headlong, companies of hundreds before handfuls of five, ten
thousands before hundreds by many ways for the one by which
they came.
(b. Some stricken by fear):
(95) Some, without even any pursuer save fear,
will turn their backs and present admirable targets
to their enemies so that it would be an easy
matter for all to fall to a man.
For "there shall come forth a man", says the oracle,
and leading his host to war he will subdue great and populous
 nations,
because God has sent to his aid the reinforcement
which befits the godly,
and that is dauntless courage of soul
and all-powerfill strength of body,
either of which strikes fear into the enemy,
and the two if united are quite irresistible.
(c. Some defeated by swarms of wasps):
(96) Some of the enemy, he says, will be unworthy to be defeated by men.

He promises to marshall against them to their shame and perdition swarms of wasps to fight in the van of the godly.

(d. The victory):

(97) They will win not only a permanent and bloodless victory in the war, but also a sovereignty which none can contest bringing to its subjects the benefit which will accrue from the affection or fear or respect which they feel.

For the conduct of their rulers shows three high qualities which contribute to make a government secure from subversion, namely dignity, strictness, benevolence, which produce the feelings mentioned above.

For respect is created by dignity, fear by strictness, affection by benevolence, and these when blended harmoniously in the soul render subjects obedient to their rulers.

Praem. 93–97 draws on the biblical story of Balak and Balaam. This story is rewritten in *Mos.* 1:289–91, which must be brought into the discussion. Balak hired Balaam to curse the Hebrew army. Instead, Balaam invoked blessings on them (*Mos.* 1:288–91):

> *The view of the Hebrew army*:
> So, setting his face to the wilderness, he looked upon the Hebrews encamped in their tribes,
> and, astounded at their number and order
> which resembled a city rather than a camp,
> he was filled with the spirit and spoke as follows:
> *The Seer's self-introduction; His visionary experience*:
> 'Thus saith the man who truly sees, who in slumber saw the clear vision of God with the unsleeping eyes of the soul'.
> *Praise of the Hebrew army (army addressed in second person)*
> How goodly are thy dwellings, thou host of the Hebrews. Thy tents are as shady dells,
> as garden by the riverside
> as a cedar beside the waters.
> *The appearance of a universal emperor (army addressed in second person)*:
> There shall come forth from you one day a man,
> and he shall rule over many nations
> and his kingdom spreading every day shall be exalted on high.
> *The conquering nation and those conquered*:
> This people, throughout its journey from Egypt, has had God as its guide, who leads the multitude in a single column.

Therefore, it shall eat up many nations of its enemies
and take the fatness of them right up to the marrow, and destroy
its foes with its far-reaching bolts.
It shall lie down and rest as a lion, or a lion's cub, full of scorn,
fearing none but putting fear in others.
Woe to him who stirs up and rouses it.
Blessing and curse:
Worthy of benediction are those who bless thee; worthy of cursing those who curse thee.

The end result of the conflict with Balak and his people was that
Moses selected the best of his men of military age, one thousand
from each tribe. The Hebrew soldiers made a slaughter of their
opponents and returned themselves all safe and sound without a single
one killed or even wounded (*Mos.* 1:306–11).

Philo thus interprets the oracle of Balaam in Numbers 24 within
the context of Moses' office as king and primarily as a warrior king.
As king of the Hebrew nation, Moses and his people had a universal
call from God, and their victory over the other peoples was partial
fulfillment of this divine call. Consequently, when Philo quotes Num
24:7ff. in *Mos.* 1:290, "There shall come forth from you one day a
man and he shall rule over many nations", he pictures a Hebrew
emperor who will bring to its full realization the universal charge of
Moses and the Hebrew nation.

It must be added that the same universal and eschatological perspective is applied to Moses' offices as legislator (*Mos.* 2:12–65), high
priest (2:66–186) and prophet (2:187–291). It has already been pointed
out that according to Philo the Laws of Moses are the specific laws
of the Hebrew nation and are at the same time the eternal principles of the universe (*Mos.* 2:45–52). Accordingly, the Laws of Moses
were translated into Greek so as to be revealed also to the Greek
half of the human race (*Mos.* 2:25–40).[5] Moses as high priest established the priesthood in Israel, and the priestly tribe was the nucleus
of all mankind as an anticipation of the blessed eschatological life to
come (2:66–186). As prophet he defended the Jewish religion and
foretold the future of the nation (2:187–291, esp. 288). Thus the central
role of the Jewish nation as the head (and ruler) of all nations is a
fundamental element of Philo's hope for the future.

---

[5] This shows that Philo's ideas about the future include the view that all nations
would become proselytes and worship the One God of the Jews. See above, Ch. 12.

Mos. *1:289–91* and Praem. *93–97*

As already stated, the passages *Mos.* 1:289–91 and *Praem.* 93–97 draw on the biblical story of Balak and Balaam.[6] In *Mos.* 1:263–305, Numbers 22–25 and 31 are interpreted. In addition to using the story about King Balak and the seer Balaam in Numbers 22–24, Philo (on the basis of Num 31:15–16) ascribes to the advice of Balaam the sins of adultery and idolatry which the Israelites committed (Numbers 25). Philo here represents a broad Jewish exegetical tradition.[7]

Praem. 93–97 belongs to the section on blessings and curses (*Praem.* 79–172). This section renders the blessings and curses spoken by Moses in Lev 26 and Deut 28.[8] When the oracle spoken by Balaam in *Mos.* 1:289–91 is examined in detail, we see that Philo paraphrases the Septuagint text of Num 24:1–9 closely. The paraphrase as such is similar to the way of rendering the Old Testament text in the targums.[9] The Septuagint translation of Num 24:7 differs from the Hebrew text in a puzzling way. It is not within the scope of the present paper to discuss this problem, although it is of great importance in itself.[10] Our task is to examine *Mos.* 1:289–90 on the basis of the Septuagint text. In Philo's paraphrase of Num 24:1–9, the following distinctive emphases can be seen:

1 Philo stresses that the Hebrews had a well-organized army. He says that the camp of the Hebrews resembled a city rather than an encampment (ὡς πόλεως ἀλλ' οὐ στρατοπέδου), although he explicitly states that the Hebrews were an army, στρατιὰ Ἑβραίων. Moreover, according to him the Hebrews went away from Egypt in the kind of military formation called a column. He interprets the Septuagint μονοκέρωτος (unicorn, Num 24:8) to mean ἓν κέρας and reads καθ' ἓν κέρας ἄγοντι. The words κατὰ κέρας ἄγειν is a technical phrase for leading

---

[6] Parts of the story about Balak and Balaam are used by Philo at various places in his works: *Leg. all.* 3:187.210; *Cher.* 32–36; *Sacr.* 94; *Det.* 71; *Immut.* 52–69.181–83; *Conf.* 64–66.72, 98.159; *Migr.* 113f.; *Mut.* 202f.; *Somn.* 1:234–37; *Virt.* 34–46.

[7] See Vermes (1961) 169ff.

[8] Parts of Lev 26 and Deut 28 are found scattered in various of his writings: Lev 26:5 in *Virt.* 47; 26:10 in *Sacr.* 79 and *Heres* 279; 26:12 in *Sacr.* 87; *Mut.* 266, and *Somn.* 1:148f., 2:248; 26:41 in *Spec.* 1:304; Deut 28:1.2.7 in *Virt.* 47–48; Deut 28:12 in *Leg. all.* 3:104; *Immut.* 156, and *Heres* 76; Deut 28:14 in *Post.* 102, 28–29 in *Heres* 250; Deut 28:49–57 in *Spec.* 1:313; Deut 28:65–66 in *Post.* 24f.; and Deut 28:67 in *Flacc.* 167.

[9] See Vermes (1961) 155–61.

[10] Cf. Hengel (1983) 679–80.

an army in marching order as a column, as over against ἐπὶ
φάλαγγος ἄγειν, to lead an army in the line of battle.[11]

2   Philo clearly places the appearance of "a man" (Num 24:7)
some time in the future, by adding ποτέ· ἐξελεύσεταί ποτε
ἄνθρωπος (there shall come forth *one day* a man). In this way he
distinguishes in time the universal reign pictured in Balaam's
oracle from the present conflict with Balak. At the same time
he makes a clear connection by adding τοιγαροῦν "for that
very reason", "therefore": ὁ λαὸς οὗτος ἡγεμόνι τῆς ἀπ' Αἰγύπτου
πάσης ὁδοῦ κέχρηται θεῷ καθ' ἓν κέρας ἄγοντι τὴν πληθύν.
τοιγαροῦν ἔδεται ἔθνη πολλὰ ἐχθρῶν . . . (*Mos.* 1:290–91). "The
people has used God as leader on the whole journey from
Egypt, God who leads the multitude (as an army) in (the
marching order of) a single column; for that very reason, it
shall eat up many nations . . ." (trans. mine). God's leadership of the Hebrew army in the Exodus of the past is the
guarantee for the people's military success in the future
encounter with many nations. This line of reasoning is in
accordance with Moses' words at the time of his death
(*Mos.* 2:288):

Then, indeed, we find him [Moses] possessed by the spirit, no
longer uttering general truths to the whole nation but prophesying
to each tribe in particular the things which were to be and here-
after must come to pass. Some of these have already taken place,
others are still looked for, since confidence in the future is assured
by fulfilment in the past.[12]

3   Philo pictures "a man" in Num 24:7 as an emperor who
shall rule over many nations, and, after he has appeared, his
kingdom will spread gradually:
Philo: "There shall come forth from you one day a man.
LXX: "There shall come forth from his seed a man
Philo: and he shall rule over many nations
LXX: and he shall rule over many nations,
Philo: and his kingdom advancing every day
LXX: and the kingdom of Gog shall be exalted

[11] See Xenophon, *Cyropaed.* 1.6.43; Liddell and Scott (1940) 941, 1913.
[12] See *Virt.* 77. See the same method of reasoning by Josephus in *Ant.* 4:125,
"And from these prophecies having received the fulfillment which he predicted one
may infer what the future also has in store"; cf. *Ant.* 10:210.

Philo: shall be exalted".[13]

LXX: and his kingdom shall be increased".

This concentration on "a man" as a glorious emperor is stressed by Philo since he omits the Septuagint reference to the eschatological enemy king Gog. Thus "a man" rules over many nations, without one particular enemy being named.

On the basis of this analysis of *Mos.* 1:298–91, how should Philo's eschatology be characterized? It is to be defined in this way: (a) From God's action in the past, Moses' prophecies for the future receive a firm basis. (b) Moses' call to kingship made him king of the Hebrew nation, the center of all nations. The Law given through Moses was at the same time the universal cosmic law.

Eschatology means then the realization of the universal aspect of Moses kingship and the universal role of the Hebrew nation and its worship and its laws. This universal realization of Moses' kingship did not take place in Moses' lifetime. It will be accomplished in the future by "a man" who will be emperor of many nations, i.e. of the world. This "man" is not a new Moses, but an emperor who, on the basis of the exodus, will continue Moses' work and bring it to its complete fulfillment. Moses' and the Hebrew army's battles with the Phoenicians and with Balak and his people are events which point forward to the Hebrew people's future eating up of many nations of its enemies.

As the eschatological emperor, the "man", although not a Davidic king, carries the features of the Messiah, in accordance with the messianic interpretation of Num 24:7 in the Targums.[14]

Moreover, as shown in the historical survey, the universal role of the Jewish people is a central theme in Jewish literature in Egypt. So also was the militaristic war tradition important, since a large number of the Jews were soldiers in the Ptolemaic army. The transfer into Roman rule brought a change; the Jews were eliminated as a military factor together with the Ptolemaic army as a whole. The military tradition of warfare was carried on, however, and led to the armed

---

[13] The translation in *PLCL* is modified.

[14] Vermes (1961) 159ff.; cf. the messianic interpretation of Num 24:17.24 in the Targums, the Dead Sea Scrolls *T12P, Sib. Or.*, and in R. Akiba's application of Num 24:17 on Simon bar Kokhba. See Vermes (1961) 165f.; Hengel (1983) 679–80; Dimant (1984) 505, 518, and 540; Neusner (1984) 241–47; Volz (1934) 180–84, 189, 193, 210, 400; Moore (1927–30) 2:329–30; Meeks (1967) 71–72.

uprising by the Alexandrian Jews at the death of Emperor Gaius
Caligula in A.D. 41, the uprising in A.D. 66 and the large-scale
revolution of Jews in Cyrene and Egypt in the years A.D. 115–117.

Philo's picture of Abraham (*Abr.* 225–35) and Moses partly as
warrior kings, and his characterization of the Hebrews in *Mos.* 1:289–
91 as a well-organized army, and his quotation of the hope for a
Jewish eschatological emperor in Num 24:7, reflect this militaristic
stream of Egyptian Jewry.[15]

As we turn from the analysis of *Mos.* 1:289–91 to *Praem.* 93–97,
we notice that Philo here paraphrases the Septuagint text in a freer
way. Although the passage is based on the blessings and curses in
Leviticus 26 and Deuteronomy 28, a quotation of Num 24:7 is
included, and as seen above, there seems to be an allusion to Isa
11:1–5 and Exod 23:28 (Deut 7:20). Again, this treatment of the
Septuagint is similar to the use of the Old Testament text in the
Aramaic Targums, in this case the freer use of the text in the Fragmentary Targum to the Pentateuch and the Targum Pseudo-Jonathan
to the Pentateuch.[16]

If the divine commandments are kept, then victory over the enemies follows as a blessing. This theme is developed in two alternatives in *Praem.* 93–97: (1) victory will be won without war, or (2) if
some attack, they will be defeated. In alternative (1) Lev 26:5 is quoted
and elaborated upon: "and war shall not go through your land"
(§ 93). In alternative (2) there is first a general description of the
futility of the attack by the enemy (§ 94). They will be forced back
by "your superior strength". Philo here paraphrases words from Lev
26:8 and Deut 28:7. Then two groups and cases are specified, as
indicated by "some" (ἔνιοι) in §§ 95 and 96.

The first case deals with "some" who flee due to fear. The fear
will be caused by the military leader. Here Num 24:7 is quoted and
elaborated upon, corresponding to the use of Lev 26:5 in *Praem.* 93:
"For there shall come forth a man, says the oracle, and leading his
army and doing battle, he will subdue great and populous nations,
because God has sent to his aid the reinforcement which befits the
godly, and that is dauntless courage of soul and all-powerfull strength

15 Hengel (1983) 655–86; Borgen (1992A) 3:1061–1072.
16 See Levey (1974) 1. Similar paraphrastic exegesis is found in the "rewritten"
Bibles, the *Book of Jubilees*, the *Genesis Apocryphon*, and the *Biblical Antiquities of the
Pseudo-Philo*. See the chapter above on rewritten Bible, and Borgen (1984) 233–34,
and Borgen (1987) 20, 52.

of body, either of which strikes fear into the enemy and the two if united are quite irresistible" (*Praem.* 95).

The second case deals with "some" who are unworthy to be defeated by men. They will be conquered by swarms of wasps (*Praem.* 96). Here, as in *Praem.* 93, Philo refers to a saying by Moses (φησίν). The reference is to LXXExod 23:28 (or Deut 7:20): "I will send the wasp before thee. . . ."

The concluding part, *Praem.* 97, says that the godly ones will not only win victory, but gain ruling power of the enemies subsequent to the war.[17] *Praem.* 97 then gives a brief catalogue of three virtues which contribute to the ruling power, dignity, strictness, benefaction.

Some observations are of importance for the understanding of *Praem.* 93–97. (1) A comparison with the presentation of the virtue courage (ἀνδρεία) in *Virt.* 34–48 is illuminating. From the story about the victory in the war which the Hebrew army fought against the Midianites (the Arabians) (Num 18 and 31:1–18), Philo here sees demonstrated the blessings of Deut 28:1, 2, and 7, and Lev 26:5. The connection is made by ὅθεν, whence, therefore", in *Virt.* 47:

> Therefore, he says in his Exhortations, 'If thou pursuest justice and holiness and the other virtues, thou shalt live a life free from war and in unbroken peace, or if war arises, thou shalt easily overcome the foe under the invisible war-leader God, who makes his care mightily to save the good'.

Since in *Virt.* 34–48 the victorious wars fought by the Hebrews during the exodus from Egypt to Canaan (Num 18 and 31:1–18) served as the basis for Moses' words about the blessing of peace or victory in wars (Deut 28:1–2,7 and Lev 26:5) provided that they pursue the virtues, then those events are also presupposed as background for Moses' words in Deuteronomy 28 and Leviticus 26 about the blessings of peace or victory in war (*Praem.* 93–97). Thus it is natural that the prophecy about the future "Man" (Num 24:7), uttered during the Hebrew army's conflict with Balak and his people, has been included in the blessings (*Praem.* 93–97) based on Leviticus 26 and Deuteronomy 28.

Both in *Virt.* 47 and in *Praem.* 95, the Hebrew army is led by a

---

[17] The τοῦτο with which *Praem.* 97 begins must be changed into τούτους, esp. due to the plural subject of ἐπιτηδεύουσι later in the paragraph. The word τούτους then refers back to τῶν ὁσίων in § 96. Goodenough, Cohn and Colson read τούτους, while Bréhier reads τοῦτον (i.e. the "man" § 95). See Goodenough (1938) 115–16.

warrior king. The same word is used, στραταρχέω, "command an army". In *Virt.* 47 the commander-in-chief is God, and in *Praem.* 95 it is the "man". This double leadership corresponds to the double royal leadership of God and Moses during the exodus, with Moses' kingship derived from that of God (cf. *Mos.* 1:149–59).

Since Philo in this way has brought the oracle about the "Man" (Num 24:7) into Moses' description of blessings in Leviticus 26 and Deuteronomy 28, he has not just in a mechanical way accepted a word about Messiah from Scripture. He has deliberately placed Num 24:7 into the new context. The corresponding passage in *Virt.* 24 has God as commander-in-chief, a fact which shows that Philo could have excluded the prophecy about the "man" if he had wanted to. These points speak against the scholars who in different ways hold that Philo only pays lip service to Num 24:7 as a word from Scripture, without placing any importance on it in his own thinking or expectations.[18]

(2) U. Fischer states that instead of the enemy being killed in the war, Philo in *Praem.* 97 talks of a bloodless (ethical?) victory by the godly people. And they will reign on the basis of the virtues σεμνότης (dignity), δεινότης (shrewdness), and εὐεργεσία (doing good deeds), and not on the basis of military superiority.

Several points speak against Fischer's interpretation. First, the term "bloodless" (ἀναιμωτί) does not exclude the possibility that the enemies were killed, since the Hebrews won a bloodless victory when the Egyptians drowned in the sea when they pursued the Hebrews (*Mos.* 1:180, cf. *Virt.* 38). Bloodless means therefore that the soldiers were not involved in a direct fight. Victory was won by other means, such as through drowning or through wasps (*Praem.* 96)[19] or through terror (*Praem.* 95), with killing involved, or without.

Moreover, Fischer sees ethical virtues and military warfare as mutually exclusive entities. This is not Philo's view. He applies ethical virtues to the pursuits of war as well as to peacetime activities. Thus some of the examples given in the treatise *On Virtues* are taken from warfare (*Virt.* 22–50, 109–18), just as also is the case in the discussion of the virtue "justice" in *Spec.* 4:219–25. And the virtues

---

[18] Against Fischer (1978) 199–202, and Drummond (1888) 322; cf. Bousset (1926) 439; Barraclough (1984) 480–81. In his section on "Die messianische Erlösung", Amir (1983) 31–37, does not discuss *Praem.* 95 at all.

[19] See Philo's interpretation in *QE* 2:24 of Exod 23:28 of the assistance of wasps in warfare.

of σεμνότης (dignity), δεινότης (shrewdness), and εὐεργεσία (doing good deeds) (*Praem.* 97), are attributes associated with rulers without excluding their military engagements.[20]

In *Praem.* 93–97 Philo does not soften the thought that the Hebrew people and its "man" as general-in-chief were to enter into warfare against the enemies. Corresponding to the divine help in the wars fought under the leadership of Moses during the exodus from Egypt, God also sent aid to the "Man" and made him awe-inspiring and irresistible.

The conclusion of our analysis above of *Mos.* 1:289–91 harmonizes well with the results of our study of *Praem.* 93–97. Three distinctive features of *Praem.* 93–97 stand out:

1 While the "Man" in *Mos.* 1:289–91 is seen chiefly as the eschatological emperor who shall rule over many nations and whose kingdom will be spreading every day, he is in *Praem.* 95 chiefly seen as the commander-in-chief who will appear if needed in the eschatological war, and who brings the Hebrew nation to be rulers of the conquered enemies.

2 The eschatological blessing is in *Praem.* 93–97 conditioned upon the loyalty and obedience of the Hebrew nation to the commandments in the Laws of Moses and the virtues present in them.

3 Most important, Philo in *Praem.* 93 states clearly that the possibility of victory might be won by peaceful means, without war. At several places Philo indicates that he favors a peaceful ideological "warfare" rather than a victory won through military war. Even when war was to be fought, the aim was peace for Abraham: "So, then, the man of worth was not merely peaceable and a lover of justice but courageous and warlike, not for the sake of warring ... but to secure peace for the future ..." (*Abr.* 225).

Thus Philo's preferred approach is indicated by the statement in *Virt.* 119–20, that Moses through all his regulations desires to create unanimity, fellowship, unity of mind, blending of dispositions, whereby houses and cities and nations and countries and the whole human

---

[20] Concerning σεμνότης, see for example *Jos.* 165 and *Flacc.* 4. Concerning δεινότης, see for example *Legat.* 33. Concerning εὐεργεσία, see for example *Mos.* 1:199 and *Legat.* 148, 284, 323.

race may advance to supreme happiness. These things will, Philo believes, become facts beyond all dispute, if God, even as He gives us the yearly fruits, grants that the virtues should bear abundantly.

The regulations and virtues in Moses' Laws contained, however, stories about wars fought under the leadership of Abraham and Moses, sections on virtues and divine assistance in wars, extensive sections on kingship, as well as ideas about the Hebrew nation as the head of all nations and about a universal acceptance of the Mosaic and cosmic laws, and about the final reign of the Hebrew nation and, if needed, of its "Man", commander-in-chief and emperor, over mankind. If necessary, this goal would be accomplished through divine intervention in future wars. The conclusion is this: without using the term "Messiah," Philo looks for the possibility of a (non-Davidic) Messiah to come in the form of a "Man" who is seen as a final commander-in-chief and emperor of the Hebrew nation as the head of the nations.

Philo puts the emphasis on the cosmic order of the world made manifest in the biblical events of the past, however, and expresses the conviction that these events of the past give certainty for the fulfillment of prophecies in the future. Philo and his fellow Jews hope for shares also now in the blessings to come. Here lies a motivation for Philo's peaceful ideological warfare to bring the Law of Moses and its virtues to all nations.

Praem. *163–72*

In *Mos.* 1:289–91 and *Praem.* 93–97 a royal warrior is mentioned in an explicit way. As we turn to *Praem.* 165 we find a reference to "a vision divine and superhuman". Some scholars believe that this also is a reference to the Messiah. For this, and for other reasons, some comments need to be made on *Praem.* 163–72. This final passage follows after the section on curses, which they will suffer who disregard the holy laws (§§ 127–62). Then those Jews who confess their sins and turn back to virtue will experience restoration and their enemies will in turn suffer punishment. *Praem.* 163–72, quoted in part, shows us this:

The condition: conversion:

> If however they accept these chastisements as a warning rather than as intending their perdition, if shamed into a whole-hearted conversion

they reproach themselves for going thus astray, and make a full con-
fession and acknowledgment of all their sin, first within themselves with
a mind so purged that their conscience is sincere and free from lurking
taint, secondly with their tongues to bring their hearers to a better
way, then they will find favour with God the Savior, the Merciful,
who has bestowed on mankind that peculiar and chiefest gift of kinship with His own Logos, from whom as its archetype the human mind
was created.

From slavery to liberty:

(164) For even though they dwell in the uttermost parts of the earth,
in slavery to those who led them away captive, one signal, as it were,
one day will bring liberty to all. This conversion in a body to virtue
will strike awe into their masters, who will set them free, ashamed to
rule over men better than themselves.

Return under guidance:

(165) When they have gained this unexpected liberty, those who but
now were scattered in Greece and the barbarian world over islands
and continents, will arise and post from every side with one impulse to
the one appointed place, guided in their pilgrimage by a vision divine
and superhuman, unseen by others but manifest to them as they pass
from exile to their home.

Three intercessors:

(166–67) Three intercessors they have . . .

The change from ruin to prosperity:

(168) When they have arrived, the cities which but now lay in ruins
will be cities once more; . . .

The reversal:

(169) Everything will suddenly be reversed, God will turn the curses
against the enemies of these penitents, the enemies who rejoiced in the
misfortunes of the nation and mocked and railed at them, thinking
that they themselves would have a heritage which nothing could destroy and which they hoped to leave to their children and descendants
in due succession; thinking too that they would always see their opponents in a firmly established and unchanging adversity which would be
reserved for the generations that followed them.
(170) In their infatuation they did not understand. . . .
(171) But these enemies who have mocked at their lamentations, proclaimed public holidays of their misfortunes, feasted on their mourn-
ing, in general made the unhappiness of others their own happiness,

will, when they begin to reap the rewards of their cruelty, find that their misconduct was directed not against the obscure and unmeritable but against men of high lineage, retaining sparks of their noble birth, which have to be but fanned into a flame, and from them shines out the glory which for a little while was quenched.

New growths from the roots:

(172) For just as when the stalks of plants are cut away . . .

As already shown, some features in this section make an interesting connection with the two historical books of *Against Flaccus* and *On the Embassy to Gaius*. The central notion of return has important parallels in parts of Philo's *Allegorical Commentary*.

The section *Praem*. 163–72 is based on Lev 26:40ff. and Deut 30:1–7. Lev 26:14–39 tells about curses which will come upon the Israelites if they do not obey God and his commandments, after which repentance and restoration will take place, vv. 40ff. According to Deut 30:1–7, the people, when they return to God, will be gathered to their land from their dispersion among the nations and the curses which they have suffered will be brought upon their enemies.

Into his paraphrase of Lev 26:40ff. and Deut 30:1–7, Philo brings in ideas from Jewish eschatological traditions, as has been shown by several scholars.[21] In *Praem*. 163 the condition for the restoration is conversion. Then the change from slavery to liberty follows in § 164, and the return of the Diaspora will take place, under supernatural guidance (§ 165). Three intercessors plead for their reconciliation with the Father, God's clemency, the holiness of the patriarchs, and the reformation working in the people (§§ 166–67). The restoration will lead to new prosperity (§ 168, cf. Paul's reference to the role of the forefathers in Rom 11:28). A reversal will take place: God will turn the curses against the enemies of the penitents (§§ 169–71). Finally, new growths will shoot up from the root of the Hebrew nation (§ 172). Compare Paul's use of the picture of the olive tree of Israel, and also his hope of the final salvation of all Israel (Rom 11:17–27).[22]

Praem. 165 reads: "When they have gained this unexpected liberty, those who but now were scattered in Greece and the outside world over islands and continents will arise and post from every side with

---

[21] See Bousset (1926) 236–37; Fischer (1978) 202–13.
[22] See Haacher (1997) 216–19.

one impulse to the one appointed place, guided in their pilgrimage by a vision divine or superhuman unseen by others but manifest to them as they pass from exile to their home".

The phrase πρός τινος θεοτέρας ἢ κατὰ φύσιν ἀνθρωπίνην ὄψεως, "by a vision more divine than according to human nature", means, according to E.R. Goodenough, a vision of a "Man" who is beyond human nature and will lead them together. L. Cohn states: "Hier findet sich bei Philo auch die etwas unklare Andeutung von der jüdischen Erwartung eines persönlichen Messias. . . ."[23]

This interpretation is not probable, since the "Man" in *Mos.* 1:289–91 and *Praem.* 93–97 is not characterized as a divine vision, θεία ὄψις. In *Mos.* 2:254 it is said, however, that there was a divine vision (θεία τις ὄψις) in the cloud that guarded the Hebrews when they left Egypt. The θεία ὄψις at the eschatological return then corresponds to the cloud-vision at the Exodus, and means the future completion of the exodus to the promised land.[24]

The general conclusion reached in the discussion of *Mos.* 1:289–91 and *Praem.* 93–97 is supported by the several agreements between thoughts in *Praem.* 163–72 and the treatises *Against Flaccus* and *On the Embassy to Gaius*, as shown above in an earlier chapter of the present book. These agreements show that the principles at work according to *Praem.* 127–72 were already at work in historical events of Philo's own time. Moreover, they support the view that the national and nationalistic motifs present in *On the Life of Moses* and the *Exposition of the Laws of Moses* were central to Philo himself. U. Fischer is therefore mistaken when he tries to isolate *Praem.* 162–72 from the rest of Philo's writings.[25]

Finally, a comment should be made on the question of allegorization. Since the specific Laws and the special position of the Hebrew people reflect and are in harmony with cosmic law and cosmic citizenship, then the heavenly reality, and the general cosmic philosophical, ethical, and psychological principles are the foundation and the dynamic force at work in the life of this people and in its relationship to the rest of the world. Accordingly, when a non-Jew becomes a Jewish proselyte, he secures for himself a place in heaven, while the Jewish apostates are dragged down to hell, to Tartarus (*Praem.* 152).

[23] Goodenough (1938) 117; *PCH* 2:382.
[24] See Bousset (1926) 237; *PLCL* 8:418; Amir (1983) 33–34; Fischer (1978) 205.
[25] Fischer (1978) 202–13.

For this exchange of roles between Jews and incoming proselytes, cf.
Paul's view that the gentiles were grafted into the olive tree of Israel,
while branches of the tree were cut of because they rejected the
Gospel (Rom 11:1–17).

The key to the combination of universalism and particularism can
be seen in the hermeneutical key as formulated in, *Mos.* 2:52: "Thus
whoever will carefully examine the nature of the particular enactments will find that they seek to attain to the harmony of the universe...." The cosmic and universal principles are revealed in the
Laws of Moses so that the specific Laws are a manifestation of these
cosmic principles. From this it becomes evident that Philo held the
view that (the Greek idea about) divine reason is made concrete in
the Laws of Moses. Thus these Laws reveal the cosmic and universal
laws which in principle are the Laws which should be followed by
all. The people who have the Laws near in speech, thought and
action (Deut 30:11–14), "has its dwelling not far from God; it has
the vision of ethereal loveliness always before its eyes, and its steps
are guided by a heavenward yearning" (*Praem.* 83–84). Thus the people
of the Laws of Moses has accomplished the proper cosmic place
intended for human beings.[26]

In a recent essay J.M. Scott discusses the tension between Philo's
positive view of the Diaspora as world colonization due to overpopu-
lation in Jerusalem, and his negative view of the Diaspora as exile,
Scott reaches the plausible conclusion that both views meet in the
future hope of the restoration of the Jewish nation and the establishment of its ultimate universal sovereignty over all nations.[27]

Conclusion

Methodologically it has proved fruitful to take the starting point in a
classification of Philo's writings when investigating his views on man's
sovereignty. The collection of treatises named the *Exposition of the Laws
of Moses* was of central importance, since Philo himself gives clues to
his overall understanding of this comprehensive work. The pictures
given in *On Rewards and Punishments* of the future rewards and punishments develop ideas also found in *On the Creation*. This observation

---

[26] See Borgen (1992) 342–44.
[27] Scott (1995) 553–75.

supports the view that the treatise *On Rewards and Punishments* is and integral part of Philo's works named the *Exposition of the Laws of Moses*.

The many Rabbinic and other Jewish parallels to the passages examined show that Philo has his place within a Jewish context. The impact of Greek/Hellenistic ideas on Philo's texts was quite strong, however.

Within the context of a cosmic framework Philo finds room for both the protological and eschatological perspectives on the topic of man's sovereignty over animals and nature. In general his ideas are presented in the form of exegesis of parts of the Pentateuch. Within the eschatological outlook he also draws on messianic ideas from Isa 11.

Philo combines the cosmic and universal dimensions with a particularistic concentration on the people of the Laws of Moses. Since the cosmic principles are made manifest in the Laws of Moses, those who keep these Laws are the true human beings. Thus, even when the future blessing is related to the animal world and to nature, the people of the Laws of Moses will play the central role.

In his interpretation of man's dominion over animals and nature Philo does not see man as an autonomous despotic ruler, but as a viceroy of God. Greed, idolatry and lawlesness are central ideas in his description of mankind's falling away from his original ideal state of being, and the future restoration is conditioned upon their obedience to the Laws of Moses. Thus one aim of Philo's picture of the possible future, is to exhort his contemporary people look at their own observance of the Laws as a condition for the materialization of their hopes.

CONCLUDING SUMMARY

In the introductory survey of research it was shown that there was an increasing interest among scholars in Philo as an exegete of the Laws of Moses. It was also shown that scholars are increasingly aware of the fact that no sharp distinction can be drawn between Palestinian Judaism and Hellenistic Judaism. Thus one task is to uncover traditions current in Judaism at that time and examine the various usages, emphases and applications within this common Jewish context as well as within the wider context of the non-Jewish surroundings.

In a study on Philo as an exegete for his time questions to be asked are: What can be known about Philo and the context in which he lived? How are the forms of his expositions and his expository writings to be characterized? Is it possible to define Philo's hermeneutical key to guide us in understanding his expositions? In what ways have his interpretations been produced within the context of his own and his compatriots historical situation?

In the chapters 1 and 2 Philo's world and his place in the history of Alexandrian Judaism were surveyed. Religiously and culturally Philo identified himself with Jerusalem and Athens. In so far as the political government allowed the Jews to live in accordance with their Laws and customs, Philo expressed a positive attitude; if not, tension and conflict between the Jewish communities and the reigning powers were unavoidable.

Within the context of the history of Alexandrian Judaism the conclusion was reached that Philo continued trends from the earlier periods, such as the feeling of Jewish superiority, the employment of Greek ideas and religious traditions in the exposition of the Laws of Moses, sharp polemic against polytheistic cults, the oscillation between spiritual and military warfare and the future hope that the Jews should be the head among the nations; an apologetic defence against criticisms and attacks from the non-Jewish surroundings. In the present study it is examined how Philo's outlook and his historical situation are reflected in his exposition and application of the Laws of Moses.

In order to characterize Philo's exegetical approach further, the chapters 3 to 7 were devoted to the question of exegetical forms. A beginning was made in investigating the various expository forms which are found in Philo's expositions. Some of these forms may be characterized as direct exegesis in the meaning that the biblical material may be interpreted either by means of rewriting as a paraphrase, or a cited biblical text may be explained without a question being asked. The rewriting can elaborate on the form of blessings and curses, give a chain of biblical cases listed in support of a thesis, and explain words and phrases in a cited text by other words or by philological analysis, etc.

Philo does not only paraphrase small biblical units, but gives comprehensive presentations of the Laws of Moses to such an extent that they may be called rewritten Bibles. Philo is neither a system-building philosopher nor just an eclectic editor. He is an expositor who draws on traditions and brings in various current ideas into his interpretations, and at the same time follows certain identifiable perspectives and uniting threads in his composition.

In the series of treatises called the *Exposition of the Laws of Moses* Philo basically follows the form also found in other Jewish books in which (parts of) the Pentateuch has been rewritten, such as *The book of Jubilees*, the *Genesis Apocryphon*, the *Biblical Antiquities of Ps.-Philo*, and Josephus' *Jewish Antiquities*.

Philo's *Allegorical Commentary*, and *Questions and Answers on Genesis and Exodus* display a different structure. They are running commentaries which interpret quoted biblical texts in sequence, verse by verse. Also some of the *midrashim* and some of the Dead Sea Scrolls consist of running commentaries.

A variety of forms may be grouped under the designation 'direct exegesis', in which the meaning of a cited text is explained without a question being asked. Some such forms are brief or more extensive commentary on a cited text, the detailed explanation of words in a quoted text, units with cited text, paraphrase and *inclusio*, a lesson on a topic presented as an excursus, the reviewing of a series of biblical stories and/or cited texts as documentation of a theme, the rewritten Bible form, etc.

The form of question and answer is found in the series *Questions and Answers on Genesis and Exodus*, in the series the *Allegorical Commentary* and also in the *Exposition of the Laws of Moses*.

In the commentaries *On the Giants, On the Unchangeableness of God*, and *The Allegorical Laws*, Book 1, the structure of a running commentary is basic, and in the expositions the form of question and answer and various forms of direct exegesis are found.

Philo employs formula-like exegetical terminology, which is especially stereotyped in the question and answer form. Thus, although
Philo is an independent and inspired exegete, he has at the same
time his place within a traditional exegetical activity.

Against the background of the insights gained into Philo's world,
his place in the history of Alexandrian Jewry, and his use of various
expository forms, aspects of ideas expressed and applications made
were examined in the chapters 8 to 15.

Some of the hermeneutical principles which guided him were
identified. According to Philo the translation of the Septuagint, which
took place on the island Pharos at Alexandria in the time of Ptolemy
Philadelphus, was a decisive event in revelatory history, the goal of
which is the recognition of these Laws of Moses by all nations. Philo's
interpretation of the Laws of Moses continues the presentation of
these Laws to the Greek half of the world.

In his exposition of the Laws of Moses Philo could in different
ways interpret one and the same biblical text within the context of
a two, sometimes a three level exegesis. These levels can be characterized as

1) the specific, 2) the general and 3) the beyond
or 1) the particular, 2) the universal, and 3) the beyond,
or again 1) the concrete, 2) the abstract and 3) the beyond,
and finally as 1) the earthly, 2) the cosmic or heavenly and
3) the beyond.

The general distinction between literal and allegorical exegesis does
not give an adequate characterization of all these aspects of Philo's
two- or three-level exegesis.

The framework for Philo's hermeneutical thinking was the view
that the specific laws of the Jewish nation represent the cosmic law,
that the God of the Jews is both Creator and Lawgiver, and that He
exists 'above and beyond' His creation.

On the concrete and specific level within this hermeneutical perspective one important context is the various forms of interactions
between the Jewish community and their non-Jewish surroundings,
such as tension, conflict or peaceful mutual influence. It is probable
that the tension reflected in the *Special Laws*, Books 3–4, *On the Virtues*
and *On Rewards and Punishments* belonged to the period prior to the
pogrom against the Alexandrian Jews during the reign of the Roman
Emperor Gaius Caligula and the governor Flaccus. Thus, when Philo

was pulled down from his heavenly ascent and was drawn into the stream of troublesome civil matters, *Spec.* 3:1–6, the situation reflected seems to be this period. Philo's engagement and activity in these civil cares explain why he could be the leader of the Jewish delegation that met with the Emperor in Rome.

On the specific level the Laws of Moses were interpreted functionally by being woven into the fabric of Jewish society, in their way of life, in rites, customs, observances, ethos, commandments, and in institutional life relative to the Temple and the synagogues. Thus the practice of the Laws was a fundamental aspect of their interpretation. From this viewpoint the historical treatises *Against Flaccum* and *On the Embassy to Gaius* are to be understood. They display how the Laws of Moses played a role in the conflict, and how Philo applied scriptural and expository ideas to the events. The several points of contact between these two treatises and in particular with *The Special Laws*, Books 3–4, *On the Virtues* and *On Rewards and Punishments* in the *Exposition of the Laws of Moses,* support the understanding that *Against Flaccum* and *On the Embassy to Gaius* are to be classified as applied exegesis and are to be seen as theological interpretation of historical events. Both biblical and Hellenistic motifs have been worked into Philo's interpretation of the events.

On the one hand, Philo's expositions of the illegitimate building of the tower of Babel have a perspective which serves well as an ideological background for the illegitimate invasion into the divine realm by the Emperor Gaius Caligula.

On the other hand, Philo pictured Moses' ascent to the "darkness where God was" as his legitimate transformation into being god and king. Moses' ascent was a paradigmatic model for the ascent of the Jewish people, for example understood as "souls whose vision has soared above all created things and schooled itself to behold the uncreated and divine" (*Legat.* 5). Thus, in contrast to the illegitimate invasion of the Emperor Gaius Caligula the Jewish people had as their identity their legitimate ascent to see the uncreated and divine.

Philo's praise of the Augustus, Tiberius and others testify to the existence also of times and situations of less tension and conflict and more of positive intercourse. During such periods there were varied and complex movements back and forth between the Hebrews/the Jews and other peoples.

It should be remembered that Philo's view that the particular Laws of Moses were in harmony with the universal cosmic law, implied that the Jewish people had a universal role to play. Accordingly, also the movements of reaching out to non-Jews and of the coming in of some as proselytes, are reflected in Philo's exegesis. The founder of the Jewish nation, Abraham, was a proselyte and a model for proselytes, and Moses was the seventh generation after the proselyte founder. It should be noted that Philo interpreted the story about Abraham on two levels, both as the history of a proselyte and as a cosmic and spiritual ascent.

Since God is the creator of cosmos, the context of the Jewish people and other peoples were seen within the broader cosmic context. Here Philo's exegesis on the relationship between human beings and animals, cosmos and God's realm beyond cosmos, was examined. In the *Exposition of the Laws of Moses* Philo developed his view on human beings relative to animals and nature. He took as point of departure Gen 1:26 and 28 which were paraphrased in *Opif.* 84a:

> The Father, after having brought him into existence as a living being naturally adapted for sovereignty not only in fact but by express mandate appointed him king of all creatures under the moon, those that move on land and swim in the sea and fly in the air, for all things mortal in the three elements of land and water and air He made subject to men but exempted the heavenly beings as having obtained a portion more divine.

Human beings thus have a position in between on the one hand animals and nature and on the other hand the heavenly and divine realms.

As for Philo's expositions on biblical ethics and observance his interpretation of the virtue of *philanthropia* was dealt with in some detail. This virtue is in *Virt.* 51–174 applied to Moses' life and to a large body of Mosaic Laws, and the section is included in Philo's rewritten Bible, the *Exposition of the Laws of Moses*. Relationships between God's people, other humans, animals and plants are illuminated. It is noted that the Greek usage is not only based on universalistic ideas about the unity of man, but may also refer to patriotic affection for a city and particular affections and lifestyle among civilized people.

Within the context of a cosmic framework Philo found room for both the protological and eschatological perspectives on the topic of man's sovereignty over animals and nature. In general these ideas were presented in the form of exegesis of parts of the Pentateuch. Within the eschatological outlook he also draws on 'messianic' ideas from Isa 11.

Philo combined the cosmic and universal dimensions with a particularistic understanding of the people of the Laws of Moses. Since the cosmic principles are made manifest in the Laws of Moses, those who keep these Laws are the true human beings. Thus, even when the future blessing is related to the animal world and to nature, the people of the Laws of Moses will play the central role.

In his interpretation of man's dominion over animals and nature Philo did not see man as an autonomous despotic ruler, but as a viceroy of God. Greed, idolatry and lawlesness are central ideas in his description of mankind's falling away from his original ideal state of being, and the future restoration is conditioned upon their obedience to the Laws of Moses. Thus one aim of Philo's picture of the possible future, was to exhort his contemporarians to look at their own observance of the Laws as a condition for the materialization of their hopes.

ABBREVIATIONS

ABD	*Anchor Bible Dictionary* (New York)
ANRW	*Aufstieg und Niedergang der römischen Welt* (Berlin)
AnSt	*Anatolian Studies*
ARW	*Archiv für Religionswissenschaft*
BZ	*Biblische Zeitschrift*
CRINT	*Compendia Rerum Iudaicarum ad Novum Testamentum* (Assen)
CPJ	Tcherikover, V. and Fuks, A. 1957–64, *Corpus Papyrorum Judaicarum*, 1–3 (Cambridge, Mass.)
HUCA	*Hebrew Union College Annual*
HTR	*Harvard Theological Review*
IDB	*Interpreter's Dictionary of the Bible* (New York)
JBL	*Journal of Biblical Literature*
JBR	*Journal of Bible and Religion*
JJP	*Journal of Juristic Papyrology*
JJS	*Journal of Jewish Studies*
JQR	*Jewish Quarterly Review*
JSS	*Jewish Social Studies*
JThSt	*Journal of Theological Studies*
MGWJ	*Monatschrift für Geschichte und Wissenschaft des Judentums*
NTS	*New Testament Studies*
NTT	*Norsk teologisk tidsskrift*
PAPM	Arnaldez, R., Pouilloux, J. and Mondésert, C. (eds. and trans.), 1961–92, *Les Œuvres de Philon d'Aleandrie*, 1–36 (Paris)
Pauly Wissowa, RE	*Paulys Realencyclopädie der klassischen Altertumswissenschaft, fortgeführt von Wissowa, etc.* (Stuttgart)
PCH	Cohn, L., Heinemann, I., Adler, M. and Theiler, W. (trans.), 1962–64, *Philo von Alexandria. Die Werke in Deutscher Übersetzung*, 1–6 (reprint), 7 (Berlin)
PLCL	Colson, F.H. (ed. trans.) 1929–62, *Philo with an English Translation*, 1–10, *Loeb Classical Library* (Cambridge, Mass.)
PLCL Supplement	Marcus, R. (trans.) 1953, 1: *Questions and Answers on Genesis*; 2: *Questions and Answers on Exodus, Loeb Classical Library* (Cambridge, Mass.)
RAC	*Reallexikon für Antike und Christentum*
REJ	*Revue des Etudes Juives*
SP	*Studia Philonica*
SPA	*Studia Philonica Annual*
Str.-B.	[Strack, H.L. and] Billerbeck, P. (1961–63), *Kommentar zum Neuen Testament aus Talmud und Midrasch* 1–4 (3rd edition), 5–6 (2nd edition (München)
SVF	Arnim, Ioannes von (coll.) 1–4, 1904–24, *Stoicorum veterum fragmenta* (Leipzig)
TLZ	*Theologische Literaturzeitung*
TZ	*Theologische Zeitschrift*
TWNT	*Theologisches Wörterbuch zum Neuen Testament*
VChr	*Vigiliae Christianae*

BIBLIOGRAPHY

Main texts and translations

In general the Greek text and the English translation of Philo's writings in *Philo with an English Translation* by F.H. Colson et al., Loeb Classical Library, 1–10 (Cambridge, Mass., 1929–62) are used. The English translation of Philo's *Questions and Answers on Genesis and Exodus* is found in *Philo, Supplements*, 1–2, translated from Ancient Armenian Version of the Original Greek by R. Marcus, Loeb Classical Library (Cambridge, Mass., 1953). The Greek text and the English translation of Josephus' writings in *Josephus with an English Translation* by H.St.J. Thackeray et al., Loeb Classical Library, 1–9 (Cambridge, Mass., 1926–65) are used. In some cases modifications of these translations have been made.

For the Greek Septuagint Translation, use is made of A. Rahlfs (ed.), *Septuaginta*, 4th ed., 1–2 (Stuttgart, 1950). For the Hebrew Bible, use is made of R. Kittel (ed.), *Biblica Hebraica*, 4th ed. (Stuttgart, 1949), for the New Testament of E. Nestle (ed.) *Novum Testamentum Graece*, 25th ed. (London, 1963), and for the English translation use has been made of *The Holy Bible Containing the Old and New Testament, Revised Standard Version* (New York, 1953).

Other books and essays

Achtemeier P.J. (ed.) 1978, *Society of Biblical Literature 1978 Seminar Papers*, 1 (Missoula, Montana).
Adler, M. 1929, *Studien zu Philon von Alexandreia* (Breslau).
Aland, K. and Cross, F.L. (ed.) 1957, *Studia Patristica*, 2 (Berlin).
Alexander, P.S. 1988, "Retelling the Old Testament", in Carson and Williamson (eds.) 1988, 99–121.
Alexandre, M. 1967, "La culture profane chez Philon", in *Philon d'Alexandrie, Lyon Colloque* (Paris) 105–29.
Alon, G. 1977, *Jews, Judaism and the Classical World* (Jerusalem).
Amir, Y. 1973, "Philo and the Bible", *SP* 2, 1–8; also printed in Amir (1983) 67–76.
———. 1983, *Die hellenistische Gestalt des Judentums bei Philon von Alexandrien* (Neukirchen-Vluyn).
———. 1988, "Authority and Interpretation of Scripture in the Writings of Philo", in Mulder and Sysling (eds.) 1988, 421–51.
Apelt, M. 1907, *De rationibus quibusdam quae Philoni Alexandrino cum Posidinio intercedunt* (Leipzig).
Applebaum, S. 1979, *Jews and Greeks in Ancient Cyrene* (Leiden).

————. 1974, "The Organization of the Jewish Communities in the Diaspora", in Safrai and Stern (eds.) 1974, 464–503.
Aptowitzer, V. 1925, "Die Seele als Vogel", *MGWJ* 69, 150–69.
Attridge, H.W. 1984, "Historiography", in Stone (ed.) 1984, 157–84.
————. 1989, *The Epistle to the Hebrews*, Hermeneia (Philadelphia).
Aucher, J.B. 1826, *Philonis Judaei Paralipomena Armena. Libri videlicet quatuor in Genesin. Libri duo in Exodum. Sermo unus de Sampsone. Alter de Jona. Tertius de tribus angelis, etc.* (Venice).
Aune, D. 1983, *Prophecy in Early Christianity and the Ancient Mediterranean World* (Grand Rapids).
Aziza, C. 1987, "L'utilisation polémique du récit de l'Exode chez les écrivains alexandrins (IVème siècle av. J.-C. – Ier siècle ap. J.-C.)", *ANRW* II:20, 1, 41–65.
Bacher, W. 1899, *Die exegetische Terminologie der jüdischen Traditionsliteratur* (Leipzig, repr. Darmstadt, 1965).
Bammel, E. 1952, "Φίλος καὶ Καίσαρος", *TLZ* 77, cols. 205–10.
Barclay, J. and Sweet, J., *Early Christian Thought in its Jewish Context*, FS Morna Hooker (Cambridge).
Barraclough, R. 1984, "Philo's Politics, Roman Rule and Hellenistic Judaism", *ANRW* II:21, 1, 417–553.
Bell, H.I. 1924, *Jews and Christians in Egypt* (Westport, Conn).
————. 1926, *Juden und Griechen im Römischen Alexandria* (Leipzig).
Bergmann, J. 1912, "Die stoische Philosophie und die jüdische Frömmigkeit", in *Judaica. Festschrift zu Hermann Cohens siebzigstem Geburtstag* (Berlin).
Betz, H.D. 1979, *Galatians* (Philadelphia).
————. (ed.) 1978, *Plutarch's Ethical Writings and Early Christian Literature* (Leiden).
Betz O. Haacker, K. and Hengel, M. (eds.) 1974, *Josephus – Studien. Untersuchungen zu Josephus, dem antiken Judentum und dem Neuen Testament*, FS O. Michel (Göttingen).
Bianchi, U. (ed.) 1967, *Le Origini dello Gnosticismo*, (Leiden).
Bilde, P. et al. (eds.) 1992, *Ethnicity in Hellenistic Egypt* (Aarhus).
Birnbaum, E.B. 1992, *The Place of Judaism in Philo's Thought: Israel, Jews and Proselytes* (diss. New York).
————. 1993, "The Place of Judaism in Philo's Thought: Israel, Jews and Proselytes", in Lovering (ed.) (1993) 54–69.
Boer, M.C. de (ed.) 1993, *From Jesus to John* (Sheffield).
Bolkestein, H. 1967, *Wohltätigkeit und Armenpflege im vorchristlichen Altertum* (Groningen).
Borgen, P. 1960, "Brød fra himmel og fra jord. Om haggada i palestinsk midrasj, hos Philo og i Johannesevangeliet", *NTT*, 61 (1960) 218–40.
————. 1963, "The Midrashic Character of John 6:31–58", *ZNW*, 54 (1963) 232–40.
————. 1965, *Bread from Heaven* (Leiden, repr. 1981).
————. 1976, "The Place of the Old Testament in the Formation of New Testament Theology". Response, *NTS*, 23, 67–75.
————. 1983, *'Logos Was the True Light' and Other Essays on the Gospel of John* (Trondheim).
————. 1983A, *'Paul Preaches Circumcision and Pleases Men' and Other Essays on Christian Origins* (Trondheim).
————. 1984, "Philo of Alexandria", in Stone (ed.) 1984, 233–82.
————. 1984A, "Philo of Alexandria. A Critical and Synthetical Survey of Research Since World War II", *ANRW* II:21:1, 98–154.
————. 1987, *Philo, John and Paul* (Atlanta).
————. 1992, "There Shall Come Forth a Man. Reflections on Messianic Ideas in Philo", in Charlesworth (ed.) 1992, 341–61.
————. 1992A, "Judaism in Egypt", *ABD*, Vol. 3, pp. 1061–1072.
————. 1992B, "Philo and the Jews in Alexandria", in Bilde et al. (eds.) 1992, 122–38.

———. 1993, "Heavenly Ascent in Philo: An Examination of Selected Passages", in Charlesworth and Evans (eds.) 1993, 246–68.

———. 1993A, "John 6: Tradition, Interpretation and Composition", in De Boer 1993, 268–91.

———. 1994, "'Yes', 'No', 'How Far'?: The Participation of Jews and Christians in Pagan Cults", in T. Engberg-Pedersen (ed.) 1994, 30–59.

———. 1995, "Man's Sovereignty over Animals and Nature According to Philo of Alexandria", in Fornberg and Hellholm (eds.) 1995, 369–89.

———. 1996, *Early Christianity and Hellenistic Judaism* (Edinburgh).

———. 1996A, "In Accordance with the Scriptures", in Barclay and Sweet (eds.) 1996, 193–206.

———. 1996B, "*Philanthropia* in Philo's Writings", in Elder, Barr and Malbon (eds.) 1996, 173–88.

———. 1996C, "Philo of Alexandria – A Systematic Philosopher or an Eclectic Editor? An examination of his *Exposition of the Laws of Moses*", *Symbolae Osloenses*, 71, 115–34.

Borgen, P. and Skarsten, R. 1976–77, "Quaestiones et Solutiones. Some Observations on the Form of Philo's Exegesis", *SP* 4, 1–15.

Bousset, W. 1901, "Die Himmelreise der Seele", *ARW*, 4:136–69 and 229–73.

———. 1926, *Die Religion des Judentums im späthellenistischen Zeitalter*. Rev. by H. Gressmann, 3rd ed. (Tübingen).

———. 1915, *Jüdisch-christlicher Schulbetrieb in Alexandria und Rom* (Göttingen).

Box, H. 1939, *Philonis Alexandrini in Flaccum* (Oxford).

Bréhier, É. 1908, *Les idées philosophiques et religieuses de Philon d'Alexandrie* (Paris 1950 3rd ed.).

Carras, G.P. 1993, "Dependence or common tradition in Philo's *Hypothetica* VIII 6.10–7.20 and Josephus *Contra Apionem* 2.190–219", in *SPA*, 5, 24–47.

Carson, D.A. and Williamson, H.G.M. (eds.) 1988, *It is Written: Scripture Citing Scripture*. FS B. Lindars (Cambridge).

Chambers, R.R. 1980, *Greek Athletics and the Jews: 165 B.C.–A.D. 70*, Ph.D. diss. (Miami).

Charles, R.H. 1913, *The Apocrypha and the Pseudepigrapha*, 2 (Oxford, 1973; reprint of the first edition 1913).

Charlesworth, J.H. (ed.) 1983, *The Old Testament Pseudepigrapha*, 1 (Garden City).

———. (ed.) 1992, *The Messiah. Developments in Earliest Judaism and Christianity* (Minneapolis).

Charlesworth, J.H. and Evans, C.A. (eds.) 1993, *The Pseudepigrapha and Early Biblical Interpretation* (Sheffield).

Christ, F. (ed.) 1967, *Oikonomia*, FS Oscar Cullmann (Hamburg-Bergstedt).

Christiansen, I. 1969, *Die Technik der allegorischen Auslegungswissenschaft bei Philon von Alexandrien* (Tübingen).

Cohen, J.D. 1989, "Crossing the Boundary and Becoming a Jew", *HTR*, 82, 13–33.

Cohen, N.G. 1995, *Philo Judaeus. His Universe of Discourse* (Frankfurt am Main).

Cohn, L. and Wendland, P. 1897, *Philonis Alexandrini Opera quae Supersunt*, 1.

Cohn, L. 1899, "Einteilung und Chronologie der Schriften Philos", *Philologus Sup. 7* (Berlin).

Cohoon, J.W. 1961 (ed. & trans.), *Dio Chrysostom with an English Translation*, 1 (London).

Collins, J.J. 1983, *Between Athens and Jerusalem: Jewish Identity in the Hellenistic Diaspora* (New York).

———. 1984, "The Sibylline Oracles", in Stone (ed.) 1984, 357–81.

———. 1987, "The Development of the Sibylline Tradition", *ANRW* II:20, 1, 421–59.

Colson, F.H. 1917, "Philo on Education", *JThSt*, 151–62.

Conley, T.M. 1984, "Philo's Rhetoric: Argumentation and Style", in *ANRW* II:21:1, 343–371.

————. 1987, *Philo's Rhetoric: Studies in Style, Composition and Exegesis* (Berkeley, Cal.).

Conzelmann, H. 1963, *Die Apostelgeschichte* (Tübingen).

Cumont, F. 1912, *Astrology and Religion among the Greeks and Romans* (New York, repr. 1960).

Déaut, R. le 1964, "Φιλανθρωπία dans la Littérature Grecque jusqu'au Nouveau Testament (Tite III, 4)", *Mélanges Eugène Tisserant*, 1: *Écriture Sainte – Ancien Orient* (Rome) 255–94.

Delling, G. (1972), "Philons Enkomion auf Augustus", *Klio*, 54 (1972) 171–92.

————. 1974, "Perspektiven der Erforschung des hellenistischen Judentums", *HUCA* 45, 133–76.

————. 1984, "The 'One Who sees God' in Philo", in Greenspahn, Hilgert and Mack (eds.) (1984), 27–41.

Diels, H. 1899, *Elementum* (Leipzig).

Dillon, J. 1995, "Reclaiming the Heritage of Moses: Philo's Confrontation with Greek Philosophy", *SPA*, 7, 108–123.

————. 1977, *The Middle Platonists: a Study of Platonism 80 B.C. to A.D. 220* (London).

Dimant, D. 1984 "Qumran Sectarian Literature", in Stone (ed.) 1984, 483–550.

————. 1992 "Pesharim, Qumran", in *ABD*, 5:244–51.

Dindorf, G. 1878, *Scholia Graeca in Homeri Iliadem* (Oxford).

Doran, R. 1987, "The Jewish Hellenistic Historians Before Josephus", *ANRW* II:20, 1, 246–97.

Dörrie, H. and Dörries, H. 1966, "Erotapokriseis", in *RAC* 6, cols. 342–70.

Drummond, J. 1888, *Philo Judaeus* 2 (London).

Due, B. 1989, *The Cyropaedia. Xenophon's Aims and Method* (Aarhus).

Dungan, D.L. (ed.) 1990, *The Interrelations of the Gospels* (Leuven).

Dunn, J.D.G. 1988, *Romans. World Biblical Commentary* (Waco, TX).

Earp, J.W. 1929–62, "Index of Names", in *PLCL* 10, 189–520.

Elder, L.B.; Barr, D.L. and Malbon, E.S. (eds.) 1996, *Biblical and Humane* (Atlanta).

Engberg-Pedersen, T. (ed.) 1994, *Paul in His Hellenistic Context* (Edinburgh).

Feldman, L.H. 1963, *Studies in Judaica. Scholarship on Philo and Josephus (1937–1962)* (New York).

————. 1968, "The Orthodoxy of the Jews in Hellenistic Egypt", *JSS* 22, 215–37.

Fiorenza, E. Schüssler 1972, *Priester für Gott* (Münster).

————. (ed.) 1976, *Aspects of Religious Propaganda in Judaism and Early Christianity* (Notre Dame, Indiana).

Fischel, H.A. 1973, *Rabbinic Literature and Graeco-Roman Philosophy* (Leiden).

Fischer, U. 1978, *Eschatologie und Jenseitserwartung im hellenistischen Diasporajudentum* (Berlin).

Fitzgerald, J.T. 1992, "Virtue/Vice Lists", in *ABD*, 6:857–59.

————. 1997, "The Catalogue in Ancient Greek Literature", in Porter and Olbricht (eds.) 1997, 275–93.

Fitzmyer, J.A. 1993, *Romans. A New Translation with Introduction and Commentary* (New York).

Flasch, K. (ed.) 1965, *Parusia. Studien zur Philosophie Platons und zur Problemgeschichte des Platonismus*. FS J. Hirschberger (Frankfurt a.M.).

Fornberg T. and Hellholm D. (eds.) 1995, *Texts and Contexts*. FS Lars Hartman (Oslo).

Fraser, P.M. 1972, *Ptolemaic Alexandria*, 1–2 (Oxford).

Freedman H. and Simon M. (eds.) 1961, *Midrash Rabbah*, 3: *Exodus* (London).

Früchtel, U. 1968, *Die kosmologische Vorstellungen bei Philo von Alexandrien* (Leiden).

Fuks, A. 1951, "Notes on the Archive of Nicanor", *JJP* 5, 207–16.

Gaylord, H.E. (trans.) 1983, "3 (Greek Apocalypse of) Baruch", in Charlesworth (ed.), 1983, 653–679.

Geiger, F. 1932, *Philon von Alexandreia als sozialer Denker* (Stuttgart).

Gerhardsson, B. 1990, "The Gospel Tradition", in Dungan (ed.) 1990, 497–545.

Ginzberg, L. 1968, *The Legends of the Jews*, Vols. 1, 3, 5 (Philadelphia).

Gilbert, M. 1984, "Wisdom Literature", in Stone (1984) 283–324.

Goldenberg, R. 1979, "The Jewish Sabbath in the Roman World up to the Time of Constantine the Great", in *ANRW* II:19, 1, 414–47.

Goodenough, E.R. 1928, "The Political Philosophy of Hellenistic Kingship", in *Yale Classical Studies*, 1 (New Haven) 55–102.

———. 1933, "Philo's Exposition of the Law and his De Vita Mosis", *HTR*, 26, 109–25.

———. 1935, *By Light, Light. The Mystic Gospel of Hellenistic Judaism* (New Haven, repr. Amsterdam, 1969).

———. 1938, *The Politics of Philo Judaeus* (New Haven, repr. Hildesheim, 1967).

———. 1953–68, *Jewish Symbols in the Graeco-Roman Period*, 1–13 (New York).

———. 1962, *An Introduction to Philo Judaeus* (2nd rev. ed. Oxford; 1st ed. New Haven, 1940).

Goodspeed, E.J. 1959, *The Apocrypha* (New York).

Greenspahn, F.E.; Hilgert, E. and Mack B.L. (eds.) 1984, *Nourished with Peace*. Studies in Hellenistic Judaism in Memory of Samuel Sandmel (Chico, Ca.).

Grözinger, K.E. 1982, *Musik und Gesang in der Theologie der frühen jüdischen Literatur. Talmud Midrash Mystik* (Tübingen).

Grumach, E.I. 1939, "Zur Quellenfrage von Philos De opificio mundi 1–3", *MGWJ*, 83, N.F. 47 (1939) 126–131.

Grünbaum, M. 1893, *Neue Beiträge zur semitischen Sagenkunde* (Leiden).

Gummere, R.M. (trans.) 1920, *Seneca, ad Lucilium Epistulae Morales*, 2 (London/New York).

Gundel, H.G. and Gundel, W. 1966, *Astrologumena: Die astrologische Literatur in der Antike und ihre Geschichte* (Wiesbaden).

Haacker, K. 1997, "Die Geschichtsteologie von Röm 9–11 im Lichte philonischer Schriftauslegung", *NTS*, 43, 209–22.

Hadot, P. 1960, "Être, Vie, Pensée chez Plotin et avant Plotin", in *Les Sources de Plotin, Entretiens* 5 (Vandoeuvres-Genève) 125–26.

Haenchen, E. 1968, *Die Apostelgeschichte* (Göttingen).

Halperin, D.J. 1988, "Ascension or Invasion: Implications of the Heavenly Journey in Ancient Judaism", *Religion* 18, 47–67.

Hamerton-Kelly, R.G. 1972, "Sources and Traditions in Philo of Alexandria: Prolegomena to an Analysis of His Writings", *SP*, 1, 3–26.

Hammershaimb, E. et al. (trans.) 1970, *De gammeltestamentlige Pseudepigrafer*, 5 (Copenhagen).

Harris, H.A. 1976, *Greek Athletics and the Jews* (Cardiff).

Hartman, L. 1985, *Kolosserbrevet* (Uppsala).

Hay, D.M. 1979–80, "Philo's References to Other Allegorists", *SP* 6, 41–75.

———. (ed.) 1991, *Both Literal and Allegorical. Studies in Philo of Alexandria's Questions and Answers on Genesis and Exodus* (Atlanta).

———. 1991A, "References to Other Exegetes", in Hay (ed.) 1991, 81–97.

Hayward, R. 1982, "The Jewish Temple at Leontopolis", *JJS* 33, 429–43.

Hecht, R.D. 1978, "Preliminary Issues in the Analysis of Philo's De Specialibus Legibus", *SP* 5, 3–17.

———. 1984, "The Exegetical Context of Philo's Interpretation of Circumcision", in Greenspahn, Hilgert and Mack (eds.) 1984, 52–79.

———. 1979–80, "Patterns of Exegesis in Philo's Interpretation of Leviticus", *SP* 6, 77–155.

Heinemann, I. 1931, "Humanitas", in Pauly Wissowa, *RE*, Suppl. 5 (Stuttgart) cols. 282–310.

———. 1962, *Philons griechische und jüdische Bildung*, (repr. Darmstadt, 1st ed. Breslau, 1929–32).

Hellholm D. (ed.) 1983, *Apocalypticism in the Mediterranean World and the Near East* (2nd ed. 1989, Tübingen).

Hengel, M. 1974, *Judaism and Hellenism*, 1–2 (Philadelphia).

————. 1983, "Messianische Hoffnung und politischer 'Radikalismus' in der 'Jüdisch-hellenistischen Diaspora'", in Hellholm (ed.) 1983, 655–86.

Hilgert E. 1986, "A Survey of Previous Scholarship on Philo's *De Josepho*", in Richards (ed.) 1986, 262–270.

————. 1991, "The *Quaestiones*: Texts and Translations", in Hay (ed.), 1991, 1–15.

————. 1991A, "A Review of Previous Research on Philo's *De Virtutibus*", in Lovering, Jr. (ed.) 1991, 103–15.

Himmelfarb, M. 1993, *Ascent to Heaven in Jewish and Christian Apocalypses* (New York/Oxford).

Hirzel, R. 1912, *Plutarch* (Leipzig).

Holladay, C.R. 1983, *Fragments from Hellenistic Jewish Authors*, 1: *Historians* (Chico, Ca).

Horsley, R.A. 1978, "The Law of Nature in Philo and Cicero", *HTR*, 71, 35–59.

Horst, P.W. van der 1989, "Jews and Christians in Aphrodisia in the Light of their Relations in Other Cities of Asia Minor", *Nederlands Theologisch Tijdsschrift*, 43, 106–21.

Jonas, H. 1954, *Gnosis und spätantiker Geist*, 2:1: *Von der Mythologie zur mystischen Philosophie* (Göttingen).

————. 1967, "Discussion of M. Simon, 'Elements gnostiques chez Philon'", in Bianchi (ed.) 1967.

Kamlah, E. 1974, "Frömmigkeit und Tugend. Die Gesetzapologie des Josephus in Ag.Ap. 2, 145–295", in Betz, Haacker and Hengel 1974, 220–32.

Kasher, A. 1985, *The Jews in Hellenistic and Roman Egypt* (Tübingen).

Kloppenborg, J. and Wilson, S. (eds.) 1996, *Voluntary Associations in the Graeco-Roman World* (New York).

Köster, H. 1968, "ΝΟΜΟΣ ΦΥΣΕΩΣ: The Concept of Natural Law in Greek Thought", in Neusner (ed.) 1968, 521–41.

Lambdin, T.O. 1992, "Nile", *IDB*, 3:549–51.

Laporte, J. 1972, *La doctrine eucharistique chez Philon* (Paris).

Lauterbach, J.Z. (ed. trans.) 1933–35, *Mekilta de-Rabbi Ishmael*, 1–3 (Paperback edition, Philadelphia 1976).

Lechner, M. 1933, *Erziehung und Bildung in der griechisch-römischen Antike* (München).

Lehrman, M. 1961, "Introduction", in Freedman and Simon, 3, 1961, VII–VIII.

Leisegang, H. 1919, *Der Heilige Geist*, 1:1 (Berlin).

————. 1941, "Philon", *Pauly Wissowa, RE*, 20:1 (Stuttgart) 1–50.

Levey, S.H. 1974, *The Messiah: An Aramaic Interpretation – The Messianic Exegesis of the Targums* (Cincinnati).

Liddell, H.G. and Scott, R. 1940, *Greek-English Lexicon*, A New Edition (Oxford, repr. 1958).

Lieberman, S. 1950, *Hellenism in Jewish Palestine: Studies in the Literary Transmission, Beliefs and Manners of Palestine in the I Century B.C.E.–IV Century C.E.* (New York).

Lovering, Jr., E.H. (ed.) 1991, *Society of Biblical Literature 1991 Seminar Papers* (Atlanta).

————. (ed.) 1993, *Society of Biblical Literature 1993 Seminar Papers* (Atlanta).

————. (ed.) 1995, *Society of Biblical Literature 1995 Seminar Papers* (Atlanta).

Luck, U. 1970, "φιλανθρωπία κτλ", *TWNT*, 9 (Stuttgart) 107–08.

Lull, D.J. (ed.) 1990, *Society of Biblical Literature. 1990 Seminar Papers* (Atlanta).

Mack, B. 1974–75, "Exegetical Traditions in Alexandrian Judaism: a Program for the Analysis of the Philonic Corpus", *SP*, 3, 71–112.

————. 1984, "Decoding the Scripture: Philo and the Rules of Rhetoric", in Greenspahn, Hilgert and Mack (eds.) 1984, 81–115.

————. 1984A, "Philo Judaeus and Exegetical Traditions in Alexandria", in *ANRW* II:21:1, 227–271.

Malter, H. 1911/12, "Personification of Soul and Body", *JQR*, N.S. 2, 453–79.

Martens, J.W. 1991, "Philo and the 'Higher' Law", in Lovering, Jr. (ed.) 1991, 309–22.

Martin, Jr., H. 1961, "The Concept of *philanthropia* in Plutarch's *Lives*", *American Journal of Philology*, 82, 164–75.

Mayer, R. 1968, *Die hermeneutische Frage in der Theologie* (Freiburg).

McKnight, S. 1991, *A Light Among the Gentiles. Jewish Missionary Activity in the Second Temple Period* (Minneapolis).

Meecham, H.G. 1932, *The Oldest Version of the Bible: 'Aristeas' on its Traditional Origin* (London).

Meeks, W.A. 1967, *The Prophet-King* (Leiden).

———. 1976, "The Divine Agent and His Counterfeit in Philo and the Fourth Gospel", in Fiorenza (ed.) 1976, 43–67.

———. 1968, "Moses as God and King", in Neusner (ed.) 1968, 354–371.

Mendelson, A. 1982, *Secular Education in Philo of Alexandria* (Cincinnati).

———. 1988, *Philo's Jewish Identity* (Atlanta).

Menken, M.J.J. 1996, *Old Testament Quotations in the Fourth Gospel. Studies in Textual Form* (Kampen).

Metzger, B.M. (trans.) 1983: "The Fourth Book of Ezra", in Charlesworth (ed.) 1983, 1:517–559.

Meyer, R. 1937, *Hellenistisches in der rabbinischen Anthropologie* (Stuttgart).

Moehring, H.R. 1978, "Arithmology as an Exegetical Tool in the Writings of Philo of Alexandria", in Achtemeier (ed.) 1978, 191–227.

Moore, G.F. 1927–30, *Judaism*, 1–3 (Cambridge, Mass.).

———. 1950, *History of Religions*, 1, 3 (Edinburgh, 3rd ed.).

Morris, J. 1987, "The Jewish Philosopher Philo", in Schürer, 1973–87, 3:2, 809–89.

Mulder, M.J. and Sysling, H. (eds.) 1988, *Mikra. Text, Translation, Reading and Interpretation of the Hebrew Bible in Ancient Judaism and Early Christianity. CRINT* 2:1 (Assen).

Müller, U.B. 1980, "Rez. Ulrich Fischer, Eschatologie . . . 1978", in *TZ* 26, 238–40.

Neumann, 1894, "Amicus", in *Pauly Wissowa, RE*, 1 (Stuttgart) cols. 1831–33.

Neusner, J. (ed.) 1968, *Religions in Antiquity. E.R. Goodenough Memorial Volume* (Leiden).

———. (trans.) 1981: *The Tosefta. Fourth Division: Neziqin*, (New York).

———. 1984, *Messiah in Context* (Philadelphia).

———. (trans.) 1985: *Genesis Rabbah. The Judaic Commentary to the Book of Genesis. A New American Translation*, 1, (Atlanta).

Nickelsburg, G.W.E. 1982, *Jewish Literature Between the Bible and the Mishnah* (Philadelphia).

———. 1984, "The Bible Rewritten and Expanded", in Stone (ed.) 1984, 89–156.

Niehoff, M.R. 1996, "Two Examples of Josephus' Narrative Technique in His 'Rewritten Bible'", *JSJ*, 27, 31–45.

Nikiprowetzky, V. 1965, "Problèmes du 'Récit de la création' chez Philon d'Alexandrie", *REJ* 124, 271–306.

———. 1977, *Le commentaire de l'Écriture chez Philon de'Alexandrie* (Leiden).

———. 1983, "L'exégèse de Philon d'Alexandrie dans le De Gigantibus et le Quod Deus", in Winston and Dillon (1983) 5–75.

Nilsson, M.P. 1950, *Geschichte der griechischen Religion*, 2 (München).

Nissen, A. 1974, *Gott und der Nächste im antiken Judentum. Untersuchungen zum Dobbelgebot der Liebe* (Tübingen).

Noack, B. 1968, *Pinsedagen* (Copenhagen).

Palmer, R.B. and Hamerton-Kelly, R. (eds.) 1971, *Philomathes; studies and essays in the humanities in memory of Ph. Merlan* (The Hague).

Pearson, B.A. 1984, "Philo and Gnosticism", *ANRW* II:21, 1, 295–342.

Pohlenz, M. 1942, "Philon von Alexandreia", *Nachrichten von der Akademie der Wissenschaften in Göttingen* (Göttingen).

———. 1948, *Die Stoa. Geschichte einer geistigen Bewegung*, 1 (Göttingen).

Porter, S.E. and Olbricht, T.H. (eds.) 1997, *The Rhetorical Analysis of Scripture: Essays from the 1995 London Conference* (Sheffield).

Porton, G.G. 1992 "Midrash", in *ABD*, 4:818–22.
Reik, K. 1907, *Der Optativ bei Polybius und Philo von Alexandria* (Leipzig).
Richards, K.H. (ed.) 1986, *Society of Biblical Literature 1986 Seminar Papers Series* (Atlanta).
Richter W. 1939, *Lucius Annaeus Seneca. Das Problem der Bildung in seiner Philosophie.* Diss. (Lengerich, Westf.).
Roloff, J. 1981, *Die Apostelgeschichte* (Göttingen).
Rostovtzeff, M. 1941, *The Social and Economic History of the Hellenistic World*, 1–3 (Oxford).
Runia, D. 1984, "The Structure of Philo's Allegorical Treatises", *VChr*, 38, 209–56.
————. 1986, *Philo of Alexandria and the Timaeus of Plato* (Leiden).
————. 1987, "Further Observations on the Structure of Philo's Allegorical Treatise", *VChr*, 41, 105–38.
————. 1988, "God and Man in Philo of Alexandria", *JThS*, NS 39, 48–75.
————. 1990, *Exegesis and Philosophy. Studies in Philo of Alexandria* (Aldershot).
————. 1991, "Secondary Texts in Philo's *Quaestiones*", in Hay (ed.), 1991, 47–79.
————. 1993, "Was Philo a Middle Platonist"? *SPA*, 5, 112–140.
Sæbø, M. (ed.) 1996, *Hebrew Bible. The History of Its Interpretation*, 1:1, Antiquity (Berlin).
Safrai, S. and Stern, M. (eds.) 1974, *The Jewish People in the First Century, CRINT* 1:1 (Assen).
————. 1974, "Relation between the Diaspora and the Land of Israel", in Safrai and Stern (eds.) 1974, 184–215.
Sandelin, K.-G. 1991, "The Danger of Idolatry According to Philo of Alexandria", *Temenos* 27, 109–50.
Sandmel, S. 1954, "Philo's Environment and Philo's Exegesis", *JBR*, 22, 248–53.
————. 1971, *Philo's Place in Judaism*, Augmented ed. (New York).
————. 1979, *Philo of Alexandria. An Introduction* (New York).
Schaublin, C. 1974, *Untersuchungen zu Methode und Herkunft der antiochenischen Exegese* (Köln).
Schmidt, H. 1933, *Die Anthropologie Philons von Alexandreia* (Würzburg).
Schmidt, J. 1938, "Philanthropos (φιλάνθρωπος), Götterbeiname", in *Pauly-Wissowa*, *RE*, 19A (Stuttgart) col. 2125.
Schmitt, A. 1977, "Struktur, Herkunft und Bedeutung der Beispielreihe in Weish 10", *BZ*, N.F. 21, 1–22.
Schneider, G. 1982, *Die Apostelgeschichte*, 2 (Freiburg).
Schürer, E. 1909, *Geschichte des Jüdischen Volkes im Zeitalter Jesu Christi*, 4th ed., 3 (Leipzig).
————. 1973–87, *The History of the Jewish People in the Age of Jesus Christ (175 B.C.–A.D. 135)*. A new English Version by Vermes, G. and Millar, F. (eds.), 1–3:2 (Edinburgh).
Schwartz, J. 1953, "Note sur la famille de Philon d'Alexandrie", *Annuaire de L'institute de philologie et d'historie Orientales et Slaves*, 13, 591–602.
————. 1967, "L'Égypte de Philon", in *Philon d'Alexandrie*. Lyon 11–16 Septembre 1966. Colloque (Paris) 35–44.
Scott, J.M. 1995, "Philo and the Restoration of Israel", in Lovering (ed.) 1995, 553–575.
Seland, T. 1995, *Establishment Violence in Philo & Luke: A Study of Non-Conformity to the Torah & Jewish Vigilante Reactions* (Leiden).
————. 1996, "Philo and the Clubs and Associations of Alexandria", in Kloppenborg and Wilson (ed.) 1996, 110–27.
Sheppard, A.R.R. 1979, "Jews, Christians and Heretics in Acmonia and Eumeneia", *AnSt* 29, 169–80.
Shroyer, M. 1936, "Alexandrian Jewish Literalists", *JBL*, 55, 261–84.
Siegert, F. 1996, "Early Jewish Interpretation in a Hellenistic Style, 4: Philo of Alexandria", in Sæbø (ed.) 1996, 162–89.
Siegfried, C. 1875, *Philo von Alexandria als Ausleger des Alten Testaments* (Jena).

Simon, M. 1967, "Éléments gnostique chez Philon" in Bianchi, 1967, 359–76.
Smallwood, E.M. 1961, *Philonis Alexandrini Legatio ad Gaium* (Leiden).
———. 1970, *Philonis Alexandrini Legatio ad Gaium*, 2nd ed. (Leiden).
———. 1976, *The Jews under Roman Rule* (Leiden).
Smelik, K.A.D. and Hemelrijk E.A. 1984, "'Who Knows not what Monsters Demented Egyptian Worship' – Opinions on Egyptian Worship in Antiquity as Part of the Ancient Conception of Egypt", *ANRW* II:17:4, 1852–2000.
Sowers, S. 1967, "On the Reinterpretation of Biblical History in Hellenistic Judaism", in Christ (ed.) 1967, 18–25.
Staehle, K. 1931, *Die Zahlenmystik bei Philon von Alexandreia* (Leipzig).
Stählin, G. 1973, "φίλος κτλ", *TWNT* 9, 112–69.
Stein E. 1931, *Philo und der Midrasch* (Giessen).
Stein, S. 1957, "The Dietary Laws in Rabbinic and Patristic Literature", in Aland and Cross (eds.) 1957, 141–54.
Stendahl, K. 1954, *The School of St. Matthew* (Uppsala).
Sterling, G.E. 1990, "Philo and the Logic of Apologetics: An Analysis of the *Hypothetica*", in Lull (ed.) 1990, 412–30.
———. 1991, "Philo's *Quaestiones*: Prolegomena or Afterthought", in Hay (ed.) 1991, 99–123.
Stern, M. 1974, "The Jewish Diaspora", in Safrai and Stern (eds.) 1974, 117–83.
———. 1976–84, *Greek and Latin Authors on Jews and Judaism*, 1–3 (Jerusalem).
Stone, M. 1980, *Scriptures, Sects, and Visions* (Philadelphia).
———. (ed.) 1984, *Jewish Writings of the Second Temple Period*, *CRINT* 2:2 (Assen).
Swete, H.B. 1902, *An Introduction to the Old Testament in Greek* (Cambridge).
Tcherikover, V. 1958, "The Ideology of the Letter of Aristeas", *HTR* 51, 59–85.
———. 1963, "The Decline of the Jewish Diaspora in Egypt in the Roman Period", *JJS* 14, 1–32.
———. 1966, *Hellenistic Civilisation and the Jews* (Philadelphia).
Terian, A. 1981: *Philonis Alexandrini De Animalibus*, (The Armenian Text with Introduction, Translation, and Commentary) (Chico, CA).
———. 1984, "A Critical Introduction to Philo's Dialogues", *ANRW* II:21, 1, 272–94.
Theiler, W. 1965, *Forschungen zum Neuplatonismus* (Berlin).
———. 1965A, "Philo von Alexandria und der Beginn des Kaiserzeitlichen Platonismus", in Flasch (ed.) 1965, 199–217.
———. 1971, "Philo von Alexandria und der Hellenisierte Timaeus", in Palmer and Hamerton-Kelly (eds.) 1971, 25–35.
Thornton, T.C.G. 1977–78, "To the end of the earth: Acts I:8", *The Expository Times*, 89, 374–75.
Thyen, H. 1955, "Die Probleme der neueren Philo-Forschung", *ThR*, 23, 230–46.
Tobin, T.H. 1983, *The Creation of Man: Philo and the History of Interpretation* (Washington, D.C.).
Urbach, E.E. 1975, *The Sages: Their Concepts and Beliefs*, 1–2 (Jerusalem).
Veldhuizen, M. van 1985, "Moses, a Model of Hellenistic *Philanthropia*", in *Reformed Review*, 38, 215–24.
Vermes, G. 1961, *Scripture and Tradition in Judaism* (Leiden).
Völker, W. 1938, *Fortschritt und Vollendung bei Philo von Alexandrien* (Leipzig).
Volz, P. 1934, *Die Eschatologie der jüdischen Gemeinde*, 2nd ed. (Tübingen).
Walter, N. 1987, "Jüdisch-hellenistische Literatur vor Philon von Alexandrien", *ANRW* II:20, 1, 67–112.
Wan, S. 1993 "Philo's *Quaestiones et solutiones in Genesim*: A Synoptic Approach", in Lovering (ed.) 1993, 22–53.
Weinfeld, M. 1992, "Deuteronomy, Book of", in *ABD* 2 (New York) 168–83.
Wertheimer, S.A. (ed.) 1967–68, *Batei Midrashot*, 2. enlarged ed. (Jerusalem).

Wilson, J.A. 1962, "Egypt", *IDB* 2, 39–66.
Wilson, R.McL. 1972, "Philo of Alexandria and Gnosticism", *Kairos*, 14, 213–19.
———. 1993, "Philo and Gnosticism." *SPA*, 5, 84–92.
Winston D. and Dillon J. (eds.) 1983, *Two Treatises of Philo of Alexandria: a Commentary on De Gigantibus and Quod Deus sit immutabilis* (Atlanta).
———. 1984, "Philo's Ethical Theory", in *ANRW* II:21:1 (Berlin) 372–416.
Wolfson, H.A. 1948, *Philo*, 1–2 (Cambridge, Mass.).
Wuellner, E. (ed.) 1975, *Protocol of the Fifteenth Colloquy: 9 March 1975: 'General Education' in Philo of Alexandria* (Berkeley, CA).
Zeller, E. 1911, *Grundriss der Geschichte der griechischen Philosophie*, 10th ed. (Leipzig).
Zuckermandel, M.S. (ed.) 1881, *Tosefta* (Pasewalk).

INDEX OF REFERENCES

APOCRYPHA AND PSEUDEPIGRAPHA

NEW TESTAMENT

PHILO OF ALEXANDRIA

20-73	113-115
35-48	68
52-96	269
60ff.	91
70ff.	91
70-73	138
70-85	115-116
74-84	138
86	138
86-121	116-118
86ff.	91
87	147
87-103	138
104	91
122	91
122-123a	138
122-139	118-119
123b-135	139
136	141
140-180	139
140-183	119-121
144-180	137, 178
145	178
156	269
180	137
181-183	269
172-178	178
173-175	26

Quod omnis probus liber sit (Prob.)

26	17, 162, 171
73	141
74	26
94	141
98	141
102	22
118	22
127	22
130	22
138	141
140	22
141	17

De sacrificiis Abelis et Caini (Sacr.)
46, 103, 124, 213

9	203
11ff.	91
12	154
48	213
51	124
62	154

76-87	138
79	269
78	269
86	154
94-96	115
112	154
119	154
128	113
128ff.	91
130	23

De Sobrietate (Sobr.) 47, 103, 186, 200

15	154
33	13
55	186
66	200

De Somniis (Somn.) 47, 103, 175

1:1	103
1:5ff.	91
1:12f.	91
1:14ff.	91
1:39	151
1:41f.	91
1:53-60	217
1:77f.	23
1:92-102	151
1:112	154
1:115-120	182
1:118	114
1:133-145	106
1:138-139	237
1:146-147	246
1:148f	269
1:161	217, 218
1:234-237	115, 269
1:256	180
2:54	26
2:56	26
2:59	19, 25, 26
2:76	154
2:78-92	15
2:110-154	174
2:111	178
2:117	179
2:121f.	19
2:121	26
2:123	17, 171
2:123ff.	174, 179
2:123-132	17
2:124	17

Josephus

Dead Sea Scrolls

Commentary on Psalm 37 (4Q171, 173)
125

Genesis Apocryphon 79, 272, 283

Habakkuk Commentary (1QpHab) 125

Manual of Discipline (1QS)
2:2-10   48

Nahum Commentary (4Q169)
125

Rabbinic Literature

Mishna

m. Aboda Zara
5:5   168

m. Berakot
7:1   168

Babylonian Talmud

b. Aboda Zara (b. Abod. Zar.)
5a   237

b. Bekarot
10a   236

b. Git.
47a   166

b. Hagigah
12A   68

b. Nedarim
32a   67, 145

b. Nid
13b   237

b. Ros. Has.
10b   232
11a   232

b. Sanhedrin (b. Sanh.)
38a   88
92ab   237
98b   232

b. Shabbat
133b   253

b. Sotah
14a   253

b. Sukkah
51b   17

b. Yebamot (b. Yebam.)
15:15c   237
62a   237
63b   237

Jerusalem Talmud

y. Moed Qatan
3:82b   237

y. Sanhedrin (y. Sanh)
4:9   87

y. Yebamot (y. Yebam)
15:15c   237

Tosephta

t. Sanhedrin (t. Sanh.)
8:7   87, 88, 95, 101, 105,
              232
8:9   87, 232
9   87, 88, 101, 232

t. Sukkah
4:6   17

CHRISTIAN AUTHORS

GREEK AND LATIN AUTHORS

INDEX OF MODERN AND ANCIENT AUTHORS